UNLIKELY GENERAL

UNLIKELY
GENERAL

"Mad" Anthony Wayne
and the Battle for America

Mary Stockwell

Yale

UNIVERSITY
PRESS
New Haven & London

Published with assistance from the Annie Burr Lewis Fund.
Published with assistance from the foundation established in memory
of James Wesley Cooper of the Class of 1865, Yale College.

Yale University Press books may be purchased in quantity for educational,
business, or promotional use. For information, please e-mail sales.press@yale.edu
(U.S. office) or sales@yaleup.co.uk (U.K. office).

Set in Electra and Trajan types by Tseng Information Systems, Inc.
Printed in the United States of America.

Library of Congress Control Number: 2017953580

ISBN 978-0-300-21475-8 (hardcover : alk. paper)

A catalogue record for this book is available from the British Library.

This paper meets the requirements of ANSI/NISO z39.48-1992 (Permanence of Paper).

10 9 8 7 6 5 4 3 2 1

To Jamie

CONTENTS

Contents

ACKNOWLEDGMENTS

I must first thank my sister Roberta Stockwell, a talented artist, excellent writer and historian in her own right, and professional cartographer who made the maps for this book. I will always appreciate the fact that she took me on a trip to Valley Forge, mainly to see the statue of Anthony Wayne. Although she lived and worked in New York City at the time, she grew up, like the rest of our family, in the Maumee River Valley, not far from the Fallen Timbers Battlefield. She knew the statue of Wayne that looks out over the Maumee Rapids and was surprised to see him high on his horse at Valley Forge. Later we went to visit his estate at Waynesborough, where the guides were happy to meet people who knew the "western" Wayne.

Thanks also to the Gilder Lehrman Institute of American History for the fellowship they awarded me to study the Wayne Papers in the Bancroft Collection at the New York Public Library. The historian George Bancroft transcribed five hundred of Wayne's best letters that are housed in the Wayne Papers at the Historical Society of Pennsylvania. His transcriptions provide the Rosetta Stone for deciphering Wayne's swift-moving and often difficult to read handwriting. I am also grateful to the staff of the William L. Clements Library at the University of Michigan for awarding me two Earhart Foundation Fellowships to study the Anthony Wayne Papers, the Nathanael Greene Papers, and many other valuable collections at their institution. The staff members of the Clements Library, including Brian Leigh Dunnigan, Jayne Ptolemy, Diana Sykes, Wendy Mekins, Valerie Proehl, Barbara Bradley, and Shneen Coldiron were thoroughly professional, but also kind and welcoming. I am likewise grateful to Adina Berk, Senior Editor for History at Yale University Press, most especially for shepherding the book through the review process; her assistant, Eva Skewes; Noreen O'Connor-

Abel, for her masterful copyediting; and Chris Rogers, the former Editorial Director at Yale University Press, who accepted the proposal for *Unlikely General.*

My thanks go as well to Robert McDonald, Professor of History at the United States Military Academy, who invited me to participate in the Sons of the Father Conference on Washington and His Protégés at West Point. He edited a wonderful book entitled *Sons of the Father: Washington and His Protégés* (University Press of Virginia, 2013), which collected the papers presented at the conference, including my article "Most Loyal but Forgotten Son: Anthony Wayne's Relationship with George Washington." Thanks, too, to Paul Lamb, then a literary agent at Howard Morheim, who luckily for me had roomed in college at DePauw University with a student from Fort Wayne, Indiana. He had visited historic Fort Wayne with his roommate's family and was surprised to learn from my proposal that there was so much more to the story of "Mad" Anthony Wayne.

"I Have Fought and Bled for the Liberties of America"

Late on a Friday evening in December 1791, a soldier and his servant could be seen racing on horseback through the streets of Philadelphia. They did not stop until they reached the President's House on Market Street, just two blocks from where the Second Congress, elected the year before, was in session. After dismounting, the soldier handed the reins of his horse to his servant, hurried up the steps, and knocked on the front door. Old German John, the porter who greeted him, said the president could not be disturbed since he was having dinner with his wife and several guests. When the soldier answered that he had important dispatches, the porter sent a servant into the dining room to fetch Tobias Lear, Washington's personal secretary. Lear promised to give the dispatches to the president at the "proper time," but the soldier would not hear of it. He said he had just come from the western country with orders to place the dispatches directly in the hands of General Washington. There must have been something desperate enough in the man's voice to make Lear fetch the president.

He went back into the dining room and whispered the cause of the commotion in the hallway to Washington. Lear then took the same place he had taken for the last seven years since becoming the general's secretary and the tutor of his grandchildren. He watched the president leave the room, come back a few minutes later, and take his own seat at the table. Washington revealed nothing about what had happened in the hallway with the soldier. Instead he merely apologized for leaving his dinner guests. Lear noticed that his appearance was exactly the same when he came back into the room as when he had left. "Everything went on as usual," he later remembered, except for an odd remark, "I knew it would be so," that the president muttered to himself. When dinner was finished, Martha Washington led everyone upstairs into the drawing room on the second floor.

Here they chatted until precisely ten o'clock, the hour when the president liked to retire. The guests said good-bye to their hosts, with Washington taking the time to bid farewell to the ladies one by one. Mrs. Washington stayed with her husband and his secretary a while longer before retiring to her bedroom down the hallway at the back of the house.

What happened next would stay with Tobias Lear for the rest of his life, although he would only confess the details shortly before his death. Washington sat down on a couch in front of the fireplace and told Lear to sit next to him. Here they remained in silence side by side for some time. The expression on the president's face was just as it had been before and after he met the soldier in the hallway. But then a sudden change came over him as he struggled to control the emotions welling up inside him. Lear realized that the president had managed to suppress these feelings for the last few hours. While most people outside of Washington's inner circle always saw him in complete control of himself, his family and closest aides knew how terrible Washington's passions, especially his anger, could be when roused. On this wintry night, something in the dispatches delivered from the western country broke open the floodgates within the president. "It's all over," he said vehemently, never moving from the same spot where he first sat down on the couch, "St. Clair's defeated—routed—the officers, nearly all killed, the men by wholesale; the rout complete—too shocking to think of—and a surprise into the bargain!"

Afraid to speak, Lear sat motionless, waiting for the storm in Washington's emotions to pass or for another wave to break over him. When the president, still highly agitated, rose and paced about the room, Lear knew there was more to come. Near the door to the hallway that led back downstairs to the front door, Washington suddenly stopped, stood for a few moments, and then exploded. "Here on this very spot," he shouted, "I took leave of him; I wished him success and honor." The president seemed to have gone back in time to the last day he had seen the general. St. Clair had just been ordered to break up the Indian confederation that was blocking the advance of American settlers across the Ohio River. "You have your instructions, I said, from the Secretary of War," Washington remembered. Then he had given his old friend from their days together in the Continental Army one more command, "Beware of a surprise!" He repeated the phrase as if St. Clair was standing right before him once again. "Beware of a surprise! You know how the Indians fight us!" But somehow St. Clair had forgotten this "solemn warning." Now a third time the president cried out, "And yet! To suffer that army to be cut to pieces, hack'd, butchered, and tomahawked, by a surprise—the very thing I guarded him against! O God, O God, he's worse than a murderer!" His hands flew in the air as he hurled curses at St. Clair with his whole frame shaking. It was a huge frame—6 foot 3½ inches tall and 21 inches from shoulder to shoulder—as Lear would learn at Washington's deathbed just eight years later when he took the measurements himself and dutifully recorded them in his journal. "How can he answer to his country," the president shouted, "the blood of the slain is upon him—the curse of widows and orphans—the curse of Heaven!"

Finally, after what Lear counted as a mere thirty minutes, the storm was over. Washington sat back down on the couch next to him, clearly embarrassed and "uncomfortable" at his outburst. All his life he had struggled to control his emotions, but in this dark December they had gotten the better of him. In a tone now much "altered," he calmly said to Lear, "This is not to go beyond this room." Lear watched a new struggle break out within Washington as he again sat near him, pushing his feelings back down inside while silently berating himself for coming to conclusions so quickly. When he spoke at last, his voice was exactly as it had been during dinner before the soldier came to the front door with his dispatches. "General St. Clair shall have justice; I looked hastily through the dispatches, saw the whole disaster but not all the particulars; I will receive him without displeasure; I will hear him without prejudice; he shall have full justice."[1]

If Tobias Lear had read through the dispatches handed to the president, he might have better understood Washington's fury. They told the horrific tale of the near destruction of America's only standing army by Indian warriors about a hundred miles north of Fort Washington early on the morning of November 4, 1791. Ten days earlier, St. Clair and his army, consisting of a little more than 1,000 soldiers and close to 300 Kentucky militiamen, marched out of their fort on the Ohio River near the frontier outpost of Cincinnati. They were headed for Kekionga, better known as the Miami Villages, located where the St. Mary's and St. Joseph's Rivers came together to form the Maumee. Henry Knox, the secretary of war, had ordered St. Clair to proceed to the place, disperse the Indian warriors gathered there, along with any British agents who might be working among them, and build a fort. But somehow this plan had gone terribly awry and now at least 650 soldiers lay dead on a patch of snow-covered ground somewhere deep in the Ohio Country. Another 250 were wounded. Only a few dozen men had come through the battle unscathed.

When the president took the dispatches from the soldier standing in his hallway, he had only to glance at the opening words of St. Clair's letter to Knox, written on November 9 from Fort Washington, to understand this. "Yesterday afternoon the remains of the army under my command got back to this place, and I have now the unfortunate task to give you an account of as warm and as unfortunate an action as almost any that has been fought, in which every corps was engaged and worsted." Most of the infantry, the artillery and rifle corps, the dragoons, nearly every soldier in the battalions from Virginia, Maryland, Western and Eastern Pennsylvania, New Jersey, and New York, and six companies of Kentucky militia had lost. Reading on, Washington learned that the soldiers of the First Infantry Regiment had survived, but only because St. Clair had sent them back the day before the massacre to hunt down deserters. Upward of 400 men had run off since the army left Fort Washington. The last group of deserters had threatened to intercept the packtrains coming north from Kentucky and take all the flour and beef for themselves.[2]

St. Clair's letter to Knox clearly showed that he had ignored the warnings of his commander in chief. They had met face to face for the last time in September 1790 when St. Clair was visiting Philadelphia for talks with Secretary Knox and Washington was in the city inspecting the house chosen as the president's mansion. In the very same drawing room where a stunned Tobias Lear now sat motionless, Washington had given specific instructions to St. Clair on how to fight the Indians. Remember, the president explained, that you must never trust them. They talked of peace as they prepared for war. They signed treaties as they planned massacres. They denied every tie to the redcoats while taking deadly aim at your soldiers with their British guns and powder. Whenever an American army headed into the Indian country, the commanding general should count on the fact that warriors were traveling right by his side, shadowing his columns from behind the endless rows of trees in the forest. Keep your arms always ready, Washington had told St. Clair, from dawn until dusk and through the night. After your army has marched all day and your men want only to sleep, do not let them rest until they have fortified their camp. Vigilance, arms at one's side, fortifications—these were the only ways to prevent the surprise attack that Washington so feared.[3]

If St. Clair had dismissed every piece of advice offered by Washington, except the necessity of fortifying his position, then his army might have been spared the slaughter in the wilderness. But late on the afternoon of November 3, 1791, when his soldiers came upon a bluff facing west across a river he thought sure was the St. Mary's, he decided the high ground was so well protected that no fortifications were necessary. Instead of spending the last hours of daylight building a barricade around their camp, he let his men rest, knowing that on the following morning, when the First Regiment returned from chasing deserters, they would have to march the last fifteen miles to Kekionga and attack the Indians gathered there. St. Clair ordered the soldiers of his right column to pitch their tents on the edge of the bluff closest to the river and the left column to settle in seventy yards to the rear. He placed the artillery between the two rows along with the horses and wagons. Since the St. Mary's wound about the right side of the camp, St.

Clair saw no need to defend it further. He sent the cavalry and rifle corps to protect the more exposed left and ordered the militia who had not run off to camp due west on another bluff across the river. As his soldiers cooked their dinner, St. Clair retired to his tent set up between the two columns of his army, remembering that he would have to build some fortifications on the next day, but only to house the heavy knapsacks that his men would leave behind once they started for the Miami Villages.[4]

Even if he had forgotten all the president's warnings, but remembered a lesson he had learned as a young soldier in the French and Indian War, then his army still might have been saved. He should have recalled that even the highest ground can be taken if an army is determined enough. Newly arrived from Edinburgh, Lieutenant Arthur St. Clair, only twenty-two years old, had scaled the cliffs below the Plains of Abraham, along with 5,000 other British soldiers, and helped General James Wolfe take the walled city of Quebec, high above the St. Lawrence River, away from the French. But failing to remember this, he had led his men into a trap from which they could not escape. He understood this immediately when he awoke on the bitterly cold morning of November 4, 1791, to the sound of gunfire and what seemed like a thousand bells ringing in the distance. The bells were actually the cries of Indian warriors as they crashed into the militia and chased the terrified men across the river and up the bluff into the army camp. Having miscalculated the strength of his position the night before, St. Clair knew that his men were now surrounded by the very enemy they had come into the wilderness to destroy.

The general threw a cloak over his nightshirt and hurried from his tent toward the artillery. There he found most of the Kentucky militia who had survived the first attack standing motionless behind the cannon where they had fled, making it nearly impossible for the soldiers to load the guns. But even when they could be fired, the cannon soon fell silent once the Indians took deadly aim at the artillery officers. Terrified enlisted men now huddled with the militia, watching for flashes of musket fire in the distance and waiting to see who would crumple to the ground next. St. Clair, clearly visible through the smoke with his long white hair flowing behind him, dodged one bullet after another. Eight shots cut through his cloak. Every horse he tried to mount was shot dead beneath him. But somehow he survived even as his officers collapsed around him. He marched back and forth in front of his frightened men, reforming their broken lines and ordering them to load their muskets and shoot back at the Indians. After fighting this way for three long hours, and seeing his rifle corps gunned down along with his artillery officers, he rounded up the few men still able and willing to charge with the bayonet and sent them first down the left slope of his camp and then down the right. They pushed the Indians across the river into the surrounding woods, but with no riflemen to support them, they quickly fled back up the bluff every time.

Finally, after directing one bayonet charge after another for the next hour, and with most of his officers dead or wounded, St. Clair decided they must retreat before everyone was killed. He passed the word along the shattered columns to be ready to make for the trail that had brought them to this dreadful place. One of his few surviving officers, Colonel William Darke, would lead a last bayonet charge on the right to push the Indians back, allowing anyone who could still walk to race down the bluff toward the road that led south to Fort Jefferson. Even though Darke was shot in the action and his son Joseph fell wounded at his side, the feint worked. A few men got away before the Indians realized what was happening. St. Clair escaped at the last minute on one of the only animals left alive, a packhorse that refused to move faster than a crawl. Warriors followed the panic-stricken soldiers for several miles, murdering the weakest and stopping to pick up the guns and cartridges thrown down by the fleeing men, before turning back to join in the plunder of the camp and the torture of the wounded.

The retreat quickly turned into a rout with no one taking orders from St. Clair anymore. The soldiers hurried on for twenty miles, stumbling but never stopping, until they finally met the First Infantry Regiment coming up the trail from Fort Jefferson. Shortly after dawn, Major John Francis Hamtramck, who commanded the regiment, heard cannon fire in the distance. He quickly mustered his men and marched them toward the sound of the guns. He had gone nine miles before meeting the first terrified soldiers coming his way. They rushed past, telling him that Indians had attacked and nearly destroyed the army. Hamtramck ordered a detachment under Lieutenant William Kersey to continue on and determine what exactly had happened while he headed back to Fort Jefferson to secure the post from a possible Indian attack. Farther up the line, as more frightened soldiers ran past him, Lieutenant Kersey decided that the wounded could not have survived the wrath of the Indians, and with St. Clair nowhere in sight, turned the entire army back toward Fort Jefferson where they arrived at sundown.[5]

General St. Clair, finally coming into the fort with the last of the stragglers, let his soldiers rest. They had run nearly thirty miles in less than ten hours. But with no food at the post, he decided that any man too tired to go on should stay behind while the rest moved forward with him in the middle of the night. Leaving a few hours before midnight, they trudged through the dark until they were unable to go another step and collapsed on the trail. They awoke when the packtrain bringing supplies from Fort Washington came upon them. St. Clair took enough flour to feed his soldiers and then sent the wagons on to Fort Jefferson. On the afternoon of November 8, after racing a hundred miles in just four days, the remnants of the army arrived back at Fort Washington. An exhausted St. Clair, who was still in shock at what had happened, waited until the next day to tell Secretary Knox, and so President Washington, the horrific news that two-thirds of the American army had been killed and most of the rest had been wounded.[6]

One month to the day later, sometime before midnight on December 9, a shaken Tobias Lear finally left the president's side and climbed the stairs to the third floor where he shared a room with his wife, Polly, and their nine-month-old son, Benjamin. Whether he or Washington got any sleep that night, Lear never said. But when he rose the next morning, he found there would be little rest for either of them. Washington knew the stunning defeat of St. Clair's army in the western wilderness would soon be breaking in newspapers along the eastern seaboard. He must get ahead of the story and give the appearance at least that he was in control of the situation. Luckily for the president, by the time he first heard the story of the massacre from the soldier who interrupted his dinner party, Congress had already adjourned for the weekend. Instead of letting the Senate and House of Representatives discover what had happened by reading accounts of the disaster in the local papers, he decided to announce the terrible news himself.

On Monday morning, December 12, 1791, a letter from Washington, bound together with the dispatches from St. Clair, arrived at the Congress of the United States. "Gentlemen of the Senate and the House of Representatives," the note politely began, "it is with great concern that I communicate to you the information received from Major General St. Clair, of the misfortune which has befallen the troops under his command." The opening words echoed the first line of St. Clair's letter that had devastated Washington just three days before. While he admitted the loss was tragic, especially since so many brave men had fallen, he assured the Congress that the situation "may be repaired without great difficulty." He promised to relay further information on the matter that would allow the nation's legislature to determine what "future measures . . . may be proper to pursue." The tone of the letter showed the remarkable job Washington had done in regaining his composure, but did little to mask the magnitude of St. Clair's defeat. There had been no disaster like this since the British general Edward Braddock, with a twenty-three-year-old George Washington at his side as his aide, had been ambushed by the French and Indians near Fort Duquesne in the summer of 1755. Even in the darkest days of the American Revolution, an older and wiser Washington had lost many battles but never an entire army. Belying his confident words to Congress, he underscored the trouble that lay ahead by signing the letter not as the president, but as "George Washington, General."[7]

Washington had rightly guessed that the story of St. Clair's defeat would soon be breaking in the press. Rumors of the massacre had been filtering east by word of mouth and through letters since early November. On the same day that the soldier carrying dispatches from the western country arrived at his front door, a few lines about the disaster appeared in *Dunlap's American Advertiser*, a daily paper in Philadelphia. Within the week, bits and pieces of the horrifying tale were printed in newspapers from Richmond to Boston. People read how St. Clair's soldiers first heard cries in the distance that sounded like wolves howling or all the bells of the packhorses ringing at once. Suddenly hundreds of warriors painted red and black poured out of the woods with their muskets blazing. They encircled the soldiers, leaving no possible way to escape. Soon all the lines broke, the tents were overturned, and one officer after another fell dead. Finally, by some miracle, a few men got away, even as they left the wounded behind on the battlefield to face the scalping knife. The reaction to these frightening images was everywhere the same. How could this have happened, especially only one year after another American army under General Josiah Harmar, also sent north to disrupt the confederation centered at the Miami Villages, had been nearly wiped out by Indians just south of the place? Certainly St. Clair must bear some of the responsibility, but most of the blame had to be laid squarely at the doorstep of President Washington, not just for appointing the general in the first place, but for crafting an Indian policy that had failed miserably.[8]

How beautiful his plans had been for the Ohio Country and how terribly they now lay in ruins all about him. Washington had promised throughout his first term that he could open the territory north of the Ohio River for settlement, deal fairly with the tribes who lived there, and somehow avoid war with the British, who still manned forts on American soil along the edges of the Great Lakes. Respect for the tribes would be the hallmark of Washington's Indian policy. He would send emissaries among them to negotiate treaties in which they surrendered their rightful claims to the land in exchange for annuities. These yearly payments of money for the chiefs, guns and powder for the men, household goods for the women, and blankets for everyone would tie the Indians to the United States. So would government trading houses established throughout the west where the Indians could exchange the skins and pelts of deer, bears, panthers, wolves, otters, foxes, and raccoons for even more goods. Having lost control of the valuable fur trade with the Indians, the British would finally let go of the country they had already surrendered on paper in the treaty ending the American Revolution.

Acting the part of his nation's master surveyor, Washington would then bring about the orderly settlement of the country that stretched west to the headwaters of the Mississippi. Just as he was overseeing the transformation of the wetlands along the Potomac into an exact grid of wide boulevards and public spaces, so he would shape the forests and prairies across the Appalachians into a perfect quilt of six-mile-by-six-mile-square blocks, with every section of every block opened for sale and settlement. As the wilderness filled up with farmers and their wives and children, new states would be organized and enter the Union on an equal footing with the original colonies, all governed from the new federal city that he and his architect Pierre L'Enfant had envisioned. The nation that Washington had spent so much of his life building would not die on the vine, bottled up along the Atlantic, surrounded by hostile tribes and nations, but would instead spread west and so endure for countless generations.

The process of transforming the wilderness across the Ohio River had been under way since the Confederation Congress passed its two greatest laws, the Land Ordinance of 1785, which subdivided the western country into perfectly drawn township squares, and the Northwest Ordinance of 1787, which laid out the pattern for the western territories to become states. Arthur St. Clair had guided the implementation of both laws since winning his appointment as the first governor of the Northwest Territory. But Washington had brought a greater vision to the project when he became president in 1789, imagining his people and the Indians living peacefully side by side in the country west of the Appalachians. Maybe it would take fifty years he thought, or less than thirty as his secretary of war Henry Knox calculated, but if the settlers were patient and the warriors agreed to settle down as farmers, giving up their traditional ways, then the country north and west of the Ohio would be a wonder for the world to behold.

As rational as this plan seemed to the president, the tribes that lived in the Ohio Country did not see it this way. Their leaders told the emissaries sent among them to go back and inform Washington that the Ohio River would run red with the blood of his young men if they dared to cross it. The chiefs understood the risk involved in delivering a message like this to a man whom the Seneca called Conocotarious, the Town Destroyer. They had first granted this honorary title to Washington's grandfather before passing it on to Washington himself in 1753, but the name took on a more literal meaning after the Continental Army set fire to Indian villages throughout the Mohawk River Valley and western Pennsylvania during the Revolution. As the Seneca chief Cornplanter later told the president, the women of his tribe to this day "turn pale" and their children "cling close" to them at the mere mention of the name Conocotarious.[9]

Still Little Turtle, the Miami chief who ruled the villages at the headwaters of the Maumee, knew that Washington would have to take some risks, too, if he meant to get this country away from the Indians. His soldiers would have to leave the safety of the fort named after him near Cincinnati and come deep into the woods where thousands of warriors from tribes living from the Ohio River to the western end of the Great Lakes would surround and destroy them. To keep their country, they had already defeated Harmar and now St. Clair and planned to do the same to whatever man the president sent against them next.[10]

Washington had no intention of letting the valuable Ohio Country slip away and decided to send an even stronger army west to win it. Instead of meeting individually with the heads of his executive departments, as he had done since taking office, he now called Secretary Knox, along with Thomas Jefferson and Alexander Hamilton, into regular cabinet meetings to discuss the formation of this new army. Together they must come up with a plan to convince Congress that an increase in the nation's military was both necessary and affordable. Knox recommended creating the Legion of the United States, which would combine the infantry, cavalry, and artillery into separate sublegions. In contrast to St. Clair's army, which had fewer than 2,000 soldiers, the new Legion would have upward of 4,500 men. Dozens of officers would have to be appointed to take the places of the men who now lay dead on a snow-covered bluff somewhere south of Kekionga. Jefferson, as the secretary of state, would be responsible for signing every treaty negotiated with the Indians because the administration considered the tribes to be separate nations. He feared that the standing army necessary to subdue them would prove dangerous to a young republic like the United States, but he could think of no better way to punish the Ohio Indians for their insolence. If the new Legion could crush their resistance, then so be it. Hamilton, who oversaw the treasury, calculated the larger army would cost an extra $650,000 a year, taking military spending up to 15 percent of the nation's annual budget. Still he was certain the new tariff and tax structure he had proposed to Congress could handle the increase.[11]

The president told his cabinet that they must also be ready to explain how the administration had done everything in its power to ensure a victory for St. Clair. He directed Secretary Knox to prepare reports showing that continuing troubles north of the Ohio River, especially the murder of more than 1,500 American settlers by Indian warriors, along with the failure of the tribes to agree to any peace treaties, had led him as the commander in chief to send armies first under General Harmar and then under General St. Clair toward Kekionga, the capital of the Indian confederation causing all the misery in the western country. These reports must prove that the soldiers had been adequately supplied with arms and ammunition, food, and clothing, all requisitioned and paid for in a timely manner. When the initial drafts were less than perfect, Washington made Knox rewrite them and told Jefferson and Hamilton to compose stronger introductions.[12]

But even before his administration had fully prepared its defense, Washington learned that Congress was less than satisfied with his response to St. Clair's defeat. Signing his short note of the twelfth as "General" had not eased their anxiety but had only heightened it. The House of Representatives decided not to rely on the president for any further explanation of what had gone wrong. Instead a congressional committee would investigate why another army had been massacred in the wilderness. Once in session, the committee would call whatever witnesses it saw fit, including General St. Clair, his surviving officers, and even the secretary of war himself. The committee would likewise demand all of the administration's records on St. Clair's march toward Kekionga, especially any documents generated by the quartermaster general and the treasury that dealt with supplying the army.

Washington, who had hoped the brave face he put on after St. Clair's defeat would calm everyone, was at a momentary loss how to proceed. He called a cabinet meeting where he admitted that "he neither acknowledged nor denied nor even doubted the propriety" of the House's request "for he had not thought upon it, nor was he acquainted with subjects of this kind." Throughout the lengthy process of writing, debating, and ratifying the Constitution, no one had considered what might happen if the nation's legislative branch chose to investigate the nation's executive branch short of impeachment. Washington and his cabinet decided that some documents might have to remain secret, but ultimately the president, and not his executive officers, would decide what should or should not be handed over to Congress.[13]

Part of Washington's confusion stemmed from the fact that he still did not fully understand what had happened to the army on that terrible day in November. How could St. Clair have marched into the wilderness completely unaware that hundreds, maybe thousands, of Indians surrounded him? The president wondered to what extent the militia was to blame for this disaster. He had little faith in the fighting ability of men called from their farms on the spur of the moment to defend their country. They usually ran at the first sign of trouble. But could he say for certain that the soldiers had behaved any better? Drawn from the worst sort in the nation's cities, they signed up for short enlistments, hoping to be back home before any war actually started.

He got a better understanding when Lieutenant Ebenezer Denny arrived at his front door on the morning of December 19. One of the few survivors of the massacre, Denny was still deeply shaken by the experience. At thirty years of age, he had spent nearly half of his life in the military, serving as a post rider for the commander of Fort Pitt when he was just a boy, a soldier in the Pennsylvania Line during the American Revolution, and then an Indian fighter in the western country under General Harmar, but never had he experienced anything as terrible as the defeat of St. Clair's army. Denny had come east to Philadelphia by way of the Ohio River and the overland route from Pittsburgh. Everywhere he went people treated him like a ghost. The president's warm greeting was a welcome change. He invited Denny to have breakfast with Secretary Knox and himself. The lieutenant recalled that this was the second time he had met General Washington. In September 1781, when Washington had finally arrived at the American camp outside of Yorktown, having marched there from New York, he greeted every soldier in Denny's brigade, shaking the hand of each man one by one. Denny now took his commander's hand once again, but this time to speak not of victory but defeat.[14]

Much of what Denny told Washington and his secretary of war matched what they already knew from St. Clair's dispatches. The lieutenant remembered the cries of the warriors in the distance, the terrified militia crashing up the hill into the stunned soldiers, and the roar of the cannon as the smoke enveloped everyone. But he also recalled how quietly the Indians fought once the battle began. Everywhere Denny looked, the warriors moved in a kind of slow motion, calm, fearless, and so silent. They "seemed to brave everything, and when finally fixed around us, they made no noise other than their fire," as he had described in his diary, "which they kept up very constant and which seldom failed to tell, although scarcely heard."[15]

But it was clear from Denny's account that this awful spectacle was more than a magical dance of death. The Indians had perfectly executed their plans and controlled the battle from start to finish. Washington had long dismissed the warriors who dared to oppose him as mere "banditti," but now understood that the men who had orchestrated this massacre were far from outlaws. They were instead a highly disciplined fighting force. Their scouts had clearly identified the officers on St. Clair's march north from Fort Washington. When the battle began, the warriors gunned them down first, creating a panic among the terrified militia and enlisted men, who headed for the center of the camp where they could be easily cut down in the crossfire.[16]

Denny agreed with St. Clair that the bayonet charges which sent the Indians back across the river did little to stop the carnage. The warriors leapt from tree to tree, running ahead of every assault but then turning back when the soldiers retreated up the bluff to their camp. Denny remembered, too, the frightening moment when St. Clair decided "delay was death" and anyone still able to move must make a run for it. The order to retreat whispered down the broken columns meant many men would have to be left behind. Those still able to walk loaded muskets and pistols and handed them to the wounded as a last defense. Denny, appointed an aide-de-camp to St. Clair on the march north toward Kekionga, found the packhorse for his commander to ride and stayed with the general until ordered ahead to stop the rout of the retreating soldiers.[17]

Lieutenant Denny saw horrible things on the retreat that he would never be able to forget. He heard shot after shot go off behind him as the wounded made a last desperate fight to fend off death. He saw men carry their exhausted comrades only so far down the trail from the battlefield before throwing them to the ground and running ahead to save their own lives. He could not forget the dozens, maybe even hundreds, of women and children left mangled and dead on the battlefield. They were the wives and mistresses of the soldiers along with their sons and daughters. Some were even prostitutes. They had followed their men into the wilderness and had been cut down without mercy by the Indians. A few had been carried off, but most had been hacked to pieces with the limbs and breasts of the women cut off and the brains of the children dashed against the trees.

Denny would always remember a nameless woman who came behind his horse and clung to its tail, refusing to let go no matter how many times he threatened her with his sword or his mount kicked her. Finally, he lifted her onto his saddle and hurried toward Fort Jefferson.[18] Other soldiers farther up the line followed a tall redheaded woman called Nance who ran ahead of them. Her bright hair lit up like a torch giving the men courage to keep going in the last hours before nightfall. Terrified and exhausted, she left her two-year-old daughter somewhere along the trail, wanting more to save herself than her baby. She would spend the rest of her life searching for the girl, hoping some warrior had found the abandoned child and adopted her into his tribe, but she would never find her. The memory of it all—men, women, so many children, the cannon, guns and cartridge boxes, the dead horses, left rotting now in the snow among the wolves— was so awful that Denny planned to resign from the army.[19]

Washington and Knox had seen much of war and knew its horrors well. What they really needed was any information that Denny might have about what St. Clair and his army had done wrong. How had General St. Clair stumbled into this surprise attack and why had the men failed so badly once the battle began? The lieutenant recalled the terrible foreboding that hung over the soldiers as they prepared to march out of Fort Washington toward Kekionga. General Harmar, who had retired from the army the year before, wrote to Denny warning him that St. Clair's army would be massacred and adding that he hoped by some miracle the lieutenant might survive. Denny believed this mood of tragedy came from the fact that the soldiers were simply not ready to fight. Many had come from the streets and jails of the nation's eastern cities. They were marched straight away to

Fort Washington where no one trained them how to follow orders, fire their muskets, or fend off an Indian attack.

Was it any wonder that desertions were so high? More than a quarter of the
combined army and militia had run off by the first week of November, leaving
St. Clair with only a thousand soldiers. The officers who remained were excellent
commanders, many having served throughout the American Revolution, but few
had any experience in Indian warfare. The awful weather was another problem.
First the driving rain and then the autumn snow made marching difficult for the
army. The soldiers waded through flooded prairies and struggled along muddy
trails in the forest. They were hungry, too, a situation that Denny blamed on contractors who failed to deliver flour and beef on time.

The high ground chosen for the camp was still another problem. The bluff was
large enough to accommodate the army for the night but too small to allow the
soldiers to maneuver if attacked. Just as important, General St. Clair, who had
chosen the bluff in the first place, was a sick and tired old man, worn out from
years of fighting and now suffering from the gout, arthritis, and bouts of asthma.
The commander, who made his way north lying in a wagon, was in so much pain
that he failed to realize his army was not at the St. Mary's near Kekionga but was
instead fifty miles to the south along a branch of the Wabash. When Indians were
spotted late in the night lurking around the camp in great numbers, no one woke
the exhausted St. Clair to warn him.[20]

Even before he heard Denny's account of the battle, Washington had made up
his mind that St. Clair must go. The lieutenant's description of the confused state
of the army under the general's command only confirmed his decision. While
he might remain governor of the Northwest Territory, he would never again lead
men into battle. The president hoped that St. Clair would understand this and
resign his commission as a major general. But St. Clair had instead decided to
throw himself on the mercy of the president and was already on his way to Philadelphia to see him. He had left Fort Washington right after Denny and was now
traveling the longer southern route through Kentucky, Virginia, and Maryland
toward the nation's capital. He arrived in Philadelphia in January 1792 and made
his way to the house where the president had once warned him to beware of a
surprise.

Washington was waiting for him with his nine-year-old grandson and namesake George Washington Parke Custis at his side. The little boy, whom everyone
called "Wash," never forgot how kind his grandfather was to the old general who
hobbled forward to grab the president's outstretched hand. Later, when recalling
the meeting as a much older man, he remembered that St. Clair seemed like a
ship lost in a storm, battened down by the public and the press for his failures,

and finding shelter at last in the welcoming embrace of the president. Just by seeing him, Washington understood how sick St. Clair must have been on the march to Kekionga. He had been writing to Secretary Knox in great detail about the pains that gripped his stomach and his extremities, but no one in the War Department seemed to care about his suffering or consider how his poor health might affect his ability to command an army in the field.

All that was forgotten for the moment as St. Clair poured his heart out to Washington, telling him everything that had gone wrong on that terrible morning in the wilderness. He complained about the poor quality of his soldiers, who cared only about their pay and the date their enlistments were up. The quartermaster general and the contractors were just as disgraceful. They bought packhorses back east and marched them hundreds of miles across the mountains to the west. By the time they arrived at Fort Washington, the poor animals were worthless. St. Clair wondered what fool had ordered the march toward the Miami Villages so late in the season when such a march was next to impossible? Sending raw recruits into Indian country with winter weather approaching bordered on insanity. How could a handful of untrained soldiers defeat thousands of warriors who knew the woods and rivers of the Ohio Country like the back of their own hands? But most of all, what chance did he have of winning if his second in command, Richard Butler, was working against him?

One of the best officers in the Pennsylvania Line during the American Revolution, and Washington's own pick as St. Clair's second in command, Butler had withheld vital information about the strength of the enemy that surrounded their camp on the night before the battle. St. Clair also blamed Major Hamtramck and Lieutenant Kersey for turning the First Regiment around and taking the army back to Fort Jefferson. If not for this, he might have been able to regroup his soldiers and make another stand against the Indians. Taking no personal responsibility for the loss, St. Clair planned to retain his commission as a major general until he could defend his conduct before a military court of inquiry.[21]

Washington listened patiently to his failed general, but when St. Clair asked him to call a special military court into session, he refused, making the excuse that there were no other active major generals in the service capable of judging him. He knew St. Clair would probably tell the same sad story to the House committee investigating the massacre and so exonerate himself, but Washington would not allow him to testify before the army. He had read reports from St. Clair's surviving officers complaining of their commander's frailty and incompetence, including one published anonymously in a Philadelphia newspaper. The author was William Darke, the colonel who had led the final charge against the Indians before carrying his dying son Joseph back to Fort Jefferson. "A general, enwrapped ten-fold in flannel robes, unable to walk alone, placed on his car, bolstered on all sides with pillows and medicine, and thus moving on to attack the most active enemy in the world," Darke bitterly explained, "was a very tragic comical appearance indeed." Congress might enjoy ferreting out the deep rifts within the army's leadership, but the president would not help by making this information public. The weight of his decision to appoint St. Clair as the army's commander in chief bore heavily on Washington. He had thought the choice a wise one because St. Clair was an experienced soldier who as governor of the Northwest Territory must know the country between Fort Washington and the Miami Villages better than any other man. But it was now obvious that he had made a terrible miscalculation.[22]

Allowing St. Clair to retain his commission and so lead another army against the Indians would be an even greater mistake. The same problems that St. Clair had faced in the previous fall would await him in the next campaign. The re-cruits would still be raw, only now their officers would be equally inexperienced, the lay of the land would be just as impassable, and the same warriors would be waiting along the hidden trails of the forest to destroy this third army sent against them. Washington, who had restored such calm in his own soul, could hardly bear the thought of another defeat. The western country might be lost forever to the Indians and their British allies, whose forts would now be firmly planted at Niagara, Oswego, Detroit, and Michillimackinac, barring all passage north of the Ohio and even threatening all settlements south of it. Refusing to countenance this possibility, he could only hope that St. Clair would resign his commission and so graciously make way for his replacement.

But who should replace him? Washington planned to call his cabinet together in a month's time to discuss the matter. Preparing for this, he wrote out a list of the sixteen men still living who had been major or brigadier generals, either offi-cially appointed or by brevet in the field, at the end of the Revolution. Working sometimes with Secretary Knox but more often alone, he tried to recall the strengths and weaknesses of each man to the last detail. While only a decade had passed since Yorktown, Washington noticed how many of the men were just like St. Clair—sick, old, and tired. In his eyes, there was only one person on the list worthy of the commission of commander in chief of the Legion of the United States. That man was Charles Coatesworth Pinckney.[23]

Just thirty-four years old, Pinckney was already an accomplished leader. Son of the indigo planter Eliza Lucas, he was one of the wealthiest and best educated men in the nation. Before the war, he had studied at Oxford with the renowned jurist William Blackstone. Later he trained in law at the Temple in London and in war at the Royal Military Academy at Caen, France. Joining the Patriots early in the Revolution, he first met Washington before the Battle of Brandywine. The general took an immediate liking to him and made him an aide-de-camp. Three years later Pinckney fought bravely in the defense of Charleston where he was captured by the British and imprisoned. When the redcoats encouraged him to switch sides, he famously replied, "If I had a vein that did not beat with love for my country, I myself would open it. If I had a drop of blood that could flow dishonorable, I myself would let it out." Washington remembered him just as fondly for the key role he played in helping to draft the Constitution at the convention in Philadelphia. "He is a man of strict honor, erudition and good sense," he wrote beneath Pinckney's name.[24]

But there were problems with his nomination. Washington had already asked Pinckney to join his cabinet as either the secretary of war or the secretary of state, but he had turned down both offers. If he refused to serve in the government, would he be more willing to lead an army against the Indians in the Ohio Country? Even more troubling, Pinckney had never commanded soldiers in the field and won his generalship only by brevet in the last days of the war. Would men who had fought for years at a higher rank be willing to serve under him? Washington thought not, and what a disaster that would be for the nation if General Pinckney was cut down in another massacre because his ablest officers had abandoned the field.

If he could set aside the list in front of him, and pick the best man in the country to lead a third army toward Kekionga, Washington would choose the dashing Colonel Henry Lee, the very image of himself as a younger man. Just a year older than Pinckney, Lee had won the nickname "Lighthorse Harry" as the commander of his own cavalry unit in the Revolution. His attack on the British post at Paulus Hook was so brilliant that the Continental Congress struck a gold medal in his honor. He led his men all the way to Yorktown before resigning, exhausted and broken from so many years of fighting in the saddle. But Lee had regained his health and made a name for himself in politics. He had, in fact, just been elected the governor of Virginia. As soon as Lee learned of St. Clair's defeat, he wrote to Washington, offering to lead his state's militia all the way to Kekionga. What better man than this to secure the vast Ohio Country first claimed by Virginia in its second colonial charter? Still Washington had to admit that Lee had never risen above the rank of colonel. Despite his talents on and off the battlefield, many a proud man might refuse to serve under him.[25]

If neither Pinckney nor Lee was a real possibility, then Washington must search again through the fifteen other names on his list. He remembered each man as best he could, judging them against the three characteristics he considered most essential for the task at hand. The man chosen must be active, brave, and sober, meaning he must have enough drive to shape untested men for battle, be willing to take his army deep into the Indian country when so ordered, and have his wits about him at all times, and so he could not be a drunkard, something that Washington particularly abhorred. The president had heard the rumors that General Harmar lay drunk in his tent as his men died all about him during the campaign a year before St. Clair's defeat. He did not dare to send another sot west to take on the Indians. Still there was an even more important trait that Washington could not bring himself to mention. The man chosen for this unenviable command had to win the next battle against the Indians. He absolutely could not fail. When that terrible moment came and he found himself in the same place that St. Clair had been, on unfamiliar ground surrounded by screaming warriors with their British guns pointed at him, he must defeat them for the good of his nation and his own honor.[26]

But who was this man? Washington was dissatisfied with every other name he had written down besides Pinckney, including three of the most distinguished generals of the Continental Army: Benjamin Lincoln, Baron Friedrich Steuben, and Daniel Morgan. Although the same age as the president, Lincoln seemed to have lost all his vigor. He had been a brave if not always successful commander, losing badly at Savannah and Charleston when he led the southern wing of the army, but he was dedicated and would surely take the post if offered, although reluctantly. He would perhaps make a better negotiator with the Indians than a general against them. Steuben, a German who was just as brave as Lincoln, had given the best of his talents to his adopted country, especially his drill manual that trained the Continental Army at Valley Forge. But as a foreigner, and an impetuous one at that, he was afflicted with a keen sense of his own superiority. The men loved him as he drilled them in the terrible winter of 1778, finding him almost comical, but there would be nothing funny about an arrogant martinet molding his raw recruits in the wilderness. Washington was even more critical of the expert rifleman Daniel Morgan, the hero of Saratoga and Cowpens. He now remembered Morgan as more fortunate than talented. The old general was also quite sick, wracked with rheumatism since well before Yorktown. Even worse, Washington worried that Morgan might be a drunkard and knew for a fact he was quite illiterate, something that would not do for a commanding general who must stay in constant communication with the War Department during the next campaign.[27]

There were many generals who had served primarily in the South during the Revolution and so the president could remember very little about them since he had fought mainly in the North. He recalled that William Moultrie was a brave man who had experience fighting the Cherokee. He had just met Moultrie, now the governor of South Carolina, on his tour of the southern states the previous spring. The two men were even corresponding about gardening. But he could not say for certain that Moultrie would make a good leader. Nor could he remember much about his third cousin Mordecai Gist of Maryland. He recalled that Gist was quite spirited, fighting bravely at Long Island and with the southern wing of the Continental Army well past Yorktown, but these traits were not enough to give him command of the Legion of the United States. Lachlan McIntosh had been just as brave but now, at sixty-five years of age, was old and inactive, a fact that Washington learned firsthand when he met him in Savannah on his southern tour. A native of Georgia, McIntosh had been one of the first generals to take on the Ohio tribes during the Revolution. He built Fort Laurens on the Tuscarawas River and even planned an attack on the British at Fort Detroit. But like Moultrie and Gist, he was little known outside of the South. Even in his home state of Georgia, he was best remembered for murdering Button Gwinnett, a signer of the Declaration of Independence, in a duel. McIntosh was definitely not the man to assume command of an army whose remnants were blaming each other for their defeat.[28]

Washington was just as dissatisfied with the other men on his list who had some experience fighting Indians along the frontier. William Irvine, a top officer in the Pennsylvania Line, had defended the country around Pittsburgh at the war's end, but the president could not recall what type of officer he had been, good, bad, or indifferent. He was certain, however, that George Weedon was not suitable for the post. During the French and Indian War, Weedon had served under Washington in the Virginia militia, but as an older man, he had become addicted to ease and pleasure. He was also, as the president noted, no enemy of the bottle. Charles Scott, who witnessed the Shawnee murder his young son by cutting out his heart, had led the Kentucky militia in successful raids against Indian villages along the Wabash in the summer before St. Clair's defeat. But Washington dismissed him as a drunkard better known for his foul mouth than for any bravery on the battlefield. Rufus Putnam, a founder of the Ohio Company, had led a group of New Englanders to his frontier settlement of Marietta on the Ohio River. He was appointed one of the first judges of the Northwest Territory so he well knew the troubles of the Ohio Country. Yet Washington worried that Putnam, scholarly, squint-eyed, and not a young man to be sure, was little known outside of his native Connecticut. Like Lincoln, he might make a better negotiator than a general. The president also could not remember anything remarkable about Edward Hand, forgetting that he had commanded Fort Pitt at the start of the Revolution where he fought off many Indian attacks.[29]

Finally, Washington took a last look at the men he had known early in the war.

While many were still quite young and none was a drunkard for sure, each one had something questionable about him. Jedidiah Huntington had made a name for himself at Bunker Hill. A judicious and upright New Englander, he served at the court-martial of General Charles Lee, who had sounded the retreat too early at Monmouth Courthouse, and on the panel that condemned Major John André to death. "Sober, sensible and very discreet," wrote the President, but there was no evidence he could command an army in the Indian country. Otho Williams, a close friend of Hamilton, would be a better choice. Fighting bravely at Boston and Long Island, where like Pinckney he was captured and held for two years in a British prison, he went on to distinguish himself at Camden, Guilford Court-house, and Eutaw Springs. He was an active and brave soldier, Washington re-membered, though a bit vain. He might be the best choice if not for his delicate health, which had sent him to the mineral waters of Sweet Springs high in the Blue Ridge Mountains for the last few years. If Williams was offered the position, would he take it, and even if he accepted, how long would he survive? Another possibility was James Wilkinson, who was already serving under General St. Clair and who last year had led raids against Indian villages in the Wabash River Valley. Sensible, active, and lively, at least as far as he described himself in glowing let-ters to the War Department, Wilkinson had played a part in the attempt to topple Washington in favor of General Horatio Gates during the terrible winter at Valley Forge. Pompous and ambitious, he could definitely not be trusted with the com-mand of the Legion of the United States.[30]

There was only one man left on the list, and for the moment, Washington could not think of a single good thing to say about him. Some might consider him active and enterprising but this came at the price of his judgment and his caution. He was generous with his men, always spending more on their food and clothing than allowed. They in turn took advantage of him in part because he cared so deeply about their welfare, but also because he was terribly vain. All this made him prone to getting into scrapes where his temper exploded in de-fense of his honor. Everyone who knew him could attest to his love of brandy and Madeira, but whether he was a drunkard, Washington could not say. But cer-tainly he was like so many aging veterans of the late war. His best days were be-hind him and so he spent many a night in front of a roaring fire with his friends and a bottle or two, reminiscing about past glories. All the while, he grew older and heavier from a lingering wound and fevers, the gout, and all that wine.

But how beautiful Anthony Wayne had been when he rode into Washington's camp on Long Island in April 1776. At thirty-one years of age, he was in the prime of his life. Not quite six feet tall, he was strong and muscular, impeccably dressed with his dark hair powdered and tied back with a ribbon, his blue coat

Portrait of Wayne in 1776. William L. Clements Library, University of Michigan.

and white pants spotless, and his black boots shining. Like so many other young men who had joined the Continental Army, he was on fire for the Revolution and eager to share his plans for victory, all drawn from the ancient history books he loved. With his high forehead, dark eyes, and aquiline nose, he even looked like the Roman generals he was so fond of quoting. A child of wealth and privilege with a gentleman's education, he conversed with ease about the ancient past and rode so perfectly that his first duty was to accompany several officers on a foxhunt through the countryside.[31]

But Wayne quickly proved that he was more than a dilettante who had little to offer his commander in chief. Right from the start, Washington appreciated the "irrepressible enthusiasm" of the young colonel, and, for all his excitability, his coolness under fire. He never panicked once a battle started. No general could maneuver soldiers more quickly while fighting or retreating than Anthony Wayne. He proved this in his first contest at Three Rivers in Canada when he led the defeated Continental Army back to safety across the St. Lawrence. He had a deep well of patience within him, too, which he showed in his yearlong command of Fort Ticonderoga after the loss at Three Rivers. Even though he had a wildly passionate side, there was a calm within him and the willingness to endure any trial if so ordered.

Many thought of Wayne as daring, but Washington knew a better word for him was devoted. He was completely committed to the cause of liberty, his new nation, and his commander in chief. Washington learned this after he called him back from Ticonderoga to help defend Philadelphia. Wayne's main concern seemed to be proving himself to his commander. No general tried harder to fulfill Washington's every command than Wayne. He stayed on the heights above Chadds Ford long after Brandywine was lost. He was the only general who executed Washington's complex plans in the fog and confusion of Germantown. At Monmouth, he formed the center of the line that almost won the battle. He climbed up the cliffs of Stony Point and later raced to West Point when Arnold deserted. He tightened the snare around Cornwallis in Virginia and helped dig the trenches at Yorktown.[32]

But Wayne was far from perfect. He had a volatile temper that troubled Washington. He gave free rein to his emotions at first blush with no fear of appearing out of control. If Wayne felt something, he said so, caring little what the reaction of others might be. Maybe that was why Washington, who had spent so much of his life repressing the darker shadings of his character, was never quite at ease with Wayne. He certainly could not muster the same devotion for his brigadier that Wayne felt for him. Nor did he like Wayne's tendency, at least early in the war, to consider himself invincible. This left him open to surprise attacks, like the one near the Paoli Tavern outside Philadelphia when the British bayoneted his soldiers in the dark of night. If Washington chose Wayne to command the next army sent into the Ohio wilderness, would he make the same mistake and lead his men into another slaughter? If he survived the massacre, like St. Clair had done, would his temper explode against anyone who dared to question him and so plunge the administration into another crisis?[33]

Still there was much to weigh in his favor, especially his acute loyalty. So many times when all hope seemed lost, Washington could always count on Wayne. There was no task so meager that he would not do it if his commander asked. In the ruination of Valley Forge, with rumors of generals and politicians turning against him, Washington ordered his officers to scour the countryside for food. Wayne rounded up cattle from local farmers with no complaint, never minding that the British mocked him as the "Drover" and later the "Cow Chacer." When the Continental Army needed still more food and clothes, Washington turned to Wayne for help. He launched blistering attacks on Pennsylvania's politicians, demanding supplies even as he questioned their patriotism and very manhood. Finally, when the British left Philadelphia for New York City, Washington, wanting desperately to attack, asked his generals if they agreed. Most were tentative but not Wayne. "Fight, Sir!" was his answer.[34]

Washington grew especially close to Wayne after the Battle of Monmouth, but they lost touch with one another after Wayne headed south to fight with the Marquis de Lafayette in Virginia. They met for the last time at Yorktown where, for once in the long war, Wayne doubted whether the Continental Army would ever defeat the British, while Washington came at last to believe the final triumph was near. When all the victory celebrations were over, Washington ordered an exhausted Wayne south to help General Nathanael Greene retake the Carolinas and Georgia from the British. Although he begged his commander not to send him, asking instead to be allowed to return if only for a time to the family he had ignored since the start of the war, Wayne once again did as his commander asked.[35]

The two men did not meet again until nearly ten years later when President Washington traveled south in the spring of 1791 on his grand tour of the republic. Wayne, who was now living on a plantation outside Savannah granted to him by the Georgia legislature, helped organize the festivities in the town. However, none of Wayne's plans, not the flotilla down the Savannah, not the dinners or fancy dress ball, and not even the fireworks along the river's edge, impressed Washington. He went with Wayne to see the fortifications where Benjamin Lincoln had laid siege to the British in Savannah, noting in his diary how sad it was that every remnant of the battle had disappeared in so short a time. But he seemed more interested in leaving for Mulberry Grove, the plantation of the late General Greene, an officer he remembered far more fondly than Wayne, most especially to see his widow Catharine who had lit up many a somber night at Valley Forge. He had stopped there on his way from Columbia to Savannah and now rode to her plantation once again before heading back to South Carolina.[36]

On his way north, Washington mentioned in a letter to Tobias Lear that he had met General Wayne, but added nothing more about him. While he certainly seemed livelier than many of the other men who greeted him on his southern tour, the president failed to note how much Wayne had changed since their days together in the Continental Army. On many mornings, Wayne woke up sick from recurring bouts of malaria that he had contracted fighting in the swamps of Georgia during the last year of the war. Sometimes he was in such pain from gout and an old wound in his leg that he could barely get out of bed. As the debts against his plantation mounted, he found his days haunted by the "blue damsels" of despair, as he called his depression. In the long lonely nights, his drinking increased to a point that seemed excessive even in an age of heavy drinkers.[37]

While the president paid no attention to Wayne's troubles while visiting Savannah, he could not ignore the scandals surrounding his former brigadier once he returned to Philadelphia. Almost everyone in the highest circles knew that Wayne had flirted with bankruptcy as he struggled to make his rice plantation profitable. His creditors in Savannah and Charleston threatened to auction off his family's estate at Waynesborough near Philadelphia at a sheriff's sale. What made matters worse was the fact that Wayne did not seem to care that the loss of his ancestral home would leave his wife without a roof over her head. The ties between Wayne and his family, especially Polly Wayne, the bride of his youth, had unraveled long ago. Since the opening days of the Revolution, a string of beautiful women had flocked around him. When he came back from Georgia to serve in Congress, he entertained women as well as men at nightly parties in his lodgings in Philadelphia. He enjoyed himself up until the very moment that the candidate he had defeated in Georgia showed up with evidence that Wayne's friends had rigged the election.

Of all the scandals engulfing Wayne, Washington was most troubled by the sorry state of his personal finances. His near bankruptcy proved he had still not learned how to handle money since the war ended and therefore was no "œconomist." But the president had to admit there were more points in Wayne's favor than against him, including the fact that he came from Pennsylvania. So far, the government, under both the Confederation and the Constitution, had always appointed Pennsylvanians to handle Indian affairs in the western country. Washington, who was sensitive to the old colonial claims of both his home state of

Virginia and Pennsylvania to land across their borders, tended to bow to the leadership of Pennsylvanians like Josiah Harmar and Arthur St. Clair. Given this tradition, Washington was certain that his cabinet would accept Wayne as the next logical choice to lead the army.[38]

But the president's department heads were less than enthusiastic at the prospect of Wayne taking command of the Legion of the United States. Hamilton and Knox, who both knew him well, preferred the brilliant Pinckney. Jefferson was even less convinced that Wayne was a wise choice. While no one could doubt his courage, in the opinion of a rational person like Jefferson, he often carried his bravery to the point of stupidity. Wayne was the kind of man who continued to beat his head against a wall and keep up the fight even when all hope for victory was lost. Maybe that was why some of his men called him "Mad Anthony" behind his back. To his face, they called him "Dandy Tony." His fastidious dress in a world of unwashed men made him somewhat laughable. Washington's cabinet could only agree to appoint Wayne if worthier candidates, meaning Pinckney or Lee, would truly have a problem with more experienced men refusing to serve under them.[39]

Yet there was a remarkable thing about Anthony Wayne that Washington knew better than any man in the room. If you could get past his terrible handwriting, a rapid-fire scrawl with letters tumbling over each other as his pen raced to keep up with his mind, you would discover that he was one of the best letter writers of his generation. There was a drama in his prose, a kind of rising and falling action that betrayed his love of literature and his appreciation for a well-turned phrase. There was also a breadth and depth to his writing that brought whatever he was describing to life for his reader. He had a keen eye for laying out any situation the Continental Army found itself in and seeing every possible contingency the soldiers faced. He could explain the strengths and weaknesses of the enemy in near perfect detail and analyze what went right or wrong for both sides after the last shot was fired better than any man. He well understood the dark side of war, especially the ever-present possibility of his own death, and yet his letters to his commander in chief were usually filled with an irrepressible cheer. Before every battle, Washington could count on a letter from Wayne telling him all would be well. Julius Caesar had been in the same situation long ago and had gone on to victory. When all the fighting was over and the Continental Army had not triumphed like the Roman legions of old, Washington could expect another letter from Wayne telling him not to worry, for in the end victory was still assured.

Yes, it must be Wayne. Not only would he be the eyes and ears of Washington in the western country, but there was still one more thing in his favor. Wayne wanted the job and had been campaigning to serve his country ever since Washington became president. He had written to Washington after his election, using his surname as a freestanding noun, telling the beloved commander that the country needed "a Washington." In his opinion, the country also needed a Wayne. He asked Washington to appoint him either as the adjutant general or surveyor general of the United States. He had written to James Madison, who would be one of the top leaders in the new Congress, outlining the dangers posed by the Spanish and the Indians along the nation's southern frontier. Let me serve as the governor of all the land between Georgia and the Mississippi River, he begged, just as St. Clair was serving as the governor of the territory north of the Ohio River. Getting no firm answer from either Washington or Madison, he wrote to Knox, and since arriving back in Philadelphia to take his seat in Congress, he came often to Knox's office telling him he would serve in whatever capacity the secretary of war saw fit. When all was said and done, there seemed no person better suited to lead the army than Wayne, especially after the House of Representatives voted on March 16, 1792, to remove him from office and called for a new election in his congressional district. Only one problem remained. Before officially recommending him, Washington asked Knox to make sure that Wayne, so humiliated by Congress, would still take the position.[40]

For a man drowning in debt, estranged from his family, and now publicly shamed by his own government, taking command of his nation's army in so desperate an hour was like grabbing hold of a lifeline. Wayne, largely unaware of the terrible things being said about him behind closed doors, was sure no man deserved the position more than he. "I have fought and bled for the liberties of America" was another more crimson thread that ran through his letters. He had suffered in the deepest snows of Ticonderoga, where death stalked his men and turned the fortress meant to protect them into a "House of Carnage." He had endured the icy rains of Valley Forge, where his soldiers were "too naked to appear on the parade" ground and where he nearly lost his patience with a world grown so weary and so bad. He had survived the brutal heat of Georgia, made even worse by the fires he set to the rice plantations of Loyalists along the Savannah River and the burning hatred of the Tories and Whigs who murdered each other in the backcountry in a way that "beggars all description."[41]

Having endured so much misery for his country, Wayne accepted his commission with no illusion that the task would be an easy one. While many thought him mad in his bravery and perhaps even drunk with a love for war, nothing could have been further from the truth. He had come to hate war as a "horrid trade of blood." He especially loathed Indian warfare, where day and night a commander and his army lived on the edge, waiting for the warriors hidden deep in the forest to strike. He was certain that only careful planning and a near fanatical training of his men could save the Legion of the United States from another disaster in the wilderness. But he loved his nation far more than he hated war. In fact, he loved his country the way a man loves a woman. In the sea of women he had known since he was a boy, she was his greatest love. Even when she treated him so falsely, never paying him for his many years of service, loaning him not one penny to rebuild his fortune after the war, and finally throwing him out of Congress, he could not abandon her now but must rescue her one more time.[42]

Neither could he abandon the commander he loved so dearly. How many times before had he come to the rescue of George Washington? He had climbed the sheer cliffs below Stony Point and taken the British post high atop it all for him. Only a mad man, so many people now said, would dare such a feat. He had rounded up cows to feed his general's starving army from Valley Forge to Bull's Ferry. The reward was ridicule. He had begged him after Yorktown, when so many others were going home, to let him go, too. Instead he was ordered to retake Georgia with no food, few arms, and only a handful of men. After the war, when his beloved general had become the first president of the nation they had fought so hard to create, he tried for a post in the new government but was always turned away. Yet now in this darkest hour when lesser men had failed him, Washington turned once again to the man who would bear anything for him.

The task set for Wayne seemed impossible. He must raise an army in place of the one that lay butchered and unburied in a distant forest. After he trained his soldiers, he must lead them back into the same forest where they would have to fight the same frightening and determined foe. Wayne knew he could not fail. He must win whatever battle came his way and so he must wrap his swollen legs and arms in flannel, pack up his best brandy and Madeira and his writing table, and head west to Ohio. But before he left, he would take the time to write out his last will and testament because he was absolutely certain that he would not come back from this last campaign for the nation and commander he loved alive.[43]

"May God Shut the Door of Mercy on Us"

There were a few things that Anthony Wayne had to do before he left Philadelphia to take up his new command at Pittsburgh. First, he had to settle his many outstanding bills, especially for the food and drink he served nightly in his quarters in the city. Washington's fear that Wayne was a drunkard might have been confirmed if he knew how much Madeira his former brigadier purchased. A gallon a week, along with regular quantities of brandy and port, seemed to prove that the newly appointed commander in chief of the Legion of the United States was unfit for duty. But Wayne, who rarely shied away from defending himself, would have assured the president that he was not the only one drinking. The many guests he welcomed into his flat every evening, both "gentlemen" and "ladies," helped him down glass after glass of wine along with the dinner and dessert he provided. Wayne loved entertaining his wide circle of friends, and was as generous with them as he had been with his military family during the late war. If Washington had known him better, he might not have worried about his drinking, but instead how a man so convivial and outgoing would ever survive in the isolation of the western frontier.[1]

Once all his bills were paid, not just for wine and food, but for the seamstresses, who made him shirts with cravats and sewed golden buttons on his coats, Wayne would finally have to face the task he had been avoiding. He must tell his wife Polly that he was going away, not back to Congress which had just unseated him, but instead to another campaign. This one would take him into the lonely wilderness beyond the Ohio and would be so perilous that in all likelihood he would never return. To soften the blow, he decided to write to her before heading to Waynesborough, their estate twenty miles outside of Philadelphia, to tell her in person. In his letter, he explained, as he had done so many times before, that his duty to his country called him away again. He did not admit what truly worried him, that he would probably be killed, but instead mentioned that no man could be certain of the future and therefore an "accident" might befall him. When he received no answer from Polly, he decided to do something nice for her when he was away. He would build a new wing onto their stone house at Waynesborough with a kitchen at its center. The room would have a large window that looked out over the garden and china cabinets built into the walls from the floor to the ceiling. The old keeping room, which once served as a living room, dining room, and kitchen, would be transformed into a library with shelves for Wayne's two hundred books. The new kitchen, soon to be connected to the formal dining room, which sat beyond the blue parlor at the front of the house, would be so beautiful that Polly might forget his long absences. She might even forgive all the wrong he had done to her since the Revolution began.[2]

But Wayne did not add specific details about what he imagined would happen in the upcoming campaign. He had usually done this before every battle, but not this time as he prepared to leave for Pittsburgh. More than the strain between himself and his wife caused his reticence. For one of the rare times in his life, he simply could not see what lay ahead. He had never faced an assignment of this magnitude. As a brigadier general in the Continental Army's Pennsylvania Line, he commanded on average twelve hundred men. For a few months, after Valley Forge, he led a small light infantry corps. After Yorktown, he received his first independent command in Georgia, but never had more than five hundred soldiers at a time. But now he must help recruit five thousand men, organize them into the new formation of a Legion, and train everyone, almost singlehandedly, to fight an invisible enemy. Having begged Washington, Knox, and even James Madison for a chance to prove his worth, the goal he had for so long pursued had become a nightmare.[3]

As he prepared to leave Philadelphia, Wayne could at least see one thing clearly. He was not heading west simply to avenge the massacre of the army, but to fulfill the mission that St. Clair had failed to achieve. Above all else, he, and the army he would raise and train, must defend the treaties signed by Great Britain and the Indians which surrendered the Ohio Country to his nation. The British had given up their claims to the land in the treaty ending the Revolution, but retained key forts along the northern edge of the surrendered territory, which remained an embarrassment and a threat to the supposedly independent United States of America. For the time being, the Confederation Congress and President Washington had pushed this matter aside, preferring to deal with the more pressing issue of what to do with the many Indians who lived beyond the Ohio River.[4]

They had started by drawing a border, commonly known as the "Indian boundary," between the land clearly controlled by the United States, meaning the old colonial settlements along the eastern seaboard, and the country west of the border still controlled by the tribes. Recognizing the Indians as the original owners of the land, they sent commissioners among them to write treaties that transferred ownership of the country from the tribes to the United States. Once this was complete, the American government would open the surrendered territory for sale and settlement to its citizens. Negotiations began in the North with the Six Nations and continued in the South with major tribes like the Cherokee and Creek. As the Indians signed away their country piece by piece, the boundary between themselves and the United States moved ever westward. One day it would disappear completely and the Americans would finally take full possession of the country they had won on paper from the British at the end of the Revolution.[5]

In 1784, when Wayne was still recovering from the damage that fighting in the Continental Army had done to his body and spirit, commissioners appointed by the Confederation Congress had headed to Fort Stanwix in western New York. Here they convinced five of the Six Nations—the Seneca, Mohawk, Onondaga, Cayuga, and Tuscarora—to give up much of their traditional homeland as well as all claims to the country across the Ohio River. The commissioners drew the first official Indian boundary meant to keep the Americans safe on one side and hold the tribes at bay on the other. The line began near Fort Niagara on Lake Ontario, headed south toward Buffalo Creek, and then followed the western border of Pennsylvania to the Ohio River. In 1785, the same negotiators moved on to Fort McIntosh, a stockade built during the Revolution where the Beaver River emptied into the Ohio River. Here they met with more tribes, including the Wyandot, Delaware, Ottawa, and Chippewa, who had fought against the United States in the late war, winning their approval for a new boundary set even farther west.

Starting at Lake Erie, the line headed south along the Cuyahoga to its portage with the Tuscaroras and then along its branches to Fort Laurens, another Revolutionary War post. It next turned west to Pickawilliny, an Indian town destroyed by the French in 1752, located in the portage of the Great Miami, and from this point traveled along the southeast side of the river to the Ohio. In 1786, at Fort Finney, which was constructed at the mouth of the Great Miami, the negotiators returned and pressured the Shawnee into accepting the Fort McIntosh boundary. Three years later, just weeks before George Washington was sworn into office as president of the United States, the negotiators were back at Fort Harmar, built at the mouth of the Muskingum River, to meet with the Ohio tribes along with the Six Nations, this time including the Oneida, who agreed to the border determined at Fort McIntosh.[6]

Wayne understood that, as the Legion's commander in chief, he must uphold the boundary set at Fort McIntosh and later reaffirmed at Fort Finney and Fort Harmar. He carried copies of these treaties in a large leather trunk filled with his correspondence that he took with him on every campaign. Washington had chosen him to lead an army against tribes that had signed these treaties, but who now argued that the Ohio River, not the line set at Fort McIntosh, was the true boundary between their peoples. The president, certain his nation had secured the approval of the Six Nations, as well as major tribes like the Wyandot, Delaware, and Shawnee, for his citizens to settle north of the Ohio up to the Fort McIntosh line, maintained that a few banditti from these tribes, along with Indians living farther west on the Wabash, were fomenting resistance. These warriors preyed upon government surveyors sent out to carve up their surrendered country into townships, and without mercy murdered men, women, and even children trying to settle there. He had ordered Governor St. Clair to win a treaty with the "Wabash Indians," his administration's name for the Miami and their allies, and to establish a fort at the tribe's main town, Kekionga to the Indians and the Miami Villages to the Americans. By so doing, the United States would open a substantial portion of the Ohio Country to settlement and maybe even intimidate the British into surrendering their remaining forts on American soil.[7]

But St. Clair had failed at both tasks, and so now Wayne must secure the Fort McIntosh line and establish a fort at the Miami Villages. A surveyor himself who well knew how to read a map, he agreed completely with his nation's plans for the Ohio Country. When he peered into the future, he envisioned the *"Empire of America,"* and not a loose confederation of states, spreading westward. But he could not see the men he would have to fight to win this empire across the Appalachians. He knew only that they were frightening warriors who came storming out of the forest at dawn to hack an army to pieces. A party of Creek warriors had surprised and nearly killed him outside Savannah during the last days of the Revolution. The mere thought of what they had almost done to him, what they had actually done to St. Clair's men, and what they might do to his soldiers, who had not even been recruited yet, was almost too horrifying to imagine. Wayne had no fear of the British commanders who stood behind them and, as he believed, directed their every move. He knew them all: Guy Carleton, also known as Lord Dorchester, the governor in chief of Canada; John Graves Simcoe, the lieutenant governor of Upper Canada; and Alured Clarke, the lieutenant governor of Lower Canada. He had fought them one by one at Three Rivers on the St. Lawrence, along the James River in Virginia, and in the swamps of Georgia. But who were the warriors they commanded? How had they been able to crush every army sent against them? How should he train his soldiers to fight them? He must find the answers before he led his Legion against them.[8]

Wayne read everything on Indians he could find in Philadelphia. He talked with anyone who had real experience with them. He gained some insights from General Harmar, who had retired from the army after his loss to the Indians along the Wabash in 1790. Harmar, a fellow Pennsylvanian who served with Wayne throughout the Revolution, encouraged him to protect his supply lines. They would be stretched to the limit when the Legion marched from Fort Washington toward the Miami Villages. Wayne also turned to Rufus Putnam, a former officer in his light infantry corps. Washington decided against appointing him as St. Clair's successor, but recruited him instead to treat with the Wabash Indians. Putnam's Ohio Company held the title to 1,500,000 acres north of the Ohio River. He brought settlers there from Massachusetts in 1788 firmly believing that if he dealt fairly with the Indians, they would not attack his towns. Before founding Marietta, where the Muskingum emptied into the Ohio, he met with local chiefs, buying their land and promising that his followers would never harm them. He was therefore stunned when Wyandot and Delaware warriors attacked Big Bottom, just thirty miles up the Muskingum from Marietta, late on the evening of January 2, 1791. Settlers had felt so safe living there that they never posted sentries or finished their blockhouse. The surprise attack on their farms, which left twelve people dead and the rest marched into captivity, sent shockwaves through the nation and compelled President Washington to send St. Clair's army toward the Miami Villages later that year.[9]

Putnam taught Wayne that the Indians could not be trusted, but John Heckewelder, a longtime missionary to the Delaware, explained there was more to them than brutality. He knew the tribes across the Ohio better than any man in Philadelphia, and for this reason Washington asked him to help Putnam in the negotiations along the Wabash. Heckewelder had worked with Reverend David Zeisberger establishing missions among the Delaware Indians. He helped build the towns of Schönbrunn, Gnadenhutten, Lichtenau, and Salem on the Muskingum where converts to the faith, nicknamed the "Praying Indians," lived under the watchful eye of Christian missionaries. Knowing the Indians as well as he did, Heckewelder maintained there was more to the struggles in the Ohio Country than bloodthirsty warriors murdering innocent settlers. He had, in fact, seen much more cruelty on the frontier against Indians than anyone else.[10]

One of the worst incidents came when Wayne was fighting with the Continental Army in Virginia and later Georgia. In September 1781, warriors allied with the British, mainly the Wyandot and other Delaware, believed the Praying

Indians were not as neutral as their leader Reverend Zeisberger claimed. They forcibly removed them from Gnadenhutten to the Sandusky River to prevent them from helping the Americans. Zeisberger and Heckewelder were sent to Fort Detroit where the British tried them for treason, but acquitted and released them. Six months later, the Praying Indians, desperate for food, returned to their town on the Muskingum to collect stores of grain and harvest the corn still standing in the fields. But before they could gather in their crops and return safely to the Sandusky, militiamen arrived from Pennsylvania. They were determined to punish the people of Gnadenhutten for recent raids on their settlements. Placing the men in one hut and the women with their sons and daughters in another, they clubbed and scalped nearly one hundred people to death, more than one-third of them children. The hymns and prayers of the Indians had no effect on their executioners. Two boys survived to tell the story of the massacre. A shattered Zeisberger finally found a new home for his followers along the Tuscarawas River and stayed with them until his own death in 1808. But Heckewelder, who had seen enough bloodshed to last a lifetime, headed back to Bethlehem, Pennsylvania, in 1786 to live in peace with his wife and daughters.[11]

While many used the term "savages" interchangeably with "Indians," Heckewelder argued their character was far more complex. After all, they were children of the same God that most Americans worshipped. He found them to be deeply moral people, especially toward members of their own tribes, whom they treated with a respect that whites rarely showed one another. There was hardly a liar or thief among them. Proud to a fault, the Indians were highly intelligent with a keen knowledge of history. They remembered every wrong done to them by the "Long Knives," the name they first applied to the Virginians and later all Americans. They traced the troubles between their two peoples to one main difference. The Great Spirit had created the red men as hunters and the white men as farmers. This caused a strain between them since the Indians must range over a wide area to hunt while the whites must claim ever more territory for their farms. But no matter how much land the tribes ceded to them, the whites were never satisfied. They must have every last inch of the Indian country just as they must pile up ever more earthly treasures.[12]

Heckewelder hoped his fellow Americans would realize that their relentless quest for land had caused much of the trouble north of the Ohio. The Indians were patient at first when settlers overran their country. They endured many insults before retaliating, but a moment always came when the warriors, duty bound as any other men to protect their families, struck back, usually against the nearest settlement. They rarely attacked in broad daylight, preferring instead to strike after dusk, in the middle of the night, or just before dawn. Coming silently in single file through the woods, they were never spotted until the moment they emerged from the forest. Whether they struck an isolated settlement, or were bold enough to surround an entire army, as they had done to St. Clair, they were merciless, killing their enemy in gruesome ways. They were expert marksmen with skills far beyond the most experienced frontiersmen, but were just as likely to use the tomahawk, war club, or even the knife. They took scalps from the dead and carried them back to their people as a sign of their bravery. They sometimes brought prisoners to their villages and made them run the gauntlet to the center of town as Indians lined up on either side to beat them. Some survivors were adopted into Indian families while others were ransomed in Detroit or Montreal.[13]

But there were also times when they tortured their captives. Everyone on the frontier knew the story of Colonel William Crawford. In the summer of 1782, when Wayne was fighting his last battles in Georgia, Crawford, an officer in the Continental Army's Virginia Line, led five hundred volunteers toward Upper Sandusky, the main Indian town halfway down the Great Trail from Pittsburgh to Detroit. He was General Washington's friend and served as his agent purchasing land on the Ohio frontier. Crawford's mission was similar to the one assigned to St. Clair and now to Wayne. He was to march to the tribal village suspected of launching raids on frontier settlements and disperse the warriors who lived there. But the Delaware and their allies got word of Crawford's advance and intercepted his soldiers before they reached Upper Sandusky. Some men escaped from the ring drawn around them in the boggy woods, but Crawford was not so lucky. He was captured and dragged to nearby Tymotchee Creek where he was tortured for hours. The Indians stripped him naked, bound his hands behind his back, and then tied his hands to a pole. Men, women, and even the smallest children circled around him, beating him with their fists and shooting sixty rounds of powder into him. They poked burning sticks into his blackened skin. Finally, they cut off his ears and scalped him. When he fell to the ground, they covered his back with burning coals, and when he died at last, they threw his body into the fire. Later, if the Delaware were ever asked why they treated Crawford so cruelly, they answered he suffered the same fate as the people of Gnadenhutten.[14]

Well aware of Colonel Crawford's gruesome death, Heckewelder still maintained that the Indians were not ruthless barbarians, but were instead skilled diplomats and negotiators. They perfectly understood the realities of their political situation. They knew the Americans wanted their land and often set one tribe against the other to get it. The Indians who lived north of the Ohio River particularly resented how the United States always deferred to the Six Nations when deciding matters related to their country. This was a mistake since these tribes no longer took orders from the confederation, which had splintered during the Revolution. They were more than capable of speaking for themselves in councils with the Americans, even though they found it nearly impossible to talk frankly with representatives of so aggressive a nation. From Fort Stanwix to Fort Harmar, they had been forced to deal with a people who never took no for an answer. Americans always claimed they meant no harm to the Indians, as they demanded every inch of their land. Even worse, treaties with the United States were usually hammered out within the walls of forts where soldiers pointed guns at their chiefs. How could pieces of paper agreed to under such conditions have any lasting value?[15]

By the time he was ready to leave for Pittsburgh, Wayne had a better understanding of what motivated the Indians across the Ohio, and more important from his perspective as commander in chief of the Legion, how to defeat them. He had to train his men to fight with the same skill and determination as the warriors they would face. Wayne had only the model of General Steuben to follow. Standing in the mud and icy rain of Valley Forge, and swearing at the troops in German and French, Steuben had drilled the Continental Army to maneuver on command and thrust their bayonets into imaginary redcoats. Wayne planned to order dozens of copies of Steuben's *Blue Book* for the many new officers who were supposed to be waiting for him in Pittsburgh. Still, how practices that made sense when fighting rows of redcoats approaching across an open field would help train men who would only see the enemy when they stormed out of a giant sea of oaks and sycamores, screaming like a thousand bells ringing at once, was a question that for the moment he could not answer.[16]

When Wayne finally headed out of Philadelphia in the last week of May, he regretted leaving his friends behind, but at least he had escaped the relentless criticism he faced in the capital. The embarrassment of being ousted from Congress still troubled him. He had barely taken his seat in Congress last November when a petition arrived from his opponent, Colonel James Jackson, who had served with him during the last year of the Revolution, alleging that Wayne's friends had rigged the vote in his favor. Invited to address the House of Representatives in February 1792, Jackson read an impassioned speech praising public virtue and denouncing corrupt politicians. Certain the evidence would prove that he had defeated Wayne in the election, Jackson demanded that Congress proceed immediately with its investigation. In his defense, Wayne said only that, if there was wrongdoing on the part of his supporters, Jackson's followers were just as guilty of trying to manipulate the election's outcome. But on March 16, 1792, when the matter was finally decided, the House voted unanimously to remove Wayne from office and call another election. The fact that Colonel Jackson maintained his opponent played no part in the chicanery mattered to no one.[17]

Wayne's humiliation only increased when, at the very moment he was ousted from the House, Congress exonerated St. Clair. Since early in the Revolution, Wayne had considered St. Clair a bumbling fool who succeeded by luck rather than skill. What else could explain how a general who led his soldiers into a massacre could be forgiven for the slaughter? Even more stunning, General St. Clair remained completely unrepentant, placing the blame for his negligence on everyone but himself. He accused Secretary Knox of sending him confusing orders, and Quartermaster General Samuel Hodgdon of holding up badly needed supplies. His fellow generals, who led raids on Indian villages, namely Josiah Harmar in 1790 and Charles Scott and James Wilkinson in 1791, made it impossible for him to negotiate a treaty with the tribes. Even worse, the warriors took their vengeance out on his army, not theirs. However, St. Clair laid the greatest blame on his soldiers. Unable to shoot a gun or wield an ax, these were the incompetents that the government expected him to take into the forests north of Fort Washington and there defeat thousands of Indians trained as marksmen since childhood.[18]

Wayne was baffled why so many Congressmen despised him even as they embraced St. Clair. He knew many politicians, especially from Virginia, were furious at Washington for naming him as St. Clair's successor. James Monroe, a Continental Army veteran who had forgotten how Wayne defended Virginia before the Yorktown campaign, had tried mightily to block his appointment in the Senate. Failing at this, he comforted himself by reporting to his mentor Thomas Jefferson how much the people of Virginia despised Wayne. There was a common saying about him in Richmond. It would have been difficult to find a more "unfit" person for the position "even if some industry had been used" to select him. James Madison was just as disgusted, but tempered his complaints, saying only that Wayne's appointment went "rather against the bristles."[19]

That Monroe and Madison mocked him would not have surprised Wayne. He knew they would have preferred their state's governor, the once dashing Lighthorse Harry Lee, rather than a third general from Pennsylvania as commander of the nation's army. He may not even have been troubled that Jefferson, a man he hardly knew, had opposed his appointment. He would have been more surprised that Henry Knox and Alexander Hamilton, with whom he had served in the Continental Army, had also been dead set against his appointment, preferring the less experienced Charles Pinckney. But the fact that President Washington, whom he admired so greatly, also doubted him would have broken his heart when, after suffering so much for his country, his heart seemed past breaking.

As he made his way from the capital, stopping at Waynesborough to say goodbye to Polly, he never suspected the terrible things Washington was writing about him to comfort a disappointed Governor Lee. "You cannot be a stranger," Lee complained to the president, "to the extreme disgust which the late appointment to the command of the army excited among all orders in this state." He claimed he was not angry that the president had chosen Wayne instead of himself, even though Lee believed he was fully qualified for the position. In reply, Washington, somewhat embarrassed for recommending Wayne in the first place, made the excuse that he always chose the higher ranking officer over the lower. He had to pick Wayne, a brigadier general for most of the war and a major general by brevet at its end, rather than Lee, who had never risen above the rank of colonel. While he confessed that Wayne had "many good points as an Officer," Washington was still worried about him. He could only hope that "time, Reflection, good advice, and above all, a due sense of the importance of the trust which is committed to him, will correct his foibles, or cast a shade over them."[20]

Fortunately, Wayne, who was prone to depression, never knew what Washington said about him, at least when he was trying to comfort Colonel Lee. He was well aware, however, of the growing hostility toward a standing army among politicians and the public alike. He could not understand how anyone could oppose the Legion when so many soldiers still lay unburied on a bluff overlooking the Wabash. But what else could explain the fact that by the time he arrived in York, a hundred miles west of Philadelphia, only a few soldiers had been recruited? Robert Miscampbell, a Revolutionary War veteran from South Carolina who had just won a commission as a lieutenant colonel in the Legion, proudly told his new commander that he had signed up forty dragoons. When these were added to the troops recruited in Elizabethtown, Wayne would have at least one whole company. There were also reports of a hundred riflemen ready to serve under Captain William Faulkner, a Pennsylvania militiaman and survivor of St. Clair's defeat. None of this seemed like good news to Wayne, especially after he learned that, just as in the Revolution, his soldiers had little food and no uniforms.[21]

The magnitude of St. Clair's defeat became suddenly more apparent when he arrived in Carlisle, twenty miles past York. The town sat on the edge of the Pennsylvania frontier and served as a staging area for armies during the French and Indian War and the Revolution. It was also the hometown of General Richard Butler, St. Clair's second in command left behind on the battlefield when the few lucky survivors escaped down the trail to Fort Jefferson. Not only was Butler dead, but so were most of the officers and enlisted men from Pennsylvania, especially from the districts around Waynesborough. What made their loss even more terrible was the fact that no recruits were waiting for Wayne in Carlisle to replace them. Except for Miscampbell's dragoons and Faulkner's riflemen, along with a few hundred soldiers manning forts from the Beaver River near Pittsburgh to Vincennes on the Wabash, Wayne had no army.[22]

Of all the Pennsylvanians who died at St. Clair's defeat, Wayne most felt the loss of his friend "Dickie" Butler. A small man with bright red hair, he had moved with his parents when he was only seventeen from Dublin to Carlisle. There he worked in his father's gun shop on West High Street with his four brothers, William, Thomas, Pierce, and Edward. The brothers, all officers in the Pennsylvania Line, were known as the "Fighting Butlers." Richard, who was the eldest, fought with Daniel Morgan at Saratoga before serving as a colonel in Wayne's regiments. As soon as they met, they became fast friends. They kept up a steady correspondence during the war and afterward. Their letters were filled with talk of politics, the army, and women. Butler found the creatures as fascinating as Wayne did, and, like him, pursued them after he was married. He was even rumored to be the father of several children among the Shawnee on the Ohio frontier.[23]

Wayne knew that Butler, as the nation's first Superintendent of Indian Affairs for the northern states, negotiated the treaties that tribes across the Ohio were now protesting. Starting at Fort Stanwix and continuing to Fort Harmar, he had cajoled, pressured, and sometimes threatened chiefs into signing these treaties. From the point of view of the Indians, neither Butler nor his fellow commissioners ever truly negotiated treaties. They instead came with documents already written and told the chiefs that peace could only be achieved if every word, including every boundary line, was accepted without question. "We offer you peace on moderate terms; we do it with magnanimity and mercy," Butler explained at Fort Stanwix. "If you do not accept it now, you are not to expect a repetition of such offers." When the Indians complained of soldiers pointing guns at them in their wooden forts, they were thinking of Richard Butler.[24]

Humiliated from post to post, they waited for their chance to take their revenge. It finally came early on the morning of November 4, 1791, after General St. Clair fled the battleground high above the Wabash. They found Butler wounded, unable to move, and waiting to get off a few last shots with his pistols. They buried a hatchet in his skull, stuffed dirt down his throat for all the land he had taken from them, and then scalped his bright red hair. The Miami chief Little Turtle later sent medals taken off Butler's body to his American widow. He assured her that his body had not been desecrated even though he knew this was not completely true. After killing Butler, Indian warriors cut out his heart. What happened next remained a mystery. Some said they chopped it apart with a portion sent to every tribe that fought St. Clair. But others claimed Butler's heart, remaining intact, was carried to Joseph Brant, the Mohawk chief who tried to stay friends with the Americans, the British, and the Indians to let him know that the tribes across the Ohio no longer bowed to his broken confederacy.[25]

Realizing he might meet the same fate as Butler, Wayne wondered what would happen when he finally arrived in Pittsburgh. It would take months to train his soldiers to fight, if they were ever recruited. But what if the Indians attacked before he could accomplish this? He would have to call out the militia, but would anyone come to his aid? This seemed unlikely as he headed farther west from Carlisle. Everywhere he went a paralyzing fear of the Indians had descended upon the countryside. If an attack came, the brave citizens of Pennsylvania would probably desert him. They would flee with their families to the nearest blockhouse, leaving him to fight hundreds, maybe thousands of warriors with only a handful of soldiers.

With his mind racing ahead to every possibility that might occur, Wayne suddenly found himself worrying about his son Isaac. When he joined the Continental Army in 1775, his little boy was just three years old. Now he was a grown man of twenty, and in the intervening years Wayne had rarely seen him. He knew Isaac cared little for studying, but he had decided nevertheless that his son would become a lawyer. He had recently apprenticed him to William Lewis, his attorney in Philadelphia. Now with death staring him in the face, Wayne thought of the many things he wanted to say to his son, but could not find the words. He turned for help to Sharp Delany, his best friend who had watched over Isaac since he was small. "I have to call your attention to a business that lays near my heart," he wrote. Delany must find a place for Isaac to live in Philadelphia and teach him to manage his money properly. He must make sure the boy never became an "idler" or succumbed to "wanton prodigality." Above all else, Delany must treat Isaac as if he were his own son. He might become just that if Wayne ended up dead with a hatchet in his skull and his heart cut out.[26]

Before that terrible moment came, Wayne would try one last time to arrange his son's life, forgetting how years before his own father's plans for himself had come undone. Wayne's father, also named Isaac, had decided that his only son, Anthony, born on New Year's Day 1745, would become a farmer like he and his father had been. The elder Wayne, an ambitious and hardworking man also named Anthony, had brought his family from Ireland to Pennsylvania in 1724. Within just two years after coming to America, he had enough money to purchase a 380-acre farm in Chester County, later known as Waynesborough. Upon his death, the farm, which by now included a tannery, passed to his youngest son, Isaac. With its fields planted in wheat and rye, large herds of cattle grazing in the meadows, and high profits from the farm's tannery, Waynesborough had made Isaac Wayne a wealthy man and would one day do the same for his son. Educated with the polish of a gentleman, Anthony would take his place in society as the master of Waynesborough. He would likewise marry a respectable girl like his mother, Elizabeth Iddings, the daughter of a Quaker neighbor, well known for her devotion to her husband, her daughters, Hannah and Ann, and her youngest child, Anthony.[27]

But Wayne's life had not gone as smoothly as his father had planned. Instead a fault line ran through his future, which, when it gave way, brought unexpected changes. This line paralleled the highest ridges of the Alleghenies now clearly visible to Wayne as he rode west from Carlisle across the Cumberland Valley. They were part of the Appalachians that extended from Maine to Georgia, cutting the English colonies and now the American states, especially Pennsylvania, in two. After Wayne climbed nearly half a mile to the top of these blue-tinged peaks, he would descend along a plateau to the west, all the way down to the Ohio, the mighty waterway that started at Pittsburgh and ran a thousand miles to the Mississippi. Beyond the river lay hundreds of millions of acres of the Ohio Country, desired by every people in living memory who had come to its borders: the French, the Six Nations, the many tribes that Wayne had come west to fight, the Americans, and the British. When Wayne was still a boy, a war had broken out for control of this country in the same mountains that he was now crossing. The fault line running through his life had given way and sent him down a path that took him far from the careful plans his father had laid for him at Waynesborough.

George Washington, the commander whom Wayne had faithfully served for much of his adult life, had played a key role in the fault line giving way. In 1753, Washington, then a twenty-one-year-old major of the Virginia militia, made a journey of his own across the Alleghenies. He carried a message from Virginia Lieutenant Governor Robert Dinwiddie in Williamsburg to the French, who were building a string of forts from Presque Isle on Lake Erie to the headwaters of the Ohio. Dinwiddie's note ordered the French out of the Ohio Country, which, in the opinion of the Virginians, belonged to them ever since James I granted the colony all the land "North and Northwest" of its borders in its second charter. But young Washington never made it to Presque Isle. French soldiers and Indian warriors intercepted him short of his destination and informed him that this country belonged to them, and by God, they were going to keep it.

They sent Washington back to Virginia, but one year later, after the French started construction of Fort Duquesne at the headwaters of the Ohio, he headed west again on Dinwiddie's orders. He was to oversee the construction of a road from Virginia to the Monongahela, and thus put France on notice that the Ohio

Country belonged to the English colonies, and not to the French. Fifty miles south of the fort in a wooded glen, on May 28, 1754, Washington's forces, which included Virginia militiamen as well as Mingo warriors, under the command of Tanacharison, who had been recruited as a guide and spokesperson for the Ohio tribes, defeated a party of French soldiers who had come south from Fort Duquesne. Both sides blamed the other for starting the fight that left the French commander Jumonville badly wounded. "Tu n'es pas encore mort, mon père!" Tanacharison remarked, meaning "You are not yet dead, my father," before he buried a tomahawk in his skull, scooped out his brains, and ate them. A horrified Washington made a hasty retreat ten miles back down the trail to a flooded plain where he built Fort Necessity. Less than a week later, more French soldiers from Fort Duquesne surrounded his tiny outpost, forced him to surrender, but once again let him go.[28]

Little did the humiliated Washington know as he crossed the mountains back into Virginia that he had fought the opening battles of the French and Indian War, which would pit France and England against each other in a final contest for control of much of North America. For the colonists who joined Virginia in the fight, the war was more than a battle to uphold promises in a charter. This was a fight for the future itself. If Virginia, Pennsylvania, and the other colonies won the bloody war along the western slopes of the Appalachians, then their towns, farms, and trading posts would extend all the way to the Mississippi and the Great Lakes. But if the French won, then their fur-trading empire, run from Quebec, Montreal, and Detroit, would stand for centuries, and the tribes who supported them, the same ones Wayne was now riding over the Alleghenies to fight, would keep this country for just as long.

At first, the troubles that swept up the Virginians, the French, and the Indians in a bloody war seemed far away from the orderly fields of Waynesborough. No member of the family had taken up arms since 1690, when Anthony Wayne's grandfather and namesake fought with William of Orange against the deposed king James II at the Battle of the Boyne. The elder Wayne was then a young man in his late twenties, a loyal Protestant who had just moved from the family's ancestral home in Yorkshire, England, to Ireland. Sixty-five years later, when the French and Indian War broke out, Isaac Wayne remained safe on his farm in Pennsylvania. He only decided to fight after General Edward Braddock, sent from England in May 1755 to help the colonists take Fort Duquesne, was ambushed in the woods far from Waynesborough, with young Washington at his side.

Isaac Wayne raised a militia company in Chester County and headed west along the same routes his son Anthony was now traveling. He built forts throughout the Cumberland Valley and into the foothills of the Alleghenies, working with

Benjamin Franklin who had taken charge of Pennsylvania's defenses. When his troops disbanded in 1757, Captain Wayne raised another company and fought until Fort Duquesne finally fell, burned to the ground and abandoned by the French, with Fort Pitt, named in honor of Prime Minister William Pitt who brought the British fully into the conflict they would name the Seven Years' War, rising in its place. In honor of his bravery, Wayne's neighbors elected him to the colonial assembly each year from 1757 until peace was declared in 1763.[29]

The French and Indian War, which ultimately shifted control of the Ohio Country from France to Great Britain, also brought changes into the life of Isaac's son Anthony, then just a schoolboy. At the start of the war, his father had sent him to a local academy run by his uncle Gabriel Wayne to acquire the skills needed to become a gentleman farmer. He must learn to read, write, and keep accounts of his land and business. He must know Latin and Greek and master the history of England, his mother country, as well as the history of Rome, the greatest civilization of the ancient world. But in the excitement of the war, Isaac Wayne found that his son cared little for learning. The child was instead caught up in tales of the many battles of the day fought in faraway places like Louisburg and the Plains of Abraham.

Young Anthony had become so enthralled with the war that he often disrupted his uncle's school. He kept his schoolmates in a fever pitch of excitement, waiting impatiently for their lessons to end so he could lead them to the schoolyard where, acting as their commanding general, he directed them in battles against imaginary Frenchmen and Indian warriors. A frustrated Gabriel Wayne wrote to his brother that unless Anthony mended his ways, he would have no choice but to expel him. As he explained, "I really suspect that parental affection blinds you, and that you have mistaken your son's capacity. What he may be best qualified for, I know not—one thing I am certain of, he will never make a scholar, he may perhaps make a soldier, he had already distracted the brains of two-thirds of the boys under my charge, by rehearsals of battles, sieges, etc.—They exhibit more the appearance of Indians and harlequins than students. . . . During noon, in place of the usual games of amusement, he had the boys employed in throwing up redoubts, skirmishing, etc."[30]

Isaac Wayne had taken his son in hand by threatening to remove him from school and put him to work doing the lowliest tasks on the farm, like cleaning the stables, feeding the hogs, and chopping wood. The prospect of learning farming from the bottom up had so unsettled Anthony that he quickly became the best student in his uncle's academy. He mastered his favorite subject, mathematics, and learned to read and write Latin. By the time he was sixteen, Wayne was ready to enter the College of Philadelphia. Enrolled there for two years, he deepened his knowledge of Latin, a language he would quote for the rest of his life. His study of history led him to deeply admire Julius Caesar. He memorized his campaigns, never suspecting that he would spend his future military career viewing every battle from the perspective of Caesar. He studied geography, moral philosophy, and still more mathematics. He never mastered Greek, but he developed a love of poetry and plays, especially the works of William Shakespeare, and the new literary form of the novel, including the writings of Jonathan Swift and Laurence Sterne. He also kept up with the latest works of the Irish playwright Richard Sheridan.[31]

By the time he came home in 1763, eighteen-year-old Anthony Wayne had all the makings of a gentleman. He wrote letters in a graceful prose and maintained a fine library that might impress his neighbors enough to elect him to the colonial assembly in Philadelphia some day. He purchased a telescope and continued his studies of astronomy. His father also made certain that he dressed stylishly in the latest fashions. The lesson, that a man should look the part he played, stayed with him for the rest of his life. Young Anthony also practiced the social graces he learned in Philadelphia. He could easily converse on the day's events with men and dance gracefully with women. He was especially fond of country dances where he whirled his partner about in patterns with other couples on the dance floor. He could even fence as well as an English nobleman.[32]

But for all his outward polish, Anthony Wayne remained unsophisticated in the ways of the world. He even believed a colonial boy like himself could become a soldier. Isaac Wayne, however, realized there was no place for his son in the British army, no matter how well trained and gentlemanly his manners might be. Soldiers often purchased their commissions with the top ranks usually reserved for aristocrats. The current rate for a captaincy was £900, a sum that even the wealthiest Pennsylvania farmer could not afford. But since his son desired an active life, Isaac Wayne got him training as a surveyor. Young Anthony was soon so proficient that he set up an office at Waynesborough to survey land for his neighbors. He made perfect measurements in a careful hand, drawing out his calculations in brown ink and taking directions for his next job from his father.[33]

While talented young colonials, like Anthony Wayne, might be locked out of the army, there were other ways for them to advance, especially in Canada, which France had surrendered to England in the peace treaty signed in Paris in 1763. Two years after the war ended, Benjamin Franklin and a group of wealthy investors had decided to set up a colony in Nova Scotia. After the local Acadians were exiled to Louisiana during the French and Indian War, Nova Scotia's governor encouraged Protestants from Great Britain and New England to settle there. Franklin and his partners decided they could make a fortune renting or selling

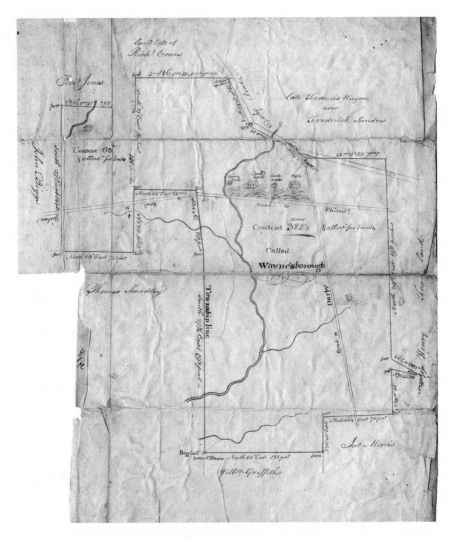

Anthony Wayne's survey of Waynesborough.
William L. Clements Library, University of Michigan.

land to the colonists and taking a percentage of their crops. But they needed the right man to "visit the territory offered for settlement, inspect the soil as regarded the purpose of agriculture, ascertain the means of commercial facility with it and then — having considered all this — locate the exact site for settlement." Knowing Isaac Wayne from his campaigns in the late war, Franklin was just as impressed with his twenty-year-old son and chose him as the agent for his colony. The two quickly became friends, with Franklin advising young Anthony while giving him a wide berth in making decisions for the colony, and Wayne in turn confiding his every success to Franklin and his partners.[34]

In March 1765, Anthony Wayne boarded the *Charming Nancy* in Philadelphia for the seven-hundred-mile trip to Nova Scotia. It was a difficult journey for a young man who had never been so far from home, especially when his ship was caught in a three-day nor'easter. Still, by the time he arrived in Halifax, he was excited about the prospects of Franklin's colony. He could barely contain his enthusiasm, a trait he would retain even in the darkest days of his life. He was confident that "any industrious man may make a fortune there in a few years." Still his job was not easy. The province's governor and a competing agent taunted young Wayne into accepting nearly impossible terms for Franklin's colony. He won 100,000 acres on the northern side of the St. John's River and another 100,000 on the Petitcodiac River. But in exchange he agreed to settle one Protestant colonist for every 200 acres, plant and fence one-third of the settlements in ten years, and deliver all the gold, silver, and coal discovered to the Crown.[35]

Wayne returned to Philadelphia and laid copies of the deeds he had filed at the Crown Land Office in Halifax before Franklin, who promised to recruit colonists. By Christmas, he was at home in Waynesborough spending the holiday with his family and enjoying his favorite pastime of fox hunting. In the following March, he was back on the *Charming Nancy*, sailing out of Philadelphia with the few settlers that Franklin was able to recruit. This time his stay in Nova Scotia was far less pleasant. The fifty settlers he brought had little to eat except for the wheat they planted on their arrival. When he tried to buy food for everyone in October and was told by local merchants that his credit was no good, he resigned his post as Franklin's agent. While he would continue writing to Franklin, especially about the politics of the day, Wayne went home to take up his place as the gentleman farmer his father had always hoped he would be.[36]

While young Wayne thought Canada held the greatest promise for Americans seeking their fortune, the people in the wagons rolling past his family's farm each day believed otherwise. For them, the Ohio Country was far more desirable than Nova Scotia. The struggle to control the land there continued even as the French and Indian War drew to a close. Warriors inspired by the Ottawa chief Pontiac were the first to rise up and fight for the country across the Ohio River. Angry over their mistreatment at the hands of British soldiers now stationed there, and certain the Master of Life supported their war against these invaders, they attacked more than a dozen posts, including Fort Pitt and Fort Detroit, in a desperate bid to drive the redcoats out of their country. While the Indians were finally defeated, Great Britain responded with the Proclamation of 1763, which drew an imaginary line along the crest of the Appalachians. West of the line, the territory, which included the Ohio Country, was declared an Indian preserve. Here the tribes could hunt, bring their furs into British forts where they would be treated with respect, and live peacefully in their villages. They would no longer have to share their country with land-hungry settlers. Any colonist who had settled west of the line must move back east immediately.[37]

But the Americans were not willing to give up the western country. Nor were they willing to pay the new taxes levied by Parliament to support the rising costs of administering a huge empire and to reduce the national debt that had doubled during the French and Indian War. Their growing opposition to the Sugar Act, the much-hated Stamp Act, and later the Townshend Acts, which included the fatal tea tax, led them to question who had the right to govern the colonies: their elected assemblies, the Parliament, or the Crown? During the ten years of debate, Anthony Wayne had grown to manhood. He became a husband, a father, and the master of Waynesborough when his father, gravely ill, handed day-to-day management of the farm and tannery over to him in 1774. Even as he found himself caught in the drift toward rebellion, he often longed for the peaceful life that his father had planned for him. "Also I hope by the next Spring that matters will be so little between the Colonies and Great Britain," he wrote in 1775 to his partner in the leather business, "that you may carry on trade as usual; when such an event happens I shall ship you a considerable quantity early." But peace never came, with protests turning into revolution and finally a war that, despite the treaty signed a dozen years before, still raged across the Appalachians. The plans that Isaac Wayne carefully laid for his only son, Anthony, finally unraveled. He left Waynesborough to fight for the "rights and Liberties of America from her Coldest to her hottest sun," as he often said, never returning to the life his father had planned for him.[38]

Now, in the spring of 1792, as he descended the last hills toward Pittsburgh, Wayne no longer worried about his own son, whose troubles seemed to have disappeared behind the mountains he just crossed. For the moment, he cared only about the country that opened before him. Everywhere he looked there was only a sea of trees. Thirty miles down the Ohio, just past Pennsylvania's western border, lay the fabled country whose destiny had shaped his life since he was a boy running wild in his uncle's academy. He had only one word for what he saw: "*Wilderness.*" This country, whose borders had been drawn so carefully in his nation's treaties with the Indians, seemed impossible to tame. The sheer size of it made the destruction of St. Clair's army understandable. How could St. Clair, even if he had a thousand soldiers perfectly trained, be expected to take it? How could Wayne secure it when no soldiers were waiting for him in Pittsburgh? The man who loved entertaining with wine and conversation flowing long into the night found himself completely alone.[39]

He could only guess what support he would receive back in Philadelphia from the government which doubted him. Ahead of him were Indian warriors he could not see, even as they laid their plans to destroy him, and British officials he could not hear, even as they wondered what the character of the latest general sent against them might be. Wayne did not pray often in his life, but in desperate hours for himself and his nation, he sometimes turned to God. This was such an hour, much like the one in early 1776 when his beloved America had not yet declared her independence. Then the "Sons of America" were on the run from "wretches who brand us with vile epithets, vain-boasters & cowards," as Wayne described the trying times from his vantage point at Fort Ticonderoga. He could do little more than hope that the Continental Army would turn and face the enemy. He also sent up a simple prayer: "May God shut the door of mercy on us." Now as he stood in Pittsburgh without any recruits beside him, he knew that after he had perfectly trained his Legion, together they would have to turn and face the enemy. Hopefully God would once again be merciful.[40]

3

"DESTINED TO EXIST . . . IN A HOWLING WILDERNESS"

Shortly after arriving in Pittsburgh, Wayne learned a few soldiers were actually waiting for him. They were not in the town, but were a quarter mile up the Allegheny River at the newly constructed Fort Fayette, named after the Marquis de Lafayette. These men included officers and enlisted men from the Second Regiment who had escaped with St. Clair on that terrible morning in the previous November. There were also forty recruits just arrived from the Cumberland Valley in May. Together they were nowhere near the thousand men that Secretary Knox promised him by midsummer, but at least they were a start. Still Wayne fretted that even if more recruits arrived in the next few weeks, there would not be enough uniforms and shoes, flour and beef, or muskets and powder for everyone. Nor was there any news on what goods had been forwarded to the Legion and when they would arrive. He finally discovered by reading a local newspaper that government contractors planned to ship six boatloads of supplies on June 16 not to his men at Fort Fayette, but downriver to Fort Washington.[1]

Disappointed in the War Department, Wayne was equally unimpressed with Pittsburgh, formerly Fort Pitt and before that Fort Duquesne, the much-fought-over point where the Allegheny met the Monongahela to form the Ohio. This was the spot George Washington had risked his twenty-one-year-old life to occupy forty years earlier. This was the spot his father Isaac Wayne had raised two militia companies to take. The location was obviously strategic. Wayne, as a surveyor, knew that to control a country, the river running along its border must be controlled. To control that river, the headwaters, where the river started, must be controlled. But after fighting for two generations, Wayne's fellow Americans had little to show for their struggles, except a few hundred log cabins and clapboard houses built on the muddy plain where the three rivers met. Beyond these streets, filled with whiskey traders and prostitutes, and pigs roaming through the garbage, lay the first rim of the Ohio forests. Even through the smoky haze, which locals told Wayne came from burning coal as their fuel, the giant sycamores with their mottled white and gray bark could be seen rising along the edges of the settlement, so high and so close together that they blocked out the sun to anyone standing beneath them.[2]

Wayne found the town crowded with settlers who fled there when word of the latest Indian attack spread through the countryside. In the same week Wayne left Philadelphia, a young mother named Massey Harbison, just twenty-two years old, had hobbled into Pittsburgh, her clothes torn, thorns sticking through her bare feet, and a one-year-old boy clinging to her side. They were the only survivors of an Indian raid on her farm. Warriors had stormed into her cabin and stole her few extra clothes and household goods. A Seneca warrior told Massey that she was now his woman and he was taking her and her three children back to his country. When her three-year-old son wept and refused to leave the cabin, an Indian took hold of him by his ankles and smashed his head against the doorpost, killing him instantly.

Later, after traveling on foot for hours, Massey's five-year-old boy complained about being tired. The Indians finished him off with a tomahawk in his skull and shoved his bleeding scalp into Massey's face. After walking for two more days, Massey and her only surviving child slipped away from their captors in the middle of the night. They wandered for four days, sometimes hiding in branches of fallen trees only a few feet away from warriors sent to track them. Finally, Massey heard a cowbell and knew she must be close to an American settlement. When her neighbors found her, sunburned, emaciated, and cut apart, she had changed so much in six days that they did not recognize her. They pulled a hundred and fifty thorns from her feet and brought her and her little boy back to Pittsburgh.[3]

The farmers huddled in the town were so frightened that they abandoned their livestock and simple possessions, and left standing in the fields the wheat that had to be harvested if they were to survive the coming winter. But few seemed happy to see General Wayne, except for Massey Harbison, who remembered him fighting at Monmouth Courthouse when she was a seven-year-old child growing up in New Jersey. Almost everyone else was as leery of him as they were of the Indians. They were sure he had come from Philadelphia to collect Hamilton's tax on their corn crop. They converted their corn into whiskey and traded it locally rather than hauling the crop over the Alleghenies. Transportation costs were so high that if they shipped their corn back east for sale, they made not a penny of profit.

Knowing this, Hamilton still recommended levying a tax on their whiskey if it was produced for public sale rather than for private consumption only. Taxes would likewise be placed on all imported spirits as well as spirits produced in America from imported materials. The money from these taxes would help pay the operating expenses of the federal government and replenish the sinking fund created to finance the national debt through the sale of bonds. As upsetting as the whiskey tax might be for small farmers in western Pennsylvania and elsewhere, Hamilton considered it preferable to taxing land or homes. The tax would also strengthen the power of the federal government and might even reduce the dependence on alcohol that Hamilton found rampant in American society.[4]

With tax collectors just arriving in their country, it was no wonder that people asked Wayne if he was a revenuer, and therefore an agent of the much-hated secretary of the treasury. He assured them that he had not come to inspect their stills or collect pennies on the dollar for every gallon they produced. He had come to defeat the Indians, the same ones who had just murdered two of Massey Harbison's children. He encouraged everyone to go home and harvest the wheat. However, he did not tell them that the one person in the government who seemed most determined to protect them was Hamilton, who was currently working on a detailed plan to fund Wayne's army from the money raised in part from the whiskey tax. His official report, sixteen pages in length and bound with a blue ribbon, finally arrived at Wayne's camp in early August. If Hamilton had his way, the citizens of Pittsburgh would have something never before seen in the short history of the United States: an army paid regularly to defend them.[5]

Wayne had turned the hostile crowds in his favor because he looked the part of a commanding general, and just as important, he spoke with an authority that never betrayed how frightened he was. In private, however, he confessed his many fears to Secretary Knox. He asked him point-blank where his army was. He had been promised a thousand men, but found less than a tenth of that number at Fort Fayette. Standing beside Pittsburgh's three great rivers, part of a network of waterways that flowed to the northern lakes and the Mississippi, he considered his situation almost comical. A "General without troops," he complained to Knox, was truly a "fish out of water." To be in this state was even more ridiculous than having to defend himself against the very people he had come west to protect.[6]

How quickly the world had changed from the opening months of the Revolution when young Anthony Wayne had joined the fight to defend liberty. Then the world glowed with an idealism that had disappeared from the present day. The country that Wayne had fought to create seemed to be fraying at the edges, as citizens along the frontier chafed against their ties to the greater whole. How different from the time in 1774 when every colony had come to the defense of Massachusetts after Parliament passed the Coercive Acts. Then Americans felt duty bound to help one another, knowing if today England closed the port of Boston, handed control of Massachusetts to an all-powerful royal governor, and sent the colony's troublesome citizens to London for trial, then tomorrow every other colony would suffer the same fate.[7]

Polly Wayne would long remember how diligently her young husband studied his nation's history. He filled his library with books and pamphlets on politics and law. Before anyone considered the colonies a separate country, Anthony spoke in terms of American independence. In Wayne's opinion, the thirteen colonies functioned as a "de facto" rather than a "de jure" republic. The colonies governed themselves with little interference from the Crown even though England never confirmed this fact in law. The self-government practiced by the colonies was what Wayne considered liberty. The Coercive Acts proved that England intended to uproot the liberty of the colonies, starting with Massachusetts and continuing down the Atlantic coast.[8]

Late in the summer of 1774, when an anonymous broadside signed by "A Freeman of Chester County" circulated in Easttown Township, Pennsylvania, almost everyone knew the author was the young gentleman farmer Anthony Wayne. The broadside called voters to the Turk's Head Tavern in West Chester to discuss the great "crisis," meaning England's attempt to overturn America's right to self-government. Wayne worried that this important issue would be lost in the frivolity that surrounded the selection of candidates for the assembly in Philadelphia. He had recently served in the provisional body established to determine Pennsylvania's response to the Coercive Acts where the delegates did not take the momentous events of the day seriously. By calling his fellow citizens to a local tavern, he hoped to convince them of the true nature of the national crisis. He would inspire them to agree on ways to defend Massachusetts even before they chose a slate of candidates for the assembly.[9]

The men who crowded into the Turk's Head Tavern in late September 1774 were amazed at the eloquence of the young man who stood before them. Three times the twenty-nine-year-old Wayne apologized for his youth, but there was nothing childish about the speech he delivered. He argued that what was happening in Massachusetts would soon happen in Pennsylvania. Parliament, whose members openly called for enslaving the colonies, had punished Massachusetts believing no colony would come to its aid. "England does not dare form on America all at once, but on one colony only," Wayne explained, "hoping that it will not be protected by its sister colonies." Parliament's "intolerable" acts were meant to control Massachusetts, thus "making a footstool of a sister colony to mount and trample on the high reared heel of American liberty." The men of Pennsylvania, he argued, no matter what their occupation or religion, must oppose this. "Forbid it, Virtue, and forbid it, Shame," he challenged his listeners. Now was the hour when all the colonies must use "moderate, constitutional means" to secure the "equitable independency" they long held within the British Empire.[10]

Wayne's words were so moving he was nominated as a candidate for the assembly. He won his election in October 1774 and again the following year. Even before fighting officially broke out, Wayne predicted the British would send armies against the colonies in their drive to crush the Americans' long-cherished right of self-government. He was certain brave soldiers would rise up to defend the political traditions of their nation. His prediction came true on the village green at Lexington, Massachusetts, on the morning of April 19, 1775. Two months later Wayne welcomed the chance to serve on Pennsylvania's Committee of Public Safety, which had been established to arm and train the colony's militia.

While serving on the committee, he came to know some of the most influential men in America, including John Dickinson, the author of *Letters from an American Farmer in Pennsylvania*, and Robert Morris, a wealthy financier who had made a fortune in ships, slaves, and trade with the Far East and West Indies. Both men became his lifelong friends. In September 1775, Wayne raised his own militia company, and finally in January 1776, he was appointed colonel of Pennsylvania's Fourth Regiment. Volunteers from townships around his family's estate rushed to serve with him. They wanted to fight at the side of the passionate and visionary Colonel Anthony Wayne.[11]

In April 1776, Wayne rode away from a life of wealth and ease, especially after his father's death the previous December made him the master of Waynesborough. He headed directly for General Washington's camp on Long Island. No matter how much he and his country might suffer, he believed they were forever bound together in a great turning point of history. Wayne agreed with his best friend Sharp Delany that America's struggle to defend liberty, in the midst of a brutal war, would "astonish future ages." But now in the haze of Pittsburgh's filthy streets, in the frightened looks of its angry citizens, and in the clueless gaze of the "rusty" veterans and callow youths who made up what there was of his army, the glory of those days seemed far away. The wonder of the Revolution faded as he realized, "I am destined to exist under a cold linnen cover in a howling wilderness with no other society than a Legion in arms protecting themselves from this dreadful trade of Death."[12]

Maybe it had not been a dream, but madness to believe that the Americans could govern themselves. Wayne knew something of madness. Years before he had been nicknamed "Mad Anthony." No soldier said this name to his face, but some muttered it behind his back. Most assumed it had something to do with his fearlessness on the battlefield. But there were other aspects of his character that made the nickname "Mad Anthony" stick. Wayne had a frightening temper that came as quickly as it went. He could let loose a string of expletives if an officer crossed him or a soldier failed to follow orders. He also had a peculiar habit of spending hours riding his horse along the edges of his camp late at night or before dawn. Then he seemed lost in thought, anticipating what might happen in the next battle and reacting in advance to every possibility. All these traits left his soldiers wondering if he was not a little mad.

Long after Wayne's death, when veterans of his campaigns tried to remember how their commander got his nickname "Mad Anthony," they told stories of Jemmy the Rover, an Irishman who served as a spy in the Continental Army. A bit mad himself, though real or feigned no one knew for certain, Jemmy easily slipped through the British lines and came back with valuable information. But Jemmy also had a tendency to drink and become disorderly. Early in 1781, a particularly trying time in Wayne's life when mutiny stirred in the Pennsylvania Line, he grew impatient with Jemmy's antics and ordered him to the guardhouse. When Jemmy was finally released, he asked the soldier who locked him up if "Anthony" was truly "mad" at him or just acting "in fun." The soldier answered that Wayne was displeased with his conduct, and if Jemmy misbehaved again, he would be sent back to the guardhouse and receive twenty-nine well-deserved lashes. "Then Anthony is mad," answered Jemmy, adding, "Farewell to you; clear the coast for the commodore, Mad Anthony's friend." He disappeared into the night, and even though Wayne told his wife to keep an eye out for him, he was never seen again.[13]

While Wayne knew some whispered he was mad, he was more upset with people who openly declared that Washington had only chosen him for the Legion's command because more valuable officers could not be spared. Delany sent word to him in Pittsburgh that he had many enemies back in Philadelphia. They claimed he was rash and had none of the qualities necessary for a good leader. "Your conduct Dear General will be well watched," Delany wrote, since many believed Washington's faith in him had been misplaced. Who were these enemies, asked a desperate Wayne, now alone in the wilderness? If they endangered his reputation, or even worse his life, then Delany must reveal their identity, he implored, so that "I may be guarded against their machinations." But no matter how much he begged, Delany never told him any specific names.[14]

Powerless to take on his secret foes, Wayne concentrated on the one task he could totally control: training his army. He knew this would not be easy for his

veterans or recruits. Experienced soldiers might resent the Legion's new struc-
ture, which Washington and Knox were still trying to determine. Survivors of
St. Clair's defeat would face special challenges all their own. They would have
to forget the horror of that awful morning and be willing to learn a better way
to fight the Indians. Edward Butler, the youngest brother of General Richard
Butler, was an example of a soldier scarred by the massacre of November 1791.
Unable to save both of his wounded brothers, he left Richard behind and lifted
Thomas onto one of the last surviving artillery horses. Hurrying away from the
battlefield, he heard Richard's last pistol shots go off behind him and the wild
cries of the victorious Indians. Still he could not believe his brother was dead.
Shortly after meeting Wayne in Pittsburgh, he won his permission to travel to
Fort Detroit and ask the British if rumors that his brother was alive were true.
A short time later he returned to Fort Fayette with eyewitness accounts that his
brother had died at the hands of Indian warriors with a tomahawk crushing his
skull and his heart torn out. Wayne had nothing but sympathy for the shattered
young man, and did his best to promote him from his aide-de-camp to his adjutant and later his inspector general.[15]

He took a liking, too, to a nineteen-year-old Virginian who had enlisted in
the army just the year before. This was Lieutenant William Henry Harrison, a
young man raised on a tobacco plantation called Berkeley on the James River.
His father, Benjamin Harrison, a close friend of George Washington, had been
a member of the Continental Congress, a signer of the Declaration of Independence, and a governor of Virginia. Young Harrison grew up watching his older
brothers go off to war. Much as Wayne had done as a boy during the French and
Indian War, Harrison dreamed of becoming a soldier like the men he saw all
around him. When he was only eight years old, he ran down the backcountry
roads along the James to catch a glimpse of Anthony Wayne, who had come
south to rescue Virginia from the British. But until the moment he joined the
army, all Harrison knew of war was what he read in his history books. He loved
the heroes of ancient Rome, and at eighteen when his father sent him to Philadelphia to study medicine, he carried the letters of Cicero with him.[16]

When their father died a short time later, Harrison's older brothers ordered
him back to Virginia, but instead he joined the army. He arrived at Fort Washington on the same day the survivors of St. Clair's massacre stumbled into the
post. They raced past him on their way to grog shops in Cincinnati, laughing at
the rich man's son who had come west to be a hero. But Harrison refused to give
up his childhood dream and, after taking much abuse from his fellow soldiers,
finally won their respect. He spent his spare time searching through Cincinnati
for anything he could read on military tactics and waiting for the chance to learn

the art of war. Harrison finally found his teacher when he met Anthony Wayne at Fort Fayette in July 1792. He had stopped at the post while escorting the family of General James Wilkinson, Wayne's second in command, from Fort Washington to Philadelphia. Wayne was so impressed with the young man that he gave him a saddle horse to ride and soon made him one of his aides-de-camp.[17]

Nearly twenty years before, after he formed his own volunteer regiment in October 1775, Wayne had done his best to understand war by reading books, much like Lieutenant Harrison was now doing. He learned the most from Maurice de Saxe, the illegitimate son of Poland's king, who led French and Russian armies to victory. For his stunning capture of Prague in a nighttime attack during the War of the Austrian Succession, Louis XV named him a marshal of France. His writings about war quickly became as famous as his deeds on the battlefield. At the start of the Revolution, Wayne had studied the works of Marshal Saxe as diligently as he once studied the campaigns of Julius Caesar during his boyhood. He readily accepted Saxe's principles, especially the notion that there was a relationship between an army's discipline and its dedication. The tougher the training of an army, including a heightened respect for rank, then the more successful its soldiers would be on the battlefield.

Wayne agreed with Saxe that an army should never hide behind fortifications. The best fortification was instead a well-formed line of soldiers marching directly toward the enemy. He accepted Saxe's dictum that a general should never wait to be attacked, but should instead choose the day and hour to strike. When that moment came, his soldiers must attack boldly, especially on the enemy's flanks, always attempting to surround them. Saxe's advice had made sense to Wayne during the Revolution and made even more sense now as he prepared for the Ohio campaign. Teaching his veterans and recruits to fight like Saxe would prepare them to face warriors who, without knowing it, followed his principles of warfare. One need only look at St Clair's defeat to see that the Indians chose the time and place of battle, bravely came out from behind their fortifications, the trees of the forest, and boldly attacked on all flanks. Wayne's men would have to do the same or they, too, would be massacred on some future morning.[18]

But knowing the sad state of his army outside Pittsburgh in the spring of 1792, Wayne also believed that only daily training, and not studying war in the abstract, would prepare his men to face the enemy. With few experienced officers, Wayne would have to do most of the work himself. He planned to drill his veterans four hours a day and his recruits two hours a day until they could handle more. This would not be easy because the thousand men who trickled into Fort Fayette by August were a sorry lot. Many suffered from smallpox and even more from venereal disease. Wayne isolated the smallpox sufferers away from his healthy soldiers until he could inoculate everyone. He did the same with those suffering from venereal disease, keeping them from Pittsburgh as he begged Knox for more medical help, especially tincture of mercury, to check the spread of the infection.[19]

Even with the pitiful condition of his men, Wayne was determined not to make St. Clair's mistake of hating his own soldiers. Instead he would take them in hand, and hopefully in no time have them maneuvering on command like Steuben had trained the Continental Army. But he would also make sure they moved with greater flexibility than Saxe or Steuben demanded. They must form their lines quickly, standing with room between each other rather than shoulder to shoulder. Their columns must be flexible because they would not be facing rows of redcoats coming at them across a field, but thousands of warriors racing in every direction from the surrounding woods. Wayne would train his infantry to fire at the Indians while his dragoons charged the enemy on both flanks. He got much needed help in drilling his mounted men from Colonel Miscampbell, the enthusiastic recruiter he had met on the road to Pittsburgh, who turned out to be an excellent cavalry officer.[20]

One of the most disturbing things Wayne discovered about his troops, whether veterans or recruits, was their general inability to load a musket and fire with any accuracy. He now better understood St. Clair's near despair over soldiers who could not shoot, even if their lives depended on it, against Indians who were expert marksmen since their youth. To train his men to shoot like Indians, Wayne ordered daily target practice from eleven to noon. He knew this would be expensive, but he wanted everyone, both soldiers and their horses, to get used to the sound and flash of gunfire. He reduced the cost by ordering his men to dig the lead balls out of the trees and posts where they fired them so the artificers could melt and remold them. Every evening he gave an extra gill of whiskey to the soldier who shot best that day and an extra half-gill to the man who came in second.[21]

Still Wayne knew that aiming at targets would be far different than shooting at warriors racing from the woods. It would be even more difficult for soldiers just learning how to handle their muskets. To help them, Wayne came up with a quicker way to load their guns. Usually a soldier had to put gunpowder into his weapon twice: first, when he primed his gun by pouring a small amount of powder into the flash pan, and second, when he poured the rest of the cartridge into the barrel of his gun. Working with artificers, Wayne discovered that if the push hole, the opening in the top of the gun that allowed air to flow into the flash pan and ignite the powder when struck by the flintlock trigger, was made wider and cut at an angle rather than straight down, there would be no need for priming. The only requirement would be for the gunpowder to be of a fine grade. Wayne was so excited about his discovery that he sent carefully wrapped specimens of the powder in letters to Secretary Knox. He explained how a soldier using the modified weapon would never have to take his eye off the enemy. Instead he would keep his opponent in view as he poured the cartridge into the musket, stuffed the lead ball in place behind it, and took deadly aim. Wayne estimated that a soldier who used the modified musket could shoot half again as much when standing and twice as much more when running.[22]

Even when Knox wrote back that Washington disapproved of his changes to the army's muskets, worrying the guns would misfire, Wayne remained enthusiastic about his soldiers. "Discipline begins to make its appearance," he wrote to Knox. He was so proud of them that, when news arrived at Fort Fayette on the evening of August 8, 1792, that warriors had been spotted north of the post, he was certain they could handle an attack. He ordered his men to form their lines, and to the beat of the drums, he rode back and forth in front of them, shouting his encouragement. He raced up to the redoubts he had built north and east of the fort. He told the men stationed there to hold their positions at "any expense of blood" until he could bring up the infantry and dragoons to push the warriors back. Wayne never doubted his sentries would do as he commanded because they had practiced this maneuver many times during the last month. But as soon as he rode away, a third of his sentries fled into the night, abandoning the very spot the Indians would attack first. Wayne was horrified, especially since his men, on a much smaller scale, had behaved exactly like the Kentucky militia on the morning of St. Clair's defeat. Instead of holding their ground, they ran for their lives.[23]

When he described the failure of his soldiers to the War Department, he blamed neither himself nor his men. Instead he reminded Secretary Knox that a "defect of the human heart" could make even the best-trained soldiers abandon their posts at the mere thought of death. Wayne knew this defect all too well for he had felt it many times. Before leaving for Pittsburgh, he reminded his wife Polly that he might die. No one understood death better than soldiers going into battle, except perhaps the general who led them. During the Revolution, Wayne had been anxious for his life during every campaign, just as his soldiers were now. Throughout his entire military career, the terror that he might have only a few hours to live haunted him the evening before every battle.[24]

But earlier in Wayne's life, when he played at being a soldier in his uncle's schoolyard, the prospect of his own death had seemed far away. Nor did death trouble him when he won his first commission as a colonel in Pennsylvania's Fourth Regiment in January 1776, or later when he helped build fortifications on Long Island. Well into his manhood, war seemed like a dream to him, alive only in the books he read about the armies of the past. Caesar's gleaming legions and Marshall Saxe's elegant soldiers were phantasms compared to a musket ball, cannon blast, or sharp bayonet coming his way. Wayne never truly faced death until the late spring of 1776 when General Washington ordered his regiment to join the new army heading for Canada.[25]

The Continental Congress had decided that if American soldiers headed north across the St. Lawrence, the French would welcome them as liberators. Once Quebec and Montreal were in American hands, Canada would join England's colonies in their revolt. Congress ignored the fact that the French had been well treated by the British since the ending of the Seven Years' War. The peace treaty signed in Paris in 1763 guaranteed the right of the Catholic Church to maintain its extensive holdings. Equally important, just as the Proclamation of 1763 allowed Indians to live in peace across the Appalachians, so the Quebec Act of 1774 allowed Catholics to practice their faith without interference. The French had no complaints about high taxes, which they were used to paying, nor did they wish to tie their fate to the Puritans of Boston, whom they had fought in many wars before Lexington and Concord and who now seemed to be leading this revolution.[26]

But Congress had dismissed these facts and in June 1775 ordered General Philip Schuyler to lead an army from Albany into Canada, occupying every British post along the way before taking Montreal and Quebec. When Schuyler fell ill, Colonel Richard Montgomery, an Irish soldier who had served in the British army during Pontiac's uprising, took his place. Crossing from New York into Canada, Montgomery laid siege to Fort St. John's for several weeks, which delayed his march across the St. Lawrence. Montgomery's small army, numbering only 1,500 men, did not occupy Montreal until late November 1775. Six weeks later, in the middle of a snowstorm on New Year's Eve, they launched an attack in the narrow streets of Quebec against the town's small British garrison. Montgomery was killed instantly in the opening volley. Benedict Arnold, who had marched north to Quebec through Maine where he lost nearly half of his 1,100 men, and now with his leg shattered by musket fire, led the army out of the city. News of Montgomery's failure, which arrived in Philadelphia in January 1776, stunned the members of Congress who responded by appropriating 300 pounds sterling for a statue to be built in Montgomery's honor and placed in the hall where they met.[27]

By the spring of 1776, with Arnold now under siege in Montreal, Congress had raised a new army under General John Sullivan to march to his relief. Colonel Wayne, whose regiment was part of Sullivan's army, would finally face his first test of battle. He headed north with his own regiment, four other regiments from Pennsylvania, including one led by Colonel Arthur St. Clair, and still more regiments from New York and New Jersey, all under the immediate command of General William Thompson. They took three weeks to travel from New York City up the Hudson to Albany and Lake George, across the portage to Fort Ticonderoga and along Lake Champlain into Canada, and finally past St. John's to the town of Sorrel on the southern bank of the St. Lawrence River. During the long trek through a country Wayne described as beautiful and desolated, he seemed most concerned about the appearance of his men. He demanded that they look the part of soldiers from head to toe and arrive on the parade ground every morning clean-shaven, perfectly coiffed, and with spotless uniforms. However, far from being a martinet, he won a reputation among his fellow officers for his love of good food, fine wine, and lively conversations that lasted long into the night.[28]

But sometimes on the way north, when the marches by day and nightly festivities were done, Wayne wrote to his wife Polly that he often worried about what would become of him on the battlefield. He had prepared for this moment since he was a boy, but now not knowing for certain whether he would live or die was almost unbearable. On the long road to the St. Lawrence River, he had wondered if he would suffer the same "defect of the human heart" that now afflicted his sentries at Fort Fayette. Would he stand and fight at the crack of artillery and lead balls shot directly at him, keeping a cool head, or would he freeze in terror, freeing himself only long enough to run for his life?[29]

Wayne got his answer shortly before dawn on June 9, 1776. The night before, after learning that three hundred British regulars were fifty miles downriver at Three Rivers, Wayne and his fellow Continentals boarded boats that took them within nine miles of the town. Local guides promised to lead the Americans there safely, but instead brought them through a deep swamp three miles wide from the St. Lawrence, and then along a road so close to the river that British gunboats opened fire on them. Wayne and the hundred and fifty soldiers he commanded pressed on, finally coming out of the swamp and running headlong into a company of British regulars racing their way. Any fear Wayne might have had up until this point disappeared as he formed his men for battle. He ordered them to "wheel to the Right & left," flanking the enemy on both sides, just like Marshal Saxe had taught him, and pommeling them with a "well Armed and heavy fire," as he later described to his mentor Benjamin Franklin. Wayne's regiment fought bravely, pushing the redcoats back toward the redoubts around Three Rivers, unaware they were not facing three hundred regulars, but instead three thousand redcoats and Hessian mercenaries, under the command of General Carleton, then the governor of Quebec, and his Lieutenant General John Burgoyne. The enemy returned Wayne's fire with muskets, howitzers, and field pieces, but still his regiment pressed on.

Finally, Wayne looked through the smoke to see if other soldiers were fighting near him. He caught a glimpse of General Thompson, St. Clair and his men, and the regiment of his close friends Colonel William Irvine and Lieutenant Colonel Thomas Hartley. They were trying to advance toward his position through the heavy fire, but Wayne quickly lost sight of them. He then saw Colonel William Maxwell fighting on his left, but with artillery blasts coming "so hot" at his Second New Jersey Regiment, they pulled back, leaving Wayne's regiment to fight alone. He knew his men could not hold out much longer, but instead must retreat back along the St. Lawrence. When Maxwell and his men returned, opening fire on the British with their muskets, and thus providing a cover on his left for a retreat, Wayne, along with Lieutenant Colonel William Allen, ordered the eight hundred soldiers near them to race back toward the swamp. Unable to find General Thompson, Wayne and Allen stayed on the battlefield with only twenty soldiers and five officers. They kept up a steady fire at the British for another hour until most of the Continentals got away.[30]

Many of the soldiers with Wayne at Three Rivers never forgot how cool he was under fire, even though he was wounded in his right hand. They did not think it bragging when he wrote home to his family and friends that he and Colonel Allen had "saved the Army in Canada." Wayne and Allen guided their troops back through the swamp, collecting three hundred more on the way, and leading them toward the army's landing point on the St Lawrence. But when they arrived there, the boats were nowhere in sight. The soldiers who guarded them, worried that the British might overrun their position, had taken the boats upriver. Wayne kept everyone calm, ordering the soldiers to march through the woods along the shore toward the crossing to Sorrel. After traveling for three days, with no food and little rest, and fearing all the while that the British would intercept them, they finally arrived opposite Sorrel and boarded the waiting boats that took them across the St. Lawrence.[31]

Only when Wayne landed in Sorrel did he learn the magnitude of the Continental Army's defeat. Fifty men had been killed and nearly five times that number captured, including General Thompson and Colonel Irvine. For the disaster at Three Rivers, Congress dismissed General Sullivan and replaced him with Horatio Gates. With Carleton's army less than a day behind, Gates hurried his broken columns south to St. John's. They next headed to Crown Point on Lake Champlain. Arriving there in the first week of July, with many men sick from wounds and fevers, and most having no shoes, socks, or coats, Gates left a few soldiers there and led the main body of the army fifteen miles south to Fort Ticonderoga.[32]

Even though he had remained calm at Three Rivers, Wayne would never overcome this fear of his own death that came upon him before every battle. His anxiety only grew worse as the Revolution continued, knowing the more he fought, the more the odds of surviving were against him. Still, as soon as a battle began, he became suddenly alert and self-assured. Now in 1792, as he shaped a new army in the wilderness, he wondered how he could teach these same traits to his men, which he had never been taught nor had he ever been required to teach to anyone else. It was especially necessary now that the raw recruits arriving daily at Fort Fayette all knew the story of St. Clair's defeat. Fighting the British had been frightening enough, but it could not compare with battling Indians who tortured and scalped their opponents. The terror of what warriors might do to them was so great that many recruits, urged to flee by the very people they came west to protect, did just that, slipping away in the night back down the roads from wherever they had come. Wayne was especially distraught when fifty-seven men on their way from Carlisle in August simply disappeared, never to be heard from again.[33]

Still he was relieved to learn that he was not facing a pending attack on Pittsburgh. The large party of warriors who were supposedly about to descend upon the town turned out to be only six Indians who fled once they were discovered. But Wayne was still furious at the sentries who had deserted their post. He condemned them as base cowards whose disgraceful behavior had endangered the lives of their fellow soldiers and the citizens they had sworn an oath to protect. He offered a ten-dollar reward to anyone, military or civilian, who returned the sentries to him. One by one, Pittsburgh's citizens brought the deserters back into Fort Fayette. Wayne wanted to brand "Coward" across their foreheads, but neither Knox nor Washington approved of such a drastic measure. He had to be satisfied with lesser punishments ranging from fifty to one hundred lashes doled out to most of them at their court-martials. Soldiers who later tried to desert would have a "D" branded on their foreheads, their hair and eyebrows shaved off, and a halter placed around their necks so they could be trotted around the camp.[34]

Up until this moment, Wayne had hesitated using the death penalty as a punishment for his men. Just a week before the alarm went up of an Indian attack, he stopped the execution of a young recruit named Henry Hamilton who was scheduled to hang for striking another ensign. Hoping his mercy would inspire his soldiers to behave better, he was certain this was the last time anyone in his Legion would commit a crime punishable by death. But on August 13, after so many of his sentries had bolted at the mere thought of facing Indian warriors, he decided to make an example of one of the deserters. Sometime between eight and nine in the morning, Private Hugh Laughlin, who had abandoned his post and later stolen the horse of a poor widow, died on the gallows in front of a full parade of the Legion. However, two weeks later, Wayne hesitated when four more deserters were condemned to death by a firing squad. A French priest visited the men and found one of them, a soldier named John Elias, unwilling to make peace with God. The priest begged Wayne to spare his life, but the general ignored him. The priest walked with the soldiers to their execution, fainting just before the guns were fired. When he awoke, he learned that Wayne, just as concerned that Elias might spend eternity in hell, had pardoned him at the last second.[35]

Wayne was not a heartless commander. The suffering of his men was real to him and even understandable. Whether a man joined the army willingly, after dreaming of becoming a soldier since childhood, like Wayne and young Harrison, or in the worst case signed up when a recruiter promised him money, glory, or whiskey, army life was more often terrible than wonderful. Wayne had first glimpsed this truth after the retreat from Three Rivers when he assumed command of Fort Ticonderoga, the giant stone fort shaped like a star built by the French at the southern end of Lake Champlain. Wayne may have been too proud to desert his post, but the thought of escaping from this living hell on earth was never far from his mind in the months he spent there.

He had taken up his command at Ticonderoga on November 18, 1776, as a reward for his bravery at Three Rivers. Wayne was elated with the appointment, especially since most of his 2,500 soldiers were Pennsylvanians. He had spent much of the summer and early fall writing with great pride to his wife about his men at Ticonderoga. "I have now the finest and best Regiment in the Continental service—we are viewed with admiration and pleasure by all the Officers in the Army," he told Polly. He also found the political situation of the country clearer as he looked out from the ramparts of the old fort. He was happy that Congress had at last declared independence, a move he had anticipated two years before. Far away from the day-to-day struggles of Washington's army, he surveyed America and proclaimed, "Our Growing Country can meet with considerable losses and survive them; but one defeat to our more than Savage Enemy Ruins them forever." The British might burn a few towns along the coast, as even now they were doing on Long Island Sound, but he assured Polly, "They will never subjugate the free born sons of America."[36]

Yet the enormity of what his soldiers would have to accomplish if Ticonderoga was attacked had weighed heavily on Wayne. He did not share these concerns with his wife, but instead told Benjamin Franklin. He continued writing to his

Fort Ticonderoga from Mount Independence.
Courtesy of Fort Ticonderoga Museum; photograph by Gavin Ashworth.

old friend until Franklin left for Paris in September 1778. Sometimes in faraway Ticonderoga, when he looked east toward Boston, he confessed that he could not understand why the British had walked away from certain victory there. If they had moved into the countryside, and seen the suffering of the people, they could have easily defeated Massachusetts. He was sure the new British commander General William Howe would never make the same mistake again. Instead, he would march north from New York City, "make a junction" with redcoats coming south from Canada, led by Burgoyne now that Carleton had returned to Quebec, and thus cut the colonies in two. The only thing preventing this would be Wayne and the men be commanded at Fort Ticonderoga.[37]

But how could men "Destitute of almost every necessary fit for a soldier, shoes, stockings shirts and coats," none of which could be easily obtained, ever hold off Howe heading north and Burgoyne heading south? Wayne had fretted mightily trying to answer this question. They "look up to me for Relief," he complained, but he could offer none. If brave Washington and ten thousand men on Long Island could not defeat the British, how could his small force, growing weaker day by day, do any better? "We are not a little surprised at the evacuation of

Long Island—the surrender of that was the opening the Door to the Island of New York," he wrote to Franklin. The hopelessness of Washington's situation lost somewhere in snowbound New Jersey and his own imprisonment in frozen Ticonderoga were nightmares from which he could not awake. Unlike Washington, Wayne did not believe the Continental Army could ever win New York City back from the British while the Royal Navy sat in the Hudson and East Rivers. Warm and well fed in comfortable quarters, the redcoats would never give up the place, not even if the Continental Army launched a winter campaign to take it.[38]

No answers to his worries had ever come back from Franklin or anyone else. Wayne was left to imagine what lay ahead as he wandered Ticonderoga, which he named "Golgotha," a place of skulls that time had forgotten. God must have made this place last, Wayne often thought, finishing it in the dark. His loathing of the fort increased as his men struggled to survive. To hold their threadbare clothes together, they scraped bones from the ground to use as buttons. Wayne was certain these were the remains of General James Abercrombie's redcoats who died trying to take the fort during the French and Indian War. But he could do nothing to help his men. He was powerless to feed or clothe them, or even to stave off the cold. Two weeks before Christmas, when Lake Champlain was "one massive solid ice," as he described to Delany, he sat before a fire for three hours and could not get warm until he drank an entire bottle of wine for dinner.[39]

In the dark December of 1776, Wayne had experienced a despair he never knew before. Looking south from Ticonderoga, everything appeared hopeless. Where was Washington? Had he taught his men to stop hiding behind fortifications and fight the British in open country? Or was the war already over and were America's brave sons hurrying home to protect their families? A man could truly go mad with worry in a place like Ticonderoga, and for a time Wayne almost did. Death was so ever present that he seemed a real person: "that *Grisly Horrid Monster*—that *Caitiff* who Distinguishes neither the Gentleman, nor the Soldier, age, Sex or *State*" wreaked havoc all around him. By Christmas, Death had carried off fifty soldiers using his three favorite weapons: pestilence, famine, and the sword. If only the army had done the sensible thing of occupying the more formidable post at Crown Point, Wayne thought to himself, he might be better able to defend New York against an invasion. If only the American people knew what his men had to endure, maybe they would send help. If only he could join Washington, wherever he was, he might help him do the impossible and defeat the British.[40]

But no amount of writing to his friends in Philadelphia, many who were now serving with Franklin in the Continental Congress, or pleas to his commanding officer General Schuyler in Albany could get help for his men or release him from his imprisonment at Ticonderoga. For a brief moment, he came out of his despair when he learned Washington had surprised the Hessians at Trenton early on Christmas morning and took Princeton on the following day. But by February 1777, even after the Pennsylvania Assembly named him a brigadier general, he had fallen back into a great darkness. He was like a lion roaring in a cage all alone in the wilderness, complaining to anyone who would listen how much he hated Ticonderoga. As his soldiers melted away, through death or when their enlistments were up, he found himself surrounded by militia who were mainly old men, young boys, and local farmers who only spoke Dutch.[41]

Finally, a letter dated April 12, 1777, and posted from Morristown, New Jersey, had arrived at Fort Ticonderoga for Wayne. The words came like a trumpet calling him back from the dead. "As you are appointed in the arrangement of the army to command a Brigade of the Pennsylvania Troops, I do so order, that you will hold yourself in readiness and repair to my Headquarters, as soon, as a General Officer arrive at the post where you now command—Your presence here, will be materially wanted, and I persuade myself, you will lose no time in complying with my requisition, when the circumstance I have mentioned, puts it in your power." The letter was signed "G. Washington."[42]

An overjoyed Wayne spent his last days at the post he despised completing the "Abatis Round the Old fort," just as the French had done in 1757 when they defeated Abercrombie, and "Octagons on Mt. Independence" across Lake Champlain for increased protection. He was determined to leave the place "in a much securer and better state than we found it." His only concern was that his soldiers, many of whom had already been called away from Ticonderoga, would get too far ahead of him on the roads heading south. They might leave the army and never return. "I want much to go also—it would be in my Power to do more with them in case of necessity than perhaps any other Officer; I know these worthy fellows well and they know me—I am Confident they would not Desert me in time of Danger," he had explained to General Schuyler in anticipation of leaving the fort. But Schuyler had paid no attention to Wayne's concern, and now made him wait until the last man left for Morristown before he could join them.[43]

"They would not Desert me." Wayne had boldly written these words early in 1777. But no matter how dedicated a general might be, he had only so much control over his soldiers. After finally leaving Ticonderoga in late April, Wayne would learn this awful truth during the darkest days of the Revolution when his men deserted him and even mutinied. Now in the summer of 1792, he was just starting to build his army and already his soldiers were running away. If the Legion of the United States, which he was still trying to piece together, was to accomplish what it had been sent west to do, then he must stop them. He believed that the only way to keep his men from abandoning him was to train them perfectly. He already knew that he must teach them how to maneuver on command and load and shoot their weapons quickly and accurately. But he now understood that he must also train them not to be afraid. To do this, they must meet the Indians a hundred times over in their imaginations before they ever met them on the battlefield. By so doing, his soldiers would overcome their fears or at least control them enough to face the enemy and not run. If they did not defeat the Indians first in their minds, they would never be able to defeat them in the howling wilderness.

After too many of his men, in his opinion, had been found guilty of desertion, Wayne devised a plan to help them overcome their fears. He decided to train them in practice battles where some of his soldiers would play the part of the Indians while the rest would act as the army. The first battle was staged along the Allegheny in August 1792 with his riflemen pretending to be warriors. They stripped off most of their clothes and took to the woods across the river. They hid behind trees and let out the kind of yells that St. Clair's men heard on the morning they were massacred. Wayne also assigned scouts to move out and report back on the actions of their imaginary opponents. He ordered both sides to advance toward each other with the warriors dashing from the trees and the perfectly dressed soldiers crossing the river. When the firing commenced, Wayne directed his scouts to fall back toward the right and left, which gave his infantry time to form their lines, load their muskets, not with shots but with gunpowder only, and fire at the enemy. Once they blasted the Indians racing from the woods, the dragoons headed around them and attacked on both flanks.[44]

Wayne was astounded by how well the exercise went. So many men were caught up in the reality of combat that they were actually hurt when their faces were burned by powder blasts. "I had no idea that the mind could be so diffusively inflamed by imagination only," he wrote to Secretary Knox. Despite the injuries, Wayne knew he had found the best way to train his frightened men. His first battle mirrored what St. Clair's soldiers had encountered on the morning of November 4, 1791. Later he practiced battles with columns moving through the forest near Fort Fayette. Once again some of his soldiers took the part of the Indians. When the fighting began, they raced from the woods toward advance guards at the head of the line. They fired at the soldiers who quickly formed their lines in open order, leaving enough room for the men to load their muskets quickly and shoot back at the enemy. Through it all, Wayne could be seen and heard, whirling about on his horse, shouting orders to his troops, and helping them not to be afraid.[45]

By the fall of 1792, Wayne finally had an actual plan for training his soldiers to fight the Indians. Yet he could not continue drilling his men, whose numbers would soon grow to nineteen hundred, in the confines of Fort Fayette. He was determined to move his army deeper into the wilderness. He must also get them away from the enticements of Pittsburgh, which he now called "Gomorrah." On October 22, he rode with a small party of aides some twenty miles down the Ohio to a site on the east bank of the river. He was just eight miles from the Beaver River and only fourteen more miles from the government survey line running north and south that officially marked the start of the Ohio Country. Wayne chose the spot on a wide floodplain that would make a good place for his men to fight their imaginary battles. He knew they would stay here at least until the spring, waiting for President Washington to make up his mind whether to send more commissioners west or the Legion of the United States into the forest to confront the Indians in one great battle. After choosing the site, Wayne returned to Pittsburgh, sent two companies of men to set up the winter camp he named Legionville, and then oversaw the court-martial of three more deserters, with the ringleader shot dead by his fellow soldiers.[46]

"I HAVE THE CONFIDENCE
OF THE GENERAL"

President Washington should have well remembered the site of Legionville. He traveled there in 1752 when the now deserted bottomland was a Shawnee village called Logstown. He came with a party of Virginians sent from Williamsburg by their colony's Lieutenant Governor Robert Dinwiddie. They were to win the support of the Six Nations and tribes living across the Ohio, the same ones that Wayne was now preparing to fight, in Virginia's struggle against the French for control of the Ohio River and the country that lay beyond it. "Brethren, we have traveled a long & dark *Way* to meet you," the commissioners announced in an attempt to impress the Indians with the arduous journey they had made over the Blue Ridge Mountains and down through the Alleghenies to reach them. Here, for the first time, Washington met Tanacharison, who two years later would murder the French commander Jumonville. At the Logstown council, the Mingo chief gave his full support to the English king and his children the Virginians. The other sachems of the Six Nations, along with chiefs of the Shawnee, Wyandot, and Delaware, agreed that the colonists could settle the country south and east of the Ohio River. Together they put their marks on the Treaty of Logstown, which made their promise official. The Indians also reaffirmed a treaty between the Six Nations and Virginia and Maryland negotiated in Lancaster, Pennsylvania, in 1744, which guaranteed Virginia's right to settle in the Shenandoah Valley west of the Blue Ridge in exchange for two hundred pounds of gold.[1]

But now the Shawnee were gone, having moved into the river valleys north of Fort Washington. Tanacharison, the man who helped Washington launch the French and Indian War, was gone, too. He died of pneumonia the year the war started, in a settler's cabin on the Pennsylvania frontier. If Wayne knew any of this, he never mentioned it in letters to Secretary Knox. He was not interested in what this place had been, but only what it would be once he brought his army here. Legionville would keep his soldiers safe from harm, both from Indians who could never dislodge them, and from themselves, most especially his untrained officers who were fonder of Pittsburgh's pleasures than disciplining their soldiers. Wayne, in fact, envisioned his camp as an "academy for officers." He ordered separate quarters built for his artillery, cavalry, and infantry officers near his own quarters, while the huts for his regulars faced the parade ground where they would spend much of their time practicing maneuvers.[2]

As cabins went up for his men, each large enough for a dozen soldiers and with a fireplace, along with stables for their horses, Wayne worried that his growing army was still not properly clothed or fed. He was especially frustrated that his requests to the War Department for uniforms had been largely ignored. So were his demands for replacement clothes for deserters who were usually brought back to camp in a "state of nakedness" having sold their uniforms to finance their escape. Even his letters asking for needles and thread so his men could repair their clothes went unanswered. However, this did not stop Wayne from demanding more supplies, especially food and drink. For his soldiers to survive the winter at Legionville, and at eleven other posts from Big Beaver to Vincennes, he estimated they would need 618,700 daily rations of flour, beef, and whiskey.[3]

In early September, after Secretary Knox finally forwarded the structure of the Legion, Wayne made one more request. He had been told to organize his soldiers into four sublegions. Every sublegion would be made up of eight infantry companies and one company each of cavalry, artillery, and riflemen. This was different from the Continental Army, where separate regiments of infantry, cavalry, and artillery were joined into brigades and brigades were formed into divisions. In order to train his officers in the new organization and instill pride among his regulars in their respective units, Wayne needed flags to identify each sublegion: white for the First Sublegion, red for the Second Sublegion, and yellow and green respectively for Sublegions Three and Four. There would be four flags per sublegion, one apiece for the infantry, cavalry, artillery, and riflemen, each clearly marked with the sublegion's number and unit. The sixteen flags, all measuring two feet by two feet, would be mounted high atop eight-foot poles. By glancing at them, in practice or combat, Wayne's soldiers would always know where they were in relation to their sublegion and the rest of the army.[4]

But when Wayne made his request to the War Department, rather than receiving congratulations for training his men so carefully, Knox told him that no new flags would be delivered to the Legion. Wayne must reconfigure the ones sent a year before to St. Clair's doomed Second Regiment. Knox said they must be packed away somewhere at Fort Washington. He also told him to place a life-size image of a bald eagle, silver or white, as the president would decide, on each. Wayne did not complain that his plans were ignored, but instructed Quartermaster James O'Hara to place silver eagles on the Legion's flags without waiting for Washington to choose. Where in the wilderness O'Hara would find silver cloth, he did not say.[5]

There were many things Wayne would have liked to tell the president about the troubles in the Ohio Country if he could communicate with him directly. From the moment he was called to Washington's side at Morristown in the spring of 1777, Wayne had looked upon the man whom everyone called "His Excellency" as his close friend. Even in the darkest days ahead, Wayne never completely lost the self-confidence that, in his eyes, made him the equal of the greatest men of his age, including General Washington. Throughout the Revolution, he spoke openly to the commander in chief, never considering him aloof as so many others did. He wrote just as boldly to Washington when they were apart, sharing his ideas as freely as a younger brother might write to his favorite older brother.[6]

But now was not the time to explain the troubles across the Ohio to Washington. Wayne respected the lines of authority running from the president to the secretary of war and finally to himself. He was training his men to respect this same chain of command. He knew full well that Washington was trying to win peace with the Indians through diplomatic means. He also understood the tremendous political pressure the president was under to do so. As Secretary Knox explained in his weekly letters, Washington did not want an Indian war because the American people did not want one. The president had made "pacific overtures" to the tribes, knowing both Indians and settlers might oppose him, out of "respect to the opinion of probably the great majority of the Citizens of the United States." Wayne agreed that the military must always be subjugated to the political authority. He had guarded this principle just as jealously as Washington during the Revolution. However, what he could not agree with was the conclusion that the secretary of war had drawn. The current "tranquility of the frontiers," which Knox believed would last through autumn, "may be fairly estimated as a consequence of the Indians knowing our desires for peace."[7]

Nor could Wayne share the president's optimism that the tribes across the Ohio were determined to make peace. Instead they were lying in wait to strike the Legion at a date and time of their own choosing. Neither could he agree that the treaty, which General Putnam and Reverend Heckewelder had just concluded with the Wabash Indians in September, would have any impact on the hostile chiefs. He likewise did not share Washington's faith in the Mohawk leader Joseph Brant, who promised to convince the western tribes to give up their demand for the Ohio River as the Indian boundary. He suspected that Brant passed every bit of information he received from Washington and Knox directly on to the British in Canada. He had more confidence in the Seneca chief Cornplanter, but still considered both men leaders of a broken confederation that had little influence beyond its dwindling borders.[8]

Finally, Wayne doubted that the two commissioners just sent among the Indians with a message from the president were still alive. John Hardin, a Kentuckian who fought at Saratoga, and Captain Alexander Trueman, a veteran of St. Clair's First Regiment, had left Fort Washington in the spring of 1792 and had not been heard from by the fall. The talk they carried to all the tribes "southward of the Lakes, East of the Mississippi and to the northward of the River Ohio" might well have been their death sentence. In it, the president assured the Indians that the United States had no desire to "deprive you of your lands and drive you out of the country." Because they wrongly believed this, warriors had massacred St. Clair's men and now terrorized settlers everywhere on the frontier. Washington claimed the Americans wanted no more land than the tribes had already signed away up through the Treaty of Fort Harmar in 1789. He then revealed his plans for "bringing the blessings of civilized life" to the Indians, a policy which up until now he had failed to mention. He would teach the tribes how to "cultivate corn, to raise oxen, sheep and other domestic animals; to build comfortable houses," and "so to dwell upon the land," side by side with the settlers coming their way, in peace "forever."[9]

Wayne did not question the president's plans nor did he make the case to Secretary Knox that warriors might not wish to become farmers. Instead he explained Washington's diplomatic efforts to militia companies from Pennsylvania to Kentucky. Upon arriving in Pittsburgh, he sent out a circular to local lieutenants describing the president's attempts to win a "General Peace" on the frontier. His letter carefully followed the language of Knox's instructions to him. Until the results of Washington's "overtures" to the tribes were known, no one was to attack any Indians. However, Wayne added a caveat of his own. The prohibition against attacks did not extend to parties of warriors seen "hovering about the frontiers." He expected the lieutenants to judge for themselves how to deal with Indians who came to murder and plunder their fellow citizens in the middle of the night or at dawn's first light.[10]

Still nothing he did to instruct the local militia, or to shape the Legion, seemed to please the president. After learning that Wayne planned to set up his winter camp twenty miles outside Pittsburgh, rather than moving down the Ohio to Fort Washington, he grew so angry in a cabinet meeting that Thomas Jefferson made a note of it. Asked how this could have happened, Secretary Knox answered that

General Wayne believed flour was limited at forts farther west and therefore he needed to stay close to Pittsburgh to obtain food for the Legion. Wayne learned about the shortages in a report sent to him by the Treasury Department. "It is unfortunate, and very extraordinary," complained an angry Washington, "that we should have suspended an opinion with respect to the disposition of the army for the winter, from a vague report of Mr. Hamilton."[11]

Furious that his fears about Wayne's prodigality were coming true, he ordered Knox to tell his wayward general in no uncertain terms that the barracks at Legionville must be built with little direct cost to the public. He was, in fact, to construct minimal housing for his troops. "Only what is *indispensably* necessary to cover and secure the Officers and Soldiers from the weather," Washington explained, should be allowed, and even this must be absent of all decorations and devoid of all conveniences. After placing him under strict orders to take no actions that might upset the negotiations with the tribes, Wayne was now told to consider himself "under marching orders" to move into Indian country in the winter or spring.[12]

Just as the American people had changed since the start of the Revolution, so had George Washington. Fifteen years before when Wayne had raced from Ticonderoga to Washington's side, he could do no wrong in his commander's eyes. Even the fact that his appearance had drastically changed since their last meeting did not seem to matter. When Wayne first bounded into Washington's camp on Long Island in 1776, he had been impeccably dressed from head to toe, but now after his imprisonment in the hated Golgotha, he appeared as ragged as the men he commanded. His blue coat, ivory vest, and white pants, threadbare and worn out, had long since been discarded. Wayne was instead dressed in black with a rust-colored coat thrown over him. The only ornament on his person was the cockade that General Schuyler's daughters had made for him, stuck in his tattered lace hat. Ignoring Wayne's bedraggled looks, Washington appreciated the fact that his brigadier was still on fire for the Revolution. He seemed even less afraid of the British after Three Rivers than when they met on Long Island. He brimmed with so much confidence that many who met him claimed he behaved more like a marshal of France than a brigadier in the Continental Army. To be placed in the same company as his hero Marshal Saxe would have been the highest compliment to Wayne, if he had heard it.[13]

He had also fairly burst with pride that he was now part of Washington's close-knit circle of top generals. Over and over, throughout the campaign to defend Philadelphia in the spring and summer of 1777, he wrote to his wife that he had been called away to another conference with His Excellency. Even though he had not seen his family for sixteen months, he never rode out to Waynesborough, but instead remained at Washington's side. As he told Polly, the commander in chief had expressly forbidden him to return home. At this trying time, Wayne could not be expected to visit his family, a point he often repeated to his wife, "I can't be spared from Camp. I have the Confidence of the General, and the Hearts of the Soldiers will Support me in the Day of Action."[14]

After calling Wayne to Morristown, Washington had moved his camp to Middlebrook in the mountains just to the east. The Delawares, now waiting across the Ohio to defeat Wayne's Legion, once lived along these ridges, which they called the Watchungs or "High Hills." From these heights, encircled with trenches to protect his army, Washington kept a close eye on the British in New York City. He was ready to pursue General William Howe if he headed north to meet Burgoyne or south to threaten Philadelphia. Either way Washington would outflank him, cutting off his communications and supply lines. Clearly understanding Washington's plans, Howe sent his men into the New Jersey countryside to goad the American commander and his inexperienced soldiers into face-to-face combat. But when Washington refused to take the bait, Howe ordered his men back to Staten Island.[15]

The first task Washington gave Wayne upon his arrival in camp was to harass the redcoats of General James Grant. They had been detached from the main British army to attack General Sullivan's troops in Princeton. Washington appreciated the fact that Wayne was quick on his feet, something he had proven at Three Rivers. No general seemed as capable of wheeling an army around better than Wayne. He showed this especially during the retreat along the St. Lawrence River in the previous winter, which saved hundreds of soldiers from capture or death. Outside Princeton in the late spring of 1777, Wayne again proved how quickly he could move an army when, by his count, he maneuvered Grant's forces six times into a skirmish. As he explained in excited letters to his friend Sharp Delany, Grant's "people broke and run" every time, once fleeing before Wayne's muskets and cannon which dirtied the general's soldiers, tore off the head of his horse, and even left him bruised. Still, the redcoats could not escape forever, for as Wayne saw it, "Our people are daily gaining Health Spirits and Discipline—the spade & pick axe throw'd aside—for the British Rebels to take up—they notwithstanding affect to hold us cheap to beat up our Quarters—*if we don't* beat up theirs first which is in Contemplation, but *this in time.*"[16]

For Wayne, these were the most exciting days of his life. The drumbeat of the present intermingled with his childhood memories and made it seem that Caesar was marching once again to meet the Gauls. Everywhere he looked history was repeating itself. He let his commander in chief know that if he seized every opportunity to attack the British before they attacked him, he would be victorious like Caesar. But Washington was not Caesar, a fact that Wayne struggled to understand during the campaign to defend Philadelphia. He had none of the bravado that still made Caesar famous nearly two thousand years after his death. He was not averse to taking chances, but more often than not his caution overruled his daring, a trait that Wayne glimpsed during the summer he skirmished with General Grant. Knowing that Howe's soldiers were on their way back to New York City, Washington ordered Wayne to stay close on their heels until he brought up the rest of the Continental Army. But at the very moment that General Howe, realizing he was being followed, turned to fight, Washington ordered Wayne and the rest of the army back up into the safe heights of Middlebrook.[17]

Many of Wayne's contemporaries believed Washington resembled Quintus Fabius Maximus, who had lived two hundred years before Julius Caesar. Better known as Fabius, he became the dictator of Rome during the Second Punic War. He assumed the post in a desperate hour for his people just like the Americans faced in 1777. The Carthaginian general Hannibal had crossed the Alps and destroyed two Roman armies, first in the bitterly cold December of 218 B.C. when his soldiers ambushed the infantry at the Trebia River, and six months later, at Lake Trasimene, when for the first time in recorded history a general outflanked his opponents. After whole armies fell to Hannibal in pitched battles, Fabius decided to fight a war of attrition, harassing the Carthaginians with small parties of cavalry and disrupting their supply lines. For his tactics, he won the nickname of Cunctator, or the "Delayer." After the Continental Army collapsed in the face of the British onslaught on Long Island and Manhattan, Washington, like Fabius, had mainly fought a war of attrition. He now had to decide whether to continue doing so in late July 1777 when, from his entrenched position at Middlebrook, he could see General Howe preparing to leave the city with his huge army of redcoats and Hessians. But for where, he could not be certain.[18]

At first, Washington thought Howe might take his army north along the Hudson to meet General Burgoyne marching from Canada. He knew Burgoyne was heading south from reports of General St. Clair, who had taken command of Fort Ticonderoga after Wayne's departure. St. Clair's scouts spotted at least eight thousand British regulars, Hessians, Indians, and French Canadians making their way down Lake Champlain. When the enemy mounted their artillery on the surrounding hills, St. Clair believed he had two choices. He could put up a brave fight, winning a reputation as a doomed but valiant commander, or he could abandon Ticonderoga. "I know I could save my character by sacrificing the army," he explained to James Wilkinson, currently serving as Wayne's second in command at Fort Washington, but he was not willing to pay the price. Early on the morning of July 6, 1777, he fled the post with his entire army, a decision that stunned both Washington and Wayne. While Washington forgave St. Clair, Wayne could not. Even though he voted to exonerate St. Clair for the surrender during his court-martial, he still considered him a coward. He disliked him even more for the surrender of Ticonderoga than he did for the fact that the Pennsylvania Assembly named him a major general instead of Wayne, who remained a brigadier.[19]

Before Washington could move his army north, General Howe loaded his 17,000-man army on 265 ships and sailed away from New York City. Not even Anthony Wayne, who prided himself on his ability to anticipate the future, could say where they were going. Washington now prepared his soldiers to move toward Philadelphia, but after the British fleet appeared off the New Jersey Capes, only to disappear again, Washington and all his generals, including Wayne, were certain Howe was heading for Charleston. Being closer to General Burgoyne, they decided to move in his direction, and were just leaving for upstate New York when news arrived that Howe's fleet had been spotted in the Chesapeake Bay. Washington finally knew that the British were heading for Philadelphia. They would land at Head of Elk, and from there take the roads northward that led directly into the nation's capital.[20]

Throwing off the mantle of Fabius, Washington decided to meet Howe's army at Brandywine Creek just west of Philadelphia. Now the race was on to move his soldiers there before the British and Hessians arrived. Washington ordered his 11,000-man army to march through Philadelphia, straight down Chestnut Street from east to west, past the hall where the Continental Congress was in session. Many of his soldiers wore new hunting shirts with evergreen sprigs in their caps. To impress the people lining the streets even more, all the men's baggage, along with their wives, children, and camp followers, were sent in wagons around the city. Wayne was not a part of the parade since Washington ordered him, as soon as Howe sailed away from New York, to head for Chester County and prepare the militia for the defense of Philadelphia. Wayne mustered out his friends and neighbors, and drilled them quickly before handing over command of the militia to General John Armstrong.[21]

By the time he caught up with the Continental Army near the Neshaminy River, twenty miles north of Philadelphia, Wayne was happy to see his commander in chief acting like the heroes of old. As Julius Caesar or Marshal Saxe might have done, Washington was racing ahead to shape the future in his favor. Wayne's mind raced ahead, too, filling with plans for certain victory. Now was the hour, he believed, for Washington to act even more decisively than at Trenton or Princeton. He wrote his boldest letter to his commander in chief to date. Buoyed up by Washington's sudden nerve, he described the drama of the great battle to come and the parts they would both play in it. The Continental Army faced a situation outside Philadelphia just like the Romans had experienced against the Gauls at Amiens in 57 B.C. Wayne urged his commander to do exactly what Caesar had done then. Do not wait for the British to approach, but instead attack them first. Caesar had marched out of his camp and routed the Gauls who were besieging Cicero. The Roman general "sallied out with his cohorts," he explained to Washington, throwing the Gauls into the "utmost consternation" and obtaining "an easy victory." Wayne offered to play the part of a different General Fabius, who joined Caesar on the road from Amiens, and lead 2,500 to 3,000 of the "best armed and most disciplined troops" in the attack.[22]

Washington had other plans for him. He knew the road from the Chesapeake to Philadelphia passed over Chadds Ford, the narrowest crossing of Brandywine Creek. If Howe crossed here, his soldiers would have to wade through waist-high water, march over swampy bottomland, and finally up steep hills on their march to the capital. Washington needed a fearless officer to command the heights above the ford. There could be no man better than his brigadier who dreamed always of Caesar. Wayne's brigades, including an artillery company under Colonel Thomas Proctor, would stand guard on the bluff above Chadds Ford. The Chester County militia he had mustered out would wait on his left. Nathanael Greene, who knew Wayne from foxhunts on Long Island and skirmishes against General Grant in New Jersey, would stand to his right and anchor the center of the American line. Farther to his right, four miles up Brandywine Creek, General Sullivan would wait with his division. General William Alexander, better known as Lord Stirling, and General Adam Stephen would hold their troops in reserve behind Greene. Washington also sent William Maxwell, now a general in the New Jersey Line, across the creek to intercept Howe on his way to Chadds Ford.[23]

Early on the morning of September 11, 1777, shortly after eight o'clock, Wayne heard gunfire across the creek. Like everyone else, he assumed the leading edge of Howe's army had just encountered Maxwell's soldiers. But it was difficult to know exactly what was happening since the countryside was covered in a thick fog. Even the sun's first rays could not clear the mist away. After listening to the fighting for two hours, Wayne spotted Maxwell's men racing back across the creek and climbing up the bluff toward his position. Then a shot rang out from the fog somewhere in the distance. The sound came like a signal for the bombardment to begin on the bluff above Chadd's Ford. Suddenly Wayne could see hundreds of soldiers in bright green uniforms coming down the hills on the opposite side of the Brandywine. They moved with such precision through the shifting fog that Wayne knew at once these were Baron Wilhelm von Knyphausen's Hessians. For

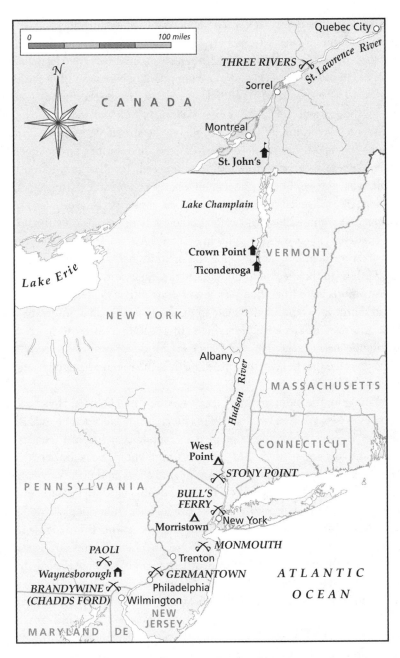

Wayne's northern campaigns. Copyright © Roberta Stockwell, 2018.

the next two hours, the hated German mercenaries bombarded his brigades with cannon and musket fire.[24]

As Proctor's artillery returned fire, Wayne wondered why the Hessians never attempted to cross the creek, and more important, where the rest of the British army was. There should be thousands of redcoats across the Brandywine, but through the fog and smoke, he only saw Hessians. Are they trying to "humor" me, Wayne asked himself? Could this merely be a feint? Was Howe even now readying his men to storm out of the fog somewhere farther up the creek? He rode to General Greene, who was just as confused. Together they found Washington, who also could not understand what was happening. Throughout the morning, he had received conflicting reports about where the redcoats actually were. He assumed first Maxwell and then Wayne were bearing the brunt of Howe's attempt to cross the Brandywine. But he received several reports that the redcoats were marching north along the opposite bank. They would probably cross farther up the creek and double back to encircle the Continental Army. If these reports were true, then Wayne was correct that Knyphausen's attack on Chadds Ford was a feint. Somewhere in the fog that still had not lifted by noon, Howe and his redcoats were preparing to attack from a different direction. Yet Washington hesitated to act after Major Joseph Spear of the Chester County militia reported that he rode the entire length of the Brandywine's opposite bank at dawn and saw no one.[25]

Assuming for the moment that Spear was wrong, and General Howe had split his forces in two, Washington decided to launch a direct attack on Knyphausen's Hessians. He ordered Wayne to prepare his men to march across Chadds Ford directly into the enemy lines. But at the very moment his brigades were ready to move, Wayne received orders from Washington to stand down. Now believing Howe had not split his army in two, he worried Wayne would be marching into a trap. A short time later, with Wayne's brigades back in position above Chadds Ford, Washington learned from Sullivan that the entire British army, 8,000 men under the command of General Howe and Lord Cornwallis, was about to slam directly into him. The officers, who had told Washington that the redcoats had crossed Brandywine Creek farther up, and therefore the Hessian attack was a feint, had been correct. Under the cover of the heavy fog, the British had marched nearly eighteen miles around Knyphausen's position and crossed the creek over two fords unknown to Washington. At this very moment they were bearing down on the American right. Howe had moved his men so quickly that they had time to stop for afternoon tea before launching their assault on Sullivan's division.[26]

Now the Battle of Brandywine began in earnest. Washington had already sent

Lord Stirling and General Stephen to a position near the Quakers' Birmingham Meetinghouse to support Sullivan. He now ordered Greene's men to hurry four miles over hilly ground to support the three generals. At the same time, Knyphausen's Hessians increased their fire on the heights above Chadds Ford before trying to storm the creek. Wayne knew his brigades must hold them back or the entire Continental Army would be surrounded. The fighting went on well into the afternoon, with high casualties on both sides, before the American right finally gave way. During the retreat from the battlefield, most of the Continental Army fled toward the town of Chester, but Wayne remained above Chadds Ford, still pounding the Hessians with cannon and musket fire. Only after Washington ordered Wayne to withdraw and join the rest of the army were Knyphausen's Hessians able to cross Brandywine Creek.[27]

Even as he fled east toward Chester, Wayne came up with a plan to turn disaster into victory. He had grown up in the rolling countryside west of Philadelphia and knew the lay of the land better than anyone. He rode to Washington's side and told him three roads led to Philadelphia and Howe had secured just two of them. The Continental Army could take the third unprotected road and cut off Howe's advance. But Washington saw only disaster in Wayne's plan and decided against it. Still, he agreed that the Continental Army should make a stand against Howe before he crossed the Schuylkill River and marched into Philadelphia. Washington led his army east along the Lancaster Road just ahead of the British and Hessians, who followed at a leisurely pace. Near the White Horse Tavern, he decided to turn and face Howe's army. He ordered Wayne to position his men directly in front of the Hessian advance guard. Wayne stationed his brigades in a cornfield and apple orchard on a small hill facing west. But, almost from the moment he ordered his men to fire into the Hessians coming their way, the skies opened and rain fell in sheets upon the ground. The storm lasted all day September 15 and continued through the next day, ruining the guns and ammunition on both sides and forcing Washington and Howe to withdraw from a contest aptly named the Battle of the Clouds.[28]

For Wayne, now marching down the mud-clogged roads toward the Schuylkill River, Washington no longer seemed to be an entirely perfect man. At Middlebrook he had noticed His Excellency's cautious streak, but at Brandywine he saw a near fatal indecisiveness that shook his faith in the commander in chief. At the same time, Washington discovered a troubling weakness in Wayne's character. If he had a difficult time making decisions, especially in the midst of battle, then his brigadier, who imagined Caesar everywhere, often made up his mind too quickly. "For God's sake, push on as fast as possible," he urged Washington immediately after the Battle of the Clouds. Proud of his ability to see all the possibilities that lay before him, once he decided exactly what was happening, Wayne denied everything occurring to the contrary. His swift thinking could be just as dangerous as Washington's ponderous reasoning, a fact proven just days after the Battle of the Clouds at the Battle of Paoli, a disaster of Wayne's own making.[29]

Washington had taken most of his soldiers across the Schuylkill River to Reading Forge, where he hoped to replenish their ruined ammunition. He was still determined to confront the British one last time before they crossed over to Philadelphia, even if he could do nothing more than capture the enemy's baggage. For this task, he turned to Wayne, who was still west of the Schuylkill, shadowing the British left. On the night of September 20, when Howe's redcoats camped along the Lancaster Road just west of the Paoli Tavern, Wayne took up a position immediately southwest of them. He hid his brigades in the surrounding hills, certain the British had not spotted him. He would wait here, just as Washington had ordered him, until Colonel William Smallwood's First Maryland Regiment joined him. General Maxwell, along with General James Potter of the Pennsylvania Line, might also join Wayne in the attack on the British rear guard. "The *cutting off* the enemy's baggage would be a great matter," Washington confided to Wayne. Knowing how important the mission was to His Excellency, Wayne convinced himself that Washington might turn the whole Continental Army around to the west and attack Howe's army from the opposite direction.[30]

Wayne's officers later remembered how anxious their commander was waiting for the rendezvous. Over and over, he pulled out his watch from his coat, checked the time, and then peered down the Lancaster Road looking for Smallwood's regiment. Finally, about nine o'clock, an old man raced into the camp. He was Morgan Jones, the father of Wayne's chaplain David Jones, who had important news for the general. The elder Jones reported that earlier in the day the British had captured a young servant in the neighborhood. The boy had just returned home claiming the British were planning to attack Wayne as he hid in the nearby hills. Wayne could not believe it. He had already made up his mind that the British did not know his position. Therefore, the rendezvous with Smallwood's Marylanders would take place as planned and Howe's baggage train would be captured. He refused to change his plans because of a rumor from a "thoroughly unmilitary" source. Nor would he abandon the position that His Excellency had expressly ordered him to take up. However, he did post a few more videttes, or mounted guards, nearby.[31]

Only the cries of the videttes that he had reluctantly posted saved Wayne from losing most of his men and perhaps his own life on the dark night of September 20, 1777. Their shouts were the first warning that the British were about to attack his camp. Led by General Charles Grey, the redcoats had swung back around their left and were now ready to pounce full force into the artillery on Wayne's right. Grey came upon Wayne's position silently, ordering his soldiers not to fire their muskets, but to use only their bayonets. Wayne immediately sent most of his men west down the hill toward the Lancaster Road with orders to head to the White Horse Tavern. He also sent a messenger in the same direction to find Colonel Smallwood and tell him to stay where he was. He then led his light infantry and the First Regiment toward the fighting near the artillery. There he found a stunned Colonel Richard Humpton, the officer in charge, and his soldiers frozen to the spot, having failed to retreat even after receiving two orders to do so. After being ordered to leave for the third time, Humpton and his men finally joined the race to the White Horse Tavern with the cannon in tow. Wayne now directed the troops who stayed with him to fire into the oncoming British just thirty yards away. The fighting continued until Wayne and the last of his soldiers joined the retreat down the Lancaster Road.[32]

Shaken and exhausted, Wayne was certain he had saved his men from disaster. But when he arrived at the White Horse Tavern, he learned that complaints of his negligence were already spreading. Some of his men blamed him for the "Paoli Massacre," as the skirmish would forever be remembered. They accused Wayne of failing to rouse them before the enemy struck their camp. They only knew they were under attack when the British came at them in the pitch-black night screaming "No Quarter!" How many men died where they slept, sliced apart by "No Flint" Grey's bloodthirsty redcoats, no one could say, but it seemed like hundreds. Wayne was horrified at these accounts of the skirmish near the Paoli Tavern. His men were wide-awake, he countered, and ready for the attack with most of them retreating quickly. Wayne guessed that perhaps a hundred and fifty had been killed, but he had gotten most of his fifteen hundred soldiers safely away. Local farmers who later came to bury the dead in a common grave agreed with Wayne that it was not a massacre. They counted fifty-three men killed, all found lying on the Lancaster Road and not in the nearby hills.[33]

No matter what the truth was about the Paoli Massacre, Wayne found himself in a position he had never known before. For the first time since taking the field at Three Rivers, he had stumbled as a commander. He was most worried that Washington would think less of him for failing to anticipate Grey's attack. He immediately wrote to His Excellency, begging him to call a military court of inquiry where he could defend himself.[34] Washington agreed, but with the Continental Army still trying to defend Philadelphia, now was not the time. Whether Wayne was officially exonerated or not was no matter to Washington. He blamed himself, not Wayne, for the surprise attack. After ordering Wayne to capture Howe's baggage train, he changed his mind about the wisdom of the plan. He sent two letters ordering Wayne to leave his position near the Paoli Tavern and join the main army as quickly as possible. But the British intercepted the letters, a matter for which Washington felt personally responsible.[35]

There was no time for either man to wallow in self-pity, especially after Washington learned that General Howe, who marched into Philadelphia on September 26, had split his forces in two. He kept some soldiers in the capital, but sent most north of the city to Germantown. The small village, made up of a few dozen stone houses, sat at the intersection of two highways: Skippack Road running from north to south and Old School Lane crossing from east to west. Howe had placed his army along Old School Lane with Knyphausen's Hessians to the west, General Grant's soldiers and a few more Hessians near the center, and the Queen's Rangers, made up of Loyalists, farther to the east. He set up headquarters for his staff just south of the main army on Skippack Road.

Now showing signs of Caesar, Washington came up with a complex plan to attack Howe's army in Germantown, with General Wayne supporting him every step of the way. Early on the morning of October 4, the Continental Army would head south over Chestnut Hill and Mount Airy along Skippack Road into Germantown. Wayne's brigades would march on the left, with General Sullivan in the center, and Thomas Conway, one of many French émigrés fighting with the Americans, on the right. Their objective was to attack the British and Hessians strung out along Old School Lane. At the same time, General Greene would bring his division farther to the left down Old Lime Road, turn west at the juncture with Old School Lane, hurry toward the center of Germantown, and smash the British right. The militia that Wayne had trained would move south around Howe's army from two directions: one to the far right along the Schuylkill and one left of Greene's division. Once both militia groups had gotten completely around the town, they would turn north, attacking the Hessians on the west and the Queen's Rangers under John Graves Simcoe on the east. If all went as planned, before the sun rose high in the sky the British would find themselves surrounded and defeated on all sides.

At dawn on October 4, 1777, Washington started his men toward Germantown. As at Brandywine, fog lay so thick on the ground that his soldiers could see no more than a hundred yards ahead of them and soon lost contact with the other regiments. Wayne first heard gunshots on his right, but in the mist he could not be certain who was firing. He assumed Sullivan's men had run into a line of British pickets posted north of Germantown. Farther to his right, he heard more gunshots and guessed Conway's soldiers had made contact with the enemy. He pressed his men forward through the fog and soon ran headlong into the redcoats himself. Although his soldiers could now see only a few feet ahead of them, they fought with a fury that stunned Wayne. He could barely control them as they cried, "Remember Paoli," and plunged their bayonets into the fallen redcoats begging for mercy. Soon neither Wayne nor his men could see anything as day turned into night all around them. Wayne thought the combination of fog that would not lift and smoke from musket fire had enveloped his men in a black cloud. He did not know that, as he approached Germantown, the British set fire to the nearby oat fields. Smoke from the burning grain had wrapped the fog and musket smoke in an immense darkness.[36]

Wayne's brigades fought on through the morning turned into night for two more hours, covering a mile and a half of ground. But where everyone else was, he could not say for certain. Somewhere in the pitch-black darkness, General Maxwell, who led the initial assault across Brandywine Creek, should be coming from the north with reinforcements, while General Greene should be making the turn down Old School Lane. Wayne heard firing behind him, but had no idea if the shots were coming from Maxwell's troops or from redcoats that had gotten around the Continental Army again. He found out later that the firing came from Sullivan's division pinned down on Skippack Road in front of a two-story stone mansion owned by Judge Chew. Over a hundred redcoats and Hessians had taken refuge there, and try as he might, Sullivan could not dislodge them.[37]

When Washington arrived at the Chew House, he called a council of war to decide what to do. Henry Knox, who had hauled the cannon from Fort Ticonderoga to threaten Boston, and whose opinions Washington accepted ever after without question, pronounced a military axiom that no army should allow the enemy to take a position to its rear. Sullivan must dislodge the enemy before proceeding. With Sullivan's division bogged down behind him, Wayne fought on alone. His beautiful roan horse was shot dead beneath him and his right hand and foot were slightly wounded. Still his soldiers hurried another mile and a half to the south until musket fire came at them from their left. Before Wayne could determine if the shots were from the British, or hopefully from Greene's division turning toward the rendezvous point, his men panicked. Certain the redcoats were about to surround them, they fled north away from Germantown. No amount of Wayne's shouting through the fire, smoke, and fog could convince them otherwise. They hurried back across the ground they had won only to discover they were running from their brothers in arms. General Stephen, commanding the right wing of Greene's division, had turned west when his men were still north of Old School Lane. He thus launched an attack directly into Wayne's brigades. Drinking heavily all morning, Stephen would later be court-martialed for his mistake and drummed out of the Continental Army.[38]

Washington's army now hurried from Germantown with General Howe, who had arrived from Philadelphia with reinforcements, close behind. He ordered Wayne to cover their retreat. Turning his artillery on the approaching redcoats, Wayne got off enough shots for Howe, after following the fleeing Americans for seven miles, to turn back. When the Continental Army finally stopped at Pawling's Mill, twenty miles north of Germantown, Wayne did not blame the loss on Washington's indecisiveness or even Stephen's drunkenness. Instead, as he wrote to Polly, the blame rested in himself and the failings of the human heart. If only he had been able to control his frightened men, they might have won the day. The war would now be over, especially since Burgoyne had surrendered at Saratoga just weeks before. Wayne did his best to comfort Washington. Refusing to brood about the past, he explained how this latest defeat was actually a win. "Our people have gained confidence—and have raised some doubts in the minds of the enemy which will facilitate their total defeat the next trial." Lest Washington entertain any doubts about the future, Wayne assured him that "you are now in my humble opinion in as good if not a better situation than you were before this action."[39]

Wayne tried one more time to convince his commander in chief to take on Howe's army. He urged him to protect Fort Mifflin and Fort Mercer, the two posts south of Philadelphia on opposite sides of the Delaware. Wayne believed these forts provided the best chance for the Continental Army to stop the flow of goods to the British. When Howe bombarded Fort Mifflin from Independence Island on the west side of the river, Wayne proposed rowing over to the island with a small company. They would spike Howe's guns and tear up his fortifications. Washington at first agreed, but when Wayne was ready to move, he stopped him, saying the plan was too risky. They would have to wait until General Gates, the hero of Saratoga, arrived from upstate New York and helped relieve Fort Mifflin. Before that could happen, the place fell to the British. Washington then ordered the few soldiers at Fort Mercer to abandon their post. The British now had free passage into Philadelphia by water as well as by land in the upcoming winter.

For the first time in the Revolution, and the only time in the many years that he would serve Washington, Wayne openly criticized his commander in chief in letters to his friends. The indecisiveness that Wayne had seen from Middlebrook to Germantown seemed to stifle Washington at every turn. How could he sit back and do nothing, Wayne complained to his friend Richard Peters, then serving as the secretary of the Board of War, when the capital of their nation had fallen to the enemy and the Continental Congress had fled to Lancaster and then York? There was still a chance to defeat Howe's army, if only Washington was a gambling man: "We have yet a Capital game to play—and if we are not too fond of keeping the Cards in our hands we may make the Odd trick."[40]

But Washington would not take a chance because he seemed to have lost the ability to make decisions on his own. Instead he preferred gathering his generals together for more councils of war. One by one he asked them what to do next and one by one they responded with not a clue. Why hold a council of war, Wayne again complained to Peters, when this was the "surest way to do nothing"? To show his contempt for the process, Wayne came to every meeting with a book in hand and sat in the corner reading. When asked a direct question, he looked up, answered with a few words, and then went back to his book.[41]

For the first time since Ticonderoga, Wayne thought about leaving the army. He could not sit idly by as his soldiers suffered through another winter. Proud of his men at the start of the war, when they paraded before him in spotless uniforms, he now could hardly look at them in their ragged clothes. Nor could he stand listening to their complaints. He passed up and down their ranks, horrified as they stood before him barefoot, hungry, and almost naked. At these terrible moments, he wished he was blind and deaf. His soldiers peered into his face, searching for any sign of relief, but he turned away, unable to give any. Refusing to leave his suffering men, he also could not abandon the commander he once believed the equal of Caesar. He would instead remain at his side, advising him when to fight and when to retreat.[42]

In the fall of 1777, when Washington asked his generals, first in October and again in November, if the Continental Army should attack the British, Wayne answered yes, and even came up with a plan. At dawn on November 26, the Continental Army should march north of Germantown where they launched their failed attack six weeks before. Washington should send a few soldiers forward to throw up redoubts. General Howe, assuming the fortifications were part of the Continental Army's winter quarters, and unwilling to call up reserves from New York to attack, would leave Washington alone. With Howe fooled into inaction, late on that same night, Washington should lead his entire army against the British redoubts around Philadelphia. Wayne assured his commander that he had nothing to lose but everything to gain. "The eyes of all the World are on you—the Junction of the Northern Army gives the Country and Congress some expectation that Vigorous efforts will be made to Dislodge the Enemy—and Oblige them to seek for Winter Quarters in a less hostile place than Phil[adelphia]," he wrote, almost challenging Washington, "It's not in our power to Command Success—but it is in our power to produce a Conviction to the World that we deserve it."[43]

But in early December, when Washington asked his generals a third time if the Continental Army should launch a winter campaign, Wayne said no. How could soldiers with no food, shoes, or blankets fight in the snow and ice against the British who were fat and happy in Philadelphia? Even though he answered no, Wayne came up with another plan. Keep the army in the field, preferably south of Philadelphia near Wilmington, Delaware, but have "a proper number Always hanging on the Skirts of the Enemy." His reasons were threefold: to protect the people from depredations, let the main army rest, and send up an alarm if the British launched a winter campaign. It went without saying that he would welcome the chance to harass the British personally.[44]

Even though Washington chose Valley Forge, and not Wilmington, as the Continental Army's winter camp, Wayne no longer doubted him. He never criticized him again, but instead became increasingly loyal, especially as cries from Washington's detractors descended from every hilltop at Valley Forge. Wayne's heart went out to Washington, who in his opinion was now unfairly compared to General Gates, the lucky victor of Saratoga. He placed him back on a pedestal as the ultimate hero. No matter how frustrated he might become in the months and years ahead, Wayne never removed him from that spot. He also felt a growing bond with Washington now that he faced relentless criticism for the Paoli Massacre.

Up until the night "No Flint" Grey snuck into his camp, no one faulted Wayne's leadership. But after dozens of his men died in the surprise attack, Colonel Humpton brought formal charges against him. He claimed Wayne ignored a clear warning of the impending danger and later failed to alert his artillery the attack was under way. Wayne was furious when Lord Stirling and Henry Knox, serving on the court of inquiry investigating him, agreed with Humpton's charges but exonerated him anyway. How could he be condemned and cleared at the same time? He demanded a court-martial to uphold his honor. Washington agreed even though he considered another trial unnecessary. Wayne's defense of his conduct before a thirteen-man panel, led by General Sullivan, was as blistering as his artillery fire against Knyphausen's Hessians at Chadds Ford. He now argued that he sent out extra videttes when warned of a possible attack and these guards alerted him of Colonel Grey's approach. He immediately ordered a retreat and stayed with his men until everyone got away. Finally, Wayne asked, how could he desert the very position that General Washington had told him to take? To do so would have been disgraceful. This time Wayne was fully exonerated and commended for his conduct.[45]

After surviving such painful scrutiny of his actions, Wayne now defended Washington as a new kind of leader fighting a new kind of war. At times His Excellency must be daring, but at other times cautious. His goal was not to pile up grand wins like Julius Caesar or Marshal Saxe, but to keep his soldiers in the field, especially after every defeat, and prepare them to fight another day. In letters written to his family and friends from Valley Forge, Wayne described Washington in almost reverential terms. He committed himself to do whatever his commander asked to help the Continental Army survive. At the same time, Washington came to appreciate the best qualities in Anthony Wayne. Proud to a fault, filled with dreams of ancient glory, and always moving on to the next grand plan, Wayne would never desert his commander or his men, no matter how unbearable conditions might become. As loyal as he was proud, Wayne would take on any task, no matter how frustrating, challenging, or demeaning.

Washington's first assignment for Wayne at Valley Forge was unleashing his pen on his state's assembly for failing to provide clothing for the Pennsylvania Line. Wayne went to work immediately, demanding shirts, vests, pants, coats, stockings, and shoes for his soldiers who were so naked they must stay in their huts all day. He sent letter after letter to Joseph Reed, Pennsylvania's president, and James Meese, the state clothier, demanding action. He also asked his friend Peters for help. Once he even went to York to confront state officials in person. But their answer was always the same: clothes and other supplies had never been authorized by the assembly and therefore could not be delivered.

Wayne soon received a second, more humiliating assignment from Washington. He and General Greene, the army's new quartermaster general, must lead five hundred soldiers across the Delaware River and look for food. Wayne did his work without complaining, unlike Greene, who muttered that farmers hid their cattle and hogs from him. On the way back to Valley Forge, with British light infantry chasing him, Wayne escaped with the help of General Casimir Pulaski's cavalry that had come from Trenton to protect him. Wayne received no credit for his work beyond winning the nickname "Drover" from the British, who mocked him from their snug quarters in Philadelphia all the way to the London stage where actors portrayed him as the "Tanner" in an oversized leather apron with a knife in his hand.[46]

Knowing how both of them and their soldiers had suffered together at Valley Forge, Wayne was certain that Washington, no longer merely the commander of the Continental Army but now the president of the United States, would be moved by the plight of his men at Legionville. They, too, were ill clad and poorly fed. Luckily, this was not the Revolution. The fools who ran Pennsylvania in 1777 were no longer in charge in 1792. Washington himself headed the government with Knox at his side. Wayne was sure the administration would fight for the Legion. He forwarded a petition from his officers to the War Department complaining that daily rations were slow in coming and inadequate once they arrived. The flour was often spoiled and the cattle, having walked for hundreds of miles "thro' a Wilderness," were little more than skin and bones. The whiskey ration had been halved and there was not a vegetable in sight. Wayne added that his men ate far less than British soldiers, who received each day a pound of bread or flour and a pound of beef or pork, and each week a half pint of rice, three pints of peas, and six ounces of butter. For once, he did not mention that these well-fed British soldiers were housed illegally on American soil. He merely added that "patriotism experience and humanity" demanded a remedy.[47]

Just after the New Year in 1793, a letter marked "Private" and dated December 22, 1792, nearly fifteen years to the day since Washington led his men into Valley Forge, was delivered to Wayne's marquee at Legionville. He and his officers were still living in tents because he had ordered the quarters for his regulars built first. The letter was from the secretary of war and contained as much anger as Knox could muster. He had never told Wayne how upset the president was at him for setting up his camp at Legionville. But he could not withhold Washington's fury over receiving a petition from the Legion's officers for better rations. Wayne must be out of his mind for sending this "extremely improper measure," which would tend "to produce insubordination and every military evil consequence thereof." How could Wayne do this when the House of Representatives, filled with hatred for standing armies, was trying to reduce the size of the Legion? As Knox explained, tempering his shock a bit, "it is the manner, more than the matter, which is considered exceptionable." He added that he could not understand why Wayne or his officers were so distraught. The rations were no different than those in the Revolution, and as far as he could remember, no one complained then about their insufficiency. Knox must have lost all memory of Valley Forge, thought Wayne, or lost his mind completely.[48]

In another letter, handed to Wayne on the same day, Secretary Knox made the same case in calmer language. He promised to mention the need for better rations in cabinet meetings, but not to Congress. When answering Knox, Wayne remained just as determined to win more rations for his men. Maybe, in the madness of Philadelphia politics, the president and his secretary of war had forgotten what it was like to be a soldier fighting for his country while he was hungry and cold. Wayne would not stop asking for more food or anything else that his Legion needed. In the future, he might temper the tone of his requests to the War Department, but not to Robert Elliott and Eli Williams, the government contractors. To them, he would write one angry letter after another demanding better food sent more quickly, not just to Legionville but to every other post in the Ohio River Valley, or the western country might be lost forever.[49]

As his fight for rations went on, Wayne continued the everyday tasks needed to run Legionville efficiently. He set up kitchens in front of the camp and regularly inspected them. He ordered latrines dug away from the water supply and assigned soldiers to keep them clean. He hired respectable married women to launder the clothes of his soldiers. He made sure that the parade ground was swept clean and ordered harsh punishments for anyone who dirtied it. He kept up daily target practice and oversaw mock battles every Sunday, weather permitting. As he shaped his army, even more deliberately in the middle of nowhere than in Pittsburgh, he had the presence of mind to keep one fact hidden from Secretary Knox in his weekly letters. Amid his complaints about poor food and lack of proper uniforms, the slowness of the recruiting process, his few trained officers, continuing desertions, endless reports of Indian attacks, the shadow of a great conspiracy of tribes beyond the forest, and British generals he had fought in the Revolution watching his every move, he did not mention how desperately sick he was.

He had done his best since taking his seat in Congress the year before to look healthy, hoping all the while that he could win a post in the government if His Excellency, now the president of the United States, thought he was not at death's door. Since winning command of the Legion, he never told Washington or Knox about the gout and fevers that plagued him. Nor did he mention there were days when he could hardly stand or nights when he could barely sleep. He had the good sense never to describe his fits of vomiting that brought up green jelly from his stomach, though he did tell the few friends who still remembered him. Once the awful substance was out of his stomach, and he had taken quinine and laudanum, he consoled himself by climbing on his horse, riding along the edges of his camp, and imagining over and over again the battle that Washington, now so angry at him in Philadelphia, had sent him west to fight.[50]

"I Have Not Been Pleased
with Madame Fortune"

Wayne kept another secret from Knox and Washington in the winter of 1793. Not only was he sick, but he was also depressed. The "blue damsels" of despair, as he named his depression, had returned in this icy winter. They came late in the day into the fine house he had finally built for himself at the northwest corner of Legionville, reminding him that in this vast wilderness he was completely alone. Not a soul back east seemed to remember him, not his wife, his son or daughter, or any living relative. Even worse for a man who knew the leading figures of his age, and charmed many of them, especially the women, to sit every evening in such silence, with not a word from anyone, was heartbreaking. There were nights when he imagined a company of dragoons marching into his camp and "metamorphosing" into a troop of "*fair* Ladies." But no matter how much he hoped for this miracle, no magical women ever appeared to "cheer the heart and bless the arms" of a lonely soldier.[1]

If the many visitors who came to Legionville on February 22, 1793, to celebrate George Washington's birthday knew how depressed Wayne truly was, they might have wondered how this was possible. Despite the fact that he was in the middle of nowhere, Wayne had built a neatly ordered village for his soldiers. The cabins lined streets that the commander in chief had laid out like a larger city. The huts were small but warm with a fireplace in each. The houses for the officers built after the New Year were grand enough for people to regret they would be abandoned when the army moved down the Ohio come spring. High on a bluff near a ravine by the river, the general's quarters, a handsome two-story house with four fireplaces and a porch facing the parade ground, was the grandest of all.[2]

How could a man who had accomplished so much ever be disheartened? A quick look around Legionville proved that Wayne had done everything in his power to feed, clothe, and arm his men. They might not have a great deal of food, yet everyone looked fit. Rations were coming down the Ohio slowly, but enough so that every day each man received a pound of flour and a pound of beef cooked for him in the camp's kitchens. When supplies of beef ran low, the cooks served up bacon or salt pork instead. Whiskey, the one item that was easy to come by in the West, was also poured out daily. All the men were clean-shaven with their hair pulled back in black ribbons under their caps. Their uniforms, stockings, and shoes were spotless.[3]

But no sight was more impressive than Wayne's soldiers maneuvering on the parade ground in honor of Washington's sixty-first birthday. The visitors to Legionville were treated to a display of military prowess the likes of which no one this far west had ever seen. Precisely at ten o'clock in the morning, with trumpets blaring and drums beating, a thousand men raced on foot from their quarters or on horseback from the stables. They quickly formed two columns in front of the waiting crowd. Soldiers with white and green facings on their uniforms and caps stood to the left amid flags of the same colors. These were the men of First and Third Sublegions. Soldiers dressed in uniforms and hats marked with red and yellow, all interspersed among flags of the same colors, stood to the right. These were the men of the Second and Fourth Sublegions. Howitzers and supply wagons were hauled between the two columns. Around the perimeters, more soldiers proudly held rifles, not muskets like the rest of the army. Behind them, high atop his horse, sat General Wayne as perfectly dressed as his men and giving no sign of the pain he was in or the despair that troubled him.[4]

What happened next was even more impressive. Upon a signal from their commander, a large body of infantry broke out from the columns and raced ahead, reforming their lines and turning back to face the rest of the army. Then, on another signal, everyone was in motion. The soldiers left on the parade ground formed a living square around the wagons. The spectators now understood the purpose of the pageant before them. The soldiers who had broken away would play the part of the Indians, while the men standing guard over the equipment would fight as Wayne's Legion. For the next half hour, a battle raged before the astonished visitors. Large quantities of gunpowder, the one item that Wayne could easily get from the War Department, were exchanged on both sides. Finally, riflemen came running at full speed out of the square around the artillery while dragoons raced forward on horseback. They charged the enemy and dispersed them to the cheers of the crowd.[5]

How could anyone, but especially the Legion's commander in chief, be depressed at the sight of the army he had so perfectly trained, and on this day when the festivities had only just begun? When the battle was over, the soldiers headed to their noonday meal, while the officers went up the bluff to Wayne's house. As once in Philadelphia, so now in Legionville, the conversation, and the Madeira, which the general had shipped in regularly from the nation's capital, flowed freely. By three in the afternoon, all the soldiers were back on the parade ground. This time General Wayne passed among them, correcting every flaw in their appearance or demeanor. When finally satisfied, he stood back and ordered them to launch three volleys of musket fire and three more volleys of cannon fire, fifteen rounds each time, into the distance in honor of the president.

Wayne's soldiers had given a glittering performance. The infantry loaded and shot their muskets and rifles quickly and accurately. They marched and whirled about on every command. The dragoons rode through their camp at lightning speed without stumbling. But their prowess on the parade ground belied the fact that all was not well in Wayne's army, especially among his officers. Preparing their charges at a fever pitch for a battle that might never come drained their nerves and spirit. Wayne had tried to promote his best soldiers through the ranks. He was greatly relieved when Congress decided not to reduce the Legion's size, and thus the number of officers, and wrote often to Secretary Knox recommending new appointments. But even with his unqualified support, Wayne's officers were often at each other's throats. They were jealous when others were promoted ahead of them, or when a soldier they considered unworthy became the general's favorite.

Wayne was determined to stop the quarreling among his officers. One of the worst fights broke out right in front of him on the parade ground on St. Patrick's Day 1793. Wayne had invited local Indians, along with the citizens of Pittsburgh, to watch another mock battle staged on Sunday, March 17. After the battle, as the soldiers returned to their columns, Edward Butler, who was now Wayne's adjutant general, and Captain William Eaton of the Fourth Sublegion, nearly came to blows. Butler had ordered Eaton to march his column from the right, but the captain refused, knowing the column should instead march from the left. After the two men exchanged angry words, Butler, who was furious that his command had been disobeyed, raced toward Eaton on horseback with his sword waving. Eaton accepted the challenge and ran at Butler with his espontoon, a steel spear mounted on a six-foot pole, raised and ready. They might have fought right there to the death if Wayne had not intervened, shouting that the parade ground was no place to fight. Both men put up their weapons and later apologized to each other: Butler for giving the wrong command and Eaton for threatening his superior officer.[6]

But Wayne did little to stop the fighting among his enlisted men. Lieutenant Harrison, who had turned twenty just two weeks before Washington's birthday celebration, remembered when he was an older man how the Legion's soldiers seemed addicted to dueling. Relatives of dead soldiers complained to Secretary Knox who in turn asked a disinterested Wayne to investigate. One incident involved the murder of Ensign William Gassaway. After Wayne ordered the Fourth Sublegion to choose a new paymaster, young Gassaway promised to vote for his fellow ensign Campbell Smith, but later changed his mind. An angry Smith mocked Gassaway as a "trifling pup and no gentleman," which led to an angry exchange, a challenge, and finally a duel. At dawn on March 23, 1793, the two ensigns met near the Ohio River with their seconds. Standing back to back, they walked ahead eight paces and then, turning toward each other, took three steps forward. Gassaway shot first, completely missing Smith, who now shot Gassaway in the right chest with the bullet lodging near his spine. After suffering for hours, Gassaway finally died. Smith and the two seconds fled for their lives, fearing prosecution since Pennsylvania had outlawed dueling. The situation was dire enough for Wayne to intervene. He sent word to the two seconds to come back to Legionville where all would be forgiven. Then he ordered Smith to take a boatload of forage to Fort Washington and stay there until the incident was forgotten. When Knox questioned Wayne about what had happened to Ensign Gassaway, he dismissed the matter as of little importance.[7]

Far from his friends in Philadelphia, and with his men fighting over the smallest slights, Wayne spent his evenings drinking brandy and finding some comfort in reading, one of his favorite pastimes. His friend Sharp Delany brought newspapers to the War Department each week and clerks forwarded them to Wayne along with Knox's correspondence. In the long nights at Legionville, Wayne studied them to keep up with the increasingly bitter politics in the nation's capital. He read his favorite Shakespeare plays that he carried with him on every campaign. He also studied a draft of "The Captain," the first part of a picaresque novel entitled *American Chivalry* written by Hugh Henry Brackenridge, a Continental Army chaplain who now ran a newspaper in Pittsburgh. His novel's main character, Captain John Farrago, bore a striking resemblance to Wayne. Like the general, he was a farmer and a soldier who had many adventures while traveling through Pennsylvania with his colorful Irish servant Teague O'Regan. Farrago was an intelligent and accomplished man who might have had a fine political career if not for the lesser men who opposed him. As Brackenridge was fond of saying, every man had a voice in a democracy, but not necessarily an equal one, because "some men had stronger lungs than others, and could more forcibly express their opinions of public affairs," a sentiment that Wayne well understood after the fiery Colonel Jackson toppled him from Congress.[8]

But Brackenridge's comic tale could not lift Wayne out of the darkness that descended upon him in the winter of 1793. Sharp Delany, the one person who continued to write regularly to him, wondered if Wayne's recent attack of gout had caused the bleak turn in his thinking. He hoped that once the episode subsided, so would his friend's depression. However, there was more to Wayne's dark mood than gout. As he finally confessed to Delany, the fear of death, which he first experienced at Three Rivers, had returned with a vengeance. He dreaded the battle that awaited him deep in the western forest and wondered how he could possibly survive. Would anyone in Philadelphia, especially the "antifederal junto" that was probably rooting for the Indians, care if he lived or died?[9]

He had taught his soldiers to channel their imaginations, but now he could barely control his own thoughts. Soon he would awake to the flash of gunfire and what sounded like a thousand bells ringing at once. Painted warriors would leap from the forest to murder his army. How his soldiers would react, and for that matter how he would react, was something he could not predict. How different this doubt was from the self-assurance he had known early in the Revolution. Then he was certain battles were won or lost in their opening moments in the hearts of the soldiers. He even had the audacity to share this conviction with General Washington. As he explained to him before the Battle of Brandywine, "This is the General rule in war; that the Irresistible Impulse of the Human Heart, which is governed by mere momentary Caprice and Opinion—Determines the fate of the day in all Actions."[10]

But it had not taken long for Wayne to realize that a battle's outcome was not completely under his control. There seemed to be a silent hand at work behind the scenes pushing men toward victory or defeat. Many of his contemporaries explained this mystery as the providence of God. Wayne, like most of them, was a Christian. When at home, he attended St. David's Episcopal Church in Radnor, which his father had helped to build. He held weekly services for his soldiers, both during the Revolution and now at Legionville, led by his friend David Jones, the son of the man who had warned him near the Paoli Tavern. But when contemplating destiny, which was woven like a dark thread through the fabric of life, he rarely saw God's handiwork, but instead glimpsed the whims of an ancient goddess.

The Romans, whom Wayne so admired, called her Fortuna, and sometimes imagined her as a young girl tossing balls in the air, thus showing that she granted her favors like a game. But more often, they portrayed her as a grown woman holding a rudder in her hand guiding men's fate, or with a small child in her arms, representing Plutus, the god of wealth. To Wayne, she was none of these things. Instead she was Madame Fortune, a beautiful but faithless woman who stalked his path, and who, after all his planning and daring, determined the outcome of every battle. She had first come into view in lonely Ticonderoga and haunted him for the rest of the war. Even now, waiting for what he believed would be his final battle somewhere in the Ohio wilderness, he could have written the same words about her that he wrote while imprisoned at the hated Golgotha. "Fortune to us has heretofore been a fickle Goddess and like many other females changed for the first new face she saw."[11]

For a time, in the years immediately following Valley Forge, she had seemed to smile on Wayne more often than not, taking him to the heights of fame, if not always to the heights of victory. He first knew the glory that Madame Fortune could drape around a man after the Continental Army left Valley Forge in the spring of 1778. General Washington had correctly surmised that Henry Clinton, the new British commander who had replaced William Howe, was about to depart from Philadelphia. On June 17, as Clinton readied his redcoats and Hessians to march from the capital, Washington asked his generals what to do next. Should he confront the British as they left Philadelphia? Attack them at their probable destination, New York City? Or train the Continental Army to fight another day? While most recommended caution, Wayne urged him to attack the enemy on the road to New York when Clinton's caravan, consisting of 13,000 men, 1,500 wagons, and countless horses, would stretch twelve miles long. Call out the New Jersey militia, Wayne advised, and let them attack the rear while Washington brought up the Continentals' full force against the head of the line.[12]

Before Washington could decide what to do, Clinton's army crossed the Delaware into New Jersey. Washington ordered his men, now numbering 11,000, to shadow the British and Hessians to the northwest, always remaining slightly behind. Following Clinton's army was an exhausting task in the sweltering heat of early summer with temperatures in the high nineties by the early afternoon. The beating sun, cloudless sky, and thunderstorms that blew in from nowhere made marching difficult for everyone. Crossing the many streams between the Delaware and the Hudson was another problem for both armies loaded down with wagons and supplies. The Continental Army had torn up most of the bridges from Philadelphia to New York and in places chopped down trees to prevent anyone from crossing. Traveling slowed to a crawl with neither side making more than six miles a day and sometimes slowing to only one.[13]

On June 24, after shadowing Clinton's army for six days, Washington again asked his generals what to do. Charles Lee, second in rank to Washington, urged him to do nothing until the enemy arrived in New York City. Henry Knox and Lord Stirling agreed, but Wayne, along with Greene, Steuben, and the young French aristocrat the Marquis de Lafayette, urged an immediate attack. Wayne reminded Washington that he might never have a chance like this again to defeat the British. He offered a new plan to take on the enemy. Send 2,500 to 3,000 men, under the command of a major general or two brigadiers, he explained, to attack the left rear of Clinton's army. After they engaged the enemy, Washington could bring the rest of his soldiers into the fight at the time of his own choosing. He did not have to add that he hoped to be one of the brigadiers chosen to lead the initial assault on Clinton's army.[14]

Ignoring the fact that Wayne's soldiers were ill clad, exhausted, and starving, Washington took his advice, along with that of Greene, Lafayette, and Hamilton. He would send a few thousand men, under the command of General Lee, a former British officer best known for his slovenly appearance and foul mouth, against the left rear of the retreating army. When Lee objected to the mission, Washington replaced him with Lafayette and increased the number of troops to 5,000, nearly twice the amount that Wayne had recommended. Lee now demanded the command for himself. Washington agreed and ordered Lee to work with Wayne and Lafayette, as well as General Maxwell, who had fought bravely at Three Rivers and Brandywine, to come up with a plan. Together they must flesh out the details of the opening assault on Clinton's rearguard, which would take place on the following morning as the enemy passed the village of Monmouth Courthouse.[15]

Right from the start, Wayne and Lee approached the coming action from two different perspectives. Wayne believed his troops were to engage the retreating British even if this led immediately to an all-out battle. If the fleeing redcoats turned and brought up their entire army, Wayne's men were to stand and fight until the rest of the Continental Army was in place. Lee, on the other hand, thought Washington had given him full authority to act as he saw fit. He could decide whether to continue the initial assault or retreat toward the main army. Unlike Wayne, who was anxious for battle, Lee worried his troops were simply not ready to take on the cream of the British army, especially if their numbers increased far past that of his own troops. He was therefore prepared to fall back, if necessary. Neither man knew that their differing opinions would soon take a toll on the American army.[16]

At dawn on June 28, 1778, Wayne marched with the soldiers under his direct command, along with the rest of Lee's men, toward the rear of Clinton's caravan near Monmouth Courthouse. He had been so excited at the prospect of fighting the British that he had even reconnoitered Clinton's camp, along with Colonel Hamilton and other officers, two nights before. Although he had long urged Washington to face the enemy on the open field of battle, he could hardly believe it was happening at last. After marching for three hours, and now drawing within a half mile of the main crossroad at the center of Monmouth, he was certain the attack would be a surprise. He was wrong. Even before his men were in position, the Queen's Rangers attacked. Wayne would never forget the "shock" of seeing General Simcoe's Loyalists coming directly at Colonel Butler's regiment on his right. Regaining his composure, he ordered them to load their muskets, fire at the enemy, and then attack with the bayonet, as Steuben had taught them at Valley Forge. Even though Butler's men threw back the initial attack, Wayne knew they could not hold out for long, especially without cavalry to support them. He sent a messenger with several frantic pleas to Lee for reinforcements. But the soldier came back with no answer. After a few reinforcements appeared on his right, and troops commanded by Brigadier General Charles Scott moved up on his left, he fought on, never doubting that victory was assured.[17]

At the same time, General Lee had concluded that victory, for the moment, was impossible. He guessed correctly that crack British troops were racing back toward the army's rear not just to halt the attack on the baggage train but to form their battle lines. His soldiers would soon be facing not just the Queen's Rangers, but the very best of Clinton's fighting force, British Grenadiers and Coldstream Guards under the command of General Charles Cornwallis, not to mention "No Flint" Grey and the same soldiers who had bayoneted Wayne's soldiers near the Paoli Tavern the year before. The British would overrun the American troops, no matter how much General Wayne dreamed of victory, long before Washington arrived.

With success impossible, especially now that his army faced at least 7,000 of the enemy, Lee decided his only choice was to fall back. He ordered everyone down the road away from Monmouth. Wayne would always claim that he never received a direct order from Lee to leave the field. He waited for more reinforcements until he realized that his men were fighting the British singlehandedly. Finally, he led them away from Monmouth and toward what he hoped would be Washington's approaching army. Although he joined the other troops, he was certain that Lee was slinking away from a winnable battle and never countenanced the fact that he might be trying to regroup. Wayne considered the general's movements a full retreat and therefore quite shameful. He could not decide if Lee was a coward or completely insane. Maybe there was an even *"Worse Cause,"* he later recalled, meaning the former British general was a traitor.[18]

A mile up the road ahead of Lee and Wayne, Washington was leading the rest of the Continental Army east toward Monmouth Courthouse. He was surprised when soldiers came running past him. He finally stopped a young musician and asked him what was happening. The boy blurted out that all the soldiers were retreating from the British. Washington let him go, but warned that if he were lying, he would be punished. Washington next recognized a large man lumbering toward him on horseback. He was Colonel Israel Shreve of the New Jersey Line. When Washington asked what was happening, a smiling Shreve answered he could not say for certain, but a retreat appeared to be under way and his men were fleeing in good order.

What happened next on the road from Monmouth Courthouse remains the stuff of legend. According to some accounts, when General Lee approached, Washington asked him, "What is the meaning of this, sir? I mean to know the meaning of this disaster and confusion." Lee supposedly answered, "By God, sir, American soldiers cannot fight British grenadiers." Still others claimed that Lee explained he had been given the full command to move his troops in any direction based on his assessment of conditions in the field. Washington, who unlike Wayne prided himself on his ability to control his temper, struggled to do so now, at least according to the memories of several officers who were with him that day. Many years later, the Marquis de Lafayette claimed he heard Washington condemn Lee as a "damned poltroon," while Charles Scott, who recalled the episode more colorfully, said the very leaves of the trees shook with Washington's fury as he swore "like an angel from heaven." No matter what was said, Washington took charge of the battle. He ordered Lee to head back toward Monmouth. Lee promptly did so and stationed his soldiers behind a long hedgerow facing the oncoming British. Washington found Wayne and several of his colonels among the retreating soldiers, and ordered them also to return to Monmouth. Wayne hurried back, determined to form the center of a new American line and hold off the approaching British until the Continental Army had time to line up alongside him.[19]

He stationed his soldiers, including men from both Pennsylvania and Virginia, in a place called the Point of the Woods, a neck of trees that jutted out south of the forest near Monmouth. For just a moment, as he watched the enemy approach, Wayne felt the same dread that Lee had experienced. Sitting high atop his horse at the center of his troops, he clearly saw the British infantry, Grenadiers, and cavalry coming in a wall of red and green directly at him. They outnumbered his men by nearly three to one. "We had just taken post when the Enemy began their attack with Horse & foot & Artillery," he would later tell his wife. His words did not capture the panic that set in among his troops. After the British fired time and again at his men, Wayne, just as Lee had done before him, was forced to fall back. He and his soldiers raced toward General Stirling's men who had positioned themselves on the American left. They were chased for a time by Colonel Henry Monckton's Grenadiers who also attacked Lee's men behind the hedgerow. The Grenadiers were finally turned back by General Greene's troops, most especially Henry Knox's artillery, that had just gotten into position on the American right.

With the fighting now extending well past noon, the battle turned into an artillery contest. At 1:30, Knox launched a barrage that lasted until nearly 4 o'clock.

During the onslaught, Wayne was finally able to bring his men back near the American center. His cannon joined Knox's guns, which were keeping up a relentless fire from the right. By now, the temperature had climbed to one hundred degrees. Wayne's soldiers stripped off their clothes down to their waists, the only time in his military career that he allowed men in battle to remove their uniforms. Exhausted from fighting with hardly a break since early morning, and suffering from the blistering sun and high temperature, many men slipped away to the nearby cedar swamp to quench their thirst in the sticky orange-stained water. Women who had followed their men into battle brought buckets of the cedar water back to them. Before the battle started, one young woman found a better stream and spent the day carrying its clear water to her husband's artillery brigade. When he collapsed, she took over swabbing and loading his gun, even braving a British cannon ball that passed between her legs and shredded her petticoat. Although no one knows for certain, she could have been Mary Ludwig Hayes whose husband William served with Wayne at Monmouth. Long after the Revolution ended, the stories of the many women who brought water to their men on many battlefields were gathered together into the legend of "Molly Pitcher."[20]

Once the cannon fire subsided, General Clinton directed three more attacks on the American line. First, he sent his troops against Stirling's position. Four times the Black Watch, foot soldiers of the Scottish Highlands in their dark green tartans, came at Stirling's men and four times they were thrown back. They finally withdrew after the Americans raced into the woods on the British right and opened fire up and down the entire enemy line. Clinton next sent his troops, including Coldstream Guards, against Greene's position. Again, the artillery joined the regular troops in gunning down the British soldiers running up the slopes toward them. At the same time, Clinton ordered his Grenadiers up the middle toward Wayne, the American officer who had first attacked his retreating caravan so many hours before. Much calmer now than he had been when his men fled from the Point of the Woods, Wayne and his men pushed the oncoming foe back three times before being forced to retreat to the safety of the hedgerow. "The Enemy began to advance again in a heavy Column," Wayne would later explain to his wife, never mentioning he had to fall back. "The Action was Exceedingly warm and well Maintained on each Side for a Considerable time—at Length Victory declared for us, the British courage failed and was forced to give place to American Valour."[21]

Wayne was right that the fight was almost over. Washington sent two brigades directly into the left and right of the British rear. But given the exhaustion of his soldiers, with many unable to take another step, the battle slowed considerably near six o'clock in the evening. Although cannon fire was exchanged on both sides for another hour, the Battle of Monmouth was finally over. Most considered the contest to be a draw, but Anthony Wayne believed that the Continental Army had won a decisive victory on this hot day in June in the New Jersey countryside. If only General Lee had stood his ground, Wayne was certain that the rest of the world would also acknowledge the win. He thus never forgave Lee for his actions. As always, Wayne wrote first to Polly back at Waynesborough describing the battle in detail, ecstatic that the Continental Army finally had beaten the flower of the British army. "Every General & other officer (one excepted) did Every thing that could be expected on this Great Occasion, but Pennsylvania showed the Road to Victory." Later, when recalling tales of the faithless women of Philadelphia chasing after British officers in their city, he could not help but gloat. As he wrote to his friend Richard Peters, after hearing how British officers dressed in brilliant costumes as knights at the grand fete honoring General Howe, "Tell the Phil'a ladies that the heavenly, sweet, pretty red Coats—the accomplished Gent'n of the Guards & Grenadiers have humbled themselves on the plains of Monmouth. 'The Knights of the Blended Rose' & 'Burning Mount'—have resigned their laurels to *Rebel* officers who will lay them at the feet of those Virtuous Daughters of America who cheerfully gave up ease and Affluence in a city for Liberty and peace of mind in a Cottage."[22]

While Madame Fortune had given Wayne a victory at Monmouth, the glory she wrapped him in did not prevent criticism from coming his way. Charles Lee, sidelined, court-martialed, and finally drummed out of the army, blamed all his troubles on Wayne. It was not Lee but Wayne who disobeyed orders, and because of his actions, the battle was lost. Arthur St. Clair joined in criticizing Wayne for the stalemate at Monmouth. Like Lee, he could point to no specific mistake Wayne had made, but told his colonels they need only remember Paoli to understand how incompetent Wayne truly was. Ignoring St. Clair's insults, Wayne challenged Lee to a duel, the first and only time in his life he ever did so. "If it is your intention to injure my military character in the eyes of the world, I know that you will have the Candour to acknowledge it, as well as courage to accept my demand of *honourable redress.*" Lee declined on the grounds he was busy preparing a pamphlet for Congress defending his actions at Monmouth, and had already been wounded in a duel with Colonel Henry Laurens, Jr., who had defended the honor of General Washington. Lee assured him that, if by some chance he ever became a general again, Wayne would be his first choice for his brigadier.[23]

After taking him to the heights of glory at Monmouth, Madame Fortune did not win him a promotion. General Washington tried, telling the Continental Congress that Wayne's "courage and bravery through the whole action deserves particular commendation," but his recommendation that Wayne be appointed a major general was ignored. The fact that Wayne had acted the part of a major general at Monmouth, directing regiments from Pennsylvania, New Jersey, and Virginia, mattered little to Congress. For the foreseeable future, he would remain a brigadier even as Arthur St. Clair won new honors. After the court-martial cleared him of wrongdoing at Ticonderoga, St. Clair had resumed his place as a major general commanding the Pennsylvania Line. He also rejoined Washington's military family. Wayne was so disgruntled that he again thought about leaving the army. But he could no more walk away from his soldiers and his commander in chief after Monmouth than he could after Germantown, Brandywine, or Three Rivers.[24]

Knowing Wayne was thinking of leaving the army, Washington promised him a winter furlough in Philadelphia, but with a catch. He must press the state assembly for food and clothes for the Pennsylvania Line. Wayne did as Washington asked. Sometimes he wooed politicians with his charm and his logic, while at others he threatened to campaign against anyone who refused to help the army. When assemblymen told him that Pennsylvania gave as much to its soldiers as any other state, Wayne showed them copies of laws from New England to Georgia proving otherwise. Countered at every turn, Wayne condemned them all as "caitiffs," his favorite word for scoundrels. He often found himself as frustrated with the old guard, who represented the wealthiest merchants and landholders, as he was with the younger radicals who spoke for the less affluent. Both sides cared more about squabbling with each other than helping the hungry, naked, and unpaid soldiers of their state.[25]

Wayne finally got the chance to speak on the floor of the Pennsylvania assembly. His pleas struck a chord among the members. They passed a series of laws that held out the promise of future support for the state's troops. If a soldier stayed in the Pennsylvania Line until the war's end, he would receive half the pay owed to him as an annuity for life. So would his widow. Based on rank, veterans were also granted "donation lands" in the western part of the state that would remain tax-free as long as they owned the property. As a brigadier general, Wayne was entitled to fifteen hundred acres. Soldiers would get new uniforms each year. Finally, they could buy rum, sugar, coffee, chocolate, tea, soap, and tobacco from state stores at prices below market value. The assembly also recommended that the Continental Congress make Wayne a major general, a request that was denied.[26]

Fully aware of how much Wayne hated lobbying politicians, and fearing again that he might leave the army, Washington offered him the command of a light infantry corps in 1779. On June 28, exactly one year to the day since the glory of Monmouth, Wayne rode into Sandy Beach on the west side of the Hudson to meet the two thousand men of his new corps. Two regiments came from Connecticut under the command of Rufus Putnam and Return Jonathan Meigs. Colonel Hans Christian Febiger, a young Danish merchant who fought at Bunker Hill and later at Monmouth, led a Virginia regiment. The rest of the soldiers were Pennsylvanians led by Richard Butler. Wayne had only one complaint. His new corps needed matching uniforms. However, Washington disagreed, refusing to grant so much as matching feathers for their caps. It would be up to Wayne to instill a sense of unity among the soldiers he placed under his command.[27]

Knowing Madame Fortune rarely smiled on an idle man, Wayne searched for a way to take his men into battle. With no specific orders from Washington, he spent his days riding south from his camp at Sandy Beach along the Hudson's western edge. He soon became fascinated with an outcropping of rock, some fourteen miles away, which rose a hundred and fifty feet directly from the water's edge. The place was called Stony Point, and just a month before the British had occupied it. They built a small fort on its summit loaded with cannon to protect King's Ferry on the eastern side of the river. The spot was especially strategic because the road from New England to New York City ran directly through here. To protect the crossing, the British also placed gunboats below the fort and a larger vessel called the *Vulture* near the Hudson's eastern shore. Wayne became convinced that if he could take Stony Point, he would deal a severe blow to British morale and inspire the Continental Army to fight on.

He was determined to come up with a detailed plan for his corps to take the massive rock jutting a half-mile out into the Hudson. He sent Butler and Febiger to the place on scouting missions, never telling them what he was planning, but asking instead for their honest opinions about the post. He studied Stony Point more closely himself, wondering how he could ever take a fort high atop a rock surrounded by water on all sides during high tide. A local man told him that after midnight, when the tide went out, a sandbar appeared in the marshy ground at the base of Stony Point allowing people to cross over from the shore. Now firmly convinced that the place could be taken, he sent larger scouting parties around its edges, hoping British patrols would take them in for questioning. When Colonel William Johnston, the post's commander, failed to take the bait, Wayne sent Captain Allan McLane into the post carrying a white flag.

Johnston was so convinced his fort was impregnable that he failed to blindfold McLane and after a short interview let him go. McLane returned to Wayne with an exact description of the British post high atop Stony Point. Redoubts surrounded the summit with guns facing out toward the river. Past the redoubts, there were two rows of abatis or logs and spikes stuck into the ground to prevent anyone from crossing over to the fort. These might be difficult to dismantle, but as McLane reported, if Wayne's corps could make it to the top of Stony Point, they would find that Colonel Johnston had failed to complete the fort's western wall. A determined group of men could storm in from that side and take the post before the British knew what hit them.[28]

Now an excited General Wayne rode north to the Continental Army's camp near West Point and headed straight for Washington's headquarters. There he laid out his bold plan for taking Stony Point. In the dead of night, he would lead a select group of men in three columns toward the post. He would station the center column at the western base of the huge rock to draw Johnston's fire, and lead the left and right columns straight up the northern and southern faces of the cliffs. With the British firing down at the soldiers of the center column, Wayne would storm into the fort and capture Colonel Johnston, his five hundred soldiers, and all the cannon. Needing more information before he could commit himself to such a daring plan, Washington sent Colonel Putnam, known for his engineering skills, to Stony Point to make sketches of the place. When Putnam returned with his drawings, Washington still worried about the plan. But after he climbed with Wayne to the crest of Thunder Mountain, or the Donderberg as the Dutch called it, and looked south toward Stony Point, he, too, believed the post could be taken.[29]

Back at his camp at West Point, Washington laid out detailed instructions for Wayne. The surprise attack would take place at midnight because even the most vigilant officer let down his guard then. Wayne's soldiers must be sworn to secrecy. They must march silently with fixed bayonets and unloaded muskets. They must wear matching white feathers or cockades in their hats so they could identify each other in the dark. A watchword must also be chosen. Any person met along on the way must be "secured," meaning taken along and not released until the fighting was over. "Prudent and determined men" must be selected to go first up the cliffs and remove the abatis in advance of the main body of troops. After Wayne's soldiers captured the post, they must turn the guns on the British across the Hudson. Having written down every possible caution, Washington added, "These are my general ideas of a plan for a surprise but you are at liberty to depart from them at every instance where you think they may be improved or changed for the better." Still, worrying at the last moment that the plan was impossible, he asked Wayne whether he truly thought storming Stony Point would succeed. Wayne answered, "General, if you give me permission, I'll storm Hell itself for you."[30]

The raid on Stony Point was set for midnight on June 15, 1779. At eleven o'clock on the morning of that same day, Wayne presided over the usual maneuvers of his men on the parade ground at Sandy Beach. But instead of allowing them to go off to their noonday meal, he readied them to march south toward Bear Mountain. Before they left, he wrote a last letter to General Washington, assuring him that all would go as planned, saying, "I am pleased at the prospect of the day & have the most happy presages of the fortune of the night."[31] As his soldiers filed out of camp, he ordered them to fix their bayonets and carry their muskets unloaded. They headed west around the base of Bear Mountain and then traveled southeast in single file along the trails of the Donderberg. Not one word was allowed to pass between them. After moving like a ghost army through a haunted landscape, Wayne halted the march at three in the afternoon and called his colonels to his side. He now revealed the plan to storm Stony Point at midnight.

The light corps would be divided into three columns. Colonel Butler would lead five hundred men on the left, Colonel Febiger, along with the help of several captains, would command six hundred men on the right, while Colonel Hardy Murfree of North Carolina would bring the rest of the men up the middle. When the attack began, a group of twenty "pioneers" would go ahead of the right and left columns, leading them across the sandbars that emerged from the water. They would go up the cliffs first and dismantle the two rows of abatis near Stony Point's crest. A hundred and twenty men specially selected by Wayne would follow close behind each group of pioneers. They would carry espontoons and rush over the broken abatis into the redoubts and capture the guns. Hopefully, if Murfree's men created a diversion at the base of Stony Point, the British would still be firing at them when Wayne and the rest of his corps stormed into the fort. There would be prize money, too, for the first three men who made it over the walls, and the entire corps would divide whatever spoils they found.[32]

Not one of his colonels balked at his orders. Instead they eagerly took the pieces of white paper that Wayne handed out and passed them to their men. They must place the paper in their hats before the attack so they could spot each other in the night. They also agreed on their watchword once the attack was a success: "The fort is ours!" If any soldier stepped out of line on the final leg of the trip, the man nearest him must run him through with a bayonet. With his orders passed through the corps, Wayne set off with his soldiers traveling again in single file through the woods in the late afternoon. At eight o'clock in the evening, they came upon the farm of David Springsteel where they waited for three more hours. Amid all the excited planning, and while working so closely with General Washington, Wayne had raced toward the future certain Madame Fortune was on his side. He was so convinced of victory that he never once thought of his own death. But now at eleven in the evening, in the silent darkness of a lonely farm, he suddenly thought of dying. He could not write to Polly as he usually did for he was certain she would never survive the report of his death. Nor could he write to Washington until Stony Point was won or lost.

He instead wrote to Sharp Delany with orders to deliver the letter to him upon his death. He began with the stark and simple words: "This will not meet your eye until the writer is no more." He gave him no details about what was happening, but simply explained that he was waiting "near the hour & scene of carnage." Facing his probable demise, all on the stage of his own making, he asked Delany to remember that he died in defense of his country and the rights of mankind. He complained that Congress, so filled with "parsimony and neglect," had brought him to this bloody moment. If Congress had supported the Continental Army, this "sanguinary campaign" would not be necessary. He suddenly found himself worrying about the commander in chief he would have to leave behind. "If ever any prediction was true it is this, and if ever a great and good man was Surrounded with a choice of difficulties," he confided to Delany, "it is General Washington."[33]

Who else would come to His Excellency's rescue once he was gone? Wayne fretted that a desperate Washington would take even more chances than the one he was planning for this night. If Washington failed again, Congress would dismiss him. That would be more terrible for his nation than his own death. All he could do now was hope that, once he fell in battle, Delany would look out for the education of his "little son & daughter." He must also take care of Polly, whom Wayne feared "will not survive this Stroke." Delany must go to her in person and remind her that "her Children claim her kindest offices & protection." Then he concluded his letter saying, "I am called to Sup, but where to breakfast, either within the enemy's lines in triumph or in the other World!"[34]

Wayne, who had been certain at eleven in the morning that Madame Fortune was with him, was just as convinced twelve hours later that death awaited him. He must push these thoughts aside if he was to lead his corps into battle. At half past eleven, he ordered his three columns to march toward Stony Point. Things went wrong as soon as they arrived there. The mysterious sand bar, which was to appear at low tide, was still two feet below the waves. He ordered his men forward, with Murfree's column reaching the base of the huge rock first. They opened fire on the British before Butler's column, aiming for the north side of Stony Point, or Wayne and Febiger's column, aiming for the south, could get into position. Luckily, this time Johnston took the bait. He sent his men toward the western edge of Stony Point, shouting all the while, "Come up, you rebels! Come up and fight!" Wayne's pioneers made their way up the north and south faces of the cliffs, with the advance guards following them and the rest of the corps right behind.

Inch by inch they climbed to the top of Stony Point with the guards coming on so fast they passed the pioneers. Though the rocky cliffs tore into their hands and feet, not one man cried out or fell back into the Hudson. Shortly after midnight, Wayne's advance corps made it over the first redoubts. Colonel Johnston heard the commotion and whirled his men away from the west side of the fort. He now ordered them to shoot their muskets directly into the Americans heading up the southern face of Stony Point. A ball grazed Wayne just above his forehead and he fainted for a moment. But he came to quickly and called for his men to help him forward. Two captains lifted him up under both arms. Though his espontoon fell from his hands and crashed into the waves below, Wayne hurried on, carried along by his officers.[35]

Colonel Louis Fleury, a French engineer in Febiger's regiment, entered the post first. Bringing down the British flag, he shouted in a thick accent, "The fort is ours!" Wayne and the rest of the right column followed him over the unfinished wall at the western end of Stony Point. At the same moment, one of Butler's men climbed over the northern wall of the post and managed to unbolt the gate to let his column in. Not long afterward, Murfree's men, the only Americans to fire any shot during the attack, but merely as a feint, climbed into Stony Point. A stunned Colonel Johnston had no choice but to surrender. Sixty-three of his soldiers lay dead, all killed by the bayonet, and many more were wounded. General Wayne counted fifteen men killed and eighty-three wounded including himself. The whole operation had taken less than two hours. Wayne's first action upon securing the post was to turn the cannon toward the British at King's Ferry and the next was to tell General Washington that the "fort & garrison with Col. Johnston are ours. Our officers & men behaved like men who were determined to be free."[36]

In the weeks following the surprise attack, Madame Fortune was more generous with Wayne than she would ever be for the rest of his life. Washington rode from West Point to look one last time at Stony Point. Back at his headquarters, he directed his aide Alexander Hamilton to invite Wayne to dinner, not once but several times. He also asked Congress to strike a gold medal in his honor. After ignoring requests for food and clothes for the Continental Army, the Congress immediately ordered a medal for Wayne. Letters of congratulations poured in from every quarter. The Pennsylvania Assembly, along with the Congress, sent their commendations. Glowing letters arrived from the Marquis de Lafayette and even Charles Lee and Arthur St. Clair. Friends from Philadelphia wrote that the name of Anthony Wayne was on everyone's lips as they recounted the daring tale of Stony Point. The next time Wayne came to the capital he would be welcomed as a member of the American Philosophical Society.[37]

But while Wayne had clearly succeeded at Stony Point, he still faced criticism. Many officers exploded in a rage at his failure to mention them in his reports to General Washington and the Continental Congress. New Englanders were especially angry with Wayne for failing to acknowledge them. They claimed

Copy of Wayne's Stony Point medal. Yale University Art Gallery,
Transfer from the Yale University Library, Numismatic Collection, 2001.

he treated them like "insignificant beings." How could Wayne list all the brave
Pennsylvanians and even the Virginians who climbed the cliffs at Stony Point,
but fail to mention a single soldier from Connecticut or Massachusetts? The Virginians complained just as mightily that Wayne had not praised them enough.
Hoping to avoid duels, he claimed he had done his best in the heat of the moment to recall exactly what had happened and never praised one group more
than another. "If I know my own heart," he explained in all earnestness, "I am
as clear of Local prejudices as any Gentleman on this ground—perhaps full as
much so, as those who effect to suspect me of it."[38]

Madame Fortune, who granted him honors one moment, casting a medal
for his bravery at Stony Point, only to plunge him into petty controversies with
the soldiers at the next, had a greater irony in store for him. Taking Stony Point
may have shocked the British, but Washington had neither the will nor the man-
power to maintain it. Just three days after capturing the post, once all the cannon
had been hauled away and the prisoners marched off to Pennsylvania, Washington abandoned the post. Within days, the British reclaimed the summit, but
in October 1779, they also gave up Stony Point. Just a few weeks later, Wayne
suffered a worse blow when Washington, at the behest of Congress, broke up his
Light Corps and sent the regiments back to their respective states.[39]

While Wayne reached the heights of glory in the summer after Valley Forge,
Washington sent him back to the humiliating task of begging for food and
clothes for the Pennsylvania Line in the following winter. This time he had the
support of Esther Reed, the wife of Pennsylvania's president Joseph Reed, and

Sarah Bache, the daughter of Benjamin Franklin. The two women organized a committee that went door to door in Philadelphia asking for contributions for the state's soldiers. Wayne was grateful for their help, but knew the Pennsylvania Line could not survive merely on begging. He warned over and over again, not just the state assembly, but also the Continental Congress, that terrible things would soon happen if his soldiers continued to suffer without adequate food, clothes, or pay. As he later explained to President Reed, he dreaded New Year's Day 1781, when the enlistments of so many of his men would be up. "When I look to a period fast approaching I discern the most gloomy prospect, distressing objects presenting themselves," he confided, "and when I consider that the mass of the people who now compose this Army will dissolve by the first of January, except a little corps enlisted for the war, that they are badly paid and worse fed, I dread the consequence."[40]

But no one listened to Wayne's concerns, and even Madame Fortune abandoned him. He knew she had departed when Washington called him to Tappan, New York, in June 1780 and gave him his next assignment. Along with Colonel Henry Lee, he was to round up livestock near the Loyalist garrison at Bull's Ferry on the Hudson directly across from New York City. Wayne, though still willing to take on any task for Washington, could barely stomach the fact that he must steal cattle from the enemy rather than fight them. Without telling his commander, he made plans to attack the Loyalists. He headed with Lee toward the farms around Bull's Ferry, but sent Colonel Irvine, along with nearly two thousand men and all the cannon, ahead toward the fort. As he and Lee rounded up livestock, Irvine launched his attack on the Loyalists. Wayne was convinced that the British, on their ships at anchor in the Hudson, would not allow the post to fall without a fight. He imagined first one ship and then another sailing across the Hudson to take on Irvine. Once Clinton saw what was happening, he would send even more soldiers across the river. General Washington would have to race south with the main Continental Army and fight a battle at last for control of New York City.

But nothing went as Wayne planned. Colonel Irvine ran into a spirited resistance from the seventy Loyalists stationed at the blockhouse at Bull's Ferry. His cannon fire only emboldened them to fight harder. They proved to be excellent marksmen who gunned down the Continental soldiers at a rate of three to one. Even when Irvine's soldiers stormed the post, tearing apart the abatis around the place as they had done at Stony Point, the Loyalists fought on, refusing to surrender. When Clinton moved not an inch, refusing to be lured into a wider battle, Wayne lifted the siege, leading Lighthorse Harry Lee, Colonel Irvine, and his soldiers back to Tappan, along with hundreds of cows to feed the Continental Army. When Washington learned of Wayne's attack on Bull's Ferry, he did not condemn him for going beyond his orders. His faith in Wayne was nearly un-shakeable since Monmouth Courthouse and Stony Point. Instead he excused his brigadier for his "intemperate valor."[41]

Wayne's actions did not go unnoticed by the British across the Hudson, especially Major John André, the officer who had staged the elaborate farewell to General Howe in Philadelphia that Wayne mocked in letters to his friends. It was now André's turn to skewer Wayne in a long poem entitled "The Cow-chace." André described Wayne in the opening canto as a loudmouth "Tanner" who inspired his barefoot soldiers with his overheated rhetoric and gill after gill of rum. When "Irving" failed to capture Bull's Ferry in Canto Two, Colonel Lee and General Wayne turned their sights on greater quarry in the final canto: livestock for Lee and women for Wayne. As his faithful colonel rounded up cattle, "Roman Anthony" chased a woodland nymph into a nearby tavern, forgetting the Battle of Bull's Ferry was under way, until he heard the "mighty Lee" lumbering down the road, "sublime upon his stirrups," with sheep, horses, goats, heifers, pigs, and chickens in tow. André concluded his poem with a final jest: "And now I've closed my epic strain, I tremble as I show it, Lest this same warrio-drover, Wayne, Should ever catch the poet."[42]

Major André could never have guessed that he would soon meet the general he so cleverly mocked. On September 22, 1780, the day "The Cow-chace" came off the presses in New York, militiamen stopped André north of the city. Convinced he was a spy, they sent him across the Hudson to West Point where General Benedict Arnold, the highest-ranking officer in the area, would interrogate him. But when André arrived at West Point, Washington, not Arnold, greeted him. Washington had paid a surprise visit to the post. He could not understand why the place was in disrepair and wondered why the commanding officer was missing. He finally learned that Arnold had let the place fall into ruin because he planned to surrender the post to the British. In return, they promised him £20,000 and a commission in their army. Arnold's accomplice was none other than the poet Major André. Washington ordered Arnold's immediate arrest, but he had already escaped to General Clinton in New York City.[43]

Washington, frantic that redcoats might be on their way up the Hudson, and with night drawing on, could think of only one man who could save him: Anthony Wayne. After Stony Point, they had become especially close. They wrote frequently to one another, and Wayne shared his many plans for future campaigns with a commander he considered his dearest friend. Washington now sent a desperate request for Wayne to come at once with his brigades to West Point. A short time later, a messenger raced into Wayne's camp and handed him Washington's urgent note. Wayne was not surprised when he learned of Arnold's treason, for he had disliked him as a self-serving spendthrift since the Quebec campaign. Still he could not believe the British would storm West Point in the middle of the night. He questioned the messenger about exactly what was happening.

As no redcoats had been spotted coming up the Hudson, he let his men, who were exhausted from their daily drills, rest for a few more hours. But at precisely two o'clock on the morning of September 27, he roused them from sleep and marched them toward West Point. They left their tents standing and their equipment behind as Wayne urged them to march as quickly as possible. They traveled sixteen miles through the dark woods, never stopping until they arrived at West Point four hours later. Wayne would always remember how His Excellency "received us like a God." Later, knowing everything was safe now that Wayne was with him, Washington said, "I again am happy."[44]

Again, Wayne knew a flash of glory, the favor of Madame Fortune for just a moment, before plunging again into misery. By the close of 1780, his long-suffering soldiers finally reached the breaking point. Now camped at Morristown, they grew angrier each day over no pay, the lack of food and clothes, and the thought of another idle winter. Knowing many of their enlistments would be up on New Year's Day 1781, Wayne worked as fast as he could to build cabins for them, hoping they would stay through the winter. Some of his best officers were also preparing to leave because they would lose their positions once Congress consolidated the Continental Army's regiments. By Christmas, there was so much grumbling in Wayne's camp that he brought large quantities of port, oysters, sugar, and green tea at his own expense. He entertained his officers for three days, while the celebration on New Year's Eve lasted six straight hours.

Just after midnight on New Year's morning, Wayne hosted a private supper for his favorite officers, Richard Butler and Walter Stewart. Suddenly the sound of gunfire and men shouting could be heard from outside his quarters. Wayne hurried toward the center of the camp with Butler and Stewart close behind. He asked Colonel Humpton, the man who had delayed retreating from the Paoli Massacre, what was happening. Humpton said he had been trying to restore order for nearly two hours, but no one was listening to him. Soldiers were racing everywhere, talking and laughing wildly, as they rushed the parade ground and the artillery. "What's this about? Why are you not in your quarters?" Wayne yelled after them, but no one answered. He finally realized that the Pennsylvania Line was in a full-blown mutiny. With General St. Clair, the line's commander, celebrating the New Year in Philadelphia, Wayne found himself the highest-ranking officer, and suddenly in charge, as years of frustration finally exploded all around him.[45]

On their own, with no officer commanding them, the soldiers formed their columns with bayonets ready and set off from the camp. Before leaving, they shot the cannon at the parade ground where Wayne had drilled them so perfectly. He raced up and down their lines, along with Butler and Stewart, begging them not to do this. He ran to the front of the columns, cocking his pistols in both hands and facing down the bayonets pointed at his chest. "We love you, we respect you, but you are a dead man if you fire," they shouted at Wayne. As they pushed past him, he chased after them in the bitterly cold night, pleading with them not to go over to the British. They shouted back as they passed him that they would kill the first man who tried to desert to the enemy. They were heading for Philadelphia to get everything they deserved for fighting so bravely for their country.[46]

Wayne could have gunned down his own soldiers, but at least three of his officers had already died trying to stop them. The mutineers injured many more with muskets, bayonets, and even rocks. Instead, he decided to follow them through the New Jersey countryside. Early on the morning of January 2, 1781, he stopped long enough to write the most painful letter of his life to General Washington. "It is with pain I now inform your Excellency of the general mutiny & defection which suddenly took place in the Penn'a line between 9 & 10 last evening," the letter began. "Every possible exertion was used by the officers to suppress it in its rise; but the torrent was too potent to be stemmed." Wayne told him what had happened to the last detail, hoping above all else that Washington would not think less of him for failing to stop the mutiny.[47]

He camped with his men at Vealtown on New Year's evening, Middlebrook a day later, and Princeton on January 3. There was only one bright spot for Wayne in the terrible ordeal. When St. Clair sent word that he was willing to meet with the mutineers, the soldiers answered that they would only deal with the one general they trusted, Anthony Wayne. When his soldiers neared Philadelphia, he rode ahead to negotiate on their behalf with the state government. The assembly agreed that any man who had completed three years of service was free to go home. Those who reenlisted were promised better conditions. The food and clothes that Wayne had requested year after year would now be granted without the asking. But a price must be paid for the mutiny. The Pennsylvania Line would be broken up. Half of the men would leave the army for good. The rest would head back to New York under the command of Arthur St. Clair. General Wayne, still a brigadier, would take command of the latest recruits from Pennsylvania at the town of York. A few of his officers, including Butler and Stewart, would stay with him, but most would be reassigned to General St. Clair. In the spring, Wayne and his new charges would head south to fight the British in Virginia under the command of the Marquis de Lafayette.[48]

It was hard for Wayne to accept the fact that his troops had mutinied. As a last measure to protect them, he petitioned Congress for a full amnesty. His request was granted, but that did not change the fact that most of his soldiers had been taken away from him. Now ordered on another furlough to Philadelphia, he found himself again making the rounds from politician to politician, this time begging for food, clothes, and arms for the fifteen hundred men he was struggling to recruit. He did not hold back in his demands. He asked for two thousand pairs of overalls and three thousand sets of shirts, stockings, coats, and even more overalls. Certain he had tried harder than any of Washington's generals to fight for his nation and the Continental Army, he now felt no man had failed both more completely. The only bright spot in the dark spring of 1781 was news of General Greene's battle against Cornwallis at Guilford Courthouse in North Carolina. Wayne declared it a victory, calling it proof that the war would soon be over and using it to win more recruits and more supplies.[49]

Finally, late in May 1781, he arrived at the camp of his new command in York. He found his soldiers restless and murmuring about mutiny. When shouts went up for "real" not "ideal" money, Wayne had a soldier in the artillery causing the most trouble arrested, court-martialed, and sentenced to death. When the enlisted men refused to go back to their tents, he had five more tried, convicted, and condemned to death by a firing squad. Although he pardoned two of these soldiers, he marched the other four to a small hill on the edge of town near a ripe field of rye. They knelt down with their backs to the field, handkerchiefs around their eyes, and their arms tied behind them at the elbows. Wayne, whose heart usually melted at the pleas of women, ignored the cries of their wives for mercy. He ordered twenty soldiers, many of them friends of the condemned men, to stand no more than twenty feet away and shoot them one after the other. The handkerchiefs over their eyes were burnt to a crisp and their heads and hands were blown off. Wayne found out later that General Washington had done the same thing when faced with a mutiny in the New Jersey Line. He had ordered the ringleaders arrested, court-martialed, and promptly shot.[50]

Wayne left for Virginia still enthralled at the sight of his men marching in perfect order to the sound of fifes and drums. But somewhere deep in his heart he no longer loved the military life so completely. For the few thrilling hours of battle, there were months, even years of drudgery, hunger, nakedness, backstabbing, and mutiny, all experienced while fighting for a people who cared not one bit for the soldiers who defended them. As he led his troops south, he was slowly losing his fascination with war. It would continue to unravel in the coming months, especially as he plunged headlong with his men into greater suffering. His faith in Madame Fortune would also diminish in the years ahead. More often than not, especially during the long southern campaign, he would complain, "I have not been pleased with Madame Fortune." Twelve years later, facing another campaign in the Ohio Country, she seemed to have disappeared completely.[51]

6

"An Event of the Utmost Consequence"

Even though he was sick and often depressed during the late winter of 1793, Anthony Wayne never lost his ability to analyze what was happening around him. When he arrived in Pittsburgh the year before, he summed up what he saw in one word: "*Wilderness.*" Now sitting alone at night in his house in Legionville, and reading through official correspondence from the War Department, letters from his loyal friend Sharp Delany, and stacks of newspapers from Philadelphia, he again explained the political state of the world in one word: "*Crisis.*" Looking into the dark future, and trying his best to see what would happen next, he came to understand the battle he had so diligently prepared his men to fight as a ripple in a wider sea of conflict that engulfed his beloved America, her archenemy Great Britain, and her first and best ally France.[1]

As Wayne surveyed the world, from his house above the Ohio River, he concluded that the struggle for American independence had never ended. The Revolution still raged across the Appalachians. The British may have signed a peace treaty in 1783, but they never accepted any redrawing of the North American map that took this country away from them. Its millions of acres of hardwood forests, deep black soil, and countless rivers that connected the inland waterways to the sea, all won first in the Seven Years' War and secured when Pontiac was defeated, still belonged to them. Because they meant to keep this country, the British refused to give up their forts on American soil at Niagara, Oswego, Detroit, and Michillimackinac. They would crush every attempt of their former colonies to grow west and thus uproot the new nation with the grand name, the United States of America, still just a dirty thumbprint on the pages of history.[2]

Wayne also understood that the British could not keep this country without the help of the Indians. Acting as the empire's advance guard, they disrupted the settlement of the country that the United States, after eight long years of fighting, had won from Great Britain. They were supplied and directed from the illegal British forts on American soil. Every attack on a blockhouse, lonely farm carved from the forests, or flatboats coming down the Ohio, as well as the murders of so many men with their wives and children carried off, happened at the behest of Wayne's former opponents, and now Canada's three top leaders: Guy Carleton, Canada's governor in chief; John Graves Simcoe, Upper Canada's lieutenant governor; and Alured Clarke, Lower Canada's lieutenant governor. Even the demand for the Ohio River as the boundary between the tribes and the United States was just a sleight of hand behind which the British kept a firm grip on their American empire.

Do not be fooled, Wayne warned Secretary Knox, and through him President Washington, into thinking that the Indians understood none of this. They were not pawns in a great international game of chess, but were instead savvy players on the world stage. "The Indians are an artful enemy," he argued, who used every trick in the book to win an advantage over their enemies. They pretended to be open to negotiations when they had decided on the Ohio River as the border between themselves and the Americans. Wayne was convinced that all the Indians, whether leaders of the Six Nations, like Joseph Brant whom the administration so trusted, or nameless chiefs of tribes living across the Ohio, would not budge an inch on this point. Wayne knew this from the Seneca leader Cornplanter, whom he entertained in his house at Legionville in the late winter of 1793. Standing next to the Ohio, Cornplanter pointed to the river and, looking back at Wayne, said, "My mind & heart is upon that river; may that Water ever continue to run, & remain the boundary of a lasting peace between the Americans & the Indians on its opposite shore."[3]

Sending more negotiators among them would not soften the Indians' position. They were preparing even now to defeat Wayne's army in order to defend this border. They would make one demand after another to weaken the Legion, including stopping the army from descending the Ohio for as long as possible. Wayne believed there was only one way to defeat them short of war. Washington must demand the "immediate surrender" of the British forts on American soil for only "the possession of them will insure a permanent peace." Without the weapons and supplies provided at these posts, the Indians would have to surrender the land between the Ohio and the Fort McIntosh line. Until that happened, Wayne must be allowed to strengthen his Legion, take his soldiers down the Ohio to Fort Washington, and head even farther north, building new posts in the valley of the Great Miami, up and down the Wabash and Maumee Rivers, and finally at the Miami Villages. Only this show of strength would convince the warriors who had slaughtered St. Clair's men to make way for the United States of America.[4]

Many times during the Revolution, Wayne had encouraged Washington not to be afraid of the British, but instead to act boldly. Now as spring approached in 1793, he did so again. Demand the "surrender of Niagara & Detroit without which, no treaty—however humiliating on our part—and embracing all the claims of the savages—will be permanently useful and expedient," he wrote to Secretary Knox. What better time to be bold, especially with Great Britain embroiled in a war against France? Wayne was so certain of this that he willed himself to recover from his many ailments. He dismissed the doctors who offered him quinine and laudanum, and treated himself with emetics instead. Then he rose early every morning, climbed onto his horse, and rode for at least two hours around Legionville, rebuilding his strength for the battle that lay ahead.[5]

For Wayne, isolated on the western frontier, Great Britain remained his nation's greatest enemy. He expected Washington to agree with him. The redcoats, whom they once opposed together on the battlefield, had simply moved their operations to Canada or to their posts on American soil. The Hessians might be gone, but Indian warriors had taken their place. Both the British and their tribal allies must be defeated. However, for Washington, no longer the commander in chief of the Continental Army, but now the president of the United States, things were not so simple. France, which had come to his nation's rescue after Saratoga, was possibly a worse enemy than Great Britain. The revolution that erupted there in 1789 had turned back in on itself. Demagogues rose and fell in a desperate bid to acquire power for their followers alone. From Washington's perspective across the Atlantic, the great fear of ancient writers that democracy would inevitably descend into anarchy had come true in France with a vengeance.[6]

One need only look at what had become of Gilbert Motier, the Marquis de Lafayette, to understand why the French Revolution so troubled Washington. The young idealist had returned to France in 1786, hoping to spread the ideals of the American Revolution throughout Europe. In 1789, when a desperate Louis XVI called the Estates General together at Versailles to raise taxes in his bankrupt nation, Lafayette gladly took his seat as a member of the First Estate. The Estates General, which represented the three medieval estates or classes of France, the nobility, the clergy, and the people, had not met since 1614. Lafayette's main goal was to strengthen the French economy, which had been badly weakened by the huge sums of money spent helping the Americans win their revolution. When the king threatened to disband the Estates General, balking at any political or economic reform proposed, Lafayette and his fellow delegates moved to the palace's tennis court. Here they declared themselves the National Assembly and set about writing a constitution for France. On July 14, 1789, after Louis tried to dismiss this body, a mob in Paris stormed the Bastille, the king's prison, killing the governor, freeing its few prisoners, and handing the key over to General Lafayette, just appointed the head of France's National Guard. Now the leader of the French Revolution, he sent the key to George Washington, who proudly displayed the trophy at Mount Vernon.[7]

Working with Thomas Jefferson, America's ambassador to France, Lafayette crafted the Declaration of the Rights of Man. In crystal clear language, he explained that every public calamity and corrupt government in human history resulted from ignoring, neglecting, or holding in contempt basic human rights. This would no longer occur in France. Instead a new government would be established that upheld principles listed in the document. People everywhere were born free and equal in their rights to property, security, resistance to oppression, and above all else, liberty. Lafayette did not define liberty as narrowly as the gentleman farmer Anthony Wayne had done at the start of his nation's revolution. Liberty was more than a person's right to elect representatives. Instead it was the freedom to do whatever one pleased as long as no one else was injured. Limits could only be placed on individual liberty as prescribed by law. The rest of Lafayette's declaration echoed many of the rights that Americans upheld in their revolution. There must be freedom of expression in all matters, even religion, in speech, writing, and the press. Likewise, there could be no arrest or imprisonment without due process.[8]

Almost from the moment Lafayette's declaration was approved in the National Assembly, the revolution, which he had hoped to lead peacefully toward a constitutional monarchy, took a violent turn he could not subdue. When the king refused to accept the declaration, mobs of angry women, whose children were starving, marched from Paris to Versailles. Lafayette reluctantly followed them hoping to restore order. He was able to protect the royal family, even kissing the hand of the hated queen Marie Antoinette, as she stood on a balcony high above the angry crowds, but still he bowed to the mob's demand that Louis, his wife, and his children be returned to the Tuilleries Palace.

Back in Paris, he could not prevent the rise of radical factions in the National Assembly. Nothing he did as the commander of the National Guard satisfied them. Even when he stopped an army of nobles from freeing the king from the Tuilleries in January 1791, his enemies accused him of treachery. Five months later, when the royal family was captured fleeing to Varennes, Lafayette was falsely accused of masterminding the escape. Standing his ground against relentless criticism, he took command of his nation's armies when Austria and Prussia declared war on France in the spring of 1792. But every loss on the battlefield only increased suspicions that Lafayette was a secret royalist conspiring with the king to restore the monarchy. Riots broke out throughout France as mobs attacked chateaus, monasteries, and churches. Thousands of aristocrats along with many Catholic priests and nuns were executed as enemies of the state. In August 1792, the National Assembly issued an arrest warrant for General Lafayette. Hoping to escape to America, he fled north into Belgium where he was captured by Austrian troops. They sent Lafayette, whom they considered a dangerous radical, from one prison to the next. By the winter of 1793, he was the prisoner of Prussia's Frederick William II at his fortress in Magdeburg. Louis XVI died in the same winter, condemned as an enemy of France and executed at the guillotine.[9]

President Washington had cheered the marquis as he launched a revolution in France. But he now abhorred the violent course that events had taken, especially the mistreatment of his friend Lafayette. Still he could not turn his back on the nation that had saved the United States. He could hardly bear the thought that France was now under attack, not just from Austria and Prussia, but also Spain, Portugal, the Netherlands, Russia, Sardinia, Naples, and finally Great Britain. According to the terms of the formal military alliance between the two nations signed in 1778, France pledged to fight with the United States until independence was achieved. Many Americans now argued that the alliance was greater than this document and the president should defend France militarily.[10]

But what soldiers could Washington send to help France against the most powerful nations in Europe? Indian warriors had destroyed two American armies in the Ohio Country, and, if General Wayne's fears were correct, they were preparing to destroy his Legion. Washington need not be reminded that, in all the years he served as the Continental Army's commander in chief, he never won a battle where soldiers marched against each other across an open field in the manner of European warfare. The few times he tried, at Brandywine, Germantown, and Monmouth, he was defeated or fought to a draw. France and the United States had also signed a commercial treaty in 1778 promising the most favored nation status for each country in their mutual trade. Washington now wrestled with whether the United States should honor this treaty if it meant reduced tariff revenues and British warships attacking American shipping. Even more troubling, how could he protect his nation's many merchant vessels without a navy?[11]

Until he could answer these questions, Washington hoped Americans would not take sides in the conflict, but this proved impossible. The events unfolding in France were so compelling that few could turn away. All the hopes and fears that Americans harbored for their own experiment in self-government seemed to be reflected in France's turmoil. They had been confident in the temperate nature of their revolution even as they toppled the old order. Any rational person could understand the self-evident truth that all men were created equal and therefore the people, not the kings or the nobility, should rule. The people's government, embodied in the Constitution, would protect the rights to life, liberty, and the pursuit of happiness embedded in human nature itself. But the French Revolution revealed something more irrational, even terrifying, in the human heart, and made Americans wonder if the rule of the people might be more tumultuous and perhaps more violent than expected. Whether that was a good or bad thing remained open to debate.

Washington bemoaned the fact that the two men in America who took up the debate most stridently were members of his own cabinet, Alexander Hamilton and Thomas Jefferson. Their disagreement over the significance of the French Revolution added to the tension building between them ever since they battled over the constitutionality of the Bank of the United States. For Hamilton, the troubles in France, which left the people reeling from one "volcano" to an-other, showed just how quickly the people's rule gave way to mob rule. He condemned France's radical factions, especially the Jacobins, and Americans who supported them as demagogues, especially Jefferson and his followers. He urged Washington to abrogate the alliance with France, even if this meant closer ties with Great Britain. Jefferson, who at first was troubled by the violence of the French Revolution, now argued that "a little innocent blood" might be necessary to give birth to a republic. He advised Washington to defend France against its many enemies, especially Great Britain. In his opinion, those who condemned the French Revolution, like Hamilton and his supporters, were reactionaries at best and monarchists at worst who hoped to restore George III to his American throne.[12]

Though he was far from the nation's capital, Wayne could not ignore the growing controversy over the French Revolution. Even if he tried to avoid it, the events of the day filled the newspapers that Sharp Delany forwarded to him every week. His opinion on the matter rested somewhere between the extremes of Hamilton and Jefferson. Like Hamilton, he despised mob rule. He had seen its terror firsthand when the Pennsylvania Line mutinied. He remembered, too, the shock that descended on Philadelphia, especially on Washington and Jefferson, when news arrived of the royal family's capture and imprisonment. Brutality and disorder seemed to be spreading everywhere in the world, especially west of the Appalachians. Since he arrived in Pittsburgh, Wayne had sensed a growing resistance among the people to their own government. Still he felt little sympathy for Louis XVI, a despot who must go the way of England's Charles I and James II. He believed the French king had brought the wrath of his people down upon himself, his wife, and his children by trying to flee. He no more wished to see him back on his throne than George III ruling America again. Like Jefferson, Wayne believed the French people should be allowed to chart their own course, no matter how traumatic, toward a republic. In his many letters to his friend Delany, he worried most that powerful nations like Austria, Prussia, and the hated Great Britain would crush France before this hope was realized.[13]

Like Washington, Wayne's greatest concern in the chaos of the French Revolution was Lafayette. He agreed with Delany that the marquis had to escape from France, especially when his attempts to set up a workable government collapsed in favor of mob rule. "Would to God," Delany complained to Wayne, "All mankind and nations had been favoured by Providence with such a Man as our beloved President." Wayne had first met the French nobleman during the campaign to defend Philadelphia in the summer of 1777. Although twelve years younger, Lafayette possessed a fiery disposition that quickly endeared him to Wayne. Their friendship deepened at Valley Forge where they closed ranks behind their beleaguered commander in chief. As Wayne launched his attacks on the Pennsylvania Assembly, demanding clothes and shoes for his men, Lafayette conducted an equally passionate campaign against the three men most determined to topple Washington from his command: Horatio Gates, the victor at Saratoga; Thomas Mifflin, the army's incompetent quartermaster general; and Thomas Conway, a fellow Frenchman. Later, when the Continental Army finally left Valley Forge, Lafayette agreed with Wayne that Washington should attack the retreating British. Not long afterward the two friends fought side by side with their beloved commander in chief in the brutal heat of Monmouth Courthouse.[14]

The ties between Wayne and Lafayette had grown even stronger in early 1781 when Washington ordered the two men to Virginia. Benedict Arnold, now a brigadier general in the British army, had set fire to Richmond in January and spent the rest of the winter raiding tobacco plantations along the James River. Wayne looked forward to hunting down the traitor, never once complaining that he had to serve as the second in command to a twenty-four-year-old major general and a foreigner at that. From the moment Lafayette learned Wayne was on his way south, he could hardly contain his enthusiasm. He sent one frantic note after another, in his tiny precise handwriting, urging Wayne to hurry. "I shall patiently wait for you," he wrote in early March, and less than a week later, "I would be extremely happy to have your assistance." By May, he confessed that "just hearing" from his brigadier "will afford the greatest pleasure." When no word came back to him, an anxious Lafayette begged Wayne to "hasten to our aid, my dear sir."[15]

Lafayette's desperate cries reflected the difficult task Washington had assigned to him. Commanding only nine hundred men, he would be hard pressed to protect Virginia's towns from Arnold's redcoats. He might have a better chance of hunting the traitor down and hanging him. Lafayette could also give chase to the hated Banastre Tarleton, commander of the British Legion, but with only infantry at his command, he probably would never catch him. Tarleton was rumored to have murdered soldiers who had surrendered and cut down refugees as they fled through the backcountry. In Virginia, he commandeered the best horses for his cavalry who raced them at lightning speed across the state. They stole military stores, torched tobacco warehouses, and destroyed the public records of the hated rebels. Lafayette reported Tarleton's handiwork to Wayne in graphic detail. He saw exhausted horses left for dead, boatloads of slaves being carried off, and a militia company, surprised in a rainstorm, sliced to pieces. Once Tarleton even came close to capturing Governor Jefferson and many of Virginia's top lawmakers, including Patrick Henry, Richard Henry Lee, and Benjamin Harrison, in their temporary capital in Charlottesville, but they escaped at the last minute. Nor could Lafayette catch Simcoe and his Queen's Rangers who roamed the state. They terrified Baron Steuben, who had been sent to help Lafayette. Steuben had tried to protect Continental Army supplies near Richmond but fled when Simcoe approached, allowing him to capture hundreds of guns, piles of powder and shot, and many barrels of rum and sugar.

But Lafayette's most difficult assignment came when Lord Cornwallis crossed over the Dan River from North Carolina with the bulk of the army. Soon two more regiments of redcoats joined him from New York. Washington ordered Lafayette to keep Cornwallis' army in Virginia with no specifics on how to accomplish this. Reports were already coming in to him that Cornwallis might take up a position at Portsmouth on the Elizabeth River or join Simcoe at the Byrd estate at Westover on the James. Lafayette did not despair because he knew Wayne was on his way with at least eight hundred men. While many would be untried recruits, and their officers might still be shaken by the recent mutinies, Lafayette was not worried, for a fearless general would be leading them. Together they would hunt down Arnold, stop the raids of Tarleton and Simcoe, and somehow trap Cornwallis in Virginia. As Lafayette explained to his brigadier, "Should you arrive before Cornwallis, I hope we may beat the enemy!"[16]

However, Wayne was not so confident. He was happy to have a new command but worried how less than two thousand men between himself and Lafayette could take on Arnold and Cornwallis, whose combined forces he estimated at ten thousand soldiers along with five hundred cavalry. Having been handed so difficult a task, he was ashamed he could only supply them by begging help from politicians. He described his humiliation to General Washington in images drawn from the ancient history he loved. "I have been knocking hard at every door," he complained, "from the council up to the Congress to little purpose, they all present me that Gorgon head,—an empty treasury."[17]

Throughout the difficult winter and spring, Washington had cheered him on, wishing him success wherever duty called him. Knowing the strain Wayne was under after thwarting another mutiny, Washington assured him that he had done the right thing by quickly executing the ringleaders. Wayne also told himself that his swift measures had restored "happiness & discipline" among his troops. But the brutality of what he had done haunted him as he wandered the streets of Philadelphia and Lancaster, collecting horses, wagons, barrels of flour and whiskey, cattle, and hopefully enough clothes and shoes for the eight hundred men he would lead to Virginia. For the moment, as he faced yet another campaign, he found himself thinking of not his own death, but the suffering that lay ahead of his men. So many had already died right before his very eyes, and now he was taking hundreds more to their probable deaths. There would be nothing to show for their sacrifice except worthless government certificates handed to their widows and orphans.[18]

On the morning of May 26, 1781, General Wayne, who was dressed in a new blue-and-white uniform, trimmed in gold thread and with golden epaulets, rode to the front of his columns and led his soldiers out of York. He placed a black-and-white cockade in his plumed hat symbolizing the colors of the French alliance. He ordered his eight hundred soldiers to wear the same cockade in their caps. He knew that down the road they would pass through Frederick, Maryland, where prisoners from Burgoyne's army were still housed. He wanted to remind them that their loss at Saratoga brought France into the war on the side of the United States. But even as he looked forward to this moment, Wayne knew all was not well with his army, especially his officers. Four of them had resigned in protest over his brutal handling of the latest mutiny. They endured a tongue-lashing from him before escaping from the Continental Army forever. Some of his remaining officers, like Captain Benjamin Fishbourne, kept up a steady stream of complaints about Wayne. "Why is there not some hidden curse in the Store of Heaven," wrote Fishbourne to General St. Clair, now the commander of the Pennsylvania Line, to "blast" men like Wayne to "perdition"?[19]

When he left York, Wayne worried about the possibility of another mutiny. His men were allowed to carry their muskets, but their ammunition was locked away in the baggage train. By the time his soldiers crossed into Maryland, Wayne found himself worrying also about the weather. Scorching heat marked the day while frightening thunderstorms kept everyone awake at night. Wayne could hardly believe the power of the lightning that crashed into his camp and the winds that overturned his army's tents. The creeks were so swollen that his men often needed an extra day to cross them. Exhausted, bedraggled in the linen overalls their commander secured for them, and sometimes shoeless, they made little impression on the British prisoners who lined Frederick's main street to sneer at them.

Wayne found the rivers in Virginia, running like parallel ribbons toward the Chesapeake Bay, even more treacherous than the streams in Maryland. He had planned to cross the Potomac at Georgetown, but after Lafayette warned him Cornwallis might be on his way there, he headed twenty miles west to Noland's Ferry. Here the river was so high that four of his soldiers drowned. Once across, Wayne followed the Carolina Road south into the piney woods past Leesburg. The weather now turned so cold that a foot of snow fell to the west along the crest of the Blue Ridge Mountains. Up until this point, Wayne let his men travel at the leisurely pace of eight or nine miles a day, sometimes less when ferrying over swollen creeks, but now he pressed them to go fifteen miles or more. When his army finally came to the flooded Rappahannock, he despaired of crossing until Virginia militiamen arrived and built rafts to take everyone to the other side. Still searching for the marquis, he marched his soldiers west to Raccoon Ford on the Rapidan River where they camped late on the evening of June 8.[20]

As he traveled south, Wayne kept up a steady correspondence with Lafayette, whom he always addressed as "My Dear Marquis." He described every trial he endured, always assuring his new commander that he was determined to join him. When they finally met at Raccoon Ford, Wayne found the excitable young man filled with plans that changed by the minute as he received the latest reports on Cornwallis' movements. Wayne never considered this indecision, but instead recognized a quicksilver mind like his own. He especially appreciated how determined the young Frenchman was to take on the British. The hated Arnold had slipped through his grasp when General Clinton recalled him to New York, but Lafayette had better luck hunting down Arnold's replacement, General William Phillips. Taking up a position across the James River from Petersburg, he bombarded the Bollingbrook Plantation where the British commander lay in the basement dying of malaria. But he could not catch Tarleton, who tried again to capture Jefferson at his home at Monticello, or Simcoe's Rangers, who had confiscated even more Continental Army supplies throughout the state. Nor had he prevented Cornwallis from destroying an arsenal at Point of Fork where the Rivanna River met the James.[21]

But Lafayette had come up with a plan to thwart Cornwallis' next move, a full-scale assault on Charlottesville. He learned from a Virginia militiaman that there was a long-forgotten road running through woods that Cornwallis would have to take on his way west. To save Charlottesville, Lafayette must get his troops onto that road before Cornwallis arrived; Wayne agreed. They set off as quickly as their tired men could march. Wayne's three regiments led the way, with the Virginia militia under Governor Thomas Nelson right behind, and Lafayette and his regiments bringing up the rear. On the evening of June 12, they found the hidden road in the woods and Lafayette ordered his axmen to clear it. Working through the night, they chopped down trees, hauled logs, and carried brush away so the army could take up a position by dawn on June 13 in the woods facing east. They waited all day, but Cornwallis never appeared. Finally, late in the evening, scouts reported that the entire British army was heading back east, perhaps to Williamsburg or maybe even back across the James.[22]

Now following Cornwallis' army at a distance, with Wayne eight or nine miles behind the redcoats and Lafayette twelve miles behind him, both men looked for a chance to attack the British as they had done at Monmouth. Twice Wayne had the enemy in his sights, first Tarleton and then Simcoe, but both times the redcoats withdrew from a fight. Butler's regiment skirmished with the Queen's Rangers at the Hot Water Plantation just west of Williamsburg, but Cornwallis continued his retreat. Remembering Stony Point, Wayne proposed a night attack, but Lafayette preferred striking Cornwallis by day. His chance finally came on July 5 when scouts reported the British were passing the Green Spring Plantation, once the home of Governor William Berkeley and now the property of the Lees. They were probably already at Jamestown Island on their way to Portsmouth.[23]

On the morning of July 6, Lafayette decided that most of Cornwallis' men must be across the river by now. He sent Wayne ahead to Green Spring, hoping to catch the British rear guard waiting their turn to cross the James. He ordered Wayne to "make a forward move" with the 500 men "under his conduct," including Colonel Stewart's regiment, more Virginia Continentals, dragoons led by Colonel John Mercer, and 150 riflemen, and "endeavor to come upon the enemy." By the time Wayne arrived at Green Spring in the early afternoon, contradictory reports were coming in about the exact location of Cornwallis' army. Mercer told him that a slave near the plantation said Tarleton was in the big house, Cornwallis was farther down the road at Green Spring Church, and most of the soldiers were along the James still waiting to cross. Lafayette soon arrived and agreed that the main British army was just south of the planation. He ordered Wayne to engage the enemy, while he headed five or six miles back down the road to call up the rest of army.

Surveying the ground ahead of him, Wayne saw that, while an attack was possible, a retreat would not be easy. His men would have to pass down a narrow wooden causeway southeast of Green Spring toward the British and take that same road back if fleeing from them. There was a swamp on his right and deep ponds on his left. A half a mile ahead, Wayne could clearly see the British cavalry stationed toward the James with the infantry and a few pickets across from them on the other side of the causeway. One of his favorite axioms of Marshal Saxe seemed to apply: never risk more than you are willing to lose. The gain of even a small victory rippling through the exhausted Virginia countryside seemed worth the risk. At two o'clock in the afternoon, Wayne noticed smoke rising south of the enemy camp. He wondered if Cornwallis was calling in his troops or maybe ordering those across the James to come back. He led his men into a patch of woods between the causeway and the James where he watched and waited.

Finally, at three o'clock, Wayne sent his riflemen ahead into open country. They hurried to a ditch behind a split-rail fence where they would be protected from a cavalry charge. Once in position, they opened fire on the redcoats and kept up their attack for two straight hours. At five o'clock, when a British column formed to flank their left, Wayne ordered Major William Galvan, a young Frenchman, to lead the infantry out of the woods to support them. He realized they could not hold out for long after another column of redcoats formed on their right. He ordered two field pieces rolled out from the woods and opened fire on the approaching British. The bombardment did little good, for the enemy quickly brought up three cannon and took deadly aim at Wayne's men. Many fell in the first blast, including Major Mercer, whose horse was killed beneath him. He used his sword to cut himself free and, mounting another horse, raced back to tell Wayne what he already knew. Three columns of British light infantry were ready to smash into the right, center, and left of his men.

Wayne finally understood that he had not attacked the last of Cornwallis' men to cross the James. Instead, he had been lured into a trap set for him by the general he now called the "fox." Rather than catching his prey, the prey had caught him. Lafayette was also aware of what was happening. Waiting near the great house at Green Spring, he rode to the James and looking downriver saw that Cornwallis' army had not yet crossed the river. Wayne's soldiers were about to attack more than ten times their number. In a panic, he sent a mounted messenger ahead with orders to retreat. For just one moment, Wayne, who prided himself on his coolness under fire and legendary ability to move an army quickly, had no idea what to do.

Then he remembered something from this war, and not from his ancient history books, that might save him. Less than a year before, an American army under Horatio Gates had stumbled upon British forces led by Cornwallis and Lord Rawdon near Camden, South Carolina. As the battle lines formed, Baron Johann de Kalb, a German general in the French army who had sailed to America with Lafayette, readied his Maryland Continentals on the left, directly facing Rawdon's men, while Gates and the Virginia and North Carolina militias faced Cornwallis' soldiers on the right. When the fighting commenced, the militiamen quickly fled the field. Kalb could have done the same, but instead he ordered his soldiers forward with a fury that belied their numbers and gave Gates and the rest of the army a chance to retreat. Remembering Kalb's bravery in an impossible situation, and just reinforced by two more Pennsylvania regiments that brought his total to eight hundred, Wayne decided his only chance was to attack or, as he would later explain: *"it was determined among a choice of difficulties to advance and charge them."* That the baron had his horse shot out from under him, that his body was riddled with ten shots, and that he died a British captive three days later were facts that Wayne pushed from his mind for the time being.

He now ordered his men to form two lines facing the enemy with muskets ready. He then rode in front of them and, coming to the center, whirled his horse about to face the oncoming redcoats. At that very moment, a shot came directly at him, missing him but slicing the plume from his hat. Ebenezer Denny, a soldier from Pennsylvania, who ten years later would bring the second message of St. Clair's defeat to President Washington, was standing right next to Wayne on his horse. He was looking up at the general at the very moment the shot hurled past him. He remembered how Wayne looked down at the fallen plume and back toward the British almost with amusement. With his men now formed in columns on either side of him, Wayne sat motionless, calmly watching the British approach, until after deciding they were close enough, he shouted, "Fire! Charge with bayonets!"

Lafayette, who could see Wayne at a distance, thought his brigadier had lost his mind. What he did not understand was that this was not an attack but a retreat. For just a few minutes, Cornwallis worried that Lafayette had arrived with thousands of reinforcements. Maybe he would be caught in the trap set for Wayne. With the British momentarily confused, Wayne sounded the retreat, ordering his soldiers back down the wooden causeway. His two field pieces must be left behind, for all the horses needed to pull them lay dead in the grass. But his men were able to save the wagons loaded with ammunition by hauling them away from the battlefield themselves. Now the race was on to make it to the safety of Lafayette's ranks. The British followed for some distance, capturing twelve of Wayne's men, before turning back as dusk fell to collect their dead and wounded, which amounted to seventy-five. Once back with the rest of the army, Wayne was disappointed to learn that his casualties were even higher: twenty-eight killed and ninety-nine wounded.[24]

In the coming weeks, letters poured into Wayne congratulating him for his daring at Green Spring. General Washington's words were the most welcome. "I with the greatest pleasure received the official account of the action of Green Spring," he wrote. "The Marquis speaks in the handsomest manner of your own behavior and that of the troops in the action." His friend Robert Morris was ecstatic that the Continental Army had won even a small victory. "It is very flattering to find our troops arrived at that degree of discipline which enables them to face with inferior numbers that proud foe who have heretofore attempted to treat our army with such contempt." But Nathanael Greene's commendation was the greatest of all. "Oh that I had you with me a few days ago!" meaning during the campaign to push Cornwallis out of North Carolina. "Your glory and the public good might have greatly advanced."[25]

However, praise for Wayne's actions at Green Spring was far from universal. For the first time, the nickname coined by Jemmy the Rover was publicly applied to him. Newspapers as far north as New Jersey condemned "Mad Anthony" for his reckless disregard for human life. For all his bravery, Wayne had lost nearly one out of five of his men. There was even some grumbling among his own ranks. Robert Wharry, a surgeon's mate who stayed behind with the women, sick, and baggage at the Chickahominy Church, was horrified at the numbers of killed, wounded, and captured, not just the rank and file, but officers, too. He took to his bed at the shock of "another Blockhouse affair," meaning another folly like Bull's Ferry. "I never such a piece of work heard of—about eight hundred troops opposed to five or six thousand Veterans on their very ground." As Wharry explained to a friend in Philadelphia, only the "*Madness*" of Mad Anthony, "by God," could explain the sheer insanity of it all.[26]

But no one criticized Wayne as much as Colonel Henry Lee. While Wayne would consider Lighthorse Harry his lifelong friend, Lee came to dislike Wayne from the moment he was appointed Lafayette's second in command. Now serving with his light dragoons in the Carolina backcountry, Lee passed on rumors to Washington that Wayne constantly disobeyed young Lafayette. Later, after the Revolution ended, his hatred grew even stronger. In his *Memoirs of the War in the Southern Department*, Lee would attack Wayne as a bloodthirsty warmonger and his Pennsylvanians as drunken Irishmen. Poor Lafayette, Lee wrote, had to endure a brigadier general with a "constitutional attachment" to the sword and his "impatient and refractory" soldiers who were good for nothing but thrusting their bayonets into the enemy at close quarters.[27]

But neither praise nor blame mattered to Wayne. Instead he cared only that his soldiers "so honorably & freely bled in defence of the Liberties of the Country." The bonds between himself and his men, once so deep that many considered Wayne the Continental Army's most popular general, had broken, seemingly past repair, after two mutinies. His veterans and recruits followed him grudgingly from Pennsylvania to Virginia. But now, seeing how bravely these same men fought at Green Spring, and remembering that just weeks before their ammunition had to be packed away from them, Wayne nearly burst with pride. Upset that he could offer them only Indian corn gruel, he bought better food for them out of his own pocket. When the wounded asked to recover in Pennsylvania, he found wagons, horses and saddles, and carriages to take them home. They, in turn, could hardly believe Wayne's kindness. His officers signed a formal petition acknowledging him as a "Gentleman whos[e] known generosity, and Parental care, has endeared him to ev[e]ry officer and Soldier under his com'd and remov'd every doubt of the Indefatigable assiduity to render their Situation Happy." As Wayne bid them farewell, they promised to "return in a short time and prove our selves worthy that notice of that General whose Ambition is the reward of the Brave."[28]

Having regained the respect of his soldiers, Wayne was still not a happy man. He was troubled by a phrase in Greene's last letter: "Be a little careful and tread softly, for, depend upon it, you have a modern Hannibal to deal with in the person of Cornwallis." Hannibal, the Carthaginian general who defeated the Romans time and again in the Second Punic War, was someone Anthony Wayne knew well. The fact that Hannibal, after humiliating the Romans at Trebia, Trasimene, and most terribly Cannae, where he again outflanked and destroyed an army twice the size of his own, finally retreated from Italy was no comfort to Wayne. Instead the gravity of his situation suddenly fell on him. His childhood sense of war as a grand adventure, which had lessened after his men mutinied, disappeared completely as he realized the monumental task before him. He must defeat a general of Hannibal's caliber with his little band of hungry, threadbare, and shoeless men. Lafayette suffered a similar reaction after Green Spring. He confessed to their mutual friend Henry Knox how terrified he actually was: "Lord C's Abilities are to me More Alarming than His Superiority of forces. I ever Had a Great opinion of Him. Our Papers Call Him a Mad man But was Ever any Advantage taken of Him where He Commanded in Person? To Speak Plain English I am Devilsh Afraid of Him."[29]

If he could not defeat Cornwallis, who had crossed the James back to Portsmouth, Wayne hoped he could at least take on Tarleton. He could not give chase to him, having lost so many horses at Green Spring, but he could intercept him.

Lafayette agreed and sent Wayne first to Chesterfield Court House, just south of Richmond, and then farther west to Goode's Bridge on the Appomattox River. After waiting there for ten days, and with no sign of Tarleton, he headed back east to Westover. Wayne might have stayed there throughout the summer, with the Byrd family swirling about him, overjoyed at his charm, beautiful manners, and brilliant conversation, but by late July, a series of frantic notes from Lafayette sent him forty miles west to Amelia Court House. A month later, an anxious Lafayette ordered Wayne back to Westover, certain that Cornwallis was on the move to Baltimore, Philadelphia, New York, or perhaps back to the Carolinas.[30]

Never once did Wayne complain about constantly crisscrossing Virginia. But by late August, when his soldiers were desperate for clothes, he grew increasingly frustrated. As he explained to Lafayette, more than three-fourths of his men were "totally destitute" of shoes while many were "bare legged rather too high up for a modest view." Knowing he would get no help from Pennsylvania, he made up his mind to take whatever supplies he came across. When he found sixteen pairs of boots, 237 pairs of men's shoes, and two thousand yards of coarse linen near the Appomattox River, he distributed the goods to his men. An angry Governor Nelson complained to Lafayette, who in turn asked his brigadier ever so gently why he had taken supplies belonging to Virginia. Wayne exploded in a string of bitter tirades. Tarleton's brigade would have taken the stores if he had left them there. If Lafayette wanted the shoes and clothes back, then nearly two hundred of his soldiers would not be able to fight. The thought of his suffering men, "marching bare foot over sharp pebbles, & thro' burning sands," particularly for ungrateful Virginians, was more than he could bear.[31]

The squabbling back and forth might have exploded into a full-blown crisis if "an event of the Utmost Consequence," as Wayne would later describe it, had not intervened.[32] On the afternoon of August 28, 1781, expecting another dispatch about taking supplies that did not belong to him, he instead received a surprising letter from Lafayette. In his breathless, tiny script, the marquis explained, "I am happy in this safe opportunity to offer my heart to you. There is an important secret which I communicate to you alone, and which I request you to keep from everybody's knowledge." The French fleet was on the way to Virginia. Lafayette had gotten the news in a letter from General Washington himself. Forgetting the near disaster of Green Spring, he now ordered Wayne to do everything in his power to keep Cornwallis in Virginia. If the British made any attempt to retreat into North Carolina, Wayne and his men, threadbare and shoeless, must stop them.[33]

Wayne could hardly believe what he was reading. But Lafayette's note helped him understand a cryptic letter he had received from Washington in the middle of summer. If everything went as planned, His Excellency said, Wayne would soon be on his way to help General Greene. He now understood Washington meant that once Cornwallis was cornered and defeated, he would be ordered to the Carolinas. In the coming days, Wayne learned the details of the plan to trap Cornwallis. Twenty-three French ships under the command of Admiral de Grasse, some of them great three-decker vessels, would soon arrive in the James, not far from Westover. They would carry thousands of soldiers under the command of the Marquis de Saint-Simon along with dozens of siege guns and field pieces. But the plan was even more staggering. At the same time, Washington, along with the rest of the Continental Army, was marching south from New York with General Rochambeau, the commander of the French forces in America, and even more soldiers. By land or sea, they were all heading to Virginia to catch Cornwallis at Yorktown.

How could this be true, Wayne asked himself, when he had foreseen none of this? After the mutiny of his men, he rarely looked ahead to any possibility of success on the battlefield. He was now in such shock that he admitted he was not as "sanguine" as he should be. After fighting for so long with no clear victories, and now commanding barefoot men in flax overalls, he could not believe the rendezvous would ever take place. But on September 2, just five days after learning Lafayette's "secret," he heard the cannon boom of the French ships as they entered the James. He sent Butler and Stewart to Bunel's Ferry to welcome Admiral de Grasse and the Marquis de Saint-Simon. They suggested Saint-Simon continue with most of the French fleet upriver to Jamestown where his soldiers could camp, while De Grasse should sail four frigates into the York River toward Cornwallis' position. After listening to his colonels describe the determination of the French commanders, Wayne admitted he almost felt sorry for the British "fox." As he explained the situation to Lafayette, "Every door is shut by the hard-hearted fellows against poor Cornwallis."[34]

Wayne hoped to greet the French commanders that evening, but was instead called to Lafayette's camp. He arrived there at ten o'clock. When a sentry demanded the countersign, Wayne gave it quickly, but the frightened man was certain Cornwallis was about to attack and shot directly at him in the dark. Wayne gave out a loud cry as the musket ball grazed the bone of his left thigh and lodged behind it. At the same moment, an agonizing shock, like a lightning bolt, ran down his leg, convincing Wayne that he had also been shot in the foot. The pain was excruciating, but the more he shouted in agony, the more he upset the advance guard called up by the sentry. With some difficulty, he finally convinced the soldiers that he was General Wayne come to meet with the marquis. He limped to the hospital tents set up in Williamsburg, now crowded with excited people awaiting the arrival of General Washington, where he would stay for the next ten days.[35]

As he lay on his cot, Wayne fretted that the town's celebrations were premature. He could not believe that Cornwallis would allow himself to be caught so easily. He imagined a British fleet under Admiral Hood, which had appeared off the Virginia Capes only to sail away, would return and entice Admiral de Grasse to follow. Hood would lure the French back to New York, and once safe in the city's deep harbors, leave De Grasse's fleet at sea to be smashed in a hurricane. British ships would then head to the James, sail up the York, and rescue Cornwallis. A downcast Wayne, unable to share in the joy of the moment, remembered how Admiral d'Estaing had failed to retake Savannah from the British just two years before, leaving the city still in enemy hands. He was at times so depressed that he believed Cornwallis could only be defeated if the elusive Madame Fortune, so fickle toward the Americans but ever faithful to the British, finally left his side.[36]

Still, his mood brightened when he wrote home to his wife, Polly. He told her he had been shot, but not to worry for he was recovering. He also let her know that, from the very moment he was hurt, he suffered terrible pains of gout in his foot. He could not understand how a gunshot could cause this ailment, but he remained confident that in a few days he would again "join the army and take an active command." Now without any doubt about what lay ahead, he assured her, "We have the most glorious certainty of very soon obliging Lord Cornwallis, with all his army to surrender prisoners of war. Everything is in readiness to commence the siege, our army is numerous & in high spirits, the French are the finest body of troops I ever viewed, & harmony & friendship pervade the whole."[37]

No matter how much pain he was in, Wayne was determined to greet General Washington. On the afternoon of September 13, leaving behind Lafayette, who had collapsed with a fever, he rode in a carriage to greet their commander in chief. Later that day, Wayne stood at his side for hours introducing soldiers from Pennsylvania to him. Washington shook the hand of every man one by one. Wayne later joined Washington, Rochambeau, Saint-Simon, and all the officers of the allied armies in the first of many dinners. He found the French gracious hosts who entertained their guests with music and opera late into the night. What amazed Wayne even more was the respect that the French showed Washington. His Excellency seemed a changed man, more decisive and certain of his plans than Wayne had ever seen him. At dawn on September 28, high atop his beautiful chestnut horse Nelson, Washington led two columns of American and French soldiers down the main street of Williamsburg toward Yorktown. Wayne, now reassigned to Baron Steuben's division, followed on horseback with his leg aching and his bedraggled regiments coming close behind.

Starting on the day Washington rode out of Williamsburg, Wayne for the first and only time in his life kept a diary. His most excited entry described the events of September 6. As evening approached, he led American and French soldiers to just a third of a mile away from Cornwallis' outer ring of forts and redoubts. All through the night, with rain falling constantly, he stood watch over his soldiers as they helped dig the first parallel around Yorktown. During the next two days, more than forty cannon were hauled into the trench. Finally, at three o'clock on the afternoon of September 9, the French opened fire on the British, and two hours later the Americans did the same. The bombardment was so intense that at least one cannon blast was fired every minute. Wayne would always remember the constant crash of the guns, far louder and hotter than anything he experienced at Chadds Ford or Monmouth Courthouse. He was especially amazed at the sight of Cornwallis' magnificent ship with forty-four guns, the *Caron*, catching fire in the night and sinking in the York. Forty-eight hours later, as the bombardment continued, Wayne crawled with soldiers from Pennsylvania and Maryland three hundred feet beyond the first entrenchment. Through the night, as he lay on the ground with musket and cannon balls flying over him, his men joined in digging the second parallel. At dawn on the following day, October 12, the guns in the new trench opened fire on Cornwallis' position.

Wayne knew the British could not hold out much longer, especially when late on the evening of October 14, Colonel Hamilton and Baron de Viomenil, with Wayne's regiments supporting them, took the last two redoubts from the British, thus completing the encirclement of Yorktown. Cornwallis tried to escape across the York River, but a horrific thunderstorm prevented his army from crossing. Finally, on the morning of October 17, as Wayne watched the bombardment from the second parallel, a boy could be seen across the way beating a drum wildly, but in the cannon fire no one could hear him. Then a British officer ran up to the boy, and grabbing hold of a white handkerchief, waved it wildly. "Cease fire!" Wayne shouted. When the guns finally fell silent, the beating of a chamade, the enemy's call for a parley, could be clearly heard down the American and French lines. Wayne ordered a soldier forward to blindfold the redcoat and take him to Washington. The Battle of Yorktown was over, a complete and stunning victory for the Continental Army at last.

Later that day, Wayne made his last diary entry: "17th. The enemy beat the chamade at 10 o'clock, A.M." Searching for an image to capture everything that had happened, Wayne turned to astronomy to explain Cornwallis' defeat. He was not a modern Hannibal, but was instead a meteor that lit up the night sky with a "momentary luster" before falling to the earth never to rise again. Wayne looked back at the long campaign in Virginia, trying to understand how the British had

The Surrender of Lord Cornwallis at Yorktown, October 19, 1781,
by John Trumbull. Yale University Art Gallery.

ever been beaten. He took no credit for Cornwallis' defeat, but instead pointed
to three other generals: "That great & good officer Gen'l Greene first lessened his
glory—he next met a Fabius in that young nobleman—the Marquis Lafayette,
and is now encompassed by a Washington."[38]

On the afternoon of October 19, 1781, as Wayne watched the redcoats and
Hessians march to the surrender field, a British fife and drum corps played the
old sea chantey "Derry Down." A poem, entitled "The World Turned Upside
Down," had recently been set to the melody. The lyrics told the story of "Goody
Bull," symbolizing Great Britain, who long abused her beautiful young daughter,
meaning America, until a farmer, the French, came along to roar in the old
woman's ears and tweak her nose. Soldiers who knew the words sang along as the
humiliated enemy passed before them. "No thanks to you, mother, the daughter
replied, but thanks to my friend here, I've humbled your pride."[39]

The world had turned upside down many times since Wayne played in his
uncle's schoolyard. In those days, France had been the enemy. But twenty-five
years later, the French, now allies of his beloved America, waited with his ragged
men outside of Yorktown. Wayne would never forget the sight of row upon row

of French soldiers standing across the road from him. Some looked somber in black and red, but most were in gleaming white uniforms faced with green, blue, or pink and matching plumes in their hats. Even the lowly drummer boys stood trimmed in silver from head to toe. Now twelve years later, with the world upside down again, he could only guess how many of these same men were victims of their country's revolution. He knew his dear marquis was languishing in a foreign prison, and that the Baron de Viomenil, who had taken the last redoubts with Hamilton, was already dead. Viomenil, who had joined the royal family's escape to Varennes, died later from wounds he received trying to protect them from the mobs at the Tuilleries Palace. Most shocking of all, within the year General Rochambeau would be waiting for his turn at the guillotine.[40]

Perhaps Sharp Delany was right: every nation needed "a Washington" at the helm. Just as cautious as he had been in the Revolution, he still weighed matters deliberately. Now in the spring of 1793, Washington at last made several important decisions. He issued a proclamation of neutrality in the war between France and her enemies, including Great Britain. The United States would "in sincerity and good faith adopt and pursue a conduct friendly and impartial toward the belligerent Powers." Any American who aided France or her opponents would face prosecution. Determined to keep his nation out of war, he would negotiate with the hostile tribes across the Ohio. He appointed three commissioners: Benjamin Lincoln, the general who had formally accepted the British surrender at Yorktown, along with Beverley Randolph, a former governor of Virginia, and Timothy Pickering, a veteran of the Continental Army. They would soon be on their way to a grand council with the Indians at Sandusky on Lake Erie.[41]

But Washington also ordered Wayne to take his men immediately downriver to Fort Washington. If the Indians refused to make peace, then he must "act with the highest vigor." He must head toward the Miami Villages, along the same path St. Clair's doomed army once marched, and there defeat the hostile tribes, if they chose to attack him. For Wayne, the waiting was finally over, and hopefully so was His Excellency's constant criticism. Knox's dispatches confirmed this. "The success of our arms, the honor of the Army and your own reputation," he wrote, depended solely on how Wayne prepared his men. The president, he added, had the "fullest confidence" in his rigorous training, which Knox finally admitted had "given him great satisfaction." While the words seemed small praise after all his efforts, they lifted Wayne's troubled spirit, if only for a moment.[42]

"I Have No Anxiety but for You and Our Children"

In April 1793, General Wayne finally received the orders he had been expecting for almost a year. He must proceed with the army he had so carefully
trained at Legionville to Fort Washington, the outpost on the Ohio River that
sat next to the muddy frontier town bearing the grand name of Cincinnati. He
had prepared his Legion for this campaign from the moment he arrived in Pittsburgh. He taught his men how to load and shoot their muskets quickly, battle
imaginary warriors in the woods, and throw up redoubts around their camp in
a matter of minutes. Wayne was proud of his soldiers; still, he could not help
but worry. What would happen when he received orders to march even deeper
into the woods north of Fort Washington? There in the dark forests and flooded
prairies, surrounded by hundreds, maybe thousands of warriors, would his men
stand and fight or awake to a catastrophe? The president, who was terrified that
the army would stumble into another massacre, could not even bear to mention
the word to Wayne. "Observe the highest degree of caution," he told him, so that
unlike St. Clair, he would never find himself in "a disagreeable situation."[1]

There was nothing new in the orders delivered to Wayne in the spring of 1793.
They were exactly the same as the ones handed to him before he left Philadelphia the previous May. He was still expected to walk a tightrope between war
and peace. He must keep his men in a fever pitch of readiness near Cincinnati.
But at the same time, he must not push them so aggressively that he upset the
upcoming negotiations with the Indians. The commissioners would soon be on
their way from New York City up the Hudson River to Albany and west past Forts
Oswego and Niagara, still in British hands, to meet with the tribes. Washington
and Knox had given the commissioners until August 1 to conclude a treaty that
would allow the Americans to settle north of the Ohio River. If they could not

win an agreement, they were to send a letter of thanks to Wayne for his support, signed by all three men, which would be the signal that the negotiations had failed. The Legion of the United States would then immediately proceed to the Miami Villages, the place that St. Clair's army had failed to reach, and raise a fort there. Knox also ordered Wayne to build smaller posts every sixteen to twenty miles as he marched north, making sure his men took no longer than a day to build each one.[2]

As he prepared his army for their departure from Legionville, Wayne fretted about many things. He had expected life to be easier for his soldiers in the Legion than it had been for his troops in the Continental Army. But his requests on behalf of his men had fallen on deaf ears. Over and over, he had begged Knox for more shirts and shoes for them. He complained they never received adequate winter clothing. Now they were heading into summer, and once again, no clothes for the season had arrived. He asked for more flags and insignia to designate each sublegion, but these, too, had never been sent. He needed experienced officers to assist him, but the promised appointments were always delayed, leaving Wayne to handle the training on his own. He blamed all this on deluded Congressmen, part of a "restless junto," who believed the army, not the Indians or British, was the greatest danger to the republic. They balked at supporting the Legion in the field and some even called for its reduction. Wayne was especially upset that many of his best young officers, who were convinced the army was about to be disbanded, despaired of ever winning a promotion and resigned their commissions.[3]

But there were times when he was just as baffled by the attitudes of Washington and Knox. Wayne wondered if the president and his secretary of war had forgotten that the United States won the western country at the negotiating table in Paris. Even in a world made more complex by the French Revolution, why should they allow Great Britain to maintain forts on American soil? Could they not see that the British were encouraging the Indians to demand the Ohio River as the boundary between themselves and the United States so they could move the Canadian border from the Great Lakes, where the peace treaty had drawn it, farther south to include the entire Ohio Country? Before any settlers crossed the Appalachians and opened farms where government surveyors were plotting out the township lines, the British would already control the territory. They would even encourage Americans to settle among them as Canadian citizens.[4]

Far from being an alarmist, Wayne had rightly guessed what Lord William Grenville, the British foreign secretary, was discussing with top officials in North America, including George Hammond, Great Britain's first ambassador to the United States, and Wayne's old nemesis from the Virginia campaign, John

Graves Simcoe, now the lieutenant governor of Upper Canada. While publicly denying they had encouraged the Indians to oppose the United States, the three officials privately searched for a way to enter the negotiations with the tribes in order to protect Canada. Grenville urged Hammond to tell officials in Washington's administration that their country would gladly give up the forts at Oswego, Niagara, Detroit, and Michillimackinac, but only if an Indian nation was established between the Ohio River and the Great Lakes.[5]

By creating this new state, Grenville believed the Americans would avoid a war they were unprepared to fight, while his nation would secure a buffer between Canada and the United States, continue the fur trade with the tribes, and gain easy access to the Mississippi River through the Indian country. Hammond repeatedly told Grenville as well as Simcoe that the United States would never accept British participation in the negotiations with the Indians. Given the overwhelming hatred Americans felt for England, even to mention such an offer would be an insult, something officials as different as Alexander Hamilton and Thomas Jefferson had both told Hammond. Still Grenville urged his ambassador to carry on with the plans, claiming all the while they came directly from the ailing King George III.[6]

Wayne would not have been surprised to learn that he rightly guessed the British plans for the Ohio Country. But for the moment, in the wet spring of 1793, he was more concerned about organizing the army's move downriver to Fort Washington. James O'Hara, the Legion's quartermaster general, had secured eight boats for supplies, thirty for the soldiers, ten for fodder, eight for horses and oxen, six for the artillery, iron forges, and military stores, and one for hospital supplies. Wayne carefully orchestrated the order the army would travel down the Ohio. A pilot boat would lead the other boats following at a distance of a hundred yards between each. Behind the pilot boat, the right column's rifle corps, dragoons, artillery, and infantry would follow. Next would come the quartermaster's supplies, fodder, and military stores. Wayne and his officers would then proceed in the *Federalist* with the hospital boat right behind them. The left column would bring up the rear, this time with the infantry, artillery, and dragoons coming in order, and the riflemen last.[7]

Wayne had planned everything down to the last detail and still he was not happy. Looking into the Ohio, which had risen steadily after ten straight days of rain, he saw himself going down the river but never ascending it again.[8] This was not the first time that thoughts of death had troubled him. Before most campaigns from Quebec to Savannah, he was certain he would be killed in battle. In the spring of 1793, when the fear returned, he told his friend Sharp Delany, but not the one person he always wrote to when haunted by the prospect of his own mortality: his wife, Polly. He had not heard from her since the previous May when he said goodbye to his family on the way to Pittsburgh. During the year he trained the army at Legionville, he received not one letter from her nor had he written one to her. The distance between them, almost from the moment he left Waynesborough for the Pennsylvania Assembly in 1774 and the Continental Army a year later, widened with every campaign. Since the war ended, the distance had turned first into coldness and finally silence.

Despite the gulf between them, Wayne was stunned to learn on April 28, the day before his army was to depart from Legionville, that Polly had been dead for more than a week. Two letters arrived in camp, one from Delany and the other from his son-in-law William Atlee, telling him that his wife had breathed her last between nine and ten o'clock on the evening of April 18. Another letter was on its way from William Hayman, the husband of Wayne's sister Ann, letting him know that his mother was also dying and would live but a few more days. Hayman was anxious to learn what was to be done with Waynesborough. Should Polly's relatives, the Penrose family, take charge of the place? Should the house be locked up until Wayne's return? Should the "old Negroes" who lived on the estate be cared for or turned out to fend for themselves?[9]

Wayne's shock at his wife's passing was surprising because he had ignored every report of her failing health for months. Letters had come to Legionville describing her steady decline and begging him to write home. Atlee was particularly frustrated with his father-in-law for ignoring his wife, his aged mother, and most especially his daughter, who was pregnant with Wayne's first grandchild. "We would be extremely happy," he wrote in November 1792, if "you would remember you have a Daughter who loves you to excess scarcely equaled." Two months later, Margaretta told her father that both his wife and mother were quite ill, and suggested that maybe he should at least write to his mother. The sting in his daughter's letter finally made Wayne take up his pen and write to her. Showing no concern for Polly or his mother, he instead defended himself against the implied charge that he cared little for his family. He reminded his daughter that she and her brother were infants when he rode off to war. Up until then, he had been an "affectionate and indulgent parent." His devotion to his country, and no lack of feeling on his part, had estranged him from his wife and children. Still Margaretta must believe that, though he seemed to have neglected them, they were never completely lost to him.[10]

But now Polly was truly lost, and after so many years of neglect, the mere thought of his abandoned wife was unbearable to him. Unable to utter her nickname "Polly" or her given name "Mary," he now remembered her as "Maria." He was so distraught that, for just a moment, he seemed not to care that his soldiers were finally boarding the many boats lined up for them in front of Legionville. Coming to his senses, especially after several boats started to leak, Wayne called off the launch set for April 29, writing to Knox that the army would move down the Ohio on the following day once the boats were repaired. He added in a postscript that he was in "a state of torture from the recent loss of my long-loved & much esteemed *Maria.*" Knox, who received the letter after Wayne's army finally left Legionville at eleven o'clock on April 30, never responded with any sympathy. In all the years Knox had known him, Wayne had never shown any concern for his wife nor had anyone in Washington's administration ever met her, either during or after the war. To say anything now, when everyone knew how badly he had treated her, would be useless at best, hypocritical at worst.[11]

How could Wayne have forgotten the beautiful girl he had fallen in love with so quickly some thirty years before? Mary Penrose was the sixteen-year-old friend of his younger sister Ann who had come to visit Waynesborough over the Christmas holidays in 1765. Known for her "modest demeanor and amiability," she was as quiet and shy as young Anthony was lively and gregarious. He had just returned from his first trip to Nova Scotia, where he had lived since the previous spring, and was full of plans for going back next year to Franklin's colony near Halifax. But this trip would have to wait, at least for a few months, since he was smitten with the bashful Mary, whom he had nicknamed Polly. He even took time away from his favorite pastime of foxhunting to be with her.

Polly was just as taken with the tall and handsome young man, so impeccably dressed, elegant in his manners, and passionate about everything, who would turn twenty-one on New Year's Day 1766. Shortly after meeting her, Wayne decided to ask for her hand in marriage. His father had no objection to Mary Penrose as his future daughter-in-law, for she was a good and devout girl just like his wife. Polly's father, Bartholomew Penrose, who had died when she was fourteen, came from a prominent family of merchants, shipbuilders, and landowners in Philadelphia, while her mother Mary traced her lineage to merchants from Barbados. Mrs. Penrose had no objection to Mary, the youngest of her five children, becoming the wife of Anthony Wayne, who already enjoyed the patronage of the most powerful men in Pennsylvania. He would make a fine match for Mary and hopefully they would have a long and happy life together. Anxious to wed before he returned to Nova Scotia, and unwilling to endure a lengthy courtship, Anthony Wayne married Polly Penrose in Christ Church, the most prominent Anglican parish in the city, on March 25, 1766, nearly three months to the day after first meeting her.[12]

Wayne took Polly with him to Nova Scotia in the spring of 1766. The trip was an adventure for him, but an agony for his bride, who had never been so far from home. She was happy to return to Waynesborough by October and rarely left the estate for the remainder of her life. The next eight years were particularly happy ones for Polly. She gave birth to a daughter Margaretta in 1770 and a son Isaac in 1772, and got along well with Wayne's mother and father, who still lived at Waynesborough. They in turn were glad to hand over the day-to-day management of the farm and tannery to their son. The leather business prospered with Wayne selling goods as far away as the West Indies. Like many wealthy landowners, he also became a banker for the local community, loaning money to dozens of his neighbors.[13]

While Polly was content to be a wife and mother, her husband was often restless. When the day's work was done, he liked to ride to the nearby taverns, most especially Howell's Tavern just north of Waynesborough in Tredyffrin Township, to talk politics with the locals. Years later, when he led his army into the Ohio Country, he still remembered the happy days he spent there under the old sycamore tree out front in summer or near the roaring fireplaces inside during winter, and ordered his men to use "Tredyffrin" as a password. From the start of the troubles with England, Wayne took the side of his fellow colonists in debates at the inn, championing their right to govern themselves and dreaming of a day when he could defend their liberty. Before the first shots were fired at Lexington and Concord, he considered himself a dedicated Whig, so much so that he refused to frequent any tavern run by proprietors fond of the crown or Parliament.[14]

Still Wayne came home every night to his wife and family. There was only one time when his socializing embarrassed them. It was in September 1771, at the end of the harvest season, when he again rode over to Howell's Tavern. While drinking with two friends, Jacob Malin and Caleb Jones, a fight broke out between Mrs. Malin, who had come to fetch her husband, and Phoebe Stewart, a tavern maid who resented the intrusion. The two women struck each other and tumbled to the ground. Malin pulled his wife away while Wayne and Jones grabbed hold of the angry Phoebe. This ended the fistfight, but the trouble between the two women continued. Malin swore out a complaint against Stewart, who in turn accused both Wayne and Jones of assaulting her. Even though the judge was a business partner in Franklin's Nova Scotia colony, he thought Wayne guilty enough to charge him a £25 bond, along with £50 for Caleb Jones and £150 for Phoebe Stewart for starting the fight in the first place. The charges against all parties were later dropped.[15]

Whatever unhappiness her husband's brawling might have caused Polly Wayne, it could not compare to the sadness that soon came into her life from an unexpected quarter. On the night of December 16, 1773, a handful of men snuck onto ships of the East India Company in Boston's harbor and threw 342 chests of tea overboard. The effects of the ruined tea darkening the waters around Massachusetts Bay were felt far beyond the colony's shores. An angry Parliament quickly passed the Coercive Acts, which threatened not just Massachusetts but every colony, as her husband explained so many times. The impact of the tea-stained waters soon reached back to Pennsylvania and all the colonies when Parliament passed a new Quartering Act, which turned every American home into a potential barracks, and the Quebec Act, which declared the Ohio Country a part of Canada, trumping the claims of Pennsylvania and Virginia to this fabled land.

Polly Wayne, who had lived in the peaceful valley outside of Philadelphia since her marriage, felt the changes, too, for they ultimately took her "dear Anthony" away from her. First, he went only as far as Howell's Tavern and other local inns to denounce Parliament's actions as "intolerable," but still he returned each night to the great stone house at Waynesborough. But in 1774, he went off to the assembly in Philadelphia and stayed away for weeks at a time. A year later, when he joined the Continental Army, he was gone for months and sometimes years. In the long separations from her husband, the happiness that Mary Penrose had known since first meeting Anthony Wayne at Christmastime in 1765 was shattered forever.[16]

Wayne played a key part in the unhappiness that came into Polly's life. Once he left Waynesborough for politics and the army, he was swept up in a new and exciting life that made him forget his wife and children. When he first went to Philadelphia, he was content to keep company with many of his neighbors, also elected to the assembly, like Richard Peters, the nephew of the minister who married him, his brother-in law John Penrose, and a new acquaintance from York, Thomas Hartley. Another newly elected assemblyman, Sharp Delany, who had emigrated from Ireland and owned an apothecary shop in Philadelphia, soon became his best friend. Away from the cares of his farm and tannery, Wayne spent his days talking politics and his nights frequenting taverns and theaters with his friends from home. But everything changed when he met Dr. Benjamin Rush, the noted physician and prominent intellectual. Wayne shared a love of books and ideas with Rush, but it was the way his new friend brought him into the most glittering salons in Philadelphia that cemented their friendship.[17]

Perfectly dressed in the latest fashions, a witty conversationalist who enjoyed trading barbs with others, and an excellent dancer, Wayne impressed everyone he met. He was comfortable with women, having grown to manhood in the company of his mother Elizabeth, his two sisters Hannah and Ann, his cousin Mary Wayne, who was the daughter of his uncle Gabriel, and later his wife Polly and his daughter Margaretta. But the women of Waynesborough were nothing like the girls who graced the many fine houses of Philadelphia. They talked freely with the men who accompanied them to afternoon teas and evening soirees, never leaving their side, but staying with them to debate politics and dance the night away. Wayne was entranced by them all, but was soon smitten with Sally Robinson, the sister of another new friend, Thomas Robinson, and her best friend Hetty Griffits. They, in fact, spent so much time with Wayne that they were nicknamed his "daughters." The women of the wealthy Biddle family, especially the dark-eyed Ann who would soon marry James Wilkinson, Wayne's brigadier in the Ohio campaign, also fell under the sway of the charming assemblyman.[18]

When Wayne joined the Continental Army, and now came calling in his colonel's uniform, many men, jealous of his appearance and his ability to attract women by merely walking into a room, mocked him as "Dandy Tony," but still the girls flocked to his side. He first understood his newfound power over women when he visited General Philip Schuyler's home north of Saratoga on his way to the failed campaign in Quebec. The general's young daughters, Angelica, Elizabeth, who would marry Washington's aide Alexander Hamilton in 1780, and Margarita, were fascinated by him and made him small favors like cockades for his hat. But finding them "such fine sweet girls," with Angelica being nineteen, Elizabeth only eighteen, and Margarita even younger, Wayne felt a twinge of conscience. Knowing how easily he could have taken advantage of them, and remembering for the moment that he had a wife and a daughter, he wrote about his dilemma to his friend Tom Robinson, who was now a captain in Wayne's battalion. "It would have been cruel to endeavour to win the affection of an innocent good girl," he explained. "I therefore studiously endeavoured to keep out of the way of temptation."[19]

Wayne, who had dreamed so long of becoming a soldier, could hardly believe that, when he finally went off to war, he most missed the company of adoring women. He had come to depend on their admiration almost as a drug. He felt their loss most terribly at Fort Ticonderoga. Here, on the icy rock of Golgotha, he endured the cold, his grieving men, and the specter of Death himself. But he suffered just as much from the lack of charming girls. He was amazed that his fellow officers could take Indian women as their "black" mistresses, something he could never do, not even in this lonely wilderness of ice and snow. His life was so solitary that he worried he had forgotten how to behave in "feminine company." He had only one female friend, Mrs. Udney Hay, the wife of a timber merchant from Quebec. With her husband frequently away on business, she acted as Wayne's hostess at his many dinner parties. In the spring of 1777, when she moved to Albany, a devastated Wayne, along with several of his officers, accompanied her to the town. Not caring that the British might appear any minute on Lake Champlain, they stopped along the way, taking tea, punch, and wine at the house of Mr. Adams and "acting as gayly as if danger was at a distance."[20]

During his long stay at Ticonderoga, Wayne kept up his spirits by writing to his two favorite admirers back in Philadelphia, Sally Robinson and Hetty Griffits. He begged them to write back, especially his favorite "daughter" Sally. "If I could only be favored once a month with a single line from you," Wayne wrote desperately to her, "I should be more than reconciled to remain in this more than bad country."[21] He was devastated to learn in September 1776 that she had married his friend Richard Peters, with Hetty Griffits as her maid of honor. Shortly after her marriage, Sally wrote a short note, consoling her distant friend and reminding him, "I can love my Husband and esteem my friend." Even though Wayne remained close to Sally's husband, who as the secretary of the Board of War kept him informed of all the doings in Congress, he enjoyed reading letters from mutual acquaintances mocking the bridegroom for failing to get his wife pregnant quickly.[22]

Sally's marriage did not stop Wayne from writing to her. He was especially frantic when stories came back to Ticonderoga about the brutality of English and Hessian soldiers as they moved ever closer to Philadelphia. In a dramatic letter, written jointly to Sally and Hetty in February 1777, he told them of his fears upon hearing that "British rebels and the savage auxiliaries were ravaging the Jersies." He could only hope that his two "Heroines" had faced these brutes with fortitude or, even better, had turned their backs on the luxuries of city life and retreated to "a little Country cottage . . . far from the din of War." Wayne confessed he was racked with conflicting emotions when he learned of their danger. Pity, revenge, and even love, though he could not speak the word, raged within him. He described how his soldiers, after learning the women were in danger, clutched their weapons and cried out, "Lead us to Death or Vengeance." Only his sense of duty, which demanded that he and the few soldiers hold off the entire British army if they marched south from Canada, kept him from flying to their side.[23]

Hetty continued to write politely to Wayne, reminding him of all the happy times they had spent together talking about books and plays. If Wayne expected more from her, she was not capable of giving it. But there was no answer from Sally. What he expected of a woman living more than three hundred miles away and now married to his close friend, he never explained in any letter to her. Instead he searched through the works of the playwright Sheridan for words that best captured his undying devotion to Sally Robinson and his loyalty to Richard Peters. Wayne found them in the libretto of Sheridan's *La Duenna*, the story of two sisters pressured by their father into marrying wealthy suitors instead of the men they truly loved. Lost in his imagination behind the lonesome walls of Ticonderoga, he copied out the opera's most popular songs, adding new titles of his own making.

Wayne found the best expression for his undying love for Sally in the lyrics of Sheridan's "Had I a Heart to Falsehood Fram'd," which he renamed "To a young Lady on her expressing some doubts of the Sincerity of a lasting Fidelity in Her Admirer." He saw the strain between his love for Sally and his loyalty to her husband reflected in Sheridan's "Friendship is the Bond of Reason," which he titled, "To a Friend when accused of Endeavouring to Supplant Him in the Affections of a Lady—and deemed by him a breach of Faith and Friendship." While Peters never wrote to him about any such worries, it was a comfort for Wayne, as he copied the lyrics in lonely Ticonderoga, to imagine that he did so: "The faith which to my friend I swore, As a Civil oath I view; But to the Charms which I adore, 'Tis Religion to be true."[24]

But even when swept away by the charms of other women, Wayne never completely forgot Polly. He sent her instructions on caring for their farm at Waynesborough, including when to lime the fields and hire workers for planting and harvesting, and how to manage the education of their children. When she became depressed over their prolonged separation, he tried to lift her spirits, not by promising to return home soon, but by explaining the causes of the unending war to her. The colonists had not sought this fight, he reminded her, but when pressed to defend their liberty, they took up arms like men and now must fight to the finish. No matter how dark the day or long the night, Wayne assured his wife that America would rise victorious. However, there would be times when he, too, sank into near despair, worried that the victory he so loudly proclaimed would never come to pass or that he would not survive the trials coming into his life because of his dedication to his country. Then no amount of flirting with other women could fill the terrible void in his heart, and he must reach out to Polly. "I have no anxiety but for you and our children," he confessed in these troubling moments.[25]

Wayne wrote his most heartfelt letters to Polly, both before every battle when his mind raced ahead to what might occur, especially his own death, and after every battle when he looked back on what had happened, including what had gone wrong. At Three Rivers, where he faced his first test of combat, he dashed off only a few lines. But later his letters became more detailed with some of the most memorable ones written before and after the fight in the fog at Germantown. At seven o'clock on the evening of October 3, 1777, he began a letter to Polly acknowledging that he always wrote to her in trying situations. "I have often wrote to you on the eve of some unexpected and uncertain event," he admitted, "but never on any equal to the present." He imagined how many brave men would die attacking General Howe's headquarters on the following morning, but for the moment he was more excited than frightened by his prospects. He was certain the Continental Army would defeat the redcoats. He could already see himself marching in the autumn light, covered with laurels, at the head of his regiment into Philadelphia. He needed no poetry from Sheridan to express what he felt in his depths. This time he could describe to Polly the emotions racing through him in poetry of his own making. "My heart sits lightly in its mansion—every artery beats in unison," he excitedly confessed, "and I feel unusual ardor for the *duel*."[26]

But even Wayne, so certain of his ability to peer into the future, had to admit that no mortal man could perfectly see what lay ahead, nor could he be certain of the exact day he would die. Maybe he was wrong about riding into Philadelphia wrapped in clouds of glory. Perhaps he would fall in the "bloody track" and expire in the last rays of the "setting sun." Either way, whether he lived or died, he assured Polly that it did not matter for in the end America would triumph. He had intended to write to his mother, his two sisters, and his mother-in-law, but there was simply no time. "I am called to Council," he explained. "Kiss our dear little children for me," he added hurriedly. "May God protect you and shield you. Adieu my dear Polly and believe me ever yours."[27]

When the battle was lost, at Germantown and so many other places, Wayne turned again to his wife. He, in fact, wrote more about what had gone wrong to her than anyone else, including General Washington. While he survived the attack on Howe's headquarters, nothing went as planned. His men fought bravely, almost savagely with their bayonets, striking down the redcoats without mercy, all to avenge the deaths of their comrades murdered in the Paoli Massacre. Still they became confused in the mist, fire, and smoke that turned the day into night. Shot at by their fellow soldiers, they retreated from the town. "The fog and this mistake prevented us from following a victory," he explained, "that in all Human probability would have put an end to the American War." He told her how his horse fell dead beneath him, shot through the breast and flank, while a bullet grazed his hand and a cannon blast bruised his foot. Polly was not to worry, for "upon the whole it was a Glorious day." The army had failed, but would succeed in the next battle that was surely only days away.[28]

But while his letters to his wife were beautifully written, perfectly structured like pieces of fine literature, with rising and falling action and stirring imagery, except for the "My dear girl" in the salutation and the "Adieu dear girl" in the farewell there was little affection in between for Polly. Never once in his many vivid descriptions of combat did Wayne ask his wife how she was, what her cares might be, or what she hoped for the future. In contrast, at least at the start of the war, Polly's letters to her husband were filled with her deep love. She fretted that his first campaign took him to frozen "Quebeck" while she and their children stayed warm before the fires of Waynesborough. That he worried about them at so great a distance, hoping the British would never force them to flee in the night, touched her deeply. She would give anything if she could fly to her husband's side. "O my Dear if a hundred miles' journey would afford me but one day with you with the most pleasure would I set off this moment to meat one that is sincere and dear to me," wrote Polly in her tiny scribble filled with misspellings. She tried to be brave and did not beg him to come home. She understood how much this war in defense of America's liberty meant to him. She knew Anthony's courage would last until the day of victory, but she could not help but wonder if his health would hold out, too.[29]

As fearless as she tried to be, Polly missed her husband terribly. Whenever she heard a rider coming up the road to Waynesborough, she ran to the front door and threw it open. She always hoped she would see him bounding off his horse and running to embrace her and their children. But it was never Anthony, and so she wept. Once, in the spring of 1776, she went by wagon to Philadelphia with little Isaac and a servant, hoping to see him, only to learn that he was on his way to far off "Quebeck," and she wept again. At times, all she could do was cry; at other times, all she could do was pray. Bring him home, Almighty God, she implored, but if you must take him, then welcome him into paradise. Polly found one more thing she could do for her absent husband. She could follow his instructions about Waynesborough to the letter and keep his farm and tannery running smoothly. "My Dear," she wrote in May 1776, "you may depend on my takeing all the Care that lays in my power in regard your Biseness and farm." This would not be easy, she explained to her husband, because with laborers scarce and work plentiful, she had to pay hired men at least £3 a month and could never get them for more than one month at a time.[30]

Polly was anxious for her husband to return home, but when he had a chance to visit Waynesborough before Brandywine, he did not take it. With his men camped only twenty miles away, he never came to see Polly or the children. Instead he stayed at his headquarters at Graeme Park, the home of Elizabeth Graeme Ferguson, a wealthy and cultured woman nine years older than Wayne, who was famous for writing poetry and for abandoning her Loyalist husband. Polly never questioned her husband about Mrs. Ferguson. Instead, waiting for news of his many battles, she slept every night in a chair before the fireplace at Waynesborough. When she finally heard heavy footsteps coming toward the house, she ran to the door, opened it wide, and called out in the dark, "Did you beat the British, General?" A soldier in a bright red uniform answered, "No, madam; the British beat the General." General Grey had sent the major to hunt down Wayne after the surprise attack near the Paoli Tavern. His soldiers searched the house, even thrusting their swords into the feather beds on the chance he might be hiding there, before leaving at daylight.[31]

As the war dragged on, and Wayne still did not come home, Polly no longer wrote to him with the same affection. She realized Anthony cared little for her troubles, and even when he did, he showed no sympathy, writing to her instead about patriotism and honor as if he was talking to his troops. "I thought you had a mind far above being Depressed at a little unfavourable Circumstance," he told her after the British captured Philadelphia, a matter of "no more Consequence" than the occupation of Boston or New York. He assured a frightened Polly that cities might fall, but the war would go on until victory was won at last. However, his detailed descriptions of battle, which seemed more the comments of a stranger than a loving husband, only increased the distance between them.[32]

As Polly wrote less frequently to her husband, Wayne complained that either her letters were not getting through to him, or maybe she had stopped writing altogether. While she continued to write, always claiming that she gave her mail to a Continental Army officer so they would be safely delivered, her letters were much shorter and colder. She still reported how things were going at Waynesborough, including the various illnesses of family and friends. She kept up her sewing for him and always asked if the new shirts and socks she made had arrived at whatever camp he was stationed. But all her descriptions of longing to be with him and flying to the door at the sound of an approaching horse disappeared from her letters. She also stopped referring to "their" children and now wrote to Wayne about all the happenings in the life of "my daughter" and "my son." She even lost any interest in coming to see him.[33]

Wayne had asked her to meet him only twice. Just days before the Battle of Brandywine, he told her to bring the children in a wagon to Naaman's Creek outside Philadelphia. She did as her husband had instructed, but could not find him among the crowds fleeing the capital as the British approached. They missed each other, with Wayne heading to Chadds Ford and Polly returning home with Margaretta and Isaac. Once during the following winter, he asked her to visit him at Valley Forge, but sensing his growing coldness toward her, she was reluctant to travel, claiming she was ill and planning to go to Maryland instead to restore her health. After Wayne fell completely under the spell of two celebrated beauties, Polly no longer wished to fly to her husband's side, while he never asked her to visit him again. The two women who would come between Wayne and his wife more than any of his previous flirtations were Catharine Littlefield, the wife of

General Nathanael Greene, and Mary Vining, the ward of Caesar Rodney, Delaware's delegate to the Continental Congress.[34]

Wayne met Catharine Greene at General Washington's headquarters at Valley Forge. She was, by all accounts, a stunning woman who most men fell in love with at first sight. She was known for violet eyes, her glossy black hair, and her translucent complexion. Her devotion to her husband was as legendary as her beauty. Catharine was only nineteen when she married Nathanael Greene, twelve years her senior, in July 1774. When the war broke out the following year, she could not bear to be away from him for long and followed him everywhere, caring little for the danger. She came first to Dorchester Heights as the Continental Army made ready to bomb Boston. She had ridden in a carriage all the way from Rhode Island even though she was pregnant. Upon meeting the army's commanding general, she told him if her child was a boy, she would name him George Washington Greene, which a short time later she proudly did. She next followed Greene to New York City, arriving in Lower Manhattan on the evening before the British launched their invasion of Long Island. She came back to her husband's side right before the disaster at Brandywine and returned again at Valley Forge, where she lived with him first in a log hut and then in the house of a local Patriot.[35]

The daring spirit of Catharine Greene, and not merely her great beauty, made her a favorite of the long list of men who came her way, including General Washington, foreign officers like the Marquis de Lafayette and Baron Steuben, and finally, Anthony Wayne. In Mrs. Greene, he immediately recognized a kindred spirit. She had a keen mind and was an avid reader, who could talk for hours about the latest books from Europe, including the novels and plays that Wayne adored. She enjoyed mocking the boorish people they both knew by making references to their favorite literary characters. She had a biting wit and could exchange barbs with Wayne and all the men who swirled about her on the dance floor, an entertainment which, like Wayne, she could keep up for hours. Wayne, a lover of elegant fashion, also admired her for her perfect wardrobe in the midst of war. She made sure before every trip to visit her husband that she had spent a small fortune on the smartest dresses. Yet Catharine had a dark cast to her character and like Wayne was prone to depression, a common trait that strengthened the bond between them.[36]

Upon their first meeting, Wayne fell hopelessly in love with her. There would be times during the war when friends gossiped that General Greene had another enemy to worry about besides the British and that enemy was Anthony Wayne, who seemed more a suitor than a friend to his wife. However, Greene never wor-

Catharine Littlefield Greene. Image copyright
© The Metropolitan Museum of Art. Image Source:
Art Resource, NY.

ried that the pair had crossed the line of mutual devotion into something more intimate. Nor did the gossip that swirled about General Wayne and Mrs. Greene ever interfere with their lifelong friendship. After the war ended, the two carried on a regular correspondence that continued for the rest of their lives. Wayne filled his letters with a deep concern for Catharine's happiness that he never expressed to Polly. He especially missed her after he moved to Pittsburgh and then Legionville. When she failed to write, he complained that the icy wind whipping through the thin walls of his tent did not "bite so keen as kindness past forget," trying his best to paraphrase a song from Shakespeare's *As You Like It*. He remained so enamored of the beautiful Caty that he was writing to her at the very moment news arrived that Polly was dead.[37]

Despite his love for Catharine Greene, an equally fascinating woman came into Wayne's life as the Continental Army prepared to leave Valley Forge. In May

John André's sketch of Mary Vining.
Courtesy of the Delaware Historical Society.

1778, a soldier who identified himself only as Captain Brown arrived at Wayne's tent and offered him a finely worked inlaid sword. The soldier, who had come from Wilmington, told him the sword was a gift from a lady who also sent this message: "I have been anxious to get it to you before, but the silversmith would not put it in my power." Wayne guessed that the present had come from the beautiful Mary Vining. He had met her briefly before the Battle of Brandywine when Lafayette took him along to meet John Vining, a delegate to the Continental Congress from Delaware, at his home in nearby Wilmington. Lafayette was quickly taken with Vining's sister, the charming Mary. She was tall and graceful with dark eyes framed by long eyelashes and dark hair piled high on her head. She flirted with Lafayette in perfect French with an accent heard only at Versailles. She seemed completely taken with the marquis, ignoring Wayne completely, until she suddenly whirled about and asked him what he had to offer her. Wayne found himself for a moment speechless at the pretty twenty-three-year-old's startling question. He finally muttered that as long as he lived his sword would be at her command. Looking at the heavy weapon he carried at his side, she answered, "For such a knight a sword should be graceful as his wit. You need, my general, a suaver sword."[38]

Wayne was grateful to Mary for the favor of the sword and proud that he had won the affections of so great a beauty. But with the Continental Army preparing to meet the British at Monmouth Courthouse, he had no time to pursue her. Nor did he seek her out in the following winter when General Washington sent him on furlough to Philadelphia to lobby the Pennsylvania assembly for more food and clothing for his troops. There would be time for Mary Vining later. For now, he was happy to pursue the sea of women waiting for him in the capital city. Wayne had already been warned by his friend Colonel Stewart that things had greatly changed in Philadelphia during the yearlong occupation of the city by the British. Before Brandywine, a man could enjoy flirting with innocent girls, like Sally Robinson and Hetty Griffits. But once the redcoats marched into the city, the bonds of morality governing relations between the sexes had completely broken down and women were now much more aggressive. A delighted Wayne discovered this for himself in the winter of 1779. He wrote to Colonel Stewart that so many women were pursuing him that he rarely stayed with any of them longer than an hour or two. "Like the bee," he explained, "I move from flower to flower and sip the honey from each rose."[39]

But suddenly, finding himself pursued by countless women, and perhaps fearing the loss of his very soul, he returned home to Waynesborough, not just once but three times over the winter and spring of 1779. What Polly had dreamed of at the start of the war finally came true. The front door of her family's stone house flew open and there stood her dear Anthony. For just a moment, he was so happy to be back with her, nine-year-old Margaretta, and little Isaac, who just turned seven, that he thought about leaving the army. Even the pleasures of wanton Philadelphia had lost their hold over him. For the first time in his military career, he wrote to friends that he had tired of war. The brutality of the British, who raped women, burned whole villages, and stole anything of value they came across, made the valor of war seem hollow. He brooded to Colonel Stewart that a "sanguine God" must require all this "human gore."[40]

However, he soon grew restless and wrote to Colonel Butler, the man whose bones would lay unburied on the bluff where he was murdered by Indians and whom Wayne was now on his way down the Ohio to avenge, that he must flee the simple pleasures of his farm, his children, and his wife, or he would never be ready to fight again. "I must try and get away from this place," he confessed, "the luxuriancy of the soil, the domestic sweets and the other pleasures and amusements which hourly present themselves have debauched me from the field." But whether he meant the field of battle or the salons of Philadelphia, he did not say. Even though he would be taking up his own light corps, it was still hard for him to leave his family. He made sure he sent barrels of beef, salt, and veal back to Polly.[41]

During the following winter, he ran headlong into Mary Vining, the woman who sent him the sword two years before. With the Continental Army now camped at Morristown, Wayne returned on furlough to Philadelphia. He and Mary were soon inseparable. They took sleigh rides together through the country-side, came arm in arm to teas among the best set in the city, and spent their evenings at dinners, dances, and the theater. Even when French officers gathered around Mary Vining, she seemed to have eyes only for Wayne. Many proposed marriage, including Axel Ferson, the rumored lover of Marie Antoinette, but she clearly had her sights set on the married Anthony Wayne. For the first time in the war, Wayne's officers grumbled that he ignored them, and even worse, that he had completely abandoned his family. He cared little about the gossip and instead willingly broke the law to make his "favorite fair," his nickname for Mary, happy. He asked a British officer, who had been taken prisoner after the raid on Stony Point, to buy him the best English fabric for sale in New York City once he returned there following a prisoner exchange. Wayne, who had scolded Sally Robinson and Hetty Griffits in the earlier, more innocent days of the Revolution, for failing to boycott tea, now openly flaunted the ban on trading with the enemy at the request of dear "Molly," another nickname for Miss Vining.[42]

But then, somewhat guilt-ridden, he went back home to Polly in March 1780. This time he loved being on his farm with his wife and children so much that he lost interest in his nation's political squabbles. "I have become so much domesticated that I am almost totally ignorant of the current of politics in the *Magnum Concilium* of States or State," he wrote to Francis Johnston, an old friend whom he had known since they were both elected to the Pennsylvania Assembly in 1774. He despised the politicians from whom he must beg help for his soldiers as "little minds" who could only make decisions on the "tottering basis of momentary popularity." Not a man given to prayer, he had come to the conclusion that only God through the "Interposition of Providence" could save his beloved America from ruin. Luckily, God had help in the "wisdom, virtue and fortitude of our good General," George Washington.[43]

Leaving war and politics in the hands of God, it was only the summons of Washington that called him away from Waynesborough and back to the humiliation of Bull's Ferry in the summer of 1780. He had gone off to Philadelphia in June, hoping to return quickly to Waynesborough, but found an express letter from His Excellency ordering him there to rejoin the army immediately. For the only time in the many years of separation between them, Wayne admitted that he was "deprived from the pleasure of visiting you." He was so hurried that he must leave the carriage, the mares, and his servant Caesar who had come with him behind in Philadelphia. He could write only a few fleeting lines to Polly that for once carried a warmth he never expressed in his previous letters. "I shall write you the first opportunity—I really am disappointed & distressed—but hope for better times. God bless you & to his protection I commit you & our little people. Adieu—farewell a *long adieu*—but that we may again meet is the sincere wish of your affectionate Anty Wayne."[44]

But this latest visit with her husband could not completely repair Polly's marriage. The rumors of Wayne's dalliances were now all too common. Even the British knew that Wayne could not resist the charms of the many women who came his way. Colonel André spent much of "The Cow-chace" describing Wayne's pursuit of a beautiful nymph as his soldiers looked for cattle to feed Washington's hungry troops. Whether truly a goddess, as André sometimes described her, or a camp follower abandoned by the British, as he also implied, the love of "mad Anthony" for women was whispered in both camps. For Polly, confirmation of her husband's infidelity came when Sharp Delany accidentally forwarded a letter to her in the summer of 1780 that Wayne had addressed to "Molly." The note was meant for Mary Vining, not his wife. Not long afterward, Polly made a trip to Philadelphia without telling her husband, probably to check on the rumors about Mary Vining herself. The following October she told Sharp Delany, who was visiting Waynesborough, that she was furious at Wayne for ignoring her. As she refused to write a "scolding letter" to her faithless husband, she would not write to him at all, at least for now. When passing through Philadelphia the following spring, on his way to join Lafayette in Virginia, Wayne never rode out to his farm to face Polly or to say goodbye.[45]

However, he also did not say goodbye to Mary Vining. Before heading to Virginia, he checked on whether the cloth he illegally purchased for her had ever arrived. But instead of saying farewell in person, he asked a friend to tell her that "she will ever live in my fond memory." He may have loved his "favorite fair," but felt no more compulsion to be faithful to her than to his wife. In the coming years, as he campaigned in Virginia and beyond, there would be still more women in his life. He would keep memories of his fleeting romances alive in letters tucked away in the great leather trunk he carried with him to preserve his correspondence. He saved notes, too, from women who asked if he remembered them, and from others who, knowing him for only a few days, could not forget him. One such woman was Mary Byrd, the mistress of Westover on the James River, whom he met while serving with Lafayette. "I shall always retain the highest sense of your politeness, & humanity, & take every opportunity of testifying my gratitude," she wrote. "May every felicity attend you in this life."[46]

As he grew older, with his body often swollen from gout and his chestnut hair turned white even before he powdered it, Wayne no longer held the same power over women. He discovered this for himself when he visited the salons of Philadelphia for the last time in the spring of 1792 before leaving for Pittsburgh. He expected the "all-conquering Miss Alexander," a beautiful young woman who was the toast of society, to fall madly in love with him, as Sally Robinson, Hettie Griffits, and the Schuyler girls had done nearly twenty years before. Wearing a new blue uniform trimmed in gold, he waited to be introduced as the Legion's commander in chief, but she passed him by, preferring to flirt with the many younger and less accomplished men who filled the room. Even with this disgrace, "Alexander" joined "Tredyffrin," along with "Robinson," "Griffits," and "Vining," as passwords for his soldiers on the Ohio frontier.[47]

But with all these women, including two whom he loved more than others, Catharine Greene and Mary Vining, there was always Polly. Even when she stopped writing to him, he never stopped writing to her, at least not until the final months of her life. When he left for Virginia in 1781, he was at the peak of his fame, and could easily throw away a wife who cared so lovingly for his farm and his children. But in the dark days ahead, when he fell from the heights of glory and knew only failure, he often remembered the girl he had married and the life he once led with her. Then he thought of the fields and meadows of Waynesborough, so carefully spaced behind chestnut fences, the whitewashed barn, and all the horses and cows. Looking back, he seemed an ancient Roman not yet called away to war and happy in the "Sabine fields" of his youth.[48]

As he once searched through Sheridan's lyrics to express his love for Sally Robinson, the first of many women who crossed his path during and after the Revolution, so now he searched through poetry for words to describe what he had lost. He copied out "The Old Soldier," not for these other women, but for the bride of his youth who rarely wrote to him.

> Once gay in life, & free from anxious care,
> I thro' the furrows drove the shining share,
> I saw my waving fields with plenty crowned,
> & Yellow Ceres joyous smile around;
> Till rous'd by Freedom at my Country's call,
> I left my peaceful home and *gave up all*,
> Now forced alas! in *distant climes* to tread,
> This crazy body longs to join the dead;

Ungrateful country! when the danger's o'er,
Your *bravest* sons, cold charity implore,
Ah! heaven for me a sympathetic sigh,
& wipe the falling tear from sorrow's eye.[49]

He never truly went home to those fields, not at the close of the Revolution nor in the decade after, not even when he had the chance. Now, in the spring of 1793, he was hundreds of miles from Waynesborough, traveling down the Ohio on yet another campaign. As his flotilla approached the small settlement of Marietta, named for the doomed French queen, where Indians had murdered upward of 150 people in the vicinity during the previous year, he allowed his men to go ashore. If his soldiers met the survivors of Indian raids, they might better understand why they had been ordered west. The town's leaders took him on a tour of Campus Martius, the huge fort at the center of Marietta, and another stockade to the north, which they built after St. Clair's defeat. Wayne's mood, which had been downcast since leaving Legionville, brightened as he inspected the sturdy outposts. But when the settlers led him to the farms that surrounded their town, laid out just like the New England villages from where they had come, he was visibly upset and ordered his men back on their boats. Seeing the fields measured so perfectly, after he had abandoned Polly and Waynesborough, was unbearable to him.[50]

They did not go ashore again until May 6 when they finally arrived at Cincinnati. Three hundred people lined the river to greet him, including Arthur St. Clair, no longer the commander of the army, but still the governor of the Northwest Territory. All animosity between himself and Wayne disappeared completely. The hour was too desperate for their nation to carry on petty grievances from their younger days. Happy to see St. Clair again, Wayne soon became restless as the town's celebration wore on. After seeing the enticements in Cincinnati that might induce his men to flee, as he once fled to the pleasures of Philadelphia, he ordered them to set up camp a mile downriver. In a few weeks, he would learn that his mother had died the day before he landed in Cincinnati. Knowing he had ignored her just as much as his wife, he went into a depression that haunted him for the rest of the campaign. Standing at the edge of the wilderness his army must enter someday, Wayne took little comfort in remembering he had abandoned his family not for any flesh-and-blood woman, but for another more elusive one. Like other men, he had gone off to war to defend his nation's liberty, but throughout the Revolution, he always imagined America as a woman. More demanding than any earthly creature, and more unpredictable even than Madame Fortune, she was a mystery whose future lay unrevealed to him. She could be faithless, too, especially to soldiers like Wayne who served her best. But still he had given up everything to rescue her and could not abandon her now.

Wayne had tried to tell Margaretta weeks before that he had no choice; he must defend America. The soldiers he had brought into the wilderness had no choice, either; they must defend her, too. When the tents of his army went up in neatly ordered rows along the Ohio, General Anthony Wayne, commander in chief of the Legion of the United States, named his new camp Hobson's Choice after the famous London stable owner who always made his customers take the horse nearest the door. Like them, General Wayne and his troops had only one choice; not in the horses they would ride, but in the fact that they must protect America, a woman more beautiful and faithless than Madame Fortune, to their last dying breaths.[51]

"They Ought to Unite
as a Band of Brothers"

Describing Hobson's Choice to Secretary Knox, Wayne noted his new camp on the Ohio did not face south toward the river, but north toward the woods where his Legion would one day face the warriors who humiliated St. Clair. Here on a flat plane a mile west of Fort Washington, he built huts for his men, larger quarters for his officers, and a house for himself in that order. Past the swampy ground in front of the camp lay the Ohio Country that stretched all the way north to the huge freshwater Great Lakes and west to the still mysterious Mississippi. When his men rose every morning, they looked directly at the land they had come west to win from the Indians and the British. To accomplish this, Wayne would train his men at Hobson's Choice as he had at Legionville. They would maneuver on a new parade ground, practice loading and shooting their guns quickly, and fight imaginary battles in the woods every Sunday afternoon. He would also make sure his men stayed away from the Gomorrah of Cincinnati where "Caitiff wretches" poured the "ardent poison" of whiskey that could ruin his army.[1]

If Wayne thought his plans for Hobson's Choice would impress Washington, he was wrong. Two months after setting up his camp, he received an angry letter from Knox, brimming with presidential fury, asking why Wayne had taken his Legion downriver from Cincinnati. While there was no chance that Wayne would order his soldiers into the cramped quarters of Fort Washington, Knox still listed the reasons why they should never have moved there in the first place. The price of rations would now increase. The cattle would arrive even stringier and the flour would have more of a chance of spoiling. If finally ordered to fight, Wayne's army would have a longer way to go from Hobson's Choice than Fort Washington. But most terrible of all, Wayne's aggressive move might endanger the work of Benjamin Lincoln, Beverley Randolph, and Timothy Pickering. The

Indians would refuse to sign a treaty. They might even murder the three commissioners as they had killed Captain Trueman and Colonel Hardin. Their bloody deaths would be on Wayne's head.[2]

Wayne, who had never criticized Washington since the dark days between Germantown and Valley Forge, did not do so now. But he still considered the president wrongheaded in believing his commissioners could win a treaty with the Indians. Wayne understood that Washington was as cautious today as he had been while commanding the Continental Army. But caution at this late hour simply blinded the president to reality. Wayne saw this more clearly than ever from his house at Hobson's Choice. Looking past the ancient forests that extended as far as the eye could see, broken only in a few places by prairies and swamps, he believed the tribes dwelling there would never give up without a fight. They were not banditti, as the president and his secretary of war once labeled them, but were instead a grand confederacy. They had formed a living chain around the green sea that stretched beyond the Ohio to keep the United States from taking this beautiful country away from them.[3]

While Washington and Knox might disagree with him, Wayne was correct that the tribes at the eastern end of the Ohio Country were determined to hold this land forever. They had settled here only recently; at the very same time, in fact, that the Waynes were establishing their farm and tannery in Chester County, Pennsylvania. The tribes were only allowed into the territory when the Six Nations, whom many called the Iroquois or "Snakes," no longer claimed the land as their private hunting grounds. For Indians who migrated there, the Ohio Country was a refuge from fighting elsewhere on the continent. The land was rich beyond belief. In the forests and grasslands, the men could hunt deer, bear, buffalo, and a long list of furbearing animals to feed their people and trade with the French and English for manufactured goods, especially guns, cloth, and whiskey. They could fish in the many rivers and streams while the women grew corn, squash, and beans in the deep soil of the bottomlands.[4]

The Wyandot, a remnant of the once mighty Huron, came first, fleeing from wars with the Iroquois in Canada, and settling south of Lake Erie along the Sandusky River. For all they had suffered, the other tribes, who followed them into Ohio, called them the grandfathers. They kept copies of every treaty signed with the white man. The Miami, known as fearsome warriors and masterful farmers, followed the Wyandot from Canada. They headed down rivers named after them, before settling along the Wabash and Maumee River Valleys. A short time later, the Seneca, themselves members of the dreaded Iroquois Confederation, left their homes along the Mohawk River. They headed west across the southern edge of Lake Erie and settled on both sides of the Cuyahoga River. Called the Mingo, a nickname that also meant "Snakes," they welcomed refugees from other tribes like the Cayuga, Munsee, and Erie to live with them.[5]

The Ottawa led the last tribes into Ohio. They came from Canada and settled near the Miami, often accompanied by members of their brother tribes, the Pottawatomi and Chippewa. They were skilled traders who collected furs from other Indians, traded them at Fort Detroit, and returned to their villages loaded down with manufactured goods for distribution. The Shawnee, considered even greater warriors than the Miami, arrived next from the south. They remembered wandering across a body of water, settling for a time in Pennsylvania and then west across the Ohio, before heading down the Appalachians to escape the wrath of the Iroquois. Everywhere they went they left their name, from the town of Savannah to the Sewanee River, before returning north to the valleys of the Scioto and Great Miami Rivers. The Delaware, who came last into the Ohio Country, had welcomed William Penn to his colony before being pushed west into the rugged hills along the Muskingum and Tuscarawas Rivers. Suffering much at the hands of the white man, they were honored as the uncles of the tribes. For all these Indians, the war to hold onto their new homeland, which began in Jumonville Glen in 1754, had never ended and still continued as Wayne watched them from his house at Hobson's Choice.[6]

But who led these many tribes? This was a question that troubled Wayne throughout the spring of 1793. He finally got his answer when a young man with bright red hair came into his camp asking to join the Legion. He was twenty-three-year-old William Wells, who had lived with the Indians since he was four-teen. Warriors had captured Wells and three friends while they were hunting bears near Louisville on the Kentucky frontier. They took the boys across the Ohio River where Wells was separated from the rest and marched two hundred miles along the Wabash River to the Miami town of Kenapakomoko. Here he was adopted into the family of the aged warrior Kaweahatta, the Porcupine, and given the name Apekonit, meaning "wild carrot" for the color of his hair. His older brothers finally found him after searching for five years. By then, he considered himself a Miami and barely remembered living among the whites. He was even married to a young Wea woman and had a child. Apekonit returned to Kentucky for a visit, but quickly hurried back to the Miami. A short time later, after American soldiers carried off his wife and child, he distinguished him-self as a warrior fighting against General Harmar's army. The Miami war chief, Michikinikwa, was so impressed with his bravery that he gave his daughter Sweet Breeze to him as his second wife.[7]

Wells told Wayne that Michikinikwa, better known among the Americans as Little Turtle, was the mastermind behind St. Clair's defeat. Little Turtle had won fame among his people for defeating Augustin Mottin de La Balme, a French cavalry officer and veteran of the Seven Years' War who fought with the Americans in the Revolution. Late in 1780, when Wayne was struggling to avert a mutiny in the Pennsylvania Line, La Balme launched an elaborate scheme to capture Fort Detroit from the British. Leading a hundred men down the Ohio to Kaskaskia, he then traveled back up the Wabash toward the Miami Villages, attacking Indian towns and British trading posts along the way. He planned to cross the portage to the Maumee, follow that river to its mouth, and head overland to Detroit, which he would take by surprise. But at dawn on November 5, 1780, not far from Kenapakomoko, where young Wells would soon live, Little Turtle led a daring raid against Le Balme's fortified camp on the Eel River, killing the Frenchman and most of the sixty men still with him. Nearly a dozen years later, as General St. Clair prepared to march toward the Miami Villages, the tribes chose Little Turtle to lead them against the American army. They were certain if he could defeat La Balme, he could do the same to St. Clair.[8]

From Wells' own eyewitness testimony, Wayne learned how Little Turtle was able to defeat St. Clair's soldiers on that terrible morning in November nearly two years before. His methods for preparing his troops were as masterful as Wayne's. He first made certain that the American soldiers were kept under constant surveillance. Setting up his headquarters at a place called Roche de Boeuf, a huge limestone outcropping in the rapids of the Maumee River, two hundred miles north of Cincinnati, he sent scouting parties under a young Shawnee warrior named Tecumseh to spy on Fort Washington. With the Ottawa chief Egushawa, a son of Pontiac, acting as his lieutenant, Little Turtle constantly monitored St. Clair's movements and troop strength. He also implemented a new method for supplying his army in the field. He organized his fourteen hundred warriors into groups of twenty that moved independently from one another. Hunters from every group brought game into their respective camps at noon each day, thus making sure the warriors were regularly fed.

As soon as St. Clair started north from Fort Washington, Little Turtle sent his war parties, gathered from more than a dozen tribes, toward the approaching army. In late October, they crossed the St. Mary's River. By early November, they moved into position around St. Clair's army now stumbling toward the Wabash. Little Turtle's scouts reported that the American general, clearly not a well man, never fortified his camp at night. Even knowing these facts, Little Turtle still worried that an attack on the American army would not be easy. But after his scouts told him St. Clair had sent his First Regiment back to Fort Jefferson, he decided to be as bold as he had been on the morning he struck La Balme.

At dawn on November 4, 1791, as his fourteen hundred warriors let out an ear-piercing cry, Little Turtle launched his attack. He sent Wapacomegat, a Mississauga from Canada, and his war party directly into the Kentucky militia. At the same moment, he ordered his son-in-law's warriors to gun down the artillery officers. They fell before them like target practice. Apekonit and his men then rushed up the bluff toward the big guns and killed the soldiers huddled there in hand-to-hand combat. He hacked so many Americans to death with his tomahawk that he could no longer lift his arm. The bloodshed finally ended, not when the last of St. Clair's men escaped from the battlefield, as the Americans believed, but when Little Turtle gave the signal to stop the killing. Before leaving the battlefield, he ordered his warriors to collect the cannon he so feared and throw them into the Wabash.[9]

Why Apekonit decided to leave the Miami and live among the Americans again was unclear. He had met General Putnam at the negotiations with the Wabash Indians in 1792, where he served as an interpreter, and was greatly impressed with his generosity. He also regretted the many Americans he killed at St. Clair's defeat and worried he might have murdered his own relatives. Years later his children, the descendants of Little Turtle, would claim that Apekonit made a pact with their grandfather to pursue peace together. Little Turtle would try to influence the Indians, while Apekonit, now William Wells once again, would work among the Americans. Anthony Wayne wondered himself why this young man, after shedding so much American blood, would ask to join his army. He feared he might be a spy. But after interviewing him for several hours, he decided Wells was trustworthy and hired him as a "confidential agent."[10]

Wells had provided valuable insights to Wayne about the leadership and fighting methods of the Indian confederation arrayed against him. But he also clarified the specific way the tribes in the Ohio Country worked with British officials. The key rested in their agents, enlisted by the Canadian Indian Department, who lived among the tribes, supplying guns, powder, and ammunition, and encouraging them to resist the American advance across the Ohio every step of the way. Chief among these intermediaries were the Girty Brothers: Thomas, James, George, and Simon. Born in Pennsylvania and close to Wayne in age, the brothers endured traumatic childhoods growing up on the colonial frontier. When Delaware warriors captured their family, the four brothers, along with their mother and younger half-brother, watched as their stepfather was tortured and finally killed by the Indians. The family was broken up, parceled out among the Wyandot, Seneca, and Delaware. Later ransomed from the tribes, the Girtys first joined the Americans in the Revolution before fleeing from Pittsburgh to Detroit in 1778 to fight the British and their Indian allies.

Since coming west, Wayne often heard of Simon Girty, the most infamous of the Loyalist brothers. His name was synonymous with mindless cruelty on the frontier, especially after he stood by and watched Colonel Crawford tortured at the stake near Tymotchee Creek in June 1782. Crawford begged him to put an end to his misery, but Girty ignored him. Later he joined in brutal raids of Loyalists and Indians at Bryan Station and Blue Licks on the Kentucky frontier. So many settlers were killed along the western slopes of the Appalachians in the final months of the Revolution that the Americans who lived there called 1782 the "Year of Sorrow." After the war ended, Girty fought with the Wyandot up through St. Clair's defeat, where he came upon a wounded Richard Butler, writhing in pain and unable to walk. Butler cried out to him to kill him before the Indians found him, but Girty ignored his pleas. He instead told a warrior standing nearby that Butler was a "high officer" in St. Clair's army. The warrior promptly buried a tomahawk in his skull, scalped him, and cut out his heart. During the next two years, Girty came to every council held among the tribes, sometimes being the only white man present, and always urged the Indians to never give an inch of ground to the Americans.[11]

Wayne also learned more about Alexander McKee, another name he heard often since taking up his command in Pittsburgh. Like the Girtys, he was a Loyalist from Pennsylvania who fled to Fort Detroit in 1778. He was now the British Indian agent in Detroit. He worked closely with Governor Simcoe in Upper Canada and ran a trading post on the Maumee seven miles downriver from Roche de Boeuf. Matthew Elliott, another Loyalist from Pennsylvania, whom Wayne described as an "artful designing man," worked as his assistant. Together they collected guns, ammunition, food, clothes, and whiskey for the tribes. They distributed the goods at their post on the eastern side of the Maumee overlooking a place called the Foot of the Rapids. They helped Little Turtle's warriors launch his attack on St. Clair, and they were ready to supply them again as they prepared to take on Wayne's Legion. They were so generous that the Indians had abandoned the Miami Villages, moving northeast along the Auglaize River and toward the Maumee Rapids.[12]

For Wayne, all the pieces of the puzzle finally fell into place. His conviction that the British and Indians were working together to defeat the Americans had been proven beyond a shadow of a doubt. He wrote to Secretary Knox more boldly than ever. "It does not require a Microscopick eye," he explained, "to see thro' this insidious policy." The British were at this very minute disrupting the negotiations in which President Washington had placed his faith. They were doing this to secure the Ohio River as Canada's southern border. Remember, Wayne told Knox, that the Indians had promised to come to a council when the "leaves were out," but later said they would arrive when the "grass was three inches high." These might sound like typical Indian phrases, but they were actually direct orders from government officials in Canada. To prove his point, Wayne repeated McKee's own words from an intercepted letter to Governor Simcoe's secretary where he recommended "further procrastination until every thing is matured." He was certain the British were delaying negotiations until they learned the outcome of the war against France. If the British defeated the French republic, they could turn their attention to building an even greater Indian confederation in the Ohio Country to stop the American advance. Wayne reported that Creek and Cherokee warriors had been spotted crossing the Ohio on their way to join the hostile tribes in a massive chain of resistance. He even worried that the British were trying to lure the Choctaw and Chickasaw, faithful allies who served him as his scouts, to their side.[13]

As he had done since the opening days of the Revolution, Wayne came up with a plan for Washington to follow. The president must break up the steady stream of supplies to the Indians at the Maumee Rapids. He proposed that upward of seven hundred mounted volunteers be immediately raised on the Pennsylvania and Virginia frontiers. He did not recommend calling the Kentucky militia, especially after their pitiful performance at St. Clair's defeat. He stated flatly that they were good for nothing but burning a few wigwams and capturing women and children. Carrying out their destruction with little opposition, they returned triumphant heroes to their homes across the Ohio and left the army to deal with the avenging Indians. Instead only militias capable of following real military objectives, meaning the men he had finally come to respect around Legionville, should be sent on this mission. They should rendezvous at Big Beaver, then march north to Lake Erie, and quickly move west along its southern shore, first to the Sandusky River and then to the Maumee Rapids. With the Indians busy monitoring the Legion at Hobson's Choice, the mounted volunteers could torch McKee's trading post and return safely home before any warriors knew what had happened.[14]

While he waited for Knox's response, Wayne readied his men for the battle that was sure to come. He ordered the road through the woods connecting Forts Washington, Hamilton, St. Clair, and Jefferson widened to sixty-five feet across. Knowing Indian spies were watching his every move, he told his axmen to pile up the first trees they felled on either side of the road to protect themselves from an attack. He wrote with increasing fury to the government contractors, Elliott and Williams, demanding they send more flour and cattle to his outlying posts. The soldiers already stationed there were going hungry. The increased rations at the head of the line would also be necessary once the negotiations failed and the Legion had to move against the Indians. He told his captains to keep the cattle close to the walls of their forts and cut down the surrounding grass to prevent surprise attacks. He welcomed the latest recruits from as far away as Bennington, Vermont, and Richmond, Virginia, bringing his total up to three thousand. He was especially happy when Thomas Posey, who served with him during the Revolution in Virginia and Georgia, arrived as his new brigadier. Wayne, who spent five to six hours a day on horseback training his men, would now get much-needed help.[15]

When Knox and Washington read Wayne's suggestions for sending volunteers to torch McKee's trading post, they did not immediately dismiss the idea. Instead they carefully weighed the reasons why the plan might not work. They worried that the operation would require a sophisticated level of cooperation that militia companies, no matter how much faith Wayne placed in them, were simply incapable of executing. Any misstep on their part would lead to disaster. It might be better if Wayne, on the chance he was ordered to fight the tribes, destroyed these supplies himself. Neither Knox nor Washington could truly believe that a few huts along the Maumee could tip the balance in favor of the Indians. Even if they could, sending hundreds of volunteers through the wilderness did not seem worth the risk. How could the militia arrive there safely without warriors intercepting them? If Wayne still had his heart set on destroying McKee's post, then he should call up the Kentucky volunteers, but only when he was finally ordered to march north.[16]

As Knox and Washington reviewed Wayne's plan, frantic letters arrived from Lincoln, Randolph, and Pickering. They were filled with angry recriminations against General Wayne. The commissioners explained how they traveled to Fort Niagara in late July, hoping to head to the Maumee Rapids where the Indians were holding a grand council, but the westerly winds across Lake Erie made this impossible. During the delay, a party of fifty Indians demanded a conference with them and Governor Simcoe, who just happened to be at the post. Their leader, the Shawnee warrior Cat Eyes, asked the commissioners if they had the authority to move the border between the tribes and the United States. The commissioners, who answered they had full power to negotiate for their government, were stunned when Cat Eyes told them that General Wayne had widened the road from Fort Washington to Fort Jefferson and beyond. The Shawnee warriors also accused Wayne of sending more soldiers and supplies to his outlying posts than necessary to maintain them.[17]

For one fleeting moment, the commissioners found themselves in complete agreement with the Indians: General Wayne's brazen aggression had endangered the delicate peace negotiations. They promised Cat Eyes that they would send a messenger immediately to the president alerting him of Wayne's hostile actions.

Knox, who never once doubted their report that Wayne had invaded the "Indian country," wrote a short note scolding him for disobeying orders and attached a copy of the commissioners' scathing analysis of his actions. Had Wayne forgotten the clear instructions sent to him the previous April to do nothing that "could be construed as a breach of the truce which is understood to exist on our parts until the treaty is written?" Forwarding the letters on July 20 by an express boat from Pittsburgh, Knox let Wayne know that Washington agreed. "I now Sir desire you in the name of the President of the United States," he wrote emphatically, "that if any troops should have been advanced to Forts Hamilton St. Clair or Jefferson exceeding the usual garrisons of those posts that you instantly withdraw them on receipt of this letter."[18]

With the Ohio River especially low in the summer of 1793, the express boat did not arrive until August 7. Wayne, who had waited more than a month for an answer to his plan for attacking McKee's trading post, was stunned when he read Knox's letter and the commissioners' accusations. Having toned down his colorful prose when writing to Knox during the past year, he now exploded in a rage and spent two days trying to compose a response. He filled page after page of the first draft in his rapid-fire scrawl railing against the lying Indians, the deluded commissioners, and Knox himself for accusing him of wrongdoing. The second draft, which he sent to the War Department, was shorter and calmer, but just as angry. How could Knox condemn him when he had singlehandedly molded the Legion into an army? He had done everything in his power to train his men, most of them raw recruits, so they would not be afraid to fight the Indians. He taught them to maneuver on the battlefield against a terrifying foe. He tried to improve their guns, made sure their cartridge boxes were full of the best powder, and even switched the trunnions on their howitzers from brass to iron so the guns would stay steady when firing. After accomplishing all this, and receiving only a few crumbs of encouragement, he must now defend himself against the "idle & fallacious reports of the *Hostile Savages.*"[19]

Wayne was most offended that his word was questioned. He had been ordered not to march into Indian country or establish any new posts until the outcome of the treaty was known. It was unbearable for him to think that Washington would believe he had disobeyed his orders. There had never been a time in the Revolution when His Excellency could not rely on Wayne. How could Knox, who had known him since the campaign to defend Philadelphia in the summer of 1777, forget his devotion to Washington and his country? Never once had he failed in an assignment given to him. Wayne did not recount his long and faithful service, but instead defended himself, saying, "I had presumed as Commander in Chief of the Legion of the United States, some confidence ought to have been placed in my honor as well as Conduct. . . . I also request you to inform the Commissioners that I have never forfeited either my word or honor to any living man."[20]

Looking back over the contradictory orders he had received during the past year, he now complained that Knox and Washington had placed him in an impossible position: "I real[l]y feel my situation awkward, unpleasant & embarrassing!" On the one hand, he must prepare his soldiers for battle. The only reward for his diligence was the condemnation he received among politicians for increasing the national debt. On the other hand, he must not be so vigilant that the Indians took offense and stormed away from the treaty negotiations. With the administration coddling the warriors, he must sit motionless at Hobson's Choice even as reports came into him about the latest Indian attacks on settlers. Under such constraints, Wayne found himself doomed to fail at every turn. If the negotiations collapsed, it was his fault. If a war started, it was his fault. If his soldiers, unprepared and lacking supplies at the head of the line, were defeated, it was doubly his fault.[21]

Knox defended both himself and Washington against Wayne's complaints. He copied over every order sent to him since May 1792, assuring him that neither he nor the president wanted to upset him. "It is not the intention of the Government to perplex or embarrass you," Knox wrote, "but on the contrary to aid you in the highest degree in every thing to bring the War to an honorable close, provided that the result of the Treaty should render it absolutely necessary to have recourse to the Sword." Wayne had already made up his mind what would happen next in the Ohio Country, but Knox and Washington were willing to let the future play out a little longer. Caution on their part meant no disrespect toward Wayne. On the contrary, they considered him the "agent on the spot" who would make the ultimate decisions on how to fight the Indians if he was ordered to do so. While the War Department had sent "general ideas" about Wayne's upcoming campaign, implementing those same ideas "must be left to your discretion." As Knox explained, "Your nearer view of the business will enable you to discover advantage or disadvantages which cannot be perceived at this distance."[22]

Even as Knox assured Wayne of the administration's faith in him, he kept him in the dark on two important matters affecting the Legion. First, he did not tell him the compromises that President Washington was willing to make to prevent Wayne's Legion from ever taking the field. He had authorized Lincoln, Randolph, and Pickering to abandon the Fort McIntosh treaty line, later confirmed at Fort Finney and Fort Harmar, if the tribes could not accept it. The United States would recognize the Ohio River as the boundary between their two peoples with just two qualifications. The Indians would have to honor the huge grant that Congress had made to the Ohio Company. They must also recognize the Symmes Purchase, a 330,000-acre grant in the Great Miami River Valley, owned by John Cleves Symmes, a former congressman and Revolutionary War veteran. If the Indians allowed Americans to settle in these two places, they could retain the rest of the Ohio Country. As an extra prize, Fort Harmar and Fort Washington would be abandoned and dismantled. The government would immediately pay the Indians a lump sum of $50,000 plus $10,000 annually into the indefinite future.[23]

Knox also did not tell Wayne that there was a graver problem facing the Legion than his usual list of complaints. Even more troubling than the lack of officers, the slow delivery of rations, and the need for proper uniforms, Wayne's second in command, Brigadier General James Wilkinson, despised him. Knox knew this from letters he received regularly from Wilkinson. The fact that Wilkinson, who had commanded the army after St. Clair's defeat, resented the major general appointed over him was no surprise to Knox. But Wilkinson's refusal to accept his place in the new chain of command was worrisome. He continued to communicate with the War Department even after Knox warned him to deal only with General Wayne. If Wilkinson's resentment was not checked, its poison could spread through the Legion and make success against the Indians, on the outside chance a battle against them might be needed, impossible. Keeping Wayne in the dark, Knox did his best to remind Wilkinson that Wayne was in charge and that he must respect him. As Wilkinson's letters continued, and became more critical of his commander, Knox made a conscious decision to keep the matter from Wayne.[24]

The secretary of war did not realize that Wayne had already been warned about Wilkinson. Right before the Legion descended the Ohio to Fort Washington, he received a letter from Captain John Armstrong, a soldier who served in the Pennsylvania Line after Monmouth Courthouse. Armstrong told his old commander that Wilkinson was doing everything in his power to drive Wayne's veterans from the army. His recent trouble with him was a case in point. After making an offhanded remark about the brigadier, Armstrong found himself facing a court-martial over trumped-up charges. Wilkinson accused him of stealing army horses, burning off their official brands, and marking them as his own. Nothing he said in his defense mattered because Wilkinson had already lined up witnesses to testify against him on charges of "speculation, theft, fraud, usurpation of power, and insubordination."[25]

While Wilkinson seemed largely motivated out of sheer cruelty, there was something more at work. As Armstrong explained to Wayne, Wilkinson was a man of easy virtue. He was always scheming for a way to make money. He could lure inexperienced officers into his plots, but not Wayne's veterans who "pos-

James Wilkinson by Charles Willson Peale.
Courtesy of Independence National Historic Park.

sessed too much virtue." Beware of Wilkinson, Captain Armstrong warned, for he was an "artful designing Jesuitical man" who was "working, in his way to obtain the command of the army." He also told Wayne that, as strange as it might seem, the author of the many articles calling for the Legion's reduction in newspapers from Pittsburgh to Philadelphia was none other than General Wilkinson. If he had to destroy the Legion to rid himself of Wayne, then he would do it.[26]

Wayne simply refused to believe Armstrong. Like most everyone who knew James Wilkinson, he considered him a charming and intelligent man. From the moment they first met as the Continental Army hurried away from Three Rivers, he never once questioned his honor or decency. Wilkinson, then just eighteen years old, was an aide to General Benedict Arnold. With his commander trapped in Montreal, he rode alone up the northern shore of the St. Lawrence to scout whether Burgoyne was heading downriver to trap Arnold. He returned with news that the British were indeed marching toward Montreal. Wilkinson then crossed the St. Lawrence and headed south to find a Continental Army officer willing to rescue Arnold. He searched day and night until his horse collapsed beneath him. He commandeered a horse from a local parish priest and hurried on until he himself collapsed in an abandoned cottage. Later, he caught up with General Sullivan, and then Colonels Maxwell and St. Clair, who all refused to help him. He finally came upon Colonel Allen, who had led the initial retreat from Three Rivers. Allen told him, "This army's conquered by its fears. Try Colonel Wayne; if anyone can help you, he's your man."[27]

Amid the long columns of soldiers, horses, and wagons trudging south toward Crown Point, Wilkinson finally saw Wayne. Unlike the bedraggled men all about him, he sat high atop his horse, straight backed and sure, "as much at ease as if he was marching to a parade exercise." Never hesitating for a moment when Wilkinson approached him, Wayne rode to a nearby bridge, posted a guard, and ordered any man crossing who still looked ready to fight to join him. In just minutes, he gathered a company and set out for Montreal. Wilkinson later remembered, "The very men who only yesterday were retreating in confusion before a portion of the enemy, now marched with alacrity against their main body." They had only gone two miles when a messenger from Arnold stopped them with news that the general had fled Montreal, escaping from Burgoyne just in time. Wayne turned his men back south to join the retreating Continentals. When they came upon the rear guard, they could hear the panicked drums pounding the alarm that the British were nearby. Wilkinson would never forget how Wayne took out his spyglass, looked into the camp, and "seemed to enjoy the panic he had caused." But realizing the danger the army was still in, he sent a soldier ahead to let them know Colonel Wayne was approaching, not General Burgoyne.[28]

When he was appointed commander in chief of the Legion, Wayne was happy to learn that Wilkinson would serve as his second in command. "I feel a singular pleasure, in having with me, a Gentleman who I have always esteemed as a friend," he immediately wrote to his brigadier at Fort Washington, "and who I know will be a brave and experienced officer." He was equally delighted that he would soon see Wilkinson's wife, Ann, whom he had known in Philadelphia in the opening years of the Revolution. In the summer of 1792, he welcomed her, along with her four sons, and Lieutenant Harrison, to Fort Fayette on their way to Philadelphia. Wayne let Wilkinson know that he had given two fine saddle horses to his family, one for his wife and the other for his sons. He looked forward to welcoming General Wilkinson into his military family once he moved downriver from Legionville.[29]

Even before he came to Cincinnati, Wayne relied on his brigadier as his eyes and ears in the western country. Wilkinson kept Wayne informed of the movements of the Indians down to the last detail. Wayne was especially impressed when Wilkinson noticed that the hundred warriors who appeared before the walls of Fort Jefferson were all dressed in new shirts, which could only have come from British traders. If they were supplying the Indians with new clothes, then they were also supplying them with new guns in preparation for the upcoming battle against the American army. When Wayne finally arrived at Hobson's Choice, he was greatly relieved that he had a general of Wilkinson's caliber to help him move troops and supplies up the line to the outlying posts. He also appreciated the fact that whenever Wilkinson seemed to overstep his bounds, especially in the area of promoting officers and managing court-martials, his brigadier always apologized.[30]

But his trust in Wilkinson did not blind him to the fact there was trouble in the army at Hobson's Choice just as there had been at Legionville, especially among his officers. "They ought to Unite as a Band of Brothers" would become Wayne's frequent complaint. He knew competition to win his favor, and so secure a promotion, was a constant source of conflict among them. But his enlisted men were just as restless, a fact apparent in the rising number of court-martials. Most cases dealt with "bad conduct," ranging from minor offenses like a slovenly appearance or ruined uniform to more serious ones like striking a fellow soldier or using disrespectful language to an officer. What bothered Wayne most about these court-martials was the fact that half of them were tied to drunkenness. Despite his best efforts to keep his soldiers safe from Cincinnati, many slipped away to buy whiskey and get drunk in the town. Still other soldiers were guilty of stealing, sleeping on duty, or leaving camp without permission. Desertion remained the worst crime, punishable by death, but with every soldier needed for the upcoming campaign, only repeat offenders were sent to the gallows or a firing squad.[31]

As tensions spread through the ranks, Wayne grew closer to a handful of loyal officers. Brigadier General Posey became his right-hand man, especially as the Legion prepared to march out of Hobson's Choice. Adjutant General Butler remained his special favorite no matter how much the other officers complained. Captain Miscampbell, the enthusiastic recruiter Wayne first met on the road from Philadelphia, was placed in charge of the cavalry, including his favorites, the Black Horse Dragoons. Major Hamtramck, who had witnessed firsthand St. Clair's failures as a general, admired Wayne's strict discipline of his men. From the moment Wayne took charge of the Legion, Hamtramck considered him a friend as much as a commanding officer. Captain Caleb Swan, the Legion's hard-pressed paymaster, worshipped Wayne as a hero for the ages. Lieutenant Harrison looked up to him like a father. A student of ancient history like Wayne, Harrison often joined his commander in exploring the mysterious Indian mounds near Hobson's Choice. His young friend from New York, Solomon Van Rensse-laer, also became a favorite of Wayne, who in turn put him in charge of the Sor-rell Horse Dragoons.[32]

Even as he drew loyal officers to his side, Wayne searched for an underlying pattern in the increasing unhappiness of his men. Never once did he blame Wil-kinson's double-dealing for the troubles in his camp. He never guessed that his gallant brigadier was hard at work gathering a clique of disloyal officers around him. Wilkinson drew Major Henry Burbeck, commandant of the Legion's ar-tillery, to his side. He enjoyed exchanging letters with Burbeck, a Continental Army veteran who had served with General Knox, mocking the dedicated Wayne throughout the Ohio campaign. He enlisted Captains Ballard Smith and Thomas Cushing, two young men who had been passed over for promotions, along with Ensign Campbell Smith, the son of a wealthy Baltimore attorney. Wilkinson also took Lieutenant William Clark of the Fourth Sublegion under his wing. Clark was the younger brother of George Rogers Clark, the Virginia frontiersmen fa-mous for his raids on Shawnee towns and the British outpost at Vincennes during the Revolution. He even won over Dr. John Scott, an army surgeon who served with Wayne in Georgia. Scott at first admired Wayne for his diligent training of the Legion, but later agreed with Wilkinson that he was a tyrant who drove his soldiers past the point of human endurance. Long into night, both at Hobson's Choice and later on the march north, Wilkinson entertained his followers with references to Wayne as "Tony Lumpkin," the main character of Oliver Gold-smith's new play *She Stoops to Conquer* who was infamous for his duplicity. Wil-kinson also called him "Mars" and the "Old Horse," while at the same time de-manding that he be addressed as "General," the only person in the Legion whom he believed deserved the title.[33]

Knowing none of this, Wayne blamed the Legion's troubles not on Wilkinson, but on the upheaval of the French Revolution spreading across the Atlantic. Wayne read accounts in the newspapers he still received weekly from Sharp Delany describing France's descent into chaos as competing factions fought for absolute control of the republic. First, in the spring of 1793, the Girondins held power. Wayne was furious when their envoy to the United States, the arrogant Citizen Genêt, traveled the country outfitting American privateers to fight the British navy, all the while ignoring President Washington's proclamation of neu-trality. By the late summer, the more radical Jacobins were on the rise. Control-ling the new Revolutionary Tribunal, which was charged with bringing counter-revolutionaries to justice, they launched "La Grande Terreur" in early September to hunt down and execute their enemies. French men and women by the thou-sands, across all social classes, now died beneath guillotines set up in Paris and towns throughout the republic. Wayne believed the bloody self-destruction had ruined the French armies and left them open to defeat by foreign powers. He hoped, with Wilkinson's help, to prevent the "fatal effects of want of discipline & dire insubordination," which now afflicted France, from infecting the Legion of the United States.[34]

Wayne also worried that France's troubles were disrupting American politics. The same people who had opposed the Constitution, the "anti-federal junto" as Wayne called them, had not fallen by the wayside. Instead, they regrouped as the loyal opposition to Washington. The president, standing at the center of the current political storm, as he once stood in the whirlwind of the Revolution, tried his best to pull the competing interests of his country together. Like a great centripetal force, he strengthened the ties to the nation with his policies on the bank, taxation, and even his proclamation of neutrality. But his enemies, like a great centrifugal force, pulled in the opposite direction. They were the Congressmen who opposed Wayne's appointment to head the Legion. They were the citizens of western Pennsylvania who refused to pay the whiskey tax. They were the politicians who threatened to dismantle the army. All these people, whom Wayne would nickname the "Demoncratic party," fought the president with the fury of French revolutionaries. To them, Washington was another Louis XVI standing in their way. Wayne was determined to hold the Legion together, no matter how much his disobedient officers and soldiers pulled away. If he failed, the western country would be lost forever. He might disagree with Washington's cautious approach to the troubles across the Ohio, but he would still stand with him.[35]

Just as the tension in the Legion seemed to reach the breaking point, Wayne finally received the news that he had long been expecting. The negotiations with the Indians had failed. The tribes would not budge in their demand for the Ohio River as the border between their people and the Americans. William Wells, who had attended the latest Indian council on Wayne's orders, brought the news first. Soon afterward, official notification came from Lincoln, Randolph, and Pickering, and later Secretary Knox. Wayne was not surprised to learn the commissioners never got the chance to address the Indians. After arriving in Detroit on July 21, they waited anxiously at the home of Matthew Elliott, who was attending the council at the Maumee Rapids, for an invitation. It never came. Instead, on July 30, two war chiefs, Bluejacket of the Shawnee and Buckongehelas of the Delaware, along with Sawaghdawunk, the headman of the Wyandot, knocked at their door. They brought one question from the council: did the commissioners have full authority to fix the Ohio River as the border between their two peoples? Following Knox's instructions, the commissioners answered they were authorized to move the border if the Indians agreed that Americans already living on Ohio Company land and in the Symmes Purchase could stay there. If the tribes said yes, the United States would give them large sums of money, not just once, but every year from then on, and even dismantle Fort Harmar and Fort Washington.

The three Indians seemed satisfied with the answer. They returned to the council, carrying a long written speech from the commissioners. The document explained how the United States had won the western country from the English king, and then, recognizing the Indians' claims to the land, negotiated treaties to acquire the country from the tribes. The commissioners were hopeful when small parties of Indians visiting Detroit told them Joseph Brant and his Mohawks were arguing for peace with the United States. The Shawnee, Wyandot, and Delaware were still for war, along with the Miami, but even among these tribes, close to half of their members wanted to accept the commissioners' offer. There were even rumors that Colonel McKee was telling the Indians to take the deal offered by the Americans.

But on August 16, two Wyandot runners returned from the Maumee Rapids with a written speech from the tribes. They would not accept the commissioners' proposals. They instead reminded them that, while the United States had signed a treaty with the English king, the Indians had never participated in these negotiations. They had signed treaties with the United States, but only because the army's guns were pointed at them. They would keep their country all the way south to the Ohio River and needed none of the riches that President Washington offered. "Brothers, money to us is of no value," they explained, "and to most of us is unknown." They recommended that instead the money be given to the poor farmers who had settled north of the Ohio so they could move elsewhere.[36]

Now Secretary Knox exploded in a rage. He could hardly believe the tribes had turned down Washington's generous offer: the entire Ohio Country handed back to them except for a handful of settlements. Just weeks since scolding Wayne for his aggressive moves, Knox railed at the "audacious savages" who rejected peace in favor of the sword. After trying so hard to win a treaty, he could now only think of the horrible warfare that would soon engulf the country across the Appalachians. Warriors from countless tribes would "murder helpless Women and Children." Starting in the Muskingum and Great Miami River Valleys, they would strike farther south into Kentucky and along the western slopes of Virginia and Pennsylvania. The only thing standing between them and the bloodshed they would unleash was General Wayne, whom he had criticized for much of the past summer, and his untried Legion, still waiting for food and uniforms at Hobson's Choice. Knox now claimed all the promised rations were on their way to

Wayne's camp. He also sent more uniforms from Philadelphia. Once they arrived in Pittsburgh, he ordered them to be "smoked" in case they were infected with a "malignant putrid fever" that had just descended on the capital.

When looking for words to encourage and still caution Wayne, he reminded him how his country was depending on him. He told him one last time that he must take no chances. For Knox, the Legion was not facing another Stony Point or Green Spring, but instead another Yorktown. When Wayne finally led the Legion into battle, against real Indians, not imaginary ones, he and his men must be fully prepared for the critical task assigned to them. Above all else, they could not fail, since "a defeat in the present time and under present circumstances would be pernicious in the highest degree to the interests of our Country." Having said all this, Secretary Knox, who was not a deeply religious man, sent up a final prayer, commending Wayne and his men to "the protection of the Supreme Being," before escaping from Philadelphia and the yellow fever raging through the city.[37]

"They Shall Not Be Lost"

As Wayne prepared to move his Legion from Hobson's Choice in September 1793, he once again viewed the world against the backdrop of ancient Rome as he had done so many times in the Revolution. During the fight to defend Philadelphia in the summer of 1777, he had laid plans for the Continental Army that matched Julius Caesar's actions at Amiens. Later, while fighting in Virginia, he had traced the connections between the present moment and the Second Punic War. Then Cornwallis seemed another Hannibal, while young Lafayette appeared a second Fabius. Now facing the Indians in the Ohio Country, Wayne remembered Caesar's final campaign against the Gauls, especially his great victory at Alesia in 52 B.C. But looking ahead to a crucial battle of his own, he no longer identified with Caesar, but instead with Vercingetorix, the leader of the Gauls who opposed him.

In another September, some eighteen hundred years before, Vercingetorix, the Arveni chieftain who had united the Gauls in an uprising against Caesar, then the governor of Gaul, took a position in the fortress of Alesia high atop Mount Auxois. He was certain his army would be safe in the walled city of 80,000 people, for even Caesar would not be brave enough to attack a fortified position. But Vercingetorix was wrong. Caesar ordered his legions to encircle Alesia with a fortress of his own. Running eleven miles around the city, its timber walls rose twelve feet high. Thirteen watchtowers were placed at regular intervals around the perimeter. A trench filled with water, twelve feet wide and twelve feet deep, was dug in front of the walls facing toward Alesia. Before Caesar could complete his circumvallation of the Gauls' city, Vercingetorix's cavalry escaped through an opening in the Roman lines.

Knowing they would soon return with 60,000 reinforcements, Caesar ordered his men to build another fortress around the first. This contravallation, with nine more watchtowers and multiple camps for his cavalry and infantry, faced out toward the oncoming relief army. Vercingetorix's forces tried time and again to destroy the first wall surrounding Alesia. With the siege cutting off food to his people, he sent the women and children out of the town, hoping the Romans would take pity on them. Instead Caesar let them starve in the no man's land between Alesia and the closest ring around the city. After the relief army failed to break through the outer fortress, Vercingetorix rode alone out through the main gate of Alesia toward Caesar's camp where he threw himself down in front of him, surrendering the town at last. The Battle of Alesia was over, a complete victory for Rome and Caesar.[1]

In Wayne's opinion, his beloved America was in the same position as Vercingetorix atop the fortress of Alesia. He believed himself safe even as two rings of fortifications went up around him. A tribal confederation was building the first ring on the western frontier. The walls grew stronger every day as more Indians joined the confederacy. Warriors from as far away as Canada and the headwaters of the Mississippi were already part of it, while the Cherokee, Creek, and maybe even the Choctaw and Chickasaw, would soon fight with them. The British were busy constructing the second ring. From their illegal forts on American soil, they stood ready to direct the Indians in a bloody war first in the Ohio Country and later everywhere west of the Appalachians. If the Legion did not break through these two encirclements, America and her citizens were as doomed as Vercingetorix and his Gauls.

Sadly, from Wayne's point of view, he was the only person who seemed to understand this. Knox and Washington certainly did not. Nor did the officers and soldiers in his Legion who cared more about fighting each other than the Indians. Even the mounted volunteers he would have to call from Kentucky showed little interest in the fate of America. When General Charles Scott, the commander of the volunteers, who had fought with Wayne from Brandywine to Monmouth, wrote that he could only enlist a few hundred men, and not the one thousand originally promised, Wayne exploded. "This is not a common, or little predatory war made by a few tribes," he railed. "It is a confederated war forming a chain of circumvalation round the frontiers of America from Canada to east Florida, and unless the fire kindled at the Miami of the Lakes is extinguished by the blood of the Hydra, a little way in our front it will inevitably spread along the borders of Pennsylvania, Virginia, Kentucky, the Territory S.W. of the Ohio, South Carolina and Georgia inclusive."[2]

For the sake of his nation's future, he knew he must march his Legion against the tribes, but he dreaded the thought of fighting the Indians in a fall campaign.

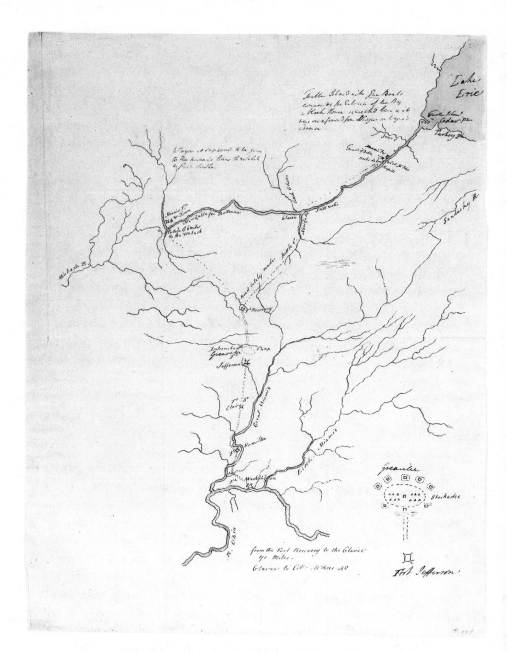

General Clinton's map of Wayne's Ohio campaign.
William L. Clements Library, University of Michigan.

This was the time of year when the tribes held a distinct advantage over his soldiers. With the harvest just completed, corn was plentiful, while the woods were full of deer. "Strong ferocious & full of the spirits," the Indians would choose the day and the hour to attack his army. In contrast, Wayne's Legion would suffer from a want of fodder for their horses and cattle. In the forests past Hobson's Choice, the first frost might have already killed the grass in the meadows. As Wayne's soldiers traveled north, their animals would starve to death. As fall gave way to winter, the chances grew stronger that his Legion would go down to defeat just like St. Clair's army.

Wayne would have preferred to fight the tribes in the spring. Then the warriors were weak. They had traveled far from their villages in search of game. Leaving their families in makeshift camps, they hunted for weeks on end in the frozen woods. The most terrible time for the Indians came in February. Known among the northern tribes as the Hunger Moon, the days were filled with snow, ice, and starvation. Wayne was certain that the best time to strike the Indians was just a few weeks later as spring approached. In late March and early April, the warriors were exhausted, tired from hunting all winter and more concerned about getting their families back safely to their villages than fighting. Then his soldiers could move swiftly against the Indians, with the horses and cattle finding plentiful fodder in the meadows that dotted the country all the way north to the Miami of the Lakes.[3]

As much as he regretted the timing, there could be no turning back for Wayne or his Legion. Even as he waited through the late summer of 1793 for news on the treaty negotiations, he had continued to prepare his men for battle. Relying on the authority granted to him as the Legion's commander in chief, he reorganized the sublegions to function more like Continental Army divisions. Each one now had a staff of officers, First and Second Battalions of infantry, a Third Battalion of riflemen, and separate units of dragoons, light infantry, and artillery. At seven o'clock every Sunday morning, Wayne ordered his sublegions to form on the parade ground with their daily rations prepared in advance. They then spent the day marching in columns, throwing up redoubts in record time, and fighting in mock battles. Wayne also drilled his soldiers in recognizing the signals of the drum and bugle corps: prepare to march, march, quicken the march, halt, form for action, call in the infantry, call in the rifle corps, commence firing, cease firing. His men had to respond immediately to these signals, for their lives would soon depend on it. Despite the near constant pain of gout, Wayne sat on his horse all day, directing his soldiers from early in the morning until late in the afternoon.[4]

As he watched his men maneuver before him, Wayne worried that he had trained them in only fifteen months. His own experience taught him that men needed three years to become soldiers. It took them that long to learn how to care for their weapons and uniforms, and also how to live off their rations. But Wayne had never been able to calculate how many years it took a soldier to be ready for actual combat. Instead he could only hope his men were fully trained for battle. Still he fretted that all the knowledge he had poured into them had come from his fighting the British, not the Indians. No matter how brutal the late war had been, combat against the redcoats had been orderly. At Three Rivers, they waited behind redoubts. At Brandywine, they came in rows across a creek and open fields. At Germantown, they stood along the town's main roads. At Monmouth and Green Spring, they approached in regular columns. At York-town, they never moved even as they were bombarded. This would not be the case in the upcoming battle. Instead, in some dark woods at dawn or tangled meadow at twilight, thousands of screaming warriors would race at the Legion from every direction. Wayne could not help but wonder how his men would react when that dreaded moment came. He confessed to Secretary Knox, "How they will behave in action, is yet to be determined."[5]

He knew one thing for certain. Under no circumstances would he allow his soldiers to flee the battlefield. To keep this from happening, Wayne decided to make them as afraid of him as they were of the Indians. He had done this on the way to Stony Point when he told his army that any man who stepped out of line would die at the hands of the soldier next to him. He now issued a general order that went far beyond any threat he previously made to his troops. He told his men if they tried to run, they would die at the hands of their fellow soldiers, not the Indians. If the rifle corps should "*shamefully give way*—or attempt to fall back before they are called or supported—the cavalry in this case will have orders to charge & put them to the Sword." If the riflemen stood firm, but the cavalry should "*shamefully give way*," the light infantry would be "ordered to direct the most deadly fire at them." If the riflemen and Cavalry held steady, but this time the light infantry, after being ordered to charge, "*attempt to retire* without having routed & dispersed the enemy," then "the fire of the artillery & musketry of the columns will be directed at them to total extirpation!" What he would do if the regular infantry and artillery panicked and ran, he did not have to say, for the battle would be lost and the Legion, along with its commander in chief, would be massacred.[6]

Wayne would not let this happen. A year before when he asked Knox for flags to train his men, he promised none of the standards would ever fall to victo-rious warriors. "They shall not be lost" was his pledge then. As he prepared to leave Hobson's Choice, he promised he would not leave his army massacred on some forgotten battlefield. He regretted that he had been angry with Knox and Washington for daring to question him. He understood the terrible position they were in politically both at home and on the world stage. He no longer railed against their caution, but instead embraced it. The three of them were allies, even brothers, not enemies. Let nothing trouble you, he wrote to the secretary of war, and assure the president to have no fear for his nation or himself. Wayne knew how the "critical situation" of their "infant nation" was deeply entwined with the "reputation of the government." He had spent much of his life defending both and would give his "latest breath" to uphold them now. Knowing Washington was worried that he might stumble into a massacre, just like St. Clair had done, or into a surprise, as he had done at Green Spring, Wayne tried his best to calm him. He promised that "I will not commit the legion unnecessarily; and unless more powerfully supported than I have reason to expect, I will content myself by taking a strong position in advance of Fort Jefferson, and by exerting every power, endeavour to protect the frontier, and to secure the posts and army during the winter, or until I am favored with your further orders."[7]

In late September, he was finally ready to lead his army, numbering 2,650 and not the 5,000 originally promised, north from Hobson's Choice. He hoped his rigorous training would save them from defeat and certain death. He had faith in the "Prowess, Conduct, & Fortitude of every Corps" and was sure he would never have to turn the guns and artillery on them. He never once considered how much his threats might have dampened the spirit of his men. Dr. Scott, who once admired Wayne for the "unequalled military discipline of the army," saw this in the many soldiers who came his way. Amidst all their aches and pains, he noticed their main complaint was General Wayne. Even an old friend like Scott ridiculed him as *"our great chief"* who, like an Achilles reborn, had turned his frightened infantry and dragoons into an army of "Myrmidons." Instead of reliving Caesar's *Commentaries on the Gallic War*, the old warrior was lost in dreams of Homer's *Iliad*.[8]

Wayne realized many of his soldiers were sick, not from hating him, but from fevers, agues, and the kinds of illnesses common in army camps. He was especially distressed when sixty recruits arrived at Hobson's Choice, all suffering from smallpox. When a strange "Malady called Influenza," as he described the sickness to the secretary of war, swept through the ranks, he delayed the march north. Wayne, like almost everyone else in camp, suffered from severe vomiting and could barely rise from his bed. But as he reported to Knox, his doctors assured him the disease was not fatal, and that his soldiers, with few exceptions, would recover. Even though the Kentucky volunteers had not yet arrived, the clothes that Knox forwarded to Pittsburgh were damaged, and the contractors refused to answer his letters, he was determined to lead the Legion out from Hobson's Choice in the first week of October.[9]

Early on the morning of Monday, October 7, 1793, Wayne ordered his men to form their columns and march north toward Fort Hamilton, twenty miles away. If all went as planned, they should arrive there in two days. Governor St. Clair came out from Cincinnati to see the soldiers off on the same path that had taken his soldiers to their deaths. He could not help but notice the wonder of the day, more beautiful in fact than he could ever remember, with "not a drop of rain, and no frost yet." The sky was the perfect sapphire blue of early autumn, with no clouds on the horizon, and a warm wind making it seem summer had returned. The terrible weather that helped defeat the army in November 1791 might never come. St. Clair, now a close friend of Wayne, had full faith in his abilities as a commander. Even after learning that a thousand Indians might be waiting for the Legion at the spot where he had been defeated two years before, he did not doubt that Wayne, unlike himself, would be successful. "He will give a good account of them," he assured the State Department, but still he could not help but say a prayer for him "fervently & sincerely."[10]

If Wayne noticed the beauty of the day, he did not record his impressions in letters to Knox or friends back in Philadelphia. Instead he took his place at the head of the Legion that he had organized so perfectly. Every man protected every other man in a great chain; together they guarded the horses, pack animals, and cattle, and the few women allowed to go with them. The scouts led the way in an arc around the front of the columns. Wayne on horseback rode behind them with his top officers, including his brigadiers Posey and Wilkinson, his adjutant Edward Butler, and his aide de camp Harrison, at his side. Two long columns of regular soldiers followed close behind. They marched on opposite sides of the road cleared from Fort Washington to six miles past Fort Jefferson. The First Sublegion, walking amid their white flags, came first on the right with the Fourth Sublegion, following yellow flags, behind them. Across the road, marching with red flags, came the Second Sublegion. The Third Sublegion walked behind them in a sea of green flags. The two columns protected the artillery, which was pulled along in wagons down the center of the road. Directly behind the artillery, also in between the two columns, came wagons loaded with military supplies, horses in long packtrains, and herds of cattle. Beyond them came the women allowed to follow their men if they left their children behind at Fort Washington. If they were also willing to do laundry or take care of the sick, he would provide them daily rations, but no pay. Farther out to the right and left of the columns came the dragoons and light infantry. Past them on both sides came the riflemen.[11]

Wayne had trained his Legion so perfectly that, if Indians attacked from any direction, his soldiers would instantly wheel about to face them. They had practiced this time and again in the woods near Legionville and the hills around Hobson's Choice. At the first sign of trouble, the scouts would send up an alarm. The riflemen, dragoons, and light infantry would race toward the enemy and hold them off until the rest of the Legion could form behind them. Soldiers assigned to the artillery would drag the guns from the rear and await Wayne's orders to position the cannon and open fire. The First and Second Sublegions would quickly take up their position in a long row in front from right to left. The Third and Fourth Sublegions would line up behind them from left to right. The officers would make sure their men did not stand shoulder to shoulder but instead had enough room between them to maneuver. They would also spread out so the Indians could never outflank them. When the columns were ready to fire, Wayne would call the riflemen, light infantry, and dragoons back to the flanks of their respective sublegions. As the two rows of his sublegions commenced firing, Wayne would direct his light infantry, dragoons, and artillery to join them as he saw fit. After all his careful planning, Wayne was convinced that from the moment thousands of painted warriors came rushing at his army from the surrounding woods, they would face an impenetrable wall of soldiers, horses, and firepower that they could never defeat.[12]

He was just as determined to protect his Legion from Indian attacks when they rested every evening. He would make sure their camp was always set up before nightfall. Early in the afternoon, when his soldiers were still on the march, he would send the Legion's quartermaster, an engineer, the quartermasters of every sublegion, and the head of the artillery up the road to find a suitable place for the army to camp. The place must be on level ground near streams with clear water and grass for grazing the animals. Once his officers found the perfect spot, they would mark out four giant squares in a grid pattern with the road cutting north and south up the middle. As the army came into the campground, the First and Second Sublegions would peel off to the right and left into their designated squares and immediately set up their tents. Coming past them up the road, the Third and Fourth Sublegions would do the same, peeling off to the left and the right, and also quickly setting up their tents. In a perpendicular line cutting across the center of the giant grid, Wayne directed the artillery be stationed to the right, along with the supply wagons, while he and his officers would set up their tents to the left.

Soldiers would then be sent into the woods to chop down trees as quickly as possible. They would carry the logs back to the camp and pile up the lumber in breastworks around all four sides of the camp. Knowing the corners were vulnerable to attack, the men would construct four bastions there pointing out like an actual fort. While the breastwork was under construction, the light infantry and dragoons would stand guard around the entire camp with firm orders to "Sustain all Attacks of the Enemy." This was still not enough protection for Wayne. He would send out picket guards, drawn from each of the four sublegions, to throw up redoubts 300 yards beyond the corners of the fortifications. After the breast-works were complete, the light infantry and dragoons would construct four more redoubts 300 yards from the center of each side. The entire camp would thus have extra protection at eight key points on the perimeter matching the main points of the compass: north, northeast, east, southeast, south, southwest, west, and northwest.

But Wayne demanded still more protection. Several hundred yards to the north of the camp, he would station a final series of advance guards. He would place a rear guard at the same distance back down the road toward the south. Though his men might be exhausted by the time they finally fell asleep on the ground beneath their blankets, they could rest certain in the knowledge that no Indian warrior would attack such a well-fortified camp. Wayne, who would stay awake long into the night writing letters to government contractors and the War Department, could be justly proud of the fact that while it took Caesar four to five hours to set up his camp, the Legion could do it in just one.[13]

Wayne kept his Legion on schedule during the two-day march to Fort Hamilton. The soldiers traveled at the expected pace of two miles an hour. Starting at ten in the morning, they continued until three in the afternoon. As his army marched through the rolling country north of the Ohio, soldiers wrote of the beauty of the land in the diaries they kept. The hills were covered in sugar maples and black walnuts. The leaves of the maples were already turning orange and red, while the walnuts would soon be bright yellow. Past Fort Hamilton on the way to Fort St. Clair, the woods, which would thin out a bit up ahead, were full of giant buckeyes and white oaks. Beyond Fort St. Clair, the country would flatten into prairies dotted with oak and beech trees. This was a rich land where a man need only reach out for a wild plum, apple, or pawpaw hanging above him. The soldiers who grew up on farms could easily see that the soil, once cleared of trees and tall prairie grass, and with the swamps drained, would be perfect for growing corn and wheat. Herds of deer and buffalo in the open prairies, rabbits and wild turkeys by the hundreds in the thickets, geese in the fields, pigeons and squirrels high in the trees, and foxes and bears everywhere made the land seem like an untouched Garden of Eden. There were so many animals, in fact, that Wayne ordered his men to stop firing at them, fearing the shots might alarm sol-diers farther up or down the line.[14]

He also addressed every problem that came up during the march to Fort Hamilton. With the army stretched out for five miles, he ordered his brigadiers to take charge of the two columns: Wilkinson would direct the First and Fourth Sublegions on the right, while Posey would command the Second and Third Sublegions on the left. Noticing that many soldiers seemed weighed down under heavy loads, which included their weapons and ammunition, a two-day supply of rations, and personal belongings, Wayne ordered everyone to throw away their scabbards, the sheaths around their swords, and their frogs, the pieces of leather that connected the scabbards to their belts. As wagons broke down, with their wheels stuck in ruts in the road or their axles split apart when dragged over rocks, Wayne directed them to the side of the road. Here they could be repaired as the army continued around them.

After the Legion passed Fort Hamilton, Wayne grew anxious for his soldiers to move faster. On the morning of October 10, he started them on their march earlier. By the time they stopped in the late afternoon, they had gone twelve miles. They camped for the night at Five Mile Spring, so named because it was five miles past the winding Great Miami River. On the following day, Wayne pushed his men to go another twelve miles. The Legion traveled only ten miles on October 12, but even with the return to a slower pace, many soldiers could not keep up and fell back toward the rear guard. As his men grew more exhausted, Wayne worried even more about an Indian attack. He was especially concerned that no one, not the scouts marching ahead of the columns or any light infantry, rifleman, or dragoons moving on the flanks, had seen or even heard a whisper of a warrior. Were they waiting to strike his tired soldiers in the early afternoon as they set up their camp for the night? Were they leading his men deeper and deeper into an unfamiliar country where thousands of Indians stood ready to attack? Or had the sheer size and careful organization of the Legion so overawed the tribes that a battle against them would be unnecessary?[15]

On October 13, as the columns approached Fort Jefferson, Wayne's soldiers were at the breaking point from sheer exhaustion and the tension of waiting for the Indians to attack. When shots rang out toward the head of the line, panic set in, especially at the rear of the columns. Soldiers marching there wondered if the long-awaited battle had commenced. The Third and Fourth Sublegions now hurried ahead to catch up with the First and Second Sublegions that even now might be holding off thousands of warriors. Over the loud rumbling of the heavy wagons at the center of the columns, the officers of the rear guard could not be certain what was happening. Finally, believing they heard musket shots ahead of them, they raced toward the front of the line only to discover that the gunfire was coming from Fort Jefferson. Colonel Hamtramck, the commander of the post, had taken his men outside the walls, and there in the surrounding meadows, he was leading his soldiers in a sham battle against imaginary Indians.[16]

The Legion made camp that night one mile south of Fort Jefferson. On the following morning, the soldiers marched seven more miles and stopped in a wide prairie. They had come to the end of the road opened through the forest during the previous year. Having pushed his army to go ninety miles in just eight days, Wayne realized his men could go no farther, especially since the beautiful weather had disappeared. Now rain fell for hours at a time, frost killed the grass in the meadows at night, and snow blanketed the ground every dawn. Even worse, Wayne found himself growing steadily sicker as he traveled north. He complained of headaches and the near constant pain of gout in his arms, legs, and joints. After managing every aspect of his Legion down to the last detail, he now fretted that events were spinning out of his control from the weather to his health and most terribly to the delivery of rations to his troops.[17]

Before his soldiers marched north from Hobson's Choice, Wayne ordered Elliott and Williams, the government contractors, to deliver 4,125 individual rations for every day the army was on the road. Another 250,000 daily rations were to be waiting for them at Fort Jefferson. The day's rations for each man included a pound of bread or flour, a pound of beef or three-quarters of a pound of pork, and a half-gill of whiskey. Weekly rations for every one hundred soldiers included one quart of salt, two quarts of vinegar, two pounds of soap, and two pounds of candles. But when Wayne arrived at the prairie six miles past Fort Jefferson, he received a letter from the contractors stating they could not collect the huge amount of rations Wayne had demanded in so short a time. Even if by some miracle they could acquire all these rations, drawn mainly from Kentucky, they did not have enough horses or oxen to deliver the goods to the Legion.

Furious that his requests had been dismissed, Wayne ordered Quartermaster O'Hara to purchase 250 horses and sixty oxen, and then send the bill for the animals to Elliott and Williams. The contractors protested by reminding Wayne that buying horses would solve nothing. A horse could only carry three bushels of corn. Needing two bushels for fodder, each horse would arrive at Wayne's camp carrying only one bushel of corn. The expense would not be worth the effort and would ultimately bankrupt the company that Wayne must depend on to feed his Legion. Dismissing their pleas, Wayne threatened to buy fourteen hundred packhorses, forward the bill to Elliott and Williams, and haul the goods himself from Cincinnati to Fort Jefferson. His soldiers would use the fortifications built by the Legion every afternoon on the way north to protect the flour, cattle, and other supplies from Indian raids.[18]

Wayne needed daily rations not just for the Legion, but also for the mounted volunteers who finally arrived from Kentucky on October 19. Expecting only three hundred, he was stunned when General Scott rode into his camp with a thousand men. They informed Wayne they had come a long way over rough country for one purpose only and that was to kill Indians. When Wayne told them that, at the moment, there were no Indians to fight, they railed against him for calling them away from their farms at harvest time. Their grumbling grew even louder when they learned Wayne had little food for them and no fodder for their horses. Still believing the Kentucky volunteers were little better than cold-blooded murderers, rather than disciplined soldiers like his Legion, Wayne suggested that they march ninety miles north to the point where the Auglaize River met the Maumee, and there singlehandedly take on thousands of warriors gathered at the Grand Glaize.

But when he proposed the mission to Scott and his top generals, Robert Todd and Thomas Barbee, both known for daring raids against Indians on the Kentucky frontier, all three said no. Scott and Barbee claimed their small force could not take on so many warriors. Todd, a Continental Army veteran who fought with General Greene at Eutaw Springs, answered Wayne even more directly. A tenth of the mounted volunteers were sick and would have to be left behind. If Wayne was so terrified of the Indians that he had to call in the Kentuckians, then how could he expect nine hundred mounted men, one-third the size of his Legion, to defeat countless warriors, especially when those same Indians were "accustomed to success" after massacring St. Clair's army? Wayne could ask the question because he never expected the Kentuckians to say yes. His suggestion was more a dare than an order. However, when Major William McMahon, an officer in the Fourth Sublegion, offered to lead a small party to the Grand Glaize, along with Simon Kenton, the most famous Indian fighter on the Ohio frontier, Wayne sent eighty-four riflemen and sixty-three mounted volunteers with him. Finding no Indian villages along the Auglaize, but spotting instead many well-worn trails, obviously trod by thousands of warriors, McMahon and Kenton returned to the Legion's camp without firing a shot. Wayne mockingly agreed that their decision not to fight the Indians was a brave one.[19]

With barely enough food for his own men, and with no plans to mount an offensive so late in the year, Wayne had no choice but to send the volunteers home. He ordered them to head to Fort Jefferson, where rations and supplies would be issued to them. They could then travel west to the headwaters of the White River where the Delaware had set up their fall hunting camps. An attack on warriors at this spot might dissuade them from raiding settlements in Kentucky during the winter. Finally, the volunteers were to ride to Fort Washington, where they would be officially relieved of their service in the Legion, at least for the foreseeable future. General Scott left with close to a thousand men, but by the time they arrived at Fort Jefferson, just six miles south of Wayne's camp, half of them had deserted. Scott led the rest to the White River, but finding the country empty of Indians, except for one man who fled at their approach, the disgusted volunteers headed home by their own route, completely bypassing Cincinnati.[20]

For Wayne, the Kentucky volunteers, whom he had begged to join him against the growing circumvallation of America's frontier, had proven to be useless. Slow to assemble, unruly once they arrived, and incapable of understanding military strategy, they could do little to ward off the increasing Indian attacks north of the Ohio, especially in the country between Fort Washington and the Legion on the march. On the same day the mounted volunteers arrived at Wayne's camp past Fort Jefferson, warriors from a tribe that no one could identify attacked White's Station at a crossing over Mill Creek. A handful of farm families lived there in six cabins on one side of the creek surrounded by a split rail fence near a small blockhouse. Three more cabins stood on the other side of the creek. As dusk approached, dogs barked wildly in the hills that surrounded the station. William Gobel, a young man living at the settlement, was certain they were barking at raccoons and crossed the creek to investigate. When he had gone a hundred yards beyond the blockhouse, thirty warriors emerged from the trees and shot him dead.

Seconds later, they took aim at a four-year-old girl playing along the creek and gunned her down with one musket ball to her head. Her mother, a young widow named Elizabeth Pryor who was standing in the doorway of her family's cabin, grabbed hold of her two-year-old son and raced across the creek as shots flew all around her. She and her little boy made it to the safety of the blockhouse, but the newborn infant she left behind was not so lucky. The warriors now raced down the hill, screaming as they always did when they attacked, and headed for the cabin where the baby slept. They carried the child by the ankles out the front door and smashed its brains out against a tree stump. The Indians then stormed the blockhouse where women loaded muskets and handed them to the men to shoot at the warriors. After fighting for a half hour, the settlers finally gunned down the leader of the raiding party, whom they later described as a "large and powerful man." Only then did the Indians flee back into the dark woods at the top of the hills from whence they had come.[21]

Wayne could do little to prevent the random attacks of warriors on isolated settlements. Instead he must rely on Governor St. Clair to call out the local militia to protect settlers, and in the case of the attack on White's Station, to bury the dead. From the moment he left Hobson's Choice, Wayne's main responsibility was to keep his soldiers ready to meet and hopefully defeat the Indian army gathering against them. But now with his army stalled past Fort Jefferson, he worried they were not prepared for the upcoming battle. Even with the strict discipline he imposed on them, drunkenness and disorderly conduct remained major problems. Wayne realized this after he set up a convoy system to bring rations from Fort Washington to the Legion in the field. Captain Jacob Melcher led one of the first packtrains north from Fort Hamilton. He sent word to Wayne that most of his men, along with the supplies they were escorting, had safely made the ten-mile trip up from Fort St. Clair. The few soldiers farther back down the road were struggling with the packhorses and their loads but should arrive shortly.

Anxious to keep supplies moving, and troubled by the tone of Melcher's letters, Wayne sent Major McMahon to find out what was actually happening. When he arrived at Fort St. Clair, McMahon was shocked to see that Melcher and only four soldiers had made it there. The rest of the detachment was strung out along the ten-mile route between the two forts. The soldiers had ransacked the army's supplies, and a hundred pounds of flour and salt were missing. Even worse, the entire detachment was so drunk that McMahon claimed ten Indians could have massacred the lot of them. He promptly arrested Melcher, who would leave the army in disgrace, but could barely get the rest of the men to follow orders. Luckily, there were no Indians in sight, and McMahon was able to bring the supplies that had not been stolen back to Fort Jefferson.[22]

An even more terrible incident, which occurred a week later, made Wayne completely doubt the readiness of his men. Major John Buell, who was the officer of the day on October 16, rode along the edges of the Legion's camp looking for a way to cross between the fifth and sixth pickets. As he searched, he heard Captain Abner Price shouting that Indians had just passed by. Buell raced back to Wayne's tent to alert him that warriors were about to attack. At the same moment, Cornet William Blue led a dozen dragoons into the prairie to graze their horses. Blue noticed a rustling of feathers in the grass ahead and thought this might be wild turkeys. When he realized they were Indians, he ordered the dragoons to follow him. He raced on horseback toward the warriors, waving his sword all the while, never suspecting that only two sergeants and one private were riding behind him. After chasing the Indians for a hundred yards toward the nearby woods, Blue saw more Indians rising up from behind logs in front of him. He turned back to cheer on his men only to see that just three soldiers were following him. As shots rang out all around him, he saw the two sergeants fall dead from their horses. Now only a frightened private remained at his side. They chased the Indians into the woods before returning to the Legion's camp.

When Wayne learned what had happened, he exploded in a rage. All his months of training seemed to be for nothing. The dreadful moment he had long drilled his soldiers to meet, when they faced Indian warriors bent on killing them, had come at last and most of them had run for their lives. He ordered the dragoons who had fled arrested and court-martialed. He laid most of the blame for their cowardice at the feet of Private Daniel Davis, who had led the dragoons away from the fight. A furious Wayne charged him with misbehavior before the enemy, abandoning his post, and retreating when he had been told to charge. After the two dead sergeants were brought back from the meadow and buried, he ordered the graves of Davis and the cowards who joined him dug even before the results of their court-martials were known. The men were found guilty on all charges and sentenced to death by a firing squad. Wayne would have executed them if his officers had not intervened. They begged him for leniency, especially since the Legion had only just started on its campaign against the Indians. Wayne must be patient, and if only this once, merciful.[23]

He finally relented, and after calming down, ordered the entire Legion to form their columns immediately in front of him. For half an hour, riding back and forth on his horse, he railed against their cowardice, and stated again in the strongest terms possible what he would do if they fled from an attack. If they ran at the start of a battle, they would die at the hands of their fellow soldiers, not the Indians. If the rifle corps gave way, he would order the dragoons to charge them with swords drawn. If the riflemen stood their ground, but the dragoons gave way, he would command the light infantry to gun them down. If the riflemen and dragoons held steady, but the light infantry, after being ordered to charge and disperse the enemy, ran for their lives, he would order the infantry and the artillery to destroy them. As he had done when he first gave this warning in a general order last September, he did not have to explain what would happen if the rest of the soldiers fled the field. They would all die, along with their commander in chief, massacred at the hands of the victorious Indians, just like most of St. Clair's men. On the next day, to prove that soldiers would pay with their lives for disobedience, he ordered two men found sleeping while on guard duty court-martialed and shot.[24]

In what seemed like a lifetime ago, as Wayne suffered through the Virginia campaign, the thought of war as a grand adventure had slowly slipped away from him. Now for the soldiers who waited with him on the prairie north of Fort Jefferson, any similar sense about the upcoming battle against the Indians also disappeared. In just a few short months, mainly spent training at Legionville and Hobson's Choice, and with only a few days on campaign, they learned the painful lesson that Wayne took years to understand. Rather than triumph and glory, war was a draining experience marked by exhaustion, drudgery, and the sheer anxiety of waiting for something to happen. While spending every Sunday afternoon battling imaginary warriors in the woods and hills along the Ohio had been stressful, waiting day after day in the middle of nowhere to fight invisible Indians was even more unbearable.

But threatened within an inch of their lives at the mere thought of fleeing from the Indians, and knowing a court-martial and execution awaited if they tried to escape before the battle began, the soldiers of the Legion of the United States had no choice but to wait. They must wait for the Indians to appear at last and fight them like men, not phantoms. They must wait for the long packtrains to bring food and supplies up from Cincinnati. Flour, meat, whiskey, salt, vinegar, soap, and candles, these were the only comforts in a beautiful but frightening wilderness. They must wait for their commanding general to right himself when caught up in a fury over their failures or sunk in pain and despair. They must wait to see whether his archenemy Brigadier Wilkinson could gather enough followers to defeat Wayne even before the Indians did. In the weeks and months ahead, the waiting would take its toll on everyone, especially the officers and soldiers who tried with all their might to remain loyal to their commander in chief. Dark days were coming when even a man as devoted to Wayne as Major Hamtramck, the commander of Fort Jefferson who looked up to him as the army's savior, confessed, "There's no doubt about it; the old man is really mad."[25]

"This Horrid Trade of Blood"

If Colonel Hamtramck, one of Wayne's most loyal officers, considered him mad, how much more so did the enlisted men who suffered under his command? The general kept his soldiers on edge, one moment organizing their camp down to the last detail to keep them safe, and the next ordering their graves dug even before the verdicts of their court-martials were announced. Some could bear it no longer and slipped away into the surrounding woods, hoping to find their way back home or at least to the nearest frontier settlement. The possibility that Indians might capture them or a hangman's noose awaited them if they were dragged back to camp seemed a chance worth taking. Almost any fate was preferable to living in the light and shadow of their commander's ever-changing moods.

To his officers, Wayne seemed like two different people; not just to Wilkinson, who despised him, but also to those who admired him. He could be a most convivial host, entertaining them with his finest brandy and Madeira. He knew more about history and literature than anyone in the army. He could regale them with stories of the living heroes of the age, including Washington, Franklin, and Lafayette, who were all his friends. But his mask of charm could dissolve in an instant if they did not perform at the perfect level he demanded, not just of them, but himself. At times it was simply best to leave the old man alone: before dawn when he rode on horseback along the edges of his camp, imagining the coming battle with the Indians; in the evenings when he sat in his tent with his pen ablaze, raging at government contractors who were slow in supplying his army; or at night when racked with pain from gout, fevers, and the old wound in his thigh, he tossed and turned in his camp bed.

Where had the dashing Anthony Wayne of the Revolution gone? His daring was legendary. Everyone knew the stories of his rescuing the army in the dead of winter at Three Rivers, climbing up the cliffs below Stony Point on a hot summer night, and spurring his men to escape from Cornwallis at Green Spring. But now his soldiers called him mad for the demons that seemed to torture his soul with dark memories and strange forebodings. Even on his best days, when the shadows lifted for a moment, the madness settled into his obsessive control of every detail of army life. His men must dress the part of soldiers, from their powdered hair tied back with ribbons, to their spotless uniforms, and finally down to the gleaming buckles of their shoes. They must march, ride, and shoot perfectly. They must throw up fortifications around their camp every night that would be the envy of great Caesar himself. They must be ever on alert, and when that awful moment came and the Indians attacked, they must not bolt and run, but instead must stand and fight to the last man.

In part, Wayne's irascible temper came from the burden placed on him. He had begged Washington, as well as Knox and even Madison, to give him any task necessary, no matter how difficult, to defend the United States. The one finally handed to him seemed like salvation when he was drowning in debt and facing expulsion from Congress. Then the prospect of training soldiers and taking them deep into the wilderness to fight Indians did not seem quite so overwhelming. But now to be in the midst of this impossible task crushed Wayne's spirit. He had been ordered to shape an army on his own in a just few short months, a feat that had taken Washington years to achieve with the likes of Baron Steuben at his side. The responsibility had been too much for lesser men like Harmar and St. Clair and now seemed even more onerous for a commander like Wayne, who weighed the outcome of every possibility before acting and knew the terrible cost of leading a third army to ruin in the Ohio Country.

Yet there seemed more to Wayne's unpredictable temper than the burden of command or the thought that his carefully trained army might be massacred. He was troubled deep within himself in a place that no one seemed able to reach. At least no man could reach it until he dared to approach Wayne and ask for the one favor he sometimes granted: a leave. From the moment he arrived in Legionville until his army marched north out of Hobson's Choice, soldiers slipped letters to him, usually written on scraps of paper in the simplest scrawl, but sometimes elaborately decorated, begging to go home. Older soldiers, who had fought Indians even before Harmar and St. Clair had come west, told him they were exhausted and must rest for a while in the milder climate of Kentucky. Younger men, who had left brothers and sisters behind, said they must go back home and help their parents. Some even confessed that recruiters, who were paid for every man they signed up, got them drunk. Before they knew what had happened, they were shivering and hungry in Wayne's army with no coats to keep them warm and little food to sustain them.[1]

Wayne was sympathetic to men who asked for a leave because in what seemed like a lifetime ago he, too, had asked to go home and his commander had said no. He did not know it at the time but in that one word, his life would change forever. Wayne would head down a path that turned him into the commander his soldiers knew in the Ohio wilderness. The dashing brigadier of the Revolution would disappear and the troubled major general who now terrorized his soldiers would take his place. The unraveling of his life had begun twelve years before in the last warm days of October. Then he had waited with his "ragged and barefeet" Continentals along the road from Yorktown to the field where the British would surrender. Across the way the French stood in their elegant uniforms. Ivory banners covered with gold and lilac fleur-de-lis waved above them. As the enemy passed before Wayne, with the redcoats hunched beneath their heavy knapsacks and the Hessians still marching straight as arrows in their bright green coats, he could think of only one thing. The war was about to end, maybe not today or tomorrow but soon, and he must go home.

Since leaving his farm in 1774, Wayne seldom worried about the two children he left behind there beyond urging their mother to make sure they received the rudiments of education. Margaretta was then just four while Isaac was only two. But now they were eleven and nine and needed their father to find a place for them in the world. Margaretta must have fine dresses, and learn music, dancing, French, and drawing so she could become a great lady and make a good marriage. Isaac must be well groomed and educated in a profession, perhaps the law, to support a family of his own in the style of a gentleman. All this would take money and suddenly Wayne, who had never given a thought to making a living throughout the war, could only think about how to make a great deal of it quickly. Amidst the endless round of festivities where French and British officers entertained themselves long into the night, Wayne, who loved parties better than any man, spent his days searching about the American camp for something he could buy cheap and sell dear. He finally came upon barrels of sugar. If he could sell them in Philadelphia, where he hoped to be heading once the French departed from the Chesapeake, then he would have enough money to start Margaretta and Isaac on their way.[2]

Certain his leave would be granted, Wayne sent a short note to his commander on November 4 asking to go home. "The campaign in this quarter being gloriously terminated under your Excellency's auspices," he wrote, "I have to request the indulgence of a short respite from the field." He had been in the saddle for half a year, fighting at Lafayette's side along the James River and holding Cornwallis, Tarleton, and Simcoe at bay until Washington and Rochambeau finally caught him. He was exhausted and still suffering from the wound in his left leg. His chest sometimes hurt and he worried this might be the first sign of consumption, a horrible illness and a still more horrifying death. No man deserved a long rest more than Wayne, or so he thought. After all, Lafayette had gone home to Paris to see his family and win more help for the Americans at Versailles. Still, hedging his bet, Wayne added if he must stay with the army, then he asked to be allowed to "advance by easy degrees" to the next campaign.[3]

Wayne was surprised when the commander whom he had served so faithfully responded on the very same day with a curt note of his own. Washington, clearly upset over Wayne's request, could not understand why his brigadier, who knew the Continental Army was heading to the Carolinas, would ask to go home at this critical time. The Pennsylvania Line had been ordered to take Wilmington before marching on to the Carolinas to help drive the British from Charleston. Perhaps Wayne could not stomach the thought of serving under Arthur St. Clair, who would command the line. Regaining his composure, Washington told his brigadier to decide for himself whether he wanted to stay with his men or go home. "I shall add no more on the subject," he concluded, "but leave you to act as you have requested, or, if it is more agreeable to you to be absent from the Army for a while, to consent to that also."[4]

The letter hit its mark. Wayne was crushed that Washington questioned his motives and quickly dashed off another note. His commander must believe that he would never do anything to "injure the cause" to which he had given his life and his property, a clear reference to his money troubles. "As a *friend*, I told you that my feelings were hurt," an angry Wayne confessed, "as a *soldier*, I am always ready to submit to difficulties." After all he had done for Washington from the moment he rode into his camp on Long Island right up until the siege of Yorktown, how could he imply that Wayne cared not a whit for his men or the outcome of the war? To be so insulted merely because he had asked for a leave was almost more than Wayne could bear. Still the implication of Washington's final sentence remained clear. Wayne knew he had no choice in the matter; he must fall in with the rest of the Pennsylvania Line and head south. "I only requested leave of absence for a short time," he now explained, but "your Excellency has set it upon a ground which prevents me from accepting it." He asked again if he might be allowed to travel to the Carolinas at his own pace, "independent of command," until he joined General Greene.[5]

Washington was correct that Wayne knew the army was heading to Wilmington. Greene had sent him letter after letter during the Yorktown campaign, praising his daring and promising to give him command of the army that would take Wilmington. Wayne was also well aware that Yorktown had not ended the war. He had written to friends back home, worrying that Americans would let down their guard after their great victory and allow the British to launch a counteroffensive. For the moment, he did not even care about serving under St. Clair, in his opinion an incompetent who had somehow cast a spell over Washington. Wayne still considered St. Clair treasonous for surrendering Ticonderoga, the hated Golgotha that he had so diligently protected. But the fact that St. Clair outranked him no longer bothered him. Unlike many of Washington's officers, Wayne rarely complained when others received honors he deserved. He was simply tired and hurting, worried about his children, and filled with a sudden dread that if he marched to the Carolinas, he would never go home.

For the moment, Washington was not interested in listening to Wayne's troubles for he had worries of his own. The British still held much of the country south of Virginia. To the west, an Indian war raged across the Appalachians. Since Yorktown, the French seemed to be allies in name only. Admiral De Grasse refused his request to transport the Continental Army to the Carolinas, claiming he had already stayed too long in the Chesapeake and must be on his way before hurricane season overtook his fleet. Washington had family worries, too, the likes of which Wayne, with children still so young, had not yet known. His stepson, Jack Custis, just twenty-six years old and the only surviving child of Martha Washington's first marriage, had visited him at Yorktown where he contracted camp fever. He had been taken to his uncle's house in Eltham some thirty miles down the road toward Mount Vernon where he now lay sick and probably dying. Washington, in fact, was making preparations to head there when he received Wayne's second request for a leave.[6]

In no mood to argue, he immediately dictated an even sharper response, saying he was "distressed" over his brigadier's latest note. He had already granted leaves to Wayne's colonels, Walter Stewart and Richard Butler. What would the soldiers of the Pennsylvania Line, who had mutinied less than a year before, think if another of their top officers was allowed to go home? The answer was all too obvious to Washington. The whole line would be discouraged and he would be censured for bowing to such an improper request. If he had to choose, he would prefer that Wayne travel on his own to Greene's camp, rather than heading back to Pennsylvania. But again he left the decision up to his brigadier. "Under this exposition of my sentiments," he concluded, "I leave you at liberty to follow the dictates of your own Judgment." Certain he had silenced Wayne at last, Washington set off for Eltham on the morning of November 5, arriving just in time to say goodbye to Jack, who passed away within hours. He did what he could to comfort his distraught wife Martha and made provisions to raise Jack's youngest children, two-year-old Nellie and seven-month-old "Wash" Custis, as his own. After escorting his family back to Mount Vernon, he set off for New York to take up the waiting game once again outside the city still occupied by the British.[7]

Three days after Washington left, Wayne, with his wounded leg still aching, started down five hundred miles of backcountry roads to the Continental Army's camp in South Carolina. Stopping every night at plantations or local inns, he took the time to write to General Greene, telling him the journey was rather pleasant, especially since the British had withdrawn from the country south of the James River all the way to Wilmington shortly after Yorktown. He told his friends in Philadelphia that regrettably he would not be sitting with them in front of a roaring fire this winter, and instructed Margaretta that she must apply herself to her studies and so become a great lady. But he sent not a word to the two people he always wrote to before every campaign: no letter went to General Washington or to Polly Wayne. He had disappointed his commander by asking for a leave and would soon disappoint his wife by failing to come home. But just as important, he could not see what lay ahead and so could not tell them, as he had always done before, how he planned to handle whatever came his way.[8]

Not being able to see the future, he turned his attention to what lay all about him on the long trip south. Plantation owners from Mary Byrd, the mistress of Westover who had entertained him the previous August, to Colonel Theodoric Bland, whose plantation at Kippax across the James still showed signs of a British attack, invited him to rest for a night or two in their stately homes. Kippax, in fact, was the only place Wayne passed in Virginia that reminded him of the fighting he had tried to escape. The main house was still standing, but the redcoats had torched most of the outlying buildings. Yet everywhere else the war seemed only a memory. Wayne met gracious men who talked politics with ease and fascinating women who made him forget for a moment that he had ever asked for a leave. Though taken with a beautiful girl who played the harpsichord for him at her father's inn in Petersburg, he left her when an invitation came from the Bolling family to visit their plantation just west of the town. Wayne found his hostess, Elizabeth Bolling, a charming gossip who knew stories about all the famous men of Virginia, but who was even more captivating when she took him on a tour of her barns and gristmill. He was amazed at a machine she showed him called a "gin" made of two wooden cylinders that turned and combed the seeds from tufts of cotton. Mrs. Bolling explained this was the only way to make a profit from growing the crop.

But the country changed dramatically when he crossed into North Carolina. Here the people were poorer and the taverns, little more than log cabins with a spare room for travelers, were at least a day's ride apart. The marks of war

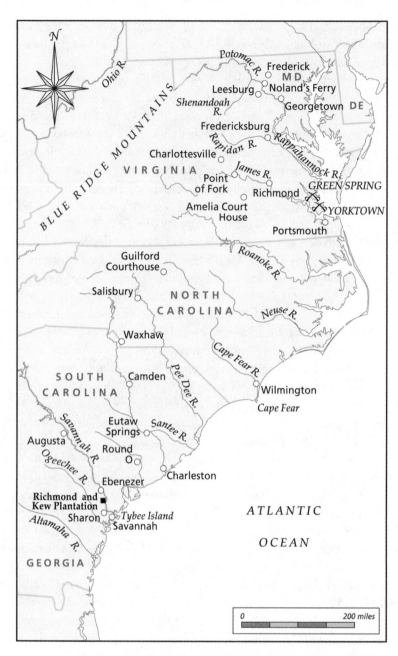

Wayne's southern campaigns. Copyright © Roberta Stockwell, 2018.

were clearer here, too, than in Virginia. His horse struggled through deep ruts in the red soil where wagons and artillery had passed. He toured the battlefield at Guilford Courthouse and counted many broken muskets and cannon strewn upon the ground. Wayne noticed a blue haze hanging over the land by day and a bright red light on the horizon by night. Innkeepers set his mind at rest by telling him these were the telltale signs of forest fires burning in the piney woods that stretched to the western mountains. Wayne saw something else that troubled him, a black man's head stuck on a sapling and a black hand nailed to a tree limb. He was told this was what became of any slave who dared to raise his hand against his master; the black man had been hung and chopped to pieces and left to rot as a warning to others.

In late December, at Waxhaws, the last settlement before crossing into South Carolina, Wayne finally caught up with the Pennsylvania Line. He sent a note to General St. Clair, telling him that Washington had given him permission to travel on his own and offering to carry any messages ahead of the main army to Greene's camp. But once he passed them by, his trip slowed considerably. If North Carolina had been fire to him, then South Carolina was water. He dismounted often, leading his horse through swamps, sometimes with the water as high as his knees, and searching every night for a dry spot of ground where he could camp. Here was a land of canebrakes, palmetto trees, and croaking frogs in the tall grass. How many times had his friend Benjamin Rush warned him of the danger of swamps and the miasma that came up from their dank waters? "Avoid the evening air, drink wine moderately, wear flannel next to your skin and take a dose of bark every day." There was no chance of doing any of this until a message came from the wealthy Le Conte family asking Wayne to join them at their estate near Camden. He arrived on Christmas, a day so warm that the Le Contes entertained their guests without building a fire in their home's main hearth. But Wayne was soon back wading through the swamps with snakes circling his horse's legs and flocks of green parakeets flying above him. On his thirty-seventh birthday, New Year's Day 1782, he headed toward the first of twelve streams that he had to pass on his way to the Edisto, the last river he would have to cross before finally arriving at the Continental Army's camp at a place called Round O on January 4.[9]

To meet Greene after so long a descent through the South was a comfort to Wayne. Just three years older than himself, and standing a little under six feet tall with the same high forehead and broad chin, Greene might have been taken for his brother. He was similar in spirit, too, having the same readiness to take on whatever Washington asked of him, no matter how difficult or demeaning. Each man had an almost boyish enthusiasm for what lay ahead, with Greene's holding steady even after the bloody battle at Eutaw Springs the previous September and Wayne's beginning to slip away only after Yorktown. Like Wayne, Greene loved literature and could entertain his officers with imitations of characters from the works of his favorite author, Jonathan Swift. Both men had a fondness for beautiful women. Greene's wife, Catharine, now the mother of four children, remained the vivacious girl who had enlivened many a solemn night at Valley Forge. Wayne, still in love with the dark-eyed Caty, was happy to learn she was on her way to Round O. She would have arrived in time for the feast that Greene prepared for his generals if she had not been delayed by a snowstorm in Philadelphia.[10]

But there was something more that bonded the two men together. Greene, unlike Washington, understood Wayne. He knew the man, with whom he shared so many traits, was not quite as steady as himself. Wayne's enthusiasm stood more on a precipice, going over the edge in fits of anger and frustration and, for the first time in this long war, despair. If Wayne had finally lost his way, then Greene would set him back on the right path with a plan to wrest South Carolina and Georgia from British control. Most of the soldiers who had just come from the North, including the Delaware, Maryland, and Pennsylvania Lines, would stay with Greene on the outskirts of Charleston and cut off General Arthur Leslie's communication with the backcountry. But he would send a few hundred mounted men toward Savannah to bottle up General Alured Clarke's redcoats and Hessians in the town. Greene could think of no better officer to command this small army than Anthony Wayne. Together the two friends would guarantee the place of South Carolina and Georgia in the United States, no matter how tired and hungry their soldiers might be, and no matter how much Great Britain tried to redraw the map in their favor at the negotiating table.[11]

Georgia's revolutionary leaders had begged Greene to send help from the moment he took command of the southern department. Their situation had changed dramatically since the summer of 1776 when they stormed into Savannah and established a provisional government for the state. Then they had been powerful enough to drive the royal governor, Sir James Wright, and his council onto a warship waiting for him in the harbor. But two years later, the British recaptured the city with Wright taking command of his colony once again and putting the rebel leaders to flight. In October 1779, the Continental Army under Benjamin Lincoln laid siege to Savannah, with the help of the French Admiral Charles d'Estaing and the Polish cavalry officer Casimir Pulaski, who had protected Wayne when he rounded up cattle near Valley Forge. After bombarding the city for five days and then fighting along its defenses for eight more, the Americans finally withdrew, having lost nearly a thousand men, wounded, captured — or

General Nathanael Greene. Yale University Art Gallery.

killed like the gallant Pulaski. A succession of revolutionary governors and as-semblymen now found themselves permanently on the run, sometimes meeting long enough to pass laws for their state, which they could never implement, be-fore mounting their horses and racing for their lives once again. A last chance for their very survival came when Greene promised to send General Wayne, an officer whose military exploits made him "conspicuous both in America and Europe," to their rescue. For Wayne, who still brooded that he would never re-turn home, and so never see his little girl and boy again, the beautiful heroism of the command offered to him brought him back for a moment from the darkness into the light.[12]

Still Wayne would have to face terrible things if he led an army into Georgia. For six long years, Loyalist and Patriot militias had terrorized the state's back-country. They murdered and plundered at will, harassing the lives and property of their supporters as well as their foes. The brutal war in the salt marshes of the coastal plain and the pine forests of the uplands had gone on for so long that many people could not remember what started the fighting in the first place. Partisanship among political opponents had given way to settling old scores be-tween neighbors. Beyond the defenses of Savannah and the few British outposts stationed along the tidal rivers, the rule of law had broken down completely. Here the ancient fear that the people could never govern themselves had come true with a vengeance. As the old order collapsed, leaving every man for him-self, the Georgia backcountry descended into a state of nature. This was a broken world that a much younger Wayne never envisioned when he met his neighbors in taverns near his family's estate and challenged them to uphold liberty. This was a frightening place that bore no resemblance to the orderly universe that John Locke had imagined in his *Second Treatise of Government*. Here no law was written on men's hearts to uphold their rights when government dissolved all around them. Instead this was the brutal landscape that Thomas Hobbes had glimpsed in *De Cive*. Here there was only *bellum omnium contra omnium*, the war of all against all.[13]

But the thought of rescuing the people of Georgia was so appealing to Wayne that for the moment he could leave whatever fears he had for himself and the family he left behind. Perhaps it was the way Greene described his new com-mand that inspired him. Wayne would not be heading south primarily to win victories on the battlefield. Instead he must "open wide a door" of forgiveness to Whigs and Tories alike. He must end the murder and plunder that set neighbor against neighbor. He must take command of Georgia's First Continental Army Battalion, as well as state troops and militiamen who were waiting across the Savannah River for him, but he must discipline them only as much as their "nature and constitution" could bear. He must help Governor John Martin and his assemblymen establish a real working government, and once established, he must urge them to pardon the Loyalists who had taken up arms against the United States. He must never burden the people he had come to serve, but instead must unite them in a final push against the British. Wayne must "invite all the people to join you," Greene explained, to "do honor to yourself" and perform an "essential service to your country."[14]

Something in the phrase "open wide a door" renewed the sense of possibilities in Wayne that had disappeared after Yorktown. If he could help establish government in a ruined place where law and order had broken down, then he would experience a kind of glory he had never known before. Renown had come to him already in the Revolution, but only for fleeting moments: the retreat through Quebec, up the sheer cliffs of Stony Point, and away from the trap at Green Spring. But all these feats had the aura of a passing glory while the fame of this campaign might be more permanent. He and his new commander General Greene must truly secure the Revolution. They must protect and sustain suffering men, women, and even children until their own duly elected representatives could do the same. With a hundred soldiers from Virginia and Pennsylvania, including Colonel Stephen Moylan's Light Dragoons, and a detachment of artillery, Wayne left Round O on January 9. Three hundred South Carolina dragoons from General Thomas Sumter's Brigade were to join him by early February. He knew he would quickly lose Sumter's brigade when their enlistments were up, but for the moment this did not bother him. Another 170 volunteers would be waiting for him in Georgia. He led his small army up along pine barrens that rose from the sand and down through tangled oaks in the swamps, some eighty miles toward a ferry crossing on the Savannah River called Two Sisters. He was buoyed up by the image of the door opened wide for all the people and troubled only by one nagging thought. Was Madame Fortune on his path again, enticing him with promises of victory even as she prepared to abandon him?[15]

Wayne suspected Madame Fortune might be toying with him when he arrived across from Two Sisters on the Savannah. Instead of soldiers ready at attention or anxious civilians lining the shore, there was no one waiting for him on either side of the river. Neither was there a ferry or any other boat to take his soldiers and their artillery and horses over to Georgia. His men would have to row themselves and their cannon across in the canoes they could round up, while their horses would have to swim the icy river. Before this happened, Wayne called upon the help that Greene had promised him in Georgia. He wrote first to Governor John Martin, letting him know the Continental Army was waiting across the Savannah. His soldiers needed boats to cross the river and then food for themselves and fodder for their horses when they arrived on the other side. Only then did he remember Greene's image of opening the wide door to all the "deluded" citizens who had gone over to the Tories. They must be forgiven, Wayne explained to Martin, for the British probably pressured them to switch their allegiance. Be merciful to them, he advised, and they would respond with renewed loyalty. He reminded Martin that gratitude for a kindness offered along with self-interest were the two forces that governed the human heart.[16]

Next, he wrote to Colonel John Twiggs, the commander of the Georgia militia, telling him he had come to defeat the British, but also to open a door to the wretched Loyalists who had joined them. You must have received General Greene's letters explaining all this, dashed off a desperate Wayne. The implication of his note was clear. Why wasn't Twiggs waiting for him across the Savannah at Two Sisters? Wayne delayed three more days on the South Carolina side of the river, but still there was no answer and no one appeared. So on January 17, he wrote to Colonel James Jackson, the commander of Georgia's state troops, no longer reminding him of why the Continental Army had come to Georgia nor that a wide door must be opened to the people. Wayne simply commanded Jackson to bring his men immediately to Two Sisters. Jackson must be there by sunrise on the morning of January 19 when Wayne's army would finally cross the Savannah River.[17]

As he waited for someone to appear on the Georgia side, Wayne could not help but think of Caesar at the Rubicon. Long ago his hero had hesitated before crossing the river south of Ravenna that marked the dividing line between Rome and its provinces. An ancient law prohibited generals from bringing their armies across the Rubicon. "Still we can retreat!" Caesar said to his soldiers, "But once lest us pass this little bridge,—and nothing is left but to fight it out with arms!" He knew crossing the river would lead to a terrible civil war and maybe even his own death. Suddenly a man playing a pipe appeared at Caesar's side. His troops gathered around him to listen to the beautiful music. The man grabbed a trumpet from one of the soldiers and ran to the Rubicon. He blasted out the call to advance and hurried across the bridge to the other side. The goddess Fortuna had tipped her hand and shown Caesar where his future was tending. "Let us go where the omens of the gods and the crimes of our enemies summon us! The die is now cast!" he declared.[18]

No sign appeared at Two Sisters telling Wayne what direction Madame Fortune was taking him as she once told Caesar. Still the Savannah seemed like the Rubicon. He was certain his life would change forever once he crossed into Georgia. All that had gone before would disappear and what would come after he could not see for sure. He thought of the last campaign leading up to Yorktown, when the world still made sense, and while not ready to write to his wife Polly or General Washington, he penned a note to Henry Lee, the dashing cavalry officer who helped push Cornwallis north across the Dan River where Wayne helped to trap him. Though Colonel Lee had already come to dislike him, Wayne still believed they were friends. Thinking the proud Virginian, who had just left the Continental Army after years of fighting in the southern backcountry, might regret his decision and so be jealous of this new command, Wayne told him not to be, a sentiment he could easily have repeated ten years later when he assumed the command in Ohio that Lee so coveted. As he explained, the "enemy in this quarter are *stronger* & we *weaker* than expected!—add to this an exhausted, & almost depopulated country, distracted by faction;—you'll then easily conclude my situation[']s not enviable."[19]

On the morning of January 19, once he had everyone across to the Georgia side, he realized even more clearly how accurate his short note to Lee truly was. He saw it in Ebenezer, the settlement ten miles downriver from Two Sisters, which he chose as his first headquarters in the state. How carefully had its founders, the Protestant Salzburgers who had fled here from Catholic Austria in the mid-1730s, laid out its town square, its intersecting streets, its house and garden plots, and its surrounding farms. But now almost everything was in ruins except for the redoubts around the settlement and one red brick church still standing. The town had been plundered so many times by Tories and Whigs, as Wayne now called the Loyalists and Patriots, that little else was left untouched.

But looking downriver toward Savannah was even more terrible, for there everything seemed to be on fire. Governor James Wright had ordered his soldiers to burn all the rice and forage in a wide sweep from Ebenezer to the Ogeechee River to hold off the "rebel general," the term he used for General Wayne in all his correspondence. The British scorched the earth as they withdrew from Mulberry Grove and Sharon, two plantations on the Savannah, and another post on the Ogeechee. They headed behind the redoubts and swamps that surrounded the capital. Seeing the smoke in the distance that masked the retreat of the redcoats, Wayne knew he had won the first victory of his very first command, but how awful this long war had become if this conflagration was a triumph.[20]

Looking past the haze of the burning fields, Wayne realized there could be no direct attack on the British in Savannah as he had boasted to Twiggs. For one thing, there were far more soldiers in the town's garrison than General Greene had estimated. Wayne had learned from a Loyalist who had just deserted from the British that there were at least eleven hundred soldiers in Savannah. These included six hundred regulars, thirty of whom were cavalry; two hundred militia led by Colonel Thomas Brown, Georgia's most hated Tory who actively promoted Indian attacks against the rebellious colonists; another two hundred Hessians; and a hundred Loyalists serving under the royal governor James Wright. A handful of men who had fled from Savannah corroborated the tally. Even though Wayne's numbers would soon increase once the dragoons arrived from South Carolina, the total was not enough to attack or lay siege to the city, especially since Twiggs and Jackson commanded only a few dozen troops. The best thing Wayne could do, not just for the sake of humanity but from a military perspective as well, was to open a wide door to the Loyalists and maybe to the Hessians. He must do this even as he sent out small parties of mounted soldiers to harass the enemy and so close off the routes that brought supplies from the backcountry.[21]

Wayne's first move was to convince Governor Martin to call his legislature together in Ebenezer and agree on a pardon for Americans who had joined the redcoats. Martin, nicknamed "Black Jack" by the British for his dark coloring, tried to explain to Wayne that winning approval for such a blanket amnesty would not be easy. In his opinion, there was another trait in human nature, besides gratitude and self-interest, which Wayne had overlooked. That trait was the inability to let go of past wrongs quickly, especially if those wrongs were as horrific as the ones inflicted on the people of Georgia. How could they forget their murdered families, their farms and fields burned to the ground, their horses stolen, their cattle taken for food, or their hogs maimed and left to rot in the woods?[22]

But Wayne would hear none of this. Nor would he sink into the mire of hatred that surrounded him like the mud of Georgia's rainy winter. He had no time to learn why Whigs despised Tories, why factions of Whigs loathed each other, or why neighbors were hell bent on murdering their neighbors. He pressed Martin to act, even writing the broadside that he would distribute once the Georgia legislature approved it. His determination paid off. On February 21, the assembly announced an amnesty for any man who had taken up arms for the British if he fought for General Wayne until the war ended or was made a prisoner by the redcoats. Wayne, with Governor Martin in tow, set out through the ruined streets of Ebenezer until he found someone who could set the proclamation in type. Once they were printed, he handed the broadsides over to his post riders with orders to distribute them throughout the countryside.[23]

Slowly the proclamation of amnesty took effect. Week after week, a trickle of men who had fought for the British came into his camp. Wayne was most impressed when Sir Patrick Houston, one of the top Loyalists, surrendered himself and his cavalry. Houston, not a young man anymore, had arrived in Georgia in 1732 as one of James Oglethorpe's original settlers. He went on to become one of the wealthiest planters in Savannah. His life was a testament to how the Revolution tore families apart. His son John had served as the second governor of the new state of Georgia in 1778 while his other son William had been elected to the Continental Congress. Within three months' time, Sir Patrick would be banished from the state and all his property confiscated once the revolutionary assembly placed him on the list of attainder as a traitor. But for now he and his fellow Loyalists would help Wayne rebuild all the roads and bridges that the British had destroyed during seven years of fighting.[24]

Soon more men, women, and children, including slaves and Indians, came into Ebenezer. They were hoping for a refuge from the endless fighting that only the Continental Army could provide. They also came looking for something to eat. Wayne finally realized why Governor Martin had turned down every request for food and fodder. The governor was not joking when he said the only crop he could offer was tobacco, which he instructed Wayne to burn near his tent to ward off swamp fever. Beyond that, his people truly had not a loaf of bread to spare or even a speck of grain to bake. They had no corn either, not for Wayne's soldiers or his horses. Nor had Martin exaggerated when he said all the livestock was gone. The cows and calves had been confiscated by whatever militia passed by last. The hogs were gone, too, killed for target practice or sliced open and left for dead in the woods. Everything had been taken away from his citizens, and so as Martin explained to the general who had come to rescue them, their burning desire for vengeance would not be easily put out.[25]

Overwhelmed at the conditions he found in Georgia, Wayne begged his commander for help. Send soldiers, even just a few veterans from the Pennsylvania Line. Greene wrote back that he could not spare anyone, but he would send a small company of Continental dragoons from Virginia under Colonel Thomas Posey, an officer who had served with Wayne since Stony Point. Send flour and beef, Wayne answered, but Greene only had rice to spare. He told his unhappy general to look for food upriver in the town of Augusta. Send clothes, too, Wayne wrote back, coats, pants, and shoes especially. He and his soldiers had not changed their uniforms for five weeks. When Posey's men, who had marched barefoot and in threadbare clothes from Virginia, finally arrived, most had to stay in their tents to hide their naked limbs.[26]

Wayne had felt like Caesar when he crossed the Savannah in January, but by late February, he seemed to have stepped out of the pages of the Bible. His usual allusions to ancient Rome disappeared from his letters, and he now filled them with images drawn from Genesis and Exodus. Surrounded by hundreds of people, whom he described as "British, Hessians, new levies, out layers, Tories, Crackers, Ethiopians & Indian allies to the number of thirteen tribes," all seeking his help and protection, he saw himself wandering through the "perfect desert" of Georgia like an Old Testament patriarch roaming the Near East with his wives and children, his servants, and his flocks. Sometimes he felt like Moses leading his people out of their captivity in Egypt to the Promised Land.[27]

But in his opinion, the suffering of the Israelites could not compare to what he had endured in Georgia. As he explained to his friend Walter Stewart, who remained behind in South Carolina with General Greene, "they had only to make brick without straw," while he and his few dragoons had formed an army without men, food, or forage, built boats and bridges with no money or material save what they took from the forests, and made Whigs out of Tories and taught them to wrest a country away from the enemy. How different this misery was from the glory they had both known along the falls of the Passaic when they marched at the head of a thousand soldiers, all wearing caps with bright red horsehair flowing behind them. Would to God, Wayne added almost as a prayer, we were there again.[28]

After nearly a month in Georgia, Wayne decided to open wide the door not just to the Loyalists and the Patriots, but to the Indians as well. On January 29, he received news that a large party of Creeks was heading down the Ogeechee Trail toward Savannah. He decided to intercept them, not with force of arms, but through a clever ruse. Knowing the South Carolina dragoons wore red uniforms, he ordered Colonel William McCoy to take a party of his state troops down the trail toward the Indians. When the Creeks were still at a distance, they were to call out that they were British soldiers come to escort them to Sir Alured Clarke's headquarters in Savannah. The ruse worked. McCoy's men brought twenty-six Indians, six white traders, and ninety-three packhorses into Wayne's camp. He ordered Colonel Jackson's Georgia volunteers to guard them, but treat them with respect. He offered them food and rum, and kept them warm with a roaring fire. He also sent Major Joseph Habersham and the entire Georgia militia to intercept a large party of Choctaw heading to Savannah using the same ruse. He was certain if he treated the Indians with kindness and generosity, explaining the war to them in simple terms, they would convince their people to stay out of the fighting once they returned home.[29]

Wayne had little experience with Indians. Like every child growing up in Pennsylvania during the French and Indian War, he heard stories of the warriors who massacred settlers across the western mountains. But he had no direct dealings with them until he commanded Fort Ticonderoga, and even then, he encountered more women than men, primarily as the mistresses of his fellow officers. He was offered still more women by Indian chiefs coming into his camp at Ebenezer, but he again refused them. Beyond these few instances, he knew nothing about the realities of tribal life. He saw the Indians as wild creatures of the forest, and had no conception of how tightly they were bound by trade with the British in Georgia and the Spanish in Florida. He had, in fact, intercepted part of the Creeks' yearly take of furs on the way to Savannah to be exchanged for manufactured goods upon which the tribe depended.[30]

Understanding none of this, Wayne instead spoke to the Creeks as if they were children, not the active business partners of colonial traders. "I am no Englishman," he explained, but instead like the Indians, "I was born on this island." His only goal was to push the redcoats back to the tiny island from whence they had come. Go home, he told the warriors, hunt deer and plant corn, and leave the Americans and British to fight out this war on their own. Keeping the Creeks as his prisoners, along with their packtrain of goods, Wayne sent the white traders home. He impressed even himself with this small victory, writing with great pride to General Greene that he made peace with the Indians without shedding a drop of blood on either side. Maybe it was possible to fight a new kind of war that did not require the death of every enemy soldier. Perhaps this revolution was not a struggle for power or territory alone, but for humanity itself and so it must be fought with reason and restraint. As Wayne had treated the Tories and the Whigs with mercy and respect, so now he would treat the Indians.[31]

He had to tell someone what he finally understood, and so for the first time in a long while wrote to his wife. A letter from Polly, dated December 10, 1781, had just gotten through to him. She thought he was coming home after Yorktown and was upset that he had gone away again. Wayne ignored her complaints as he had throughout the war and told her instead what had happened in Georgia. He had been ordered to rescue the suffering people of this ruined state and would have come on his own if he had known all the troubles they endured. Wayne described how he had driven the redcoats back behind the defenses of Savannah, more by "spirited maneuvers than by force." He had done his best to serve the "most wretched people on earth" without spilling much blood. Wayne was most proud of the fact that he had spared hundreds of Indian chiefs and warriors. Remembering a line from a work by Laurence Sterne, one of his favorite writers, he said the Irish writer was wrong when he dismissed soldiering as a profession that "made bad men worse." Surely his time in Georgia had disproved Sterne's adage. Wayne then confessed something even more startling to his "dear girl." In no uncertain terms, he told Polly, "I am *satiate* of this horrid trade of blood, & would much rather spare one poor *savage* than destroy twenty."[32]

But even as he praised his newfound faith in treating the enemy with mercy, he was already descending back into dark currents of war. In the same week he wrote to Polly, Colonel Jackson's men, who despised the Creeks and could no longer bear seeing them so well treated, let the Indians escape. Colonel Habersham returned to Ebenezer with news that the Choctaw had not fallen into the trap set for them. His militia, disgruntled that they would not be able to rob or kill Indians, had deserted him and gone off to plunder the tiny village of St. Andrew's where they murdered eleven of their fellow Americans. Furious at both the Georgia state troops and the militia, Wayne turned his rage against the British, ordering a three-pronged attack to destroy all the forage within a half-mile of Savannah. In the dead of night, his men were to torch the fodder stored at Governor Wright's plantation east of the city and on nearby Hutchinson Island while his infantry feigned an attack on Savannah from the northwest. While the British intercepted the soldiers sent to the island, killing and wounding several of them before they could set fire to anything, the rest of the operation went off as scheduled. Wayne was overjoyed to see Savannah "illuminated" in the middle of the night, all at "Wright's expense" as his plantation went up in flames. General Greene cheered him on from a distance, writing that the destruction of the enemy's forage was "capital" and noting, "How Strange to tell! That the enemy are pounded with less than one third their numbers."[33]

But the final descent into the horrors of war came a short time later. Wayne had stayed above the hating, refusing to be dragged into the world of an eye for an eye and a tooth for a tooth, even as he lit a ring of fire around Savannah, until word arrived in his camp, which had moved back to Ebenezer, that Major Francis Moore, his favorite young officer among the Georgia state troops, was dead. He had sent Moore and a small group of soldiers across the Ogeechee River toward the Altamaha to intercept parties of Tories and Indians trying to get through to Savannah. Moore had written back that the people living in the southern part of Georgia were in an even more desperate state than those living near Savannah. They were, he explained, a wretched, damned, and disaffected lot who had suffered so many abuses that they had lost any sense of humanity.[34] When he was searching for boats at Reed's Bluff to take his men across the Altamaha, shots rang out from a nearby house. Tories and Indians were hiding there, and one of them gunned Moore down. Wayne, who had witnessed hundreds of deaths on the battlefield since Three Rivers, could not accept the fact that Moore had been killed so ignominiously. He had never consoled the parents of his dead soldiers, but felt compelled to write to Moore's family. He was so distraught that Greene, who had been unable to return any of his letters for a month, especially as he faced a mutiny of the Pennsylvania Line, finally wrote back to comfort him.[35]

The man who had preached forgiveness, squelching any thought of reprisal, now felt the same burning need to avenge the death of the people he loved. When Colonel Jackson's dragoons gunned down a British officer named Major Gill, in retaliation for Moore's death, Wayne regretted only that while the man held the same rank as Moore, he was far from his equal in character. He now filled his letters to Greene with plans to dig the "caitiffs," his favorite word for villains of all stripes, out of their fortress in Savannah. His desire for revenge grew even stronger when a Choctaw warrior killed one of his dragoons and dragged the body back into the city. After cutting off his nose and upper lip, the Indians paraded his scalp through the city with Governor Wright and General Clarke, who wrongly believed the dead man was Colonel Habersham, cheering him on and giving a ball in his honor. Clarke ordered no one to bury the dead soldier on pain of death, an edict that a few slaves ignored, burying the corpse in the night. Wayne learned all of this from a captured Chickasaw. He vowed to Greene that once he got hold of a British soldier, he would kill both of them, the Indian and the redcoat, in the same manner.[36]

He saw an even greater chance to wreak vengeance on the enemy when he learned in late May that Colonel Brown's Loyalist rangers, along with a company of British infantry and dragoons, totaling about 350 men, were heading out of Savannah to escort a party of Creeks into the city. They had marched seven miles out of town toward the southwest along the Ogeechee Trail and by May 19 had made it to Harris's Bridge on the Ogeechee River, their chosen rendezvous point. After waiting for two days, and with no Creeks in sight, they hurried back toward Savannah, fearing all the while that the rebel general might attack them. If they could make it to the wooden causeway on the outskirts of the city, they believed they would be safe, for not even the daring Wayne, who had moved his camp to the Gibbons Plantation just five miles northwest of Savannah, would have the courage to come through the swamps to attack them.

But late on the evening of May 20, when Wayne learned Brown's men were approaching Savannah, he decided to lead his dragoons through the swamps and onto the causeway where he could intercept them. Shortly after midnight on May 21, the soldiers at the head of Brown's party ran straight into Wayne's men waiting for them in the dark. Wayne ordered his dragoons to charge ahead with the sword and bayonet. The redcoats fell back into the Loyalists coming up behind them. Colonel Brown could not deploy his men on the crowded causeway and fled for his life into the pitch-black swamp. Forty of the enemy were killed and eighteen wounded, but Wayne, who lost five men killed and two wounded, had no sympathy for them, only for their horses that he could hear thrashing about in the dark waters. Some of the enemy, including the hated Brown, survived, but took several days to make their way back to Savannah. Wayne followed them to the very edge of the town, but seeing that General Clarke would not come out and fight, he moved his camp back to Ebenezer.[37]

This small victory elated Wayne for the moment, but could not lift him fully out of the despair that haunted him since arriving in Georgia. Soldiers who had known him for years noticed he grew ever more depressed and anxious. He also drank far more than usual. Wayne was short with his men, often brooding in his tent with his books, but also going off alone on his favorite black horse and riding along the edges of his camp for hours on end. His friends at a distance in Philadelphia, like Benjamin Rush and Sharp Delany, got a frightening picture of Wayne's state of mind. He complained of the alligator water he was forced to drink, the abandonment of his wife and children who never wrote to him, and the certain and horrible death that awaited him. After Yorktown he had only wanted to go home, and now he was certain that he would die instead in this god-forsaken place. Greene worried that Wayne, excited one minute and downcast the next, might take chances he never would if he were calmer. Reciting what he had learned long ago from Marshal Saxe, Wayne assured his commander, "I have long adopted the Opinion of those military writers, who lay it down as a maxim, that an officer never ought to hazard a battle, where a defeat would render his situation much worse than a retreat without it."[38]

If he had been on a more even keel, Wayne might have been overjoyed that the war he tried to escape just months before was finally ending. But instead he had a difficult time admitting the truth to himself. He knew by early May that the British were on the brink of letting go of their colonies. Even before General Greene sent him official word that the war was drawing to a close, Wayne already suspected as much, primarily from intercepted letters between General Clarke and Colonel Brown. But now the man who had wanted to go home after York-town could not let go of his need to avenge the wrongs done all around him. He had been sent to Georgia to fight a new kind of war only to lose his way in a sea of hate. The war must continue, he wrote to Greene, until he finally took Savannah by the sword. "Do let us dig the Caitiffs out," he demanded, "it will give us an éclat to our Arms; to effect a business in which the armament of our great and goodly Ally failed."[39]

But in late May, when a British soldier carrying a white flag came looking for him in Ebenezer, Wayne had to face the fact that the war was ending. The guards took the man's papers and then rudely shooed him away, an act for which Wayne later apologized. The documents included a letter from General Clarke informing him that for all practical purposes the war was over and imploring him to do everything in his power to "prevent an unnecessary *effusion* of *Blood*." There was also a letter from Governor Wright asking for an end to hostilities. The man who had burned the fields around Savannah to prevent the rebel general from taking his city now promised Wayne he would do everything in his power to reconcile Great Britain and its former colonies. Wayne wrote polite letters back to both men, agreeing with their desire for peace, but explaining he was merely a soldier and could only suspend hostilities if so ordered by the Congress of the United States. But to Greene, he was less polite and almost hell-bent on a military victory. Still sunk in the mud of vengeance and despair, he wrote, "May I expect your orders by the return of the express or rather the means of possessing Savannah *vi et arms*."[40]

Wayne's determination to fight to the finish nearly got him killed a month later. Obsessed with digging the British out of Savannah, he failed to reconnoiter the countryside to see if the Creeks, who had missed their rendezvous with Colonel Brown, might be on their way to the city. Never considering such a possibility, and thus making the same mistake he had made near the Paoli Tavern, he moved his camp to the Gibbons Plantation just five miles from Savannah to keep an eye on the hated British caitiffs. On the night of June 23, he stationed most of his men toward Savannah, leaving only one guard in the rear near the artillery park facing the backcountry. Little did he suspect that the Creeks were only miles away and heading directly for his camp. They had arrived at the rendezvous point the day after Brown left and were determined to kill Wayne before heading with their packtrain loaded with furs into Savannah.[41]

Shortly after midnight on June 24, the Indians came upon the lone guard and killed him. Then their leader let out a war whoop and his men raced toward the tents where the general and his soldiers lay sleeping. Wayne, waking immediately, was certain Colonel Brown had come out from Savannah to attack his camp. He shouted to his men to fix their bayonets and die with him. Climbing onto his black horse, he was soon confronted in the dark by a man who grabbed hold of his reins. Wayne struck him down with his sword, but as the man fell, he got off one last shot with his pistol, missing the general but killing his horse. Tumbling to the ground, Wayne realized the attack was coming from the rear of his camp. He ran toward the artillery park, ordering first the cavalry and then the infantry to charge and push the enemy back into the surrounding woods.

Only when the fighting was over and he saw the dead Indians lying all about him did he realize that the Creeks, and not Colonel Brown, had attacked him. He learned, too, that the man who grabbed his reins and killed his beautiful black horse was their chief Emistersigo. Wayne was furious that the Indians he treated so mercifully had tried to murder him. When Colonel Posey brought thirty Creek prisoners back into camp, Wayne exploded, demanding to know why Posey had done this. There was something terrible in his voice that the colonel would never forget. Wayne had a way of speaking to his soldiers that

made every word sound like a challenge. This time was no different. Wayne's enraged tone, so brusque and allowing no contradiction, meant a death sentence
for the prisoners, which Posey carried out immediately.[42]

Still, there was no denying that the war was over and the victory belonged to
the Americans. With the help of Greene, who by now was writing almost daily
letters to him, Wayne gave up the need for vengeance and slowly came out of
his despair, if only for the moment. He recognized the work he had done, not
to defeat the redcoats in a grand battle but to "deprive the British of a considerable tract of territory with which they expected to go to the European market,
where the fate of America will ultimately be decided." Together the two generals had made sure the Americans could secure South Carolina and Georgia as
parts of the United States of America. Suddenly all the mercy he had shown in
his first weeks after he crossed into Georgia came back to him. He was gracious
to Loyalist merchants who came from Savannah asking that he keep their goods
safe from harm when his soldiers marched into the town. They would have six
months, he promised, to maintain their stores before they left Georgia forever.[43]

He was even more forgiving once his soldiers finally marched into Savannah
on July 11. Wayne ordered Colonel Jackson and the Georgia state troops to lead
the parade into town. His heart softened toward the city he had planned to attack
when he saw how much its intersecting streets and tree-lined squares resembled
Philadelphia. Governor Martin and his assembly came, too, but that did not prevent Wayne from making one proclamation after another for the state on his
own. The Tories would be forgiven for their crimes, with the exception of murder.
All Tory merchants could stay in business if they opened their storehouses to
Wayne, who needed clothes and food for his men. But he was not past saber rat-
tling at the British who lingered with their fleet on Tybee Island. He demanded,
on behalf of the citizens of Georgia, that they return the many slaves they had
taken with them. To all the enemy, soldiers and Loyalists alike, who might be in
East Florida, he welcomed them to join the victorious Patriots, but threatened
war if they dared to resist him.[44]

Greene was pleased that Wayne had come back from the brink but warned
him not to make grand pronouncements that he could not fulfill. He was even
more worried that Wayne, after complaining about his time in Georgia, now
seemed reluctant to leave. Every time Greene ordered him to march his men to
South Carolina, Wayne offered a new excuse why he must stay in Savannah. At
first, it was because the British had failed to leave Tybee Island on schedule. Then
there were rumors that Colonel Brown and Loyalist militia were on their way to
attack Savannah. Wayne even took soldiers south of the city to meet them, but
Brown's company fled to a nearby island at the mere thought of facing Wayne

again. There was another reason that Wayne would not leave Savannah, one that he could not tell his commander. He had fallen under the spell of a beautiful young woman, just twenty-one years old, and would not leave her side.

Her name was Mary Maxwell. She had written to him shortly after Savannah fell, sending him a black-and-white cockade that she had made for his hat. He in turn sent one flirtatious note after another to Strathy Hall, her family's plantation, begging her to come meet him. "If you leave after breakfast, you could be here for dinner with me in Savannah," he wrote. She finally rode to town and, from the moment she met Wayne, never left him. Wayne gathered a group of locals around Mary and himself, including former Tories, for nightly carousing in Savannah. Many officers, who had expected Wayne to win them promotions once the war was over, complained of his unjust treatment. Servants he hired in Savannah to cook and do his laundry complained they were never paid. Wayne forgot everyone in his mad pursuit of Miss Maxwell. Finally, guilt ridden, he dashed off two letters to Polly, reminding her to make sure Margaretta mastered her French and Isaac his Latin.

He finally came to his senses when he realized Mary was only interested in his political connections. She asked Wayne to win the release of her younger brother, a Loyalist, from prison and remove him from the state's list of attainder, which meant the loss of his property and banishment from Georgia for being a traitor. Wayne wrote to John Martin asking for his help, but the governor turned down his request. Both the governor and his assembly had grown tired of Wayne's merciful tendencies, and no longer needing his protection, they added more names to the list and confiscated even more property of the Loyalists. Wayne, who never again asked for help for the Maxwell family, now prepared to leave Savannah. Although he never wrote to Mary again, "Maxwell" would later join the names of other women as a password for his soldiers on the Ohio frontier.[45]

Wayne sent the few soldiers still with him ahead to Greene's camp at Ashley Hill while he came alone on horseback a week later. When he crossed into South Carolina, he was horrified at the barren country. Less than a year before when he arrived in the state, he had seen flocks of parakeets flying above him, but now as he traveled north only buzzards circled overhead. He knew he was close to Ashley Hill when he smelled the filthy men and the carrion on which they survived. Once he finally came into Greene's camp, he was horrified that conditions were just as terrible there as they had been in Georgia. Everywhere he looked the soldiers were in rags. Their uniforms were so worn that they buttoned their coats with thorns from locust trees. Some were so naked they stayed in their tents all day long. Everyone was anxious to be paid, to find food, and to go home. The few surviving cattle about to be slaughtered had barely any meat on their bones.

The dark despair, which had disappeared for the few weeks he chased Miss Maxwell, descended on Wayne with a vengeance. Greene did his best to cheer his friend who seemed more irascible and troubled than he ever remembered him. He was desperate to do anything to win the war that had already been won. Let me have the soldiers of Mordecai Gist, who lay sick in his tent, he begged, and I will take them to chase away the British who might come out of Charleston looking for forage. Let me take some of my men from Georgia, he implored, and hunt Tories and Indians along the Ashley and Cooper Rivers. When Greene refused all these requests, Wayne planned to take some of his Georgia veterans and pursue the enemy anyways, with or without his commander's approval, ignoring the fact that Greene had already hung soldiers in the Pennsylvania Line for disobeying him.

Greene never had to discipline his friend for disobeying orders. On September 2, as Wayne sat in his tent writing a letter to the financier Robert Morris, begging for money for the troops, he collapsed with a virulent fever. He did not rise from his cot for an entire month. Beyond sheer physical exhaustion and emotional despair, Wayne had contracted malaria. He wavered between chills and fever, shivering under a threadbare blanket and then throwing it off in an anxious sweat. Greene came often to his tent to cheer him, while camp doctors gave him cinchona bark to chew and told him to exercise. Finally, after weeks of hovering between life and death, he came out of the worst of it. By the end of October he could stand and walk, but barely. He took up his pen to finish his letter to Morris. He also wrote to Colonel Butler that if all the wealth of the Indies was waiting for him just a mile away, he could not walk an inch to take hold of it.

Even when Wayne was back on his feet, he remained a raw nerve. He could not be questioned on the smallest matter or he would launch into a mighty defense of himself. Greene had already suffered from Wayne's harangues the previous June after telling him that Congress was about to investigate the army for "want of oeconomy." If performing the "Herculean business" of securing Georgia with no provisions "be deemed want of oeconomy," Wayne answered, then "I acknowledge myself guilty!" He was furious when General Thaddeus Kosciusko accused him of taking large stores of wine, beer, and cheese for the exclusive use of his officers. When Kosciusko also charged him with letting too many civilians through to Charleston, Greene had to question Wayne's actions even though he already knew the reason. Wayne could not resist any woman who asked for his help. Whether they told him they must pass through to care for their children or run a family business, he always let them go.[46]

How could Greene question him on this, an angry Wayne shot back, after all he had done for his country? How could anyone begrudge his men a few blocks of cheese when they had suffered so much in Georgia? Or berate him for letting a few suffering women through to their children? Greene kept him calm through it all, assuring him that the questions were a mere formality. To bolster his spirits, Greene chose him to lead the army into Charleston once the British finally left. He could pick Wayne because his highest-ranking officer Mordecai Gist lay sick in his tent. On the morning of December 14, 1782, Wayne rode at the front of the army's columns into Charleston. Once the British boarded their ships and departed, Greene let his troubled friend dance the night away with his beautiful wife, Caty, in celebrations that lasted until dawn. Later he sent both of them, along with several officers, to James Island in the Charleston harbor to rest and recuperate.[47]

The short furlough did little to improve Wayne's anxious spirit. Even as the army slowly disbanded all around him, Wayne refused to go home. He could not let go of the life he had known for nearly a decade. He begged Greene to send him on one last campaign. He got his chance in April 1783 when rumors came north that a renegade band of Loyalists was about to invade Georgia from Florida. Wayne and a small company of men, this time at Greene's orders, raced south along the Atlantic coast, but no enemy appeared. He returned to South Carolina and now asked Greene to let him treat with the Indians. Brooding over the future, he worried about wars along the western frontier. Greene agreed and sent Wayne to Augusta where he called a council with the Creeks and the Choctaws, but though he waited, week after week, no one ever appeared.[48]

By early summer, when he was back with Greene in South Carolina, Wayne found a stack of letters waiting for him, not from Polly or his children, but from his many friends. Come home, wrote Benjamin Rush, and join in the political fights that were just beginning. Robert Morris, struggling to find ways to pay off the nation's war debts, and John Dickinson, now the governor of Pennsylvania, wrote, too, urging Wayne to return to the people who loved him. Only Sharp Delany, who had watched over his children in his absence, understood that Wayne, broken in body and spirit, must come home to rest and recover. We will take long walks in the countryside and go fishing in the streams near Waynesborough, he promised his friend, like we did long ago before this terrible war started.[49]

Finally, in July 1783, after almost everyone else had left, Wayne made ready to board one of the transport ships he had asked Dickinson to send to bring home the last of the Pennsylvania Line. But there was one more thing he must do before he left the war behind. He returned to the Savannah River to inspect the plantations that the Georgia legislature had granted him in honor of his service in the state. He was given land along the Altamaha, but the prize was the Rich-

Sharp Delany. Image copyright © The Metropolitan Museum of Art.
Image Source: Art Resource, NY.

mond Plantation, confiscated from Alexander Wright, the son of the royal governor, and the very fields Wayne's men had once burned, and the adjoining Kew
Plantation. All the buildings were still standing, a fine house and barns, but the
slaves were gone, having run off or been taken away by the British. The rice fields,
all the gates and dikes, lay in ruins.

Still, for the moment, he imagined himself a wealthy planter. Perhaps little
Margaretta, now thirteen, would come and live with him here and grow into a

fine lady. They might ride downriver to Mulberry Grove, the plantation that the Georgia legislature has awarded to General Greene. Hopefully Greene would live there with his beautiful Catharine, and here in the place of Wayne's greatest suffering, they would find themselves reborn into a new and gracious life. But he realized that this would take a great deal of money, and he had no more money now than when he asked Washington to let him go home after Yorktown. Awaking as if from a dream, he returned to Charleston where he boarded the last transport of soldiers out of the city and headed toward home.[50]

Broken in body and spirit, he returned to Pennsylvania but remained restless and discontented. He would never know how different his life might have been if Washington had let him go home after Yorktown. But he did know that after the Georgia campaign he could never shake the darker cast in his thinking that came from witnessing so much misery and despair. Under all his gruffness, a deep well of sympathy remained for his men. He might be impatient with them for fleeing from the first Indian attack, but not so much so that he did not understand their fears, especially when facing death at the hands of the enemy. As impatient as he had been with them on October 15, 1793, when they fled for their lives, just two days later when they failed again, he did not condemn them. Shortly after dawn on October 17, as Colonel John Lowry and Ensign Samuel Boyd led twenty supply wagons north toward the main army, Ottawa warriors attacked the convoy seven miles past Fort St. Clair. The two officers, "gallant young gentlemen" as Wayne remembered them, fought bravely but died alongside thirteen of their fellow officers and privates. Seventy-five other soldiers raced down the road toward Fort Jefferson. The Indians took ten men prisoners and stole or killed upward of seventy horses. Leaving the supply wagons for the Legion to recover later, they sent seven scalps ahead to the Indians gathered at Roche de Boeuf.

This time, when Wayne learned what had happened, he did not dig the graves of the men who had deserted the convoy. Instead, he decided that his soldiers, now camped in a broad prairie six miles north of Fort Jefferson, had gone as far as they could with winter approaching. He called a council of his generals and asked them what to do. They knew that Wayne had already decided the answer. On this spot, he would build a fort to keep his army safe. Here they would wait together until the late winter or early spring when they would finally have to face the enemy who still terrified them. He would name the place after the man who held him steady in his darkest hours. He would call the fort Greeneville.[51]

"PERSECUTION HAS ALMOST DROVE ME MAD"

Deep in the Ohio wilderness, a hundred miles north of Fort Washington, General Wayne ordered his men to build the largest wooden fort ever constructed in America. Rising from a prairie surrounded by trees that grew 50 feet before branching, the post named for his friend Nathanael Greene would cover fifty-five acres and at 900 feet by 1,800 feet would measure more than a mile around. This fortress would keep Wayne's legions safe from harm as he had never been able to protect his men during the Georgia campaign. Then his soldiers slept under threadbare blankets and tents that turned a rusty brown from the constant rain. Nor would any Indian dare to breach the ten-foot walls of Fort Greeneville and try to assassinate him as Emistersigo had done. Though he might drive his men half-mad with his obsessive care, Wayne was determined not to lose any of them in the long winter that lay ahead. Here they would wait together for the Indians to make the next move.[1]

Waiting can be terrible for any man, but most especially for Anthony Wayne. From the Golgotha of Ticonderoga to the swamps of Georgia, he found waiting for the future to unfold almost unbearable. Once he envisioned what would happen next, his only goal was to hurry forward and meet it. Why Washington, Knox, and for that matter all Americans failed to see the danger ahead of them was beyond Wayne's understanding. Out past the edge of the forest, where even now his axmen were hauling back giant trees to build his fort, Wayne could see the Indians and the British encircling the entire frontier. Just as Julius Caesar surrounded Alesia with two bigger fortresses, so now the Indians and British were building a double stranglehold to crush the United States in a hidden vise.[2]

While waiting was difficult for Wayne, he knew it could be just as trying for his army. If his soldiers did not stay busy, they would turn against each other. In such close quarters, they would imagine insults where none existed and fight each other before they ever fought the Indians. For the moment, they had a new fort to build. Wayne ordered eight blockhouses constructed at precise intervals around the perimeter. Their windows, facing out toward the surrounding prairie, must be wide enough to fire a cannon left, right, and straight ahead. Their shutters must be strong enough to withstand musket fire until they could swing open with guns blazing. Bastions, the pointed wooden structures with a sentry box in each, must jut out from the fort's corners like buttresses supporting a cathedral. Here soldiers would be posted to watch for Indian warriors racing from the woods. Wayne was so convinced the enemy was hiding in the forest to attack his men that he ordered a wall of redoubts thrown up around the site and another ring of pickets established beyond them during the fort's construction.

Within the ascending walls of his fort, Wayne laid out intersecting streets with open squares like Philadelphia and Savannah. His soldiers would be safe in the cabins arranged in two rows around the inner walls of the fort. The cabins measured eleven feet by fourteen feet with room enough for ten men who would stay warm in front of fireplaces. He ordered the chimneys raised high enough so sparks from them never set fire to roofs nearby and engulfed the fort in flames. Flour, barrels of salted beef, whiskey, and hospital supplies would be stored in wooden sheds built against the inner walls of the fort. There would be a powder magazine for ammunition and a laboratory for making lead shots. For every sublegion, Wayne ordered stables, a guardhouse, and a kitchen built nearby. There would be separate houses, too, for himself, his brigadier generals, and the lieutenant colonels of each sublegion. Even as he saw to the comfort of his men, Wayne made sure there would be no end to their training. He ordered parade grounds leveled where his men could practice their maneuvers every day.[3]

Once Fort Greeneville was completed in December 1793, Wayne worried that his soldiers would soon be restless. Alone in so vast a country, far from frontier outposts like Cincinnati or Pittsburgh, and even farther away from the homes they left behind, they might forget they had come into this awful wilderness to defeat the Indians who had slaughtered St. Clair's men. Three days before Christmas, he ordered Major Burbeck to take three hundred men out of Fort Greeneville to the site of the massacre. If not for the fact that he was suffering from a headache and another bout of the flu, he would have led them himself. Once Burbeck found the place, his men must build a fort there according to Wayne's precise instructions, which included a drawing he made of the new post. He also told Burbeck to collect the bones of the fallen soldiers and bury them in a common grave at the center of the fort that would rise over the haunted place. Wayne ordered an extra gill of whiskey for every skull that a soldier found.

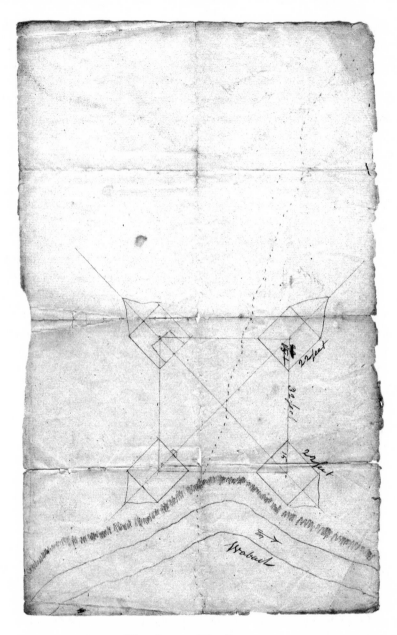

Wayne's map of Fort Recovery.
William L. Clements Library, University of Michigan.

Finally, they must find the cannon captured by the Indians and thrown into the river that encircled the place.[4]

Major Burbeck knew his soldiers were only a few miles away from the massacre site when they came upon skeletons and broken muskets strewn everywhere along the trail. They arrived at the battleground itself, on a bluff overlooking a narrow stream just like St. Clair had described in his dispatches to Secretary Knox, shortly after dawn on Christmas Eve. The melancholy place was more truly a Golgotha than Ticonderoga. By Burbeck's count, there were at least five hundred skulls strewn about the bluff, some still attached to skeletons. His soldiers found many skeletons lying side by side on the ground, the last remnants of men who had died fighting each other. It was easy to spot who was a soldier and who was an Indian. If a skull was crushed, a sure sign of a tomahawk blow, or cut and broken near the forehead, a clear mark of scalping, then it was an American.[5]

Following Wayne's instructions, Burbeck ordered most of his men to start building the fort. He sent the rest in search of the cannon that St. Clair's fleeing troops had abandoned. They found two of them, a brass three-pounder and a brass six-pounder, right where William Wells said they would be. They were in the river, a branch of the Wabash, which the Kentucky militia had stormed across on that terrible morning two years before. Once Burbeck's men found the cannon, the soldiers did something they had not been officially ordered to do. They searched for the remains of Wayne's friend Richard Butler. His younger brother Edward told Burbeck to look for Richard under a "large spreading oak tree" where St. Clair's soldiers had left him. They could identify him by examining his thighbone. He had broken his leg when he was a boy and the bone had never healed properly. Burbeck's men found Butler's skeleton with its crooked right thighbone still sitting against an oak tree.[6]

Wayne had trained his soldiers so well that the fort he named Recovery was finished by sunset on Christmas Eve. They had chopped down trees, dressed the lumber, and put up four one-story blockhouses and a wall of pickets connecting them in less than half a day. Burbeck placed the two cannon that his men found in the river, along with two more hauled from Fort Greeneville, in the blockhouses at the corners of the fort. There would be time later to build a second story on each blockhouse, but for now everyone was safe. The soldiers had done their best to bury the remains of the dead in a common grave at the center of the post, but before they could fall asleep on this holiest night of the year, they had to scrape together countless fragments of bone that still lay beneath them.[7]

While Wayne had turned down an invitation to share Christmas dinner with Wilkinson and his wife at Fort Jefferson, claiming he felt sick, he was strong enough to lead a small party of dragoons, his aides William Henry Harrison and Henry DeButts, and Dr. John Scott north from Fort Greeneville to inspect the new post. He was impressed that Burbeck had followed his instructions to the letter and that the soldiers had done their work so dutifully. He was especially happy that they recovered St. Clair's cannon. Leaving Captain Alexander Gibson in charge with a few dozen artillerymen and two companies of infantry and riflemen, Wayne led Major Burbeck and the rest of the troops back to Fort Greeneville on December 28. There had been only one serious mishap. The cannon recovered from the Wabash had misfired in a ceremony honoring the dead. Burbeck had suffered minor injuries, but beyond that, no man was lost, no soldier deserted, and no Indian had dared to attack.

Though he was still not feeling well, Wayne nearly burst with pride in his letter to Knox describing the successful mission. His soldiers had done everything he asked in record time. He was especially gratified when he watched them march on the parade ground on New Year's Day 1794 in new uniforms that had just arrived. Later that morning, he was still so elated that he rode with several officers to Fort Jefferson to celebrate the holiday, which happened to be his forty-ninth birthday, with the Wilkinsons. After surviving on bread, beef, and whiskey for so many months, Wayne's soldiers were amazed at the banquet laid out before them, including veal, turkey, mutton, venison, and even bear, vegetables of every kind, mince and apple pies, plum pudding and cake, and finally coffee, tea, and the finest wine. However, once the banquet was over, Wayne would not let his men linger and hurried them back to Fort Greeneville by nightfall.[8]

He soon grew anxious about the soldiers left behind at Fort Recovery and sent one order after another to keep them occupied. He told Captain Gibson to send out patrols and discover exactly where the Indians were camped for the winter. Find out, too, he added, what tribes were gathered at the Grand Glaize. Map the country all about paying particular attention to the rivers and streams and the lay of the land. Send a company of men some forty miles beyond Fort Recovery and find the place called Girty's Town, where James Girty, brother of the hated Simon Girty, lived. Wayne reminded Captain Gibson to protect his men and never rest at night until he had thrown up redoubts and pickets all around his soldiers. Gibson was also to keep his eyes open for any overture of peace from the tribes. If by some chance an Indian bearing a white flag came into his camp, he must not be harmed, but must instead be sent to Wayne at Fort Greeneville.[9]

Another worry for Wayne was a frightening rumor that the French, half mad in the bloodletting of their revolution, were coming up the Mississippi to recruit volunteers in Kentucky, head west to attack Spanish possessions, and thus reclaim their former empire. The execution of their hated queen Marie Antoinette, who was guillotined in the same week the Legion arrived in the prairie that would become Greeneville, had not broken the terror's fever, but instead had fueled it. Send mounted volunteers stationed between Lexington and Georgetown, Wayne wrote to Kentucky's governor Isaac Shelby, for soon we will be fighting not just the Indians, and probably the British, but the French, too. Shelby calmed the excited Wayne by assuring him there was no truth to these rumors.[10]

No French soldiers appeared and neither did any Indians, not for war or for peace. Where were they, Wayne wondered day after day? Handfuls of them had attacked his supply trains, but he had never seen the numbers of warriors that had descended upon St. Clair. Safe for the moment behind the walls of Fort Greeneville, Wayne still found the very idea of Indian warfare unnerving. The tribes, not Wayne, chose the place, the day, and the hour of battle. To defeat them, an army must be ever vigilant, ever prepared, and ever active, at every fort, along every trail, and in every convoy. Even the best men could go mad waiting for an attack. The previous year Captain John Smith, then the commander of Fort Jefferson, had lost his mind fearing an Indian raid on his post. He spent many sleepless nights wandering the fort, talking to phantom Indians wrapped in blankets who told him the names of soldiers who would be captured and killed next. Fearing for their captain's life as well as their own, Smith's officers took away his guns and sent him back to Fort Washington where he would hopefully regain his sanity.[11]

For Wayne, the stress of waiting was compounded by the fact that he had heard nothing from Philadelphia since the previous September. He knew a yellow fever epidemic was raging in the nation's capital, and many people, including Washington, had fled the city. But even when the epidemic subsided, there was still no word. A letter finally arrived from Knox saying the president was worried when he learned Wayne's convoys had been attacked. By way of Knox's letter, Washington cheered Wayne on from afar, reminding him of his full power to choose the site for his winter quarters. He even apologized for dragging the negotiations with the Indians through the summer, which meant there was no chance of leading a campaign against them until the following spring.[12]

Wayne wondered if Madame Fortune was toying with him again. Perhaps she had disappeared altogether, and the Fates, the even more mysterious goddesses who spun, measured, and cut the cloth of each man's life, were once again laying down the pattern of waiting, acting, and failing that had haunted him since he left Charleston at the war's end. How much of the past ten years had been waiting for events to turn for the better, then rushing forward in a mad dash of activity, only to run headlong into failure, often brought about by the opposition of others, or persecution as Wayne described the final stage, which began the cycle all over again. "Persecution has drove me half mad" became a favorite expression of Wayne in these years. After returning from the trauma of the Georgia campaign, he never again believed he was in total control of his life. Instead, misfortune stalked his path.[13]

He had made his way back to Pennsylvania in August 1783 so sick that he never left his bunk on the ship bringing him home. Though then only thirty-eight years of age, he appeared much older, especially after the long sea voyage from Charleston left him racked with fever and unable to keep food down. He was too weak to travel the twenty miles from Philadelphia to Waynesborough and instead stayed "forty two days or 1,008 hours," by his own count, in the city at the home of his faithful friend Sharp Delany. He did not return to his farm until mid-September, when another attack of fever laid him so low that he needed the constant care of his family. Finally back in the great stone house where he was born, reunited with Polly and his children, Wayne could think of nothing but when he could leave again. He was especially frantic that he would miss seeing Washington when he visited Philadelphia. Wayne returned to the city in October 1783, but the general was already gone. He took the time to write a thirteen-page letter to Washington describing the Georgia campaign down to the last detail.[14]

But just one month later, Wayne was back home at Waynesborough, suffering from a painful attack of gout. He felt as if the bones in his feet from his heels to his toes had been dislocated and probed "twenty & twenty thousand times over." He was most upset he would not be able to attend the farewell dinner that General Washington planned to host for his officers at the Fraunces Tavern in New York City. Nor would he able to say goodbye to him when he passed through Philadelphia on his way home to Mount Vernon. As Wayne explained to his beloved commander in letters written in the late fall, "Long want of health occasioned by the extreme of fatigue & loss of blood in assisting to vindicate the rights & liberties of Americans from her *coldest* to her *hottest* sun" deprived him of the pleasure of seeing him. But Washington need not fear that this was his "last adieu." His physicians assured him he would recover. They would meet again, Wayne promised, perhaps when he visited Mount Vernon on his way to inspect his plantation in Georgia.[15]

Wayne, who like a soldier in Caesar's legions had dreamed of returning home from the far corners of the empire, now could not bear the peace and quiet of Waynesborough. His concern for his children had all but disappeared in the swamps of Georgia, and seeing how well Polly ran the farm, he now gave little thought to the future of Margaretta or Isaac. When he arrived back in Philadelphia from the war, he bought dresses for his daughter and a suit with red velvet cuffs for his son. He also ordered a new uniform for himself and his servant Caesar after the Pennsylvania Assembly finally appointed him a brevet major general. But beyond getting new clothes for everyone, except for his wife, he showed little interest in his family's well-being. He decided to leave the management of Waynesborough in the capable hands of Polly and the details of his children's education to his friend Sharp Delany. In late December 1783, when his most recent attack of gout finally subsided, he put on a new ruffled shirt, a silk waistcoat sewn with golden thread, white pants, silk hose, and black shoes trimmed with diamond buckles, and wrapping himself in a blue coat with gold buttons and ivory facings, he climbed onto his horse and hurried back to the excitement waiting for him in Philadelphia.[16]

He was determined to get back into politics by running for a seat on Pennsylvania's Council of Censors. Established in 1776, this body oversaw the integrity of the state's constitution. Its members, two elected from every county, met every seven years. Their primary responsibility was to ensure the state's constitution was not violated. They must monitor the actions of the president, his executive council, and the legislative assembly making certain that no one overstepped the authority granted to them in the constitution. They also reviewed the collection of taxes and oversaw the proper implementation of state laws. If the censors discovered any irregularities, they could publicly censure officials, order their impeachment, and even recommend which laws should be repealed. The constitution could only be amended if the Council of Censors proposed changes and called for a convention to approve them.[17]

Wayne had been so determined to win a seat on the Council of Censors that on Election Day he rode on horseback through the streets of Philadelphia, rounding up veterans and marching them to the polling place at the state capitol. When they arrived there, he jumped down from his horse and pushed his followers past the people already waiting to vote. The judges stationed at the polling place to make sure the election was fair refused to allow Wayne and his soldiers to vote. They went looking for Thomas McKean, the Chief Justice of Pennsylvania's Supreme Court and a friend of Wayne, for his opinion on whether the election should continue, but he was out of town. So they searched for Attorney General William Bradford, who refused to take a stand on the matter. He remembered how six months earlier a raucous crowd of angry veterans so terrorized the Confederation Congress that they fled to Princeton and still refused to come back to Philadelphia. Growing ever more impatient, Wayne and his followers cursed the judges who tried to stop them. Fearing a riot, they stepped aside and let Wayne's soldiers vote, but they vowed to bring formal charges against him for disrupting the election.[18]

After spending nearly a decade ordering men about, Wayne refused to bow to the judges who dared to cross him. Even Death, whom he had stared down so many times, no longer troubled him, at least for the moment. Like Madame Fortune and America, Death still seemed a flesh-and-blood person, who stalked him first at Ticonderoga and most lately at Delany's house in Philadelphia where he stayed after returning from Charleston. This "very troublesome fellow," as Wayne now described him, asked over and over again if he was "ready for payment." He might have been troubled by such imaginary encounters when facing his end at Brandywine and Monmouth Courthouse and Yorktown, but not when he was far from the battlefield. When Death kept up a din to drag him away, Wayne's friends intervened, certain he would live at least another forty years. Finally, when nothing could satisfy Death, Wayne's doctor made an appearance, issuing a *"nolle prosequi"* to Death to drop the case and a writ of habeas corpus setting him free at once.[19]

Having escaped Death's clutches and now elected to the Council of Censors, he could dig out a whole new set of caitiffs, meaning the cowardly "Yellow Whigs," his name for radical politicians who helped foment the Revolution but who never went off to war themselves. They stayed behind and wrote the state's constitution, which Wayne condemned from the moment he learned about it in letters from his Philadelphia friends, especially Benjamin Rush, while imprisoned in Ticonderoga. He saw nothing wrong in the long list of rights granted to the citizens of the state. Men were born free and independent; they could think, speak, and write as they pleased. They could worship God as they saw fit and freely assemble to discuss whatever they chose. They could acquire property and defend it in the courts and with the arms they had every right to bear. All power in the state derived from the people who must be allowed to vote freely without interference from anyone. If accused of a crime, they had the right to a speedy trial by a jury of their peers, no cruel or unusual punishment, no excessive bail, no unreasonable search and seizure in the quest for evidence against them, and no compulsion to testify against themselves.[20]

There was nothing in the long list of rights enumerated in the constitution that bothered Wayne, especially since he spent the better part of his life defending them. He had no problem with the state's suffrage requirements, which allowed all men twenty-one years of age or older who paid taxes to vote. Such wide-open suffrage meant most of the veterans of the Pennsylvania Line could cast a ballot. Nor did he oppose the fact that everyone elected must swear their allegiance to God and their acknowledgment that the Old and New Testaments were divinely inspired. What he opposed was the disorderliness built into the structure of the government itself. The constitution placed almost all power in the hands of a unicameral legislature whose members were elected yearly. Voters also chose a twelve-man council, but the constitution made no mention of the precise duties of this body. Likewise, the assembly elected a president and vice president for the council, but for all practical purposes these two executives, who derived their power from the legislature, had no real authority. Neither did the judiciary, whose structure and duties could not be deduced by reading the constitution. There was a Chief Justice of the Supreme Court and lower courts established before the Revolution, but what purpose they served in the state government was nowhere clearly explained.[21]

Wayne now blamed all the troubles of the Pennsylvania Line on the state constitution, which gave too much power to the assembly. He had not forgotten how often he came to Philadelphia begging the assemblymen for food, clothes, and pay for his men. He and his supporters on the Council of Censors worked throughout the early winter of 1784 drafting amendments to the constitution that would dramatically change Pennsylvania's government. They proposed a governor elected by the voters, who would have real power, a bicameral legislature, and an independent judiciary. But the proposals came to nothing in the continuing furor over Wayne's questionable conduct on Election Day. Committees in both the assembly and on the Council of Censors heard the testimony of witnesses who said General Wayne had shouted down anyone who dared to cross him. They claimed he pushed his followers forward so vehemently that clerks were overwhelmed, unable to check the ages of the voters, where they lived, or what taxes they paid. Some of the soldiers were barely twenty-one years old. They had not a cent of property to their names and so had never paid any taxes. Not one of them took the required oath of loyalty to Pennsylvania and some probably came from Maryland, New Jersey, or even New England. They also carried ballots filled out for them in advance. If they wanted to change their votes, officers among them prevented them from doing so. When everything was tallied, 230 more people voted than were eligible according to the lists of taxable citizens.[22]

Despite the evidence against him, Wayne was cleared of charges that he had willfully manipulated the election. The experience left him more determined than ever to make his mark in the state's politics. If he failed on the Council of Censors, then he would try for a seat from Chester County in the assembly. He would fight for the rights of veterans against the Yellow Whigs who had begrudged them even the barest necessities during the war and who now treated them like pariahs. They still refused to pay them properly for their services. For every twenty shillings due an enlisted man, he would get only two. The half-pay for life promised to officers was merely a dream. They even balked at parceling out land they had promised to their returning soldiers. They finally set up a lottery system for granting acres west of the Allegheny River to veterans.[23]

Wayne took the seat he had won in the assembly in October 1784 and quickly learned how much the state's political mood had changed since the Revolution's

start. He came to the assembly to defend soldiers only to discover that no institution was more hated in postwar Pennsylvania than the army. Politicians railed
against the very men who had recently defended them. A standing army was
the greatest threat to a fledgling republic like the United States; one need only
look at the rise of Wayne's hero Julius Caesar to understand this lesson of history. They pointed to the Society of the Cincinnati as the first step in the army's
attempt to control the country. This organization of Continental Army officers
was thought to be especially dangerous because its membership would be passed
down to the eldest sons of its members. The Society of the Cincinnati was a
budding aristocracy and so a future tyranny. Wayne, as an active member of the
group, condemned anyone who opposed it. Cowards all, he shouted at his fellow
assemblymen, arguing that the Society of the Cincinnati would thrive no matter
what the politicians said.

But Wayne was calmer when he fought the disenfranchisement of people who
had refused to swear or affirm the oath to Pennsylvania during the Revolution.
He had worked to restore law and order in Georgia by recommending full par-
dons for Loyalists who actively supported the British. If he could open wide a
door to these people, then Pennsylvanians, who had never experienced the brutality he had seen in Georgia, could do the same. Wayne tried three times to restore the full rights of citizenship to people who had refused to take the loyalty
oath. He thought it especially unjust that these same people were banned from
voting and serving on juries but still had to pay taxes. In December 1784, he
called for readmitting to full citizenship all persons who had not actively fought
with the British. His proposal was voted down. A month later, almost in jest, he
proposed that disenfranchised people should no longer be required to pay taxes.
When this measure failed, he called for a committee to study the matter. The assembly agreed, but once formed, the committee decided the state had every right
to strip citizenship away from Loyalists.

For Wayne, the reason why his fellow assemblymen could not forgive Loyalists was beyond him. He ignored the fact that many of the disenfranchised were
wealthy Quakers who had long dominated Pennsylvania's politics. Younger politicians were happy to strip the old guard of their power. Wayne was even more
baffled at the strange puritanical streak that had settled on the assemblymen.
They were obsessed with upholding the virtues of every citizen. To accomplish
this, they closed Philadelphia's many theaters, believing they were immoral and
thus harmful to a republic. To Wayne, this seemed madness, especially since men
as virtuous as General Washington loved plays. The French who had saved the
nation at Yorktown staged operas after the great victory. For a man like Wayne
who loved Shakespeare and Sheridan, carrying copies of their works on every

campaign, the thought that he would never see these plays performed was almost unbearable.[24]

Wayne proposed a bill that would open a local theater with reasonable ticket prices. A part of the proceeds would be donated to the poor. He tried every argument he could think of to win over the assemblymen, including the fact that his friend Dr. Franklin noticed the morals of Parisians improved with theater going. Knowing soldiers as well as he did, Wayne further argued that the theater was a far more moral pastime for young men than others. But when he said the Congress, which had fled to Princeton, might return if its members could enjoy their evenings watching plays and operas, assemblymen rose to shout him down while crowds in the gallery openly mocked him for making so ridiculous a statement. They were still angry with the cowardly congressmen and wanted no part of their return. For Wayne, who began his postwar political career by shouting down judges and crowds on Election Day, now saw his political career in Pennsylvania come to an end in another shouting match, but this time he was on the receiving end of it.

He could hardly believe what was happening. A hero on the battlefield, a friend of Washington, Franklin, and Lafayette, the general who had single-handedly saved Georgia from being swallowed up by the British at the peace negotiations, laughed at in the halls of the state assembly. He had won two terms, but he would not fight for a third. Nor would he retreat to Waynesborough and wait for the world to come to its senses. Suddenly there was only one place where he wanted to go. That place was Georgia. The horrid world he tried desperately to escape from now seemed like a refuge to which he must return. On the plantation that Georgia had given him, he would throw himself again into a mad rush of activity and become a wealthy rice planter.

The Georgia assembly had awarded Wayne a plantation measuring hundreds of acres on the Savannah River, which once belonged to Alexander Wright, the son of Georgia's last royal governor. The younger Wright had purchased it for more than £10,000 in 1772. But the nation's economy had fallen so low that the estate was now worth only a third of that, but still the land had potential. The 847 acres that lay along the Savannah River, known as Richmond, was perfect for growing rice, while 573 more acres, known as Kew, that lay across Black Creek away from the river, sloping upward in a forest of pine and oak, was perfect for lumber. The awful war in Georgia had taken its toll on the place. After Wright had fled with his wife and children, Patriot militias had taken the livestock early in the war. Later the slaves were taken or they ran away.

What the Patriots began, the Loyalists completed with Wright's own father ordering Richmond's fields burned as Wayne, the "rebel general," approached in

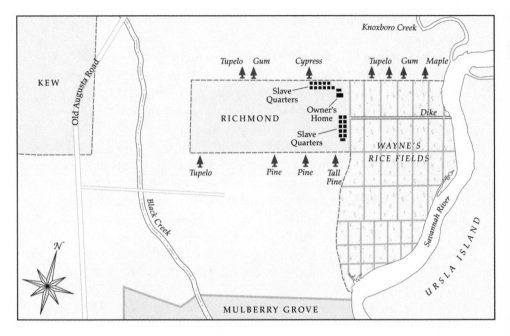

Wayne's plantation at Richmond and Kew. Copyright © Roberta Stockwell, 2018.

the winter of 1782. Alexander Wright, who stayed in Charleston through much of the war, refused to take up arms against the United States. He hoped to return to his ruined estate, but the Georgia assembly never forgave him for being the son of the hated royal governor and placed him on the list of attainder where all traitors were named, confiscating his property and banishing him from the state forever. A few days later, the assembly granted the estate to General Wayne, and in 1782, just days before he left Savannah for Charleston, he rode twelve miles upriver to survey his new property. The rice fields lay in ruins, but the main house was still standing. So were the barns and stables as well as the slave quarters. The orchards and gardens were overgrown but could be easily cleared and made beautiful again. Once all the fences were repaired, the meadows would be perfect for grazing horses and cattle. There was sure to be good fishing in the many ponds between the Savannah River and Black Creek. Even after Wayne escaped the misery of Georgia and he was back safe and sound in Philadelphia, he could never get the thought of this estate out of his mind.[25]

Before he left Georgia in the summer of 1783, Wayne tried to borrow money to buy slaves. He turned first to John Penrose, Polly's uncle, asking him for £1,000 to buy seventy to eighty "workers," a term he always used instead of slaves. Wayne counted many wealthy slaveholding Pennsylvanians among his friends and his own father had owned three who, though now quite aged, still lived at Waynesborough. He saw slavery up close for the first time in Virginia where he was shocked at the sight of naked young black men serving the daughters of planters who never once blushed at the sight. He was horrified at the black hand he saw nailed to a fence post on the way to Greene's camp. He cared for slaves who came into his camps in Georgia looking for refuge from the bloodletting. Once he even urged Governor Martin to recruit blacks to fight with the Patriots. But he also railed against the British for sailing off with thousands of slaves from Georgia and the Carolinas when the war ended. When Polly's uncle turned him down, he asked a local friend named William Gibbons to run Richmond in his absence. He asked Colonel Habersham, who stayed behind in Savannah after the war, and Richard Saunders, with whom he caroused in his last days in Georgia, to find slaves for him. Habersham assured him that fresh cargoes of fine young specimens from Senegal and Ghana would arrive any day.

Failing in Pennsylvania politics, Wayne's horrible memories of Georgia transformed into a golden glow, as dark memories sometimes do, burnished and bronzing in his depths. The place from which he had tried so hard to escape now seemed a sanctuary. Here he could throw himself into the breach of renewed activity. This was especially true once he learned that Nathanael Greene and his wife, Catharine, had decided to move to Mulberry Grove. Wayne's imagination lit up with dreams of spending his days with his old friend, walking through their fields together, riding to Savannah to talk politics with their fellow planters, and spending their evenings with the beautiful Caty. He never once thought of bringing his wife to Georgia or his son who was away at school in Virginia, where he was misbehaving quite badly according to Delany's letters. But he thought again how Margaretta, now at Mrs. Boideau's School in Philadelphia, could join him as the lady of the manor.

When he served on the Council of Censors and in the state assembly, he begged anyone he could think of for money to buy slaves. Robert Morris, who loaned money to Greene for Mulberry Grove, gave not a penny to Wayne, but recommended him to the House of Jan and Willem Willinks in Amsterdam. The mere suggestion that the Willinks might grant him a loan quickly became a certainty in Wayne's mind. In the many letters that the Willinks brothers wrote to him, there was a constant note of caution, which Wayne simply ignored. While they were glad to consider his request for a loan, which came with the endorsement of the well-respected Robert Morris, the Willinks had grave reservations about loaning any money to plantations in America. Wealthy investors had already lost huge sums on loans to planters in Surinam and Dutch islands in the Caribbean. With conditions in the United States still unstable, even after peace was restored, and with new wars looming in Europe, they were more reluctant than ever to loan money.[26]

But Wayne heard none of this. Looking ahead to the possibilities of life as a rice planter, he decided that the Willinks would give him the money. He even asked Pieter Johan van Berckel, the Dutch ambassador to the United States, what he thought of his prospects. When Van Berckel answered with cautious optimism, Wayne considered the loan a foregone conclusion. In the winter of 1785, he sent off a package of documents to the Willinks, including a power of attorney, the sworn valuation of Waynesborough, and certificates proving he owned his farm as a fee simple without any mortgages, suits, or actions against it. Then he boarded a ship for Georgia, promising Polly that he would be home by summer. But with the Delaware frozen over, he had to wait several days for the river to clear. He had already forwarded instructions to Saunders to buy slaves. When he arrived in Savannah, he learned that his friend had purchased forty-seven slaves from North Carolina from a trader named Samuel Potts with the help of a broker named James Penman and his cousin Edward Penman, a Charleston slave trader. Wayne made a list of the slaves himself, noting the men, women, and children, their ages, and their names. Many of them seemed too old or too young to work. By his estimate, only seventeen were able-bodied and ready to do the backbreaking job of planting and harvesting rice.[27]

Wayne had made up his mind that he would become a planter even though growing rice was a complex process about which he knew nothing. He was sure the people he purchased and the overseers he hired to manage them would take care of his plantation. His life would be filled with the conviviality he so loved. Rising at dawn, he would take on the most taxing part of his day. He would ride across Richmond inspecting his crops, making sure his overseer and driver had their charges working from sunup to sundown. By the time the slaves he had purchased entered the rice fields, his day's work would be done. He would breakfast at eight, head to a local tavern to talk politics with his fellow planters, and by four he would be ready for dinner, either at the Greene estate or his house at Richmond, with good food and wine, the finest tobacco, and brilliant conversation lasting long into the night.

Contrary to what he had told Polly, Wayne stayed at Richmond through the summer of 1785, coming back to Pennsylvania only briefly in the fall to run for a second term in the state's assembly, before heading back in the following winter to Georgia. This time he traveled through violent storms on the Atlantic that took his beautiful horse overboard and even drowned his new overseer. As he had done throughout the Revolution, he wrote to Polly telling her every detail of the frightening experience. He might have taken these tragic events as omens of misfortune, but for the moment Wayne saw only a bright future. He bought more slaves and paid for them with drafts on the Dutch loan that was sure to come through any day now. He ordered the best clothes for himself, laid up fine wine and cheese in his larder for his guests, and rode off to Savannah to discuss the late war with local politicians and chiefs visiting from the Creek nation.[28]

Only Sharp Delany, Wayne's oldest friend, the guardian of his wife, and the surrogate father of his children, wondered if Wayne had lost his mind. At first, he helped him in his furious efforts to become a rice planter. He found an overseer and the countless shovels that Wayne always needed for digging ditches and throwing up dikes in his rice fields. He reported back, too, all the latest news about the health of Wayne's wife and mother. But Delany became increasingly worried about his absent friend when his list of demands grew ever longer. He was also troubled by reports of Wayne's bad behavior in Georgia from the first moment he arrived there. If the rumors were true, he was spending more time carousing in Savannah than putting his plantation in order.[29]

Stories of Wayne's drunkenness even made it into Savannah's only newspaper, the *Georgia Gazette*. If the reports were correct, Wayne and his fellow Sons of the Cincinnati had passed a raucous Independence Day in July 1785 drinking thirteen toasts to their nation. By the late evening, they were drunk enough to go looking for a traveling band of actresses who had come to town. They found them at a nearby tavern and pounded on the front door, demanding that the women come out and perform for them. Wayne and his friends broke through the door, but were pushed back when the customers came at them with bayonets. After they barricaded the tavern's front door, one of them grabbed a rifle, ran upstairs, and shot at Wayne and his companions from an open window. While the actresses were saved, one of Wayne's fellow Cincinnatians was shot dead.[30]

Rumors of other women in Wayne's life filtered back to Philadelphia. The most serious rumors surrounded his relationship with Catharine Greene. She had been constantly at his side when they both arrived back in the capital in 1783, spending even more time with him than Mary Vining did. With her husband still in Charleston, she visited Wayne frequently while he was bedridden at Delany's house. When he regained his health, they went together as a couple to parties throughout the city. Pregnant with her fifth child, she spent a small fortune on new dresses that hid her condition and allowed her to dance the night away with Wayne as she had done when Charleston fell. Two years later, when Catharine and her husband finally took up residence at their estate at Mulberry Grove, their most frequent visitor was General Wayne. He enjoyed horseback riding with Caty in the late afternoon, comparing notes with her on their flower gardens, and staying for dinner. When a woman from Savannah warned Greene about the scandalous romance between General Wayne and his wife, he assured her they were merely close friends. He also added that the pair was never alone in a house filled with children and servants. Greene was grateful that Wayne was one of the few people who could cheer his wife after she lost a newborn baby girl to whooping cough in 1785 and miscarried another child less than a year later.[31]

But the happiness Wayne had found at Catharine Greene's side ended just eight short months after she arrived in Georgia. On an especially hot day in the early summer of 1786, Nathanael Greene spent the day examining his fields. Late in the afternoon, he returned home with a terrible headache and soon collapsed from heat stroke. His wife put him to bed, and sent first for the doctor and then for General Wayne. By the time Wayne arrived, Greene was totally incoherent. Wayne sat by his side as Greene once sat at his side in what seemed a lifetime ago outside of Charleston when racked with fever he had lost the will to live. Nothing could save Greene, who died in the night. A few days later Wayne accompanied Greene's casket in a boat downriver to Savannah where he was buried. Another tragedy soon followed when Catharine sailed home with her children to live with her family in Rhode Island. Wayne accompanied her to the docks in Savannah, begging her not to go. As he watched her ship sail into the distance, all the plans he had made for a new life with his daughter at Richmond went with her.[32]

However, it was not the loss of a future with Margaretta that troubled him. Rather it was the loss of Catharine Greene that sent him into despair. As soon as he returned home after bidding her farewell, he wrote a letter to her describing the deep emotion he felt while watching her leave. He tried to restrain his feelings when she descended to her cabin below deck. But when the ship sailed out of view, he felt a "sensation" unlike anything he had ever experienced. By the time he returned home, he could barely walk. He had to be helped up the stairs to his room. He tried to sleep but woke constantly from frightening nightmares. In one, he saw a terrible storm, like a tornado, tossing Catharine's ship on the waves. The storm turned the sky black as night even though it was still the afternoon. He was convinced something awful had happened to her. Unable to get her out of his mind, he could do nothing else but pray for her. "An involuntary petition to the supreme governor of the universe flowed warm from my heart," he confessed, "for her alone from whom I had so recently departed perhaps forever."[33]

The loss of Catharine Greene was only the beginning of a long period of trouble that came into Wayne's life. His plantation was finally producing five hundred barrels of rice each year, but he used all the profits for his living expenses. He had not paid cash for anything he purchased in the previous two years. Instead he bartered or wrote drafts against the Dutch loan. He had promised to pay for the slaves he purchased in installments over a five-year period, but as Penman explained to him in the summer of 1787, *"to this Hour, You have never paid One shilling of this large Purchase so Solemnly made."* Never mind, he thought, for money would surely come from Amsterdam any day now and give him enough cash to stay ahead of his creditors. But word soon arrived that the House of Willinks refused to pay any bill submitted to them. Drafts from Potts and Penman for the slaves Wayne had purchased came back across the Atlantic marked "unpaid." Potts and Penman now demanded immediate payment for the slaves they had purchased for him. They would not rest until they got all their cash back.[34]

When Wayne misread what was happening on the battlefield, most notably near the Paoli Tavern, at the Green Spring Plantation, and on the outskirts of Savannah, he always had the presence of mind to escape with his life. But now he could not escape from the financial trap that he had set for himself. Playing the part of a great planter, with his fine clothes, a carriage and horses, and nightly entertainment, all purchased on credit, he found himself bankrupt. He railed against Potts and Penman in colorful prose, especially to his friend Delany, and complained of every last thing the caitiffs dug in all around him had done to him. But he also blamed America, the faithless woman whom he still loved best, for his troubles. He had spent the best years of his life defending her as if in a dream only to awake and find himself a ruined man. As he explained to Delany, "when I reflect that the prime of my life, health & Constitution were devoted to the service of a Country—as devoid of *Justice*, as she is of *Gratitude*; when I reflect that that the very injustice precipitated me into those difficulties—I am tempted to renounce her forever."[35]

He wrote even more frightening letters to Polly, telling her for the first time in his life that he was not afraid to die. Death was no longer the flesh-and-blood person who had stalked his path since Ticonderoga. Instead, he was merely a "debt which every mortal must at one day pay." Wayne now tried to make Polly understand why he had left Waynesborough for Georgia. He had done this mad thing, not to abandon her and their children, but to make the money he had failed to make while fighting the Revolution. He was so determined to leave a substantial inheritance to Margaretta and Isaac that he did not care if he died in the process. "I feel so easy about death," he confessed to Polly, "that I would scarcely turn upon my heel to escape it was it not that I wish to put my private estate in Operation and free of any encumbrance for the benefit of our children, previous to my exit."[36]

Wayne might no longer be frightened by death, but he was terrified of debt. If he could not pay the bills piling up in Georgia, then he might end up in debtor's prison. He might also lose Waynesborough. Potts and Edward Penman were determined to take Wayne's farm and tannery in Pennsylvania away from him. In July 1787, they presented a lawsuit against the Wayne estate in the Philadelphia County Court of Common Pleas. Their demand was a simple one; in payment for money owed to them, they asked that Waynesborough be sold at a sheriff's sale. The estate would have been auctioned off immediately if not for the fact that Potts and Penman sued Wayne in the wrong county. Waynesborough was in Chester County, not Philadelphia County, and this mistake gave Wayne time to come up with a plan to counter their lawsuit.[37]

Remembering that elected officials were immune from prosecution, he reasoned if he could get elected to any political office, then he could not be jailed for the money he owed. For this reason, late in the fall of 1787, he stood for election to Pennsylvania's ratification convention for the Constitution of the United States. Wayne totally supported the proposed document. He had recommended its main features, including a strong executive, a bicameral legislature, and an independent judiciary, as a better form of state government for Pennsylvania while on the Council of Censors. But Wayne also supported the Constitution because he believed it would restore the nation's finances. A strong national government would support banks, set up a currency and credit system, and thus be a godsend for debtors. If there was a way to borrow money in the United States, rather than turning to foreign creditors like the Willinks, then life would be better for all Americans, not just Anthony Wayne.

He returned to Philadelphia in December 1787 as one of the six representatives elected from Chester County, and sat with his old friend Benjamin Rush at the ratification convention. He made only one motion: the proceedings of the previous day should be read out on the following morning. He kept few notes on the debates, preferring instead to listen to Judge James Wilson, who did most of the talking in defense of the Constitution. Wilson, who helped to draft the document, was a man like Wayne overwhelmed by debt. He would, in fact, spend his last years in a debtor's prison. But for now, his arguments won the day with the convention ratifying the Constitution by a vote of 46 to 23. Still frightened that he would be arrested while in Pennsylvania, Wayne dared not go home to see his family but sailed quickly back to Savannah. He returned to Richmond where he entertained his fellow planters long into the night. One of his guests was a widow named Mrs. McLean who lived with him throughout the winter. Still hoping to avoid prison through politics, he sought an elected office, hopefully as a senator from Georgia, but to no avail.[38]

As much as he loved his life as a planter, he decided in January 1788 to put

Richmond up for sale. He advertised his estate in a broadside that detailed the many assets of the place. When he got no takers, he offered to hand over his plantation to Potts and Penman as full payment of his debts. When they refused, demanding cash instead, he decided to put Waynesborough up for sale. Before Potts and Penman could get their hands on his family's estate, everything would be gone: the stone house, the tannery, the barns, the livestock, and all the fenced-in fields and meadows. Only shocked silence came back from his wife and children in Pennsylvania. But Sharp Delany asked him point-blank: what will become of Polly, Margaretta, and Isaac, who was still a student? He pleaded with Wayne to give up the failed dream of becoming a successful planter. Instead he should come back to his true home and there restore his health and sanity. Wayne never gave a direct answer to any of Delany's questions. Instead he was now determined to sell Waynesborough, pay off his debts in Georgia, and save Richmond.[39]

By the summer of 1788, Wayne had fallen into a deep despair. On July 16, as he started another letter to Delany, he noticed the date. Nine summers before he was the hero of Stony Point, but now he had nothing to show for his bravery but a "total reverse of fortune" and the gold medal cast in his honor. He seemed transported back to the day when, surrounded by his "Gallant corps" and "clasped in the arms of Victory," he saw General Washington approaching to congratulate him. At the moment his commander embraced him, the wound in Wayne's forehead started to bleed. Now it seemed that even deeper wounds within him would never stop bleeding until the very "last drop was drained." But Wayne soon came out of his sad reverie. He asked Delany, as he had done so many times throughout the late war, to look after his son, Isaac, now studying at Princeton, and "not to neglect Waynesborough."[40]

As Wayne brooded about his fall from grace, Potts and Penman prepared to file their suit in Chester County, Pennsylvania, to gain control of Waynesborough. A desperate Wayne turned to Aedanus Burke, a judge living in Charleston, for help. He advised Wayne that a sheriff could not sell property with claims against it. Wayne must find someone to sue him, as the owner of Waynesborough, before his farm was put up for sale. Wayne remembered that he had promised to provide an annuity for his mother after his father's death, but he had never paid her a penny. If Wayne's mother sued him for failure to pay the annuity, then according to Burke, Waynesborough could not be sold. For good measure, he also advised Wayne to have his mother-in-law sue him on the same grounds.

Now the race was on for Wayne to convince the two "old women," his term for his mother and Polly's mother, to sue him. He asked Sharp Delany to help

FOR SALE,

And may be taken Possession of immediately,

THOSE VERY VALUABLE

RICE PLANTATIONS,

SITUATE on the river Savannah, in the state of Georgia, called *Richmond* and *Kew*; in a *good pitch of tide*, twelve miles above the town, formerly the property of Alexander Wright, Efq. containing twelve hundred acres; about *three hundred* whereof are prime tide fwamp, properly and well banked, upon which there has, and may be made from 800 to 1000 barrels of *rice* per annum. The fields are equally divided between *Richmond* and *Kew* by a center canal, cut from the river to the faft land; there are dwelling houfes and a fufficient number of negro habitations on each; a commodious barn and machine houfe, (all of frame) the machine new; together with ftables, coach houfe, and other neceffary buildings.

The fettlements are high, healthy, and beautifully fituated, commanding a full view of the *rice fields*, and a number of fettled plantations on the river; there are 200 acres of provifion land cleared, of the fiift quality, and feveral never failing fprings of excellent water convenient to the dwellings.

In a word, in point of fituation, fertility of foil, and advantage of water carriage, they are equal to any plantations in the ftates of South-Carolina or Georgia, and will be fold feparate or together, as may beft fuit the purchafer or purchafers.

An indefeafable title will be made upon the payment of part of the purchafe money, and giving fatisfactory fecurity for the payment of the remainder, (with intereft) by equal inftalments of one, two and three years.

There are alfo on the premifes, and may be Purchafed,

A GANG OF

Fifty Country born and Seafoned

NEGROES;

Among whom are carpenters, coopers, fawyers and prime field flaves, together with a large quantity of Seed Rice, Indian Corn and other Provifions, a fine ftock of CATTLE, fuch as Working Oxen, Milch Cows, &c. with Waggons, Cart, Ploughs and Plantation Tools, &c.

For further particulars apply to the hon. *Ædanus Burke*, Efq. in Charlefton, to the Hon. Gen. *James Jackfon*, in Savannah, or to the fubfcriber on the premifes.

Anthony Wayne.

Charlefton, January 21, 1788.

Sale of Wayne plantation broadside.
William L. Clements Library, University of Michigan.

him and did all he could by writing in his most heartfelt manner to the wife he had abandoned years before. Under great pressure from Delany, and with Polly reading Wayne's letters aloud to her, his mother finally agreed to sue her own son, but she never forgave him for humiliating her. She immediately changed her will, leaving all her property to Margaretta and Isaac and only one dollar to her son. Polly's mother held out longer but she, too, finally agreed to sue him. By the time Wayne's creditors arrived at the Court of Common Pleas in Chester County, it was too late. Waynesborough was safe for the moment behind the lawsuits of the two old ladies.[41]

Brooding and alone well into 1789, Wayne turned to his daughter, Margaretta, with whom he had hoped to share his life in Georgia. The little girl he tried to raise money for by selling barrels of sugar at Yorktown was now all grown up at nineteen. He had spent little time with her since the war ended. When he returned home to Philadelphia from Charleston in 1783, he had bought her fine clothes and made sure she continued her studies at Mrs. Boideau's School. He even took her to see the fireworks at the docks along the Delaware River on New Year's Day in 1784. The cold wind was so blustery that his new beaver hat and her new bonnet blew away. He knew from letters from Delany that she had become a beautiful young woman, but she rarely wrote to him anymore.

The reason for her silence was finally explained in August when Delany told him that Margaretta was engaged to a young attorney named William Atlee. Wayne received a letter from Atlee himself, but he refused to answer his future son-in-law or Delany. Instead he fell into his darkest depression to date. Delany begged him to come home and attend the wedding, which was set for a year from November, but Wayne remained wrapped in silence, still terrified that he would be arrested and thrown into debtor's prison the moment he landed in Philadelphia. He was shocked at how swiftly time had passed since he begged General Washington to go home after Yorktown. He never brought his daughter to Georgia as the mistress of his plantation and he was about to lose her forever. Even Catharine Greene, who wrote letters taunting him for ignoring her, could not bring him out of his depression. Nor did he visit her like he once did when she returned to Mulberry Grove.[42]

But he finally escaped from his despair by turning his attention to another woman he loved, America. He looked past the western border of Georgia and saw America surrounded by enemies on all sides, especially the Creeks and the Spanish. In 1783, the United States had won the country north of the Gulf of Mexico to the Mississippi, at least on paper in the treaty ending the Revolution, but had not taken possession of it for real. He envisioned organizing the region into the Southwest Territory, just as the Ohio Country was now the Northwest

Territory. A governor should be appointed here, just as Arthur St. Clair had been appointed north of the Ohio River, to oversee the government's surveying of the land and the entrance of new states into the Union. Wayne sent his suggestions to James Madison, newly elected to the House of Representatives, letting him know he was willing to serve in any capacity. When Madison's response was non-committal, he wrote to Washington and Knox, also telling them that he would gladly serve in the new government. He turned to Sharp Delany, just appointed the customs collector in Philadelphia, and even to Catharine Greene, begging his two dearest friends to use their influence to win him a government position.[43]

With no response from anyone, Madame Fortune showed her hand. William Gibbons, the manager of Richmond in Wayne's absence, suggested he stand for election to the House of Representatives in Georgia's first congressional district in the fall of 1790. He could easily defeat James Jackson, the current representative, and take his seat in the House of Representatives. Gibbons even offered to manage his campaign. Likewise, and more miraculously, Potts and Penman finally agreed to accept Richmond and Kew as payment for his debts. But to win a full settlement, Wayne needed the help of the three women he had so badly treated, his wife, his mother, and his mother-in-law. Polly must sign official documents renouncing her dower rights to one-third of Richmond and Kew. The two "old women" would have to withdraw their lawsuits against Waynesborough. Once again, Sharp Delany would have to negotiate all this with the women in Wayne's family.[44]

After winning his election, Wayne came back to Philadelphia in late 1791, having a position in the government at last and also starting his climb out of bankruptcy. He took his seat in the House, where he was determined to fight for veterans and a strong military. He would likewise try to win compensation for Catharine Greene for the debts that her husband had incurred in the last months of the war to feed his soldiers. Wayne had entertained Washington in the spring when the president visited Savannah but seemed to have made no impression on him. He hoped that Washington would notice that he was not "totally ruined & depressed" and stood ready for an "appointment his services deserved." He came knocking on the president's door with ideas about America's future, especially on the western frontier, just as he had laid out battle plans for him from Brandywine to Stony Point. But when James Jackson arrived in Philadelphia, claiming Wayne's supporters had stolen the election, he could think of no plan to escape from this disaster. He retreated into his vivid imagination and wrote a short story entitled "The Old Georgians." Composed in the style of Sterne or Swift, the piece observed his troubles from afar. He now recast the stolen election in terms of native Georgians despising newcomers to their state. "Excited by curiosity," his tale began, "I went to visit the hustings on the day of election in Savannah in company with a gentleman to whom I had been particularly introduced upon my arrival in this state, we had not been long upon the ground when we frequently heard these kind of declamations—let's have no *New Commers*—let's have *Old Georgians*—they are the only men proper to represent us."[45]

Wayne had finally come back to reality when Henry Knox asked him, early in 1792, if the president offered him the position of the Legion's commander in chief, would he accept it? Now a year and a half later, having said yes, Wayne sat waiting in the massive fort his soldiers had built in the prairie past Fort Jefferson. Once again, all his frantic activity, this time building the Legion of the United States, had come to nothing. He wandered the walls of Greeneville as he once wandered the ramparts of Ticonderoga. There was nothing left for him to do but wait for the Indians to make a move. Finally, on a cold winter night in mid-January 1794, his sentries noticed a small party of warriors, carrying a white flag of truce, approaching across the meadow. Wayne ordered his artillery to fire a salute in their honor. He welcomed the Delaware chief George White Eyes and his companions into the fort and laid out a banquet for them. Calling himself Washington's "chief warrior," he assured the Indians that the "eyes and ears of the President of the United States are ever open to the voice of peace." He asked them to stop listening to the British, give up their raids on settlers, and return the Americans they had taken on the frontier.[46]

The chief answered he had not come to make peace, but to ask that the three Indian girls kidnapped by Captain Gibson's men at Fort Recovery be returned to their people. Wayne promised he would do as the chief asked. Before they left, he wrote out a speech to all the tribes for George White Eyes to take to his people. He also took the Indians on a tour of Greeneville, walking its inner circumference and showing him the thousands of soldiers he commanded. After they left, Wayne ordered Captain Gibson to return the women to their people, with a message asking for Little Turtle to meet with him at Greeneville by the next full moon. Wayne waited for a month, but no answer ever came back. Not one Indian, in fact, was spotted in the surrounding woods or prairies in the entire time. Wayne's plans had failed again and he had to take up the waiting game once more.[47]

He never guessed the impact he had already made on the man he most wanted to meet. Little Turtle, after listening to George White Eyes describe Greeneville, was more convinced than ever that Wayne could not be beaten. Like Wayne, he believed in fortune's mysterious movement among men. The Indians had defeated the armies of Harmar and St. Clair. They should not expect a third victory. "The Americans are now led by a chief who never sleeps," Little Turtle warned, "night and day are alike to him." None of the young men sent against him had surprised his army. "Think well of this," he added, "There is something whispers to me, it would be prudent to listen to his offers of peace." As Wayne wandered his fortress, certain he had failed, Little Turtle worried he had already won.[48]

"A Savage Enemy in Front, Famine in the Rear"

There were times when General Wayne, while waiting with his Legion at Greeneville, wrote in glowing terms about his life. This was especially true in his letters to Catharine Greene. As he once spoke about their flower gardens in Georgia, so he now described the beautiful country surrounding the fort named for her husband. The prairies extended in every direction as far as the eye could see. Stands of great oak trees rose up like islands in a rolling dark sea. Hoping she might worry about him, he confessed that, despite the wonder of the countryside, he was still in danger. Thousands of hostile Indians waited for him in the forest that started up again just past the edge of the prairies. However, he assured his beautiful friend that he would be victorious. There was only one chance that he might be defeated: if Madame Fortune, that "Capricious female," intervened against him. Since giving him command of the Legion of the United States, she had been noticeably absent from his life, or as Wayne explained to his beloved Caty, "I may no longer be a favorite."[1]

But to Sharp Delany, he felt no compulsion to describe his fate with any charm. He instead wrote in the depressed tone he used during the Georgia campaign. The whole world, including his daughter and son, his many friends in Philadelphia, and even Secretary Knox and President Washington, had completely forgotten him. There were few friendly faces at Greeneville. His officers squabbled to win his favor, and even more for promotions, which were less frequent now that the Legion had taken shape. Tired of the fighting, he instituted a lottery system to fill the few open positions. Wayne's officers also pressed him for furloughs. He had granted them generously from Legionville to Hobson's Choice. But knowing the army would soon march north from Greeneville, he let fewer men go home, which further enraged his officers. Some of the younger ones even tendered their resignations. Wayne saw something more sinister in their be-havior than the normal restlessness of an army waiting to go into battle. A dark mood had settled on Greeneville in the winter of 1794 more completely than in the previous fall. The Legion had literally divided into two camps. Officers and soldiers lined up on opposing sides. Caught between the Indians ahead of him and the lack of supplies behind him, Wayne described his position to Delany in dire terms. "I am to contend with a choice of difficulties," he explained, "a savage enemy in front, famine in the rear, and a baneful leaven in the center of the Legion."[2]

As he had done throughout the previous year, Wayne blamed the leaven on the troubles of the age. The horror of France in flames as the Jacobins murdered at will, all in the name of the rights of man, continued to cast frightening shadows on American politics. The president's many political opponents, both in and out of Congress, attacked him as if they were fighting at Robespierre's side. Every good thing Washington accomplished for his nation, including the Bank of the United States, the new system of tariffs and excises, especially the tax on whiskey, and even the Legion, was condemned as proof that the republic was descending back into a monarchy. Many were calling for armed rebellion if anyone tried to tax their homemade whiskey. Across the nation, people opposed to the presi-dent formed Democratic-Republican Societies, where they cheered the bloody upheaval in France, even as they waited to topple what they saw as Washing-ton's corrupt administration. For them, "Federalist" had become a dirty word. Sneering back at them, Wayne called the rising opposition the "Demoncrats."[3]

Wayne could name specific officers stirring up the baneful poison in his Legion, like Captain Isaac Guion, who was court-martialed for fighting with a fellow officer over a woman. But as winter gave way to spring, he had to admit that there was another actor working behind the scenes. That man was James Wil-kinson. Wayne could no longer ignore the fact that his most faithful officers had warned him about Wilkinson's treachery. Major William McMahon, who led the failed attack on the Grand Glaize, told him that officers were resigning under direct orders from Wilkinson. Rest assured, he swore to Wayne, "I shall be one of the last to turn my back on you." Cornet Blue, who tried to lead the dragoons against the Indians in October, told Wayne a disturbing rumor he heard from a Philadelphia merchant visiting Cincinnati. Senators were calling for Wayne's im-peachment on the grounds he was an embezzler. The person behind the charges was none other than General Wilkinson. Thomas Posey, who had brought his half-naked Virginians to fight with Wayne in Georgia, told him point-blank that Wilkinson, the man whose company he seemed to enjoy, was his worst enemy.

By February 1794, Posey could bear the backstabbing no longer. He resigned his commission and returned to Virginia.[4]

During the Revolution, Wayne experienced the jealousy common among officers, particularly in his dislike of St. Clair, which had now completely disappeared. But with this exception, he had never hated any officer simply for outranking him. He now struggled to believe that General Wilkinson despised him so thoroughly that he would turn half the Legion against him. He had no idea the lengths to which his brigadier had already gone to destroy him. Wilkinson wrote constantly to Senator John Brown of Kentucky that Wayne was a "despotic, Vainglorious, ignorant General." Brown, never doubting Wilkinson's charges, became the leading force in the Senate to impeach Wayne. Not content to let others run the smear campaign against "Old Lumpy," Wilkinson submitted several anonymous pieces to the *Centinel of the Northwestern Territory*, Cincinnati's only newspaper, signing them "A.W." for "Army Wretched." The articles described Wayne as a drunkard who could no more lead an army than St. Clair. He was likewise a thief who spent government money like his private fortune. Ignoring his best men, most obviously Wilkinson, Wayne terrorized his camp with his few loyal officers in tow, "pimps and parasites" all of them.[5]

Wilkinson inspired officers who had resigned their commissions to write even worse pieces about Wayne. An article written by a "gentleman in General Wayne's camp, who may be depended on," and first posted in the Martinsburg, Virginia *Gazette*, was widely reprinted in the nation's newspapers. The author described Fort Greeneville as a nightmarish place filled with "drinking, gambling, quarelling, fighting, and licentiousness." The fault for the scandalous behavior afflicting all ranks must be laid at the feet of General Wayne. A despotic monster, he had a feeble mind, a foul mouth, and a violent temper that he vented on his best officers. A demon himself, "acting above all laws divine and human," he profaned the Sabbath for the "extraordinary fatigues" of his sham battles. With a fiend in charge of the army, the author needed "no spirit of prophecy" to predict what would become of the third army sent against the savages. Its defeat was inevitable. To emphasize the truth of his accusations, the anonymous author signed his piece as "Stubborn Facts."[6]

Attacks in the press did not bother Wayne, especially since he found the accusations bizarre. Pay no attention to them, he told both Knox and Delany, for his accusers were nothing more than "vile calumniators," "mutinous cowards," and "dirty tools of faction." What troubled him more were rumors that Wilkinson was interfering with the delivery of rations to the Legion at Fort Greeneville. Wayne had demanded that 250,000 rations be sent to the post by December 1793. But by the end of that month, only 42,800 rations had arrived. There was slightly more beef than flour, but little salt or soap, and no vinegar or whiskey. No complaints to Elliott and Williams had any effect. The lack of supplies dragged on through May when the Legion had only an eight-day supply of food. Wayne, who considered a spring campaign against the Indians possible, realized the Legion could not march out of Fort Greeneville without food and the bare necessities of life.

When he confronted Wilkinson about the delay in rations, his brigadier responded that he found the contractors' behavior just as "inexplicable" as Wayne. He did not tell him that he had been writing to Elliott and Williams since the fall, encouraging them to ignore Wayne's every request and deal directly with him. He assured them Wayne would never follow through on his many threats, including buying fourteen hundred horses and sending them the bill. He told them instead to send only a small trickle of goods, just enough to keep the army alive but not enough to launch a campaign. Wilkinson also did not tell Wayne that, even if by some chance the army marched in the spring, he was doing his best to turn the Kentucky mounted volunteers against him. When Wayne delayed paying them until January 1794, because he did not receive the money until the yellow fever epidemic subsided in Philadelphia, Wilkinson told the militiamen that the "Old Man" had stolen the money.[7]

Faced with the troubling duplicity of his brigadier general, Wayne treated Wilkinson pleasantly at times, frequently inviting him to dinner and asking his opinion on military matters, and at other times addressing him curtly and dismissing his every concern. As he struggled with Wilkinson, along with his growing number of followers, he took some comfort in the fact that Knox and Washington stepped into the breach to defend him. Knox collected glowing statements about Wayne from his fellow officers, most especially General Scott, who had just been named major general of Kentucky's mounted volunteers. Not only was Wayne sober and responsible, but Scott also reported he had never seen a general more concerned about the well-being of every soldier in his army than the Legion's commander. Having passed these testimonials on to the *Gazette of the United States*, a Philadelphia newspaper favorable to the president, Knox assured Wayne that attacks on his character "died of their own imbecility" as soon as they arrived in the War Department. Guessing that Wayne's tough discipline, rather than any scandalous behavior on his part, lay at the heart of the complaints, Knox passed on Washington's hearty congratulations for his training methods.[8]

Despite the growing rift in his army, Wayne kept up the rigorous training of his men. He demanded they fall out on the parade ground with their uniforms perfectly clean, their powdered hair tied back with ribbons, and the buckles on their shoes shining. They must be ready to maneuver on command, practice responding to the beat of the drums, and fight as if they were in a real battle against the Indians during their Sunday field days. Wayne also kept his elite corps busy. He sent Captain Miscampbell's dragoons to Kentucky to grow stronger in the warm grasslands, and his scouts, still led by William Wells, into the Indian country for news on the location and intentions of the tribes.

As he watched over his men, Wayne worried again, as he had done since Three Rivers, whether he would survive the upcoming campaign. When Delany told him to think of pleasant days ahead, once he finally retired from the army, Wayne confessed he could not imagine a peaceful life for himself. He reminded Delany of his many responsibilities, not just military but diplomatic as well. Whether the battle against the Indians was ever fought, he still must win a treaty with the hostile tribes allowing Americans to settle north of the Ohio River. While he could envision this happening, he could not see himself ever returning to Waynesborough or Philadelphia.[9]

Again facing his own death, Wayne turned his thoughts not to his daughter, but to his son. He had stopped writing to Margaretta in the year after her mother's death and had taken no interest in the child that was about to be born to her. Instead he reached out to Isaac. He had rarely thought of him since leaving for Pittsburgh two years before. Since then, Delany had often reported that the boy needed money, first as a student at Princeton and later in Philadelphia where his father had sent him to study law. Once Isaac even demanded that his father let him live in the handsome house he bought in the city before taking up the Legion's command, a request that Wayne promptly denied. But more recently, Delany's letters were filled with praise for Isaac. Wayne's son had become an avid reader, piling up bills not from carousing like other young men his age, but for buying books. Isaac would one day own a library that rivaled his father's collection. While at first he had no interest in the law, he now applied himself to his studies, much to the delight of his mentor, Wayne's lawyer William Lewis.[10]

But would Isaac Wayne, now a grown man of twenty-two, want to communicate with the father who had ignored him for so long? Perhaps he disliked him as much as Wayne's own mother, who had left him a dollar in her will. Maybe he thought as little of him as Polly did at the end of her life. At the start of the Revolution, when she wrote frequently and with great feeling to her husband, she tried her best to keep the bond alive between Isaac and his absent father. She told Wayne how their little boy tried to remember what he looked like. When men visited the farm, pretending to be General Wayne, he would cry, "You are not my tatty." Once when Polly came looking for her husband in Philadelphia, only to learn he was in Ticonderoga, little Isaac, then just five years old, told her not to cry. To prove that he was learning like his father demanded, he practiced writing his initials in the margins of his mother's letters. He loved the gold-laced hat and sword Wayne sent him after the Battle of Monmouth and his father's few visits home while on winter furlough in Philadelphia. Whenever Polly spanked her "hardy and wild" son, he would cry, "I will take my little horse and ride to the wars to my daddy." But Isaac had probably forgotten all this and now only remembered his mother's dying words. Polly told Isaac how proud she was of him for turning into a fine young man devoted to his studies. The change in his character was especially remarkable since his father had abandoned him when he was still in his cradle, handing him off to his friend Sharp Delany to raise.[11]

Despite how he had ignored his son, Wayne was happy to learn that Isaac was willing to write to him. He again had a confidante like Polly to whom he could tell his hopes and fears as he faced his last campaign. Seeking the best way to advise Isaac, he could find no better words than those of Polonius to his son Laertes in Shakespeare's *Hamlet*: keep your thoughts to yourself; be friendly but distant; stay close to your oldest friends and make new ones carefully; avoid quarrels but once in them make sure your opponents end up fearing you; listen to everyone but speak to few; accept the censure of others but hold back your criticism; dress well but not gaudily for clothes make the man; neither a borrower or a lender be. But most of all, "to thine own self be true," a motto that Wayne had lived by, for then Isaac could not be "false to any man."[12]

Having restored his relationship with Isaac, before he lay dead on some forgotten battlefield, Wayne again waited anxiously for the Indians to make some move. Since George White Eyes had gone back into the night, he had heard nothing from them. He was especially anxious for Little Turtle to appear. He assumed the Miami war chief was organizing the warriors against him as he had done against St. Clair. Wayne did not know that Little Turtle was only one man among many now leading the confederated tribes. Two of the messengers from the council at the Maumee Rapids who met with Washington's three commissioners in Detroit the previous summer had surpassed him in importance. They were the renowned Shawnee war chief Wayapiersenwah, better known as Blue Jacket, and Buckongehelas, his Delaware counterpart. Unlike Little Turtle, who worried that Wayne, the "Black Snake Who Never Sleeps," appeared unstoppable, these two men never doubted their warriors could defeat him. Other respected Shawnee chiefs, like Black Hoof and Black Fish, and Delaware chiefs, like Captain Pipe and Big Cat, stood ready to fight with them.

They also had the full support of Egushawa, recognized by the Ottawa as the successor to Pontiac, who served as their lieutenant. He directed the scouting parties that tracked Wayne's every move, sent messages about the Legion to the tribes near and far, and disrupted the army's supply line. Egushawa had ordered Negig, or Little Otter, to attack Captain Lowry's packtrain the previous October. The Ottawa would call their brother tribes, the Pottawatomi and Chippewa, to fight against Wayne. The renowned Pottawatomi warrior Le Petit Bled would lead them. Nine chiefs of the Wyandot, including Tarhe the Crane, likewise were anxious to fight. So were the Seneca, or Mingo, who lived along the Cuyahoga River. Even Joseph Brant promised to send his Mohawks into battle. He now condemned the many treaties that handed the Ohio Country over to the United States. Brant no longer feared the Americans after British agents assured him a war was about to break out between their nation and the United States. Redcoats and Canadian militia would fight at the side of the confederated tribes against the Legion.[13]

As he prepared his soldiers to fight the Indians, Wayne still hoped the chiefs, whose names he did not know, would decide for peace in their councils at Roche de Boeuf. He knew the British were pressuring them not to negotiate with him. In a grand council with the Indians in Quebec in February, Lord Dorchester, still known to Wayne as General Guy Carleton, had urged the tribes to resist the United States. Noting America's aggression toward the tribes and Great Britain, he predicted, "I shall not be surprised if we are at war with them in the course of the present year; and if so, a line must be drawn by the warriors." Even knowing this, Wayne still wrote confidently to Knox that he could win a treaty with the chiefs by early May. But as he scanned the meadows for Indians carrying a flag of truce, he made sure the new road he opened from Greeneville to Girty's Town on the St. Mary's River was ready for his men to march against the tribes. He also welcomed the many Choctaw and Chickasaw warriors who arrived from the south to fight the northern tribes. He sent them into the Maumee River Valley as scouts, making sure he tied bright yellow ribbons in the topknots on their heads so no American soldier mistook them for the enemy. He continued to press Elliott and Williams to send more rations immediately to Fort Greeneville. He enlisted James O'Hara, the Legion's quartermaster general, and his staff to help him deal with the contractors. He even experimented with bringing rations by boat up the Great Miami River.[14]

Confident that he had done everything in his power to bring about peace while still readying his men for war, he was stunned when his scouts brought news in May 1794 that the British were building a new fort on American soil some ten miles downriver from Roche de Boeuf. Lord Dorchester had directed General Simcoe to build Fort Miamis on the site where the Great Trail from Pittsburgh crossed over the Maumee and turned north toward Detroit. Decades before, a small French fort stood there, and the British also maintained a post on the site during the Revolution. Four hundred soldiers would be stationed at the post to support nearly two thousand Delaware, Shawnee, Wyandot, Miami, and Ottawa warriors who had gathered there with their families. They awaited the arrival of at least fifteen hundred more Indians, including Mohawks and Mingo from the east and Pottawatomi and Chippewa from the northern lakes.

While the new British fort would be small, even miniscule compared to Greeneville, its strategic location was meant to disrupt Wayne's plans. The fort would stand on the west side of the Maumee along deep water where boats from Detroit could easily deliver supplies. With four of the fort's dozen cannon placed in the bastions facing the river, Wayne would not dare to attack the place from Lake Erie. But neither could he come down the Maumee to attack Fort Miamis. The post was two miles downriver from Colonel McKee's store, which sat at the Foot of the Rapids, the endpoint of a long stretch of rippling currents running over flat rocks in the riverbed that stretched all the way from Roche de Boeuf. The Maumee Rapids could only be navigated by canoe. If Wayne attempted to march west around the fort and take the trail to Fort Detroit, the many cannon in the bastions facing the rear would cut down his soldiers. If his men attempted to storm Fort Miamis, they would have to climb over rows of abatis sunk deep into a ditch surrounding the post and then up earthen ramparts that surrounded its twenty-foot walls. While brave General Wayne had taken Stony Point, Carleton and Simcoe were certain he could never take Fort Miamis.[15]

Furious at the British for establishing another illegal post on American soil, Wayne understood immediately that his old enemies, Carleton and Simcoe, had placed him in a "delicate & disagreeable" situation. His sworn duty was to defeat the Indians, break up the confederacy now blocking settlement north of the Ohio, and win a treaty with the hostile tribes. However, he had no authority to attack the British. He knew President Washington had just sent John Jay to London to resolve problems with Great Britain left unsettled at the end of the Revolution. In Wayne's eyes, the removal of the British from forts on American soil was at the top of the list. Once the British were gone, their support for the Indians would disappear, too. Wayne also hoped the border between the United States and Canada would be more clearly delineated. Trade between the United States and the British West Indies, which once helped Wayne's tannery business prosper, must be restored. He knew another concern from serving in Georgia during the Revolution: compensation for slaves taken by the British army. Likewise, he understood American shipping, now caught in the crossfire of England's war against France, must be protected. The Royal Navy had simply ignored Washington's proclamation of neutrality. To date, British warships had captured two hundred and fifty American vessels, confiscating their cargo and impressing their sailors into His Majesty's service to fight whatever faction currently held power in France.[16]

Wayne fretted that any false move on his part might upset the negotiations just under way in London and inadvertently launch a war between the United States and Great Britain. He remembered, too, how many times Knox, and through him Washington, had scolded him for appearing too aggressive. Surely, they would do the same now. He was therefore surprised in late June 1794 when Knox ordered him to proceed immediately against the Indians and, if necessary, to take on the illegal British post on American soil. "If, in the course of your operations against the Indian enemy," Knox explained, "it should become necessary to dislodge the party at the rapids of the Maumee, you are hereby authorized in the name of the President of the United States to do it." Knox added a caveat: Wayne could not fail. He must win, not just against the Indians, but the British as well. As Knox cautioned, "no attempt ought to be made unless it shall promise complete success; an unsuccessful attempt would be attended with pernicious consequences." He did not have to spell them out for the politically savvy Wayne: the Indians would be encouraged to fight on, the British would send John Jay packing and declare war, and President Washington would be ruined.[17]

Laying out his plans for Secretary Knox, as he had done long ago for General Washington, Wayne proposed moving first due north to the Maumee River. Once there, he would not turn left toward the Miami Villages, the place St. Clair had tried to reach, but would instead go right toward the Grand Glaize, the place where the Auglaize emptied into the Maumee. There was no reason to head for the Miami Villages when hundreds of warriors from numerous tribes, along with their families, had abandoned Kekionga for the Grand Glaize. Hopefully, before he reached this spot, the chiefs would treat with him. If not, he would probably have to fight them. There was still one more reason to march right rather than left. Wayne would be leaving Fort Greeneville with half the rations he demanded from Elliott and Williams. He would therefore have to feed his men and horses with the stores of corn, beans, fruit, squash, and other vegetables he would find at the Grand Glaize.[18]

Now hoping to take on the Indians before they attacked him, he was stunned when a soldier raced through the gates of Fort Greeneville on the afternoon of July 1 with news that Fort Recovery was under siege. At five o'clock the previous morning, a party of Choctaw and Chickasaw warriors, still wearing the yellow ribbons Wayne had tied in their hair, appeared at the gates of the fort. They seemed "much agitated and confused." They clearly wanted to tell the soldiers some important news, but they could not speak English nor could anyone understand their languages. Captain Gibson, who still commanded the post, realized the scouts were warning him that a large party of warriors was nearby. He sent out patrols, but when they returned having seen no signs of Indians, he ordered his men to carry on their normal duties. He sent out thirty head of cattle to graze in the grass near the fort. He also directed 264 packhorses, along with their drivers, into the meadows near the woods. Major McMahon, with dozens of dragoons and riflemen, had escorted the packhorses up from Fort Greeneville the day before. Once McMahon finished his breakfast, he and his soldiers would take the horses, now empty of their loads of flour, back to Greeneville.

At exactly seven o'clock, just after sunrise, the soldiers in Fort Recovery heard gunfire coming from the woods. Shouts of "Indians! Indians!" came across the meadows along with the screams of warriors in the distance. Without waiting for Captain Gibson to form his troops, Major McMahon mounted his horse and called the dragoons from Fort Greeneville to follow him. He shouted to Captain Asa Hartshorne, whose riflemen were also part of the packtrain's escort, to join him. They raced toward the sound of the guns through the open gates of Fort Recovery. McMahon led his mounted men toward a creek bed near the woods, while Hartshorne's riflemen hurried ahead to a small hill in the trees. They passed terrified horses and cattle running in every direction and drivers racing as fast as their legs could carry them back toward the fort.

Just as McMahon reached the creek, Indian warriors who had been hiding along its banks rose to their feet and took deadly aim at the dragoons. McMahon fell from his horse first, fatally shot through the neck. Twelve more dragoons soon lay dead, with thirteen others wounded, and at least seventeen captured by the Indians. Captain Hartshorne and his riflemen held out longer, but they were quickly surrounded by hundreds of warriors who climbed up every side of the hill where they stood. Hartshorne was shot through the leg, and after his men tried to carry him to safety, he ordered them to leave him and run for their lives. He fought off the Indians who soon surrounded him, striking at them with the espontoon he carried. Hartshorne finally died when a warrior tomahawked him; then the Indians slit open his chest and placed two leather hearts inside him as symbols of his bravery. Eight of his fellow riflemen died with him. The Indians also shot the packhorses, killing or wounding at least fifty and capturing more than two hundred along with all the cattle.

As men fortunate enough to escape from the warriors raced into the fort, Captain Gibson had ordered Lieutenant Samuel Drake to take twenty-one soldiers and rescue the dragoons and riflemen. But approaching the woods, they could barely distinguish the soldiers from the Indians in the hand-to-hand combat. Wounded almost immediately, along with ten of his men, and with another shot dead, Drake ordered his soldiers to retreat to the fort. As they crossed through the gates, Captain Gibson slammed the doors behind them. The warriors now pommeled the thick walls of the fort with musket fire. At first, Gibson ordered his soldiers to return the fire just as furiously, but after fighting for several hours and losing not one man to an Indian sharpshooter, he told them to aim only at clear targets.

Gibson's soldiers, along with the Choctaw and Chickasaw scouts, now shot at warriors who were trying to corral the few horses still alive or strip the leather saddles and pouches off the dead ones. They also fired at several warriors searching frantically for something in the creek bed. Captain Gibson surmised the Indians were hunting for the artillery left behind by St. Clair's army. He rolled out those same guns, which had been retrieved the previous December, and blasted the woods where the fight began hours before. When night fell, Gibson's men shot at warriors who came by torchlight to look for the dead and wounded. By eight the next morning, most of the Indians had disappeared. Later in the day, when Gibson led a detachment out of the fort to bury the fallen soldiers and haul the dead horses into the woods, a few warriors could still be seen moving in the thickets. Gibson taunted them to come out and fight like men. They shouted at him and took a few shots at his soldiers, but by the early afternoon they, too, disappeared.[19]

By the time Wayne received news of the attack on Fort Recovery, the battle was over. Reading through Gibson's dispatches, Wayne surmised this "coup de main" was a well-planned assault on the site of St. Clair's defeat, and not merely an attack on McMahon's packtrain. The soldiers who had fallen, all the horses taken, and even the cattle were unexpected prizes, but not the true target. The warriors had instead meant to level the post built over the scene of their greatest victory. Wayne rightly guessed that between fifteen hundred and two thousand Indians had participated in the attack, a greater number than the warriors who destroyed St. Clair's army. He was also correct that British soldiers had participated in the assault on Fort Recovery, a fact that worried him as he faced his own battle against the Indians. As he explained to Knox, "It is therefore more than probable that the day is not far distant, when we shall meet this Hydra in the vicinity of the Grand Glaize & Roche de Bout without being able to discriminate between the White & red savages."[20]

Wayne chose six o'clock on the morning of July 28, 1794, as the precise moment he would lead his Legion out of Fort Greeneville. He worried that he only had nineteen hundred soldiers, far less than the five thousand promised to him when he accepted his commission as the commander in chief two years before. He also had only eighty-four officers. He called up Captain Miscampbell and all the dragoons from Kentucky and ordered General Scott to bring as many mounted volunteers from the state as he could muster. Even if only a few hundred militiamen joined him, his army would probably equal the number of warriors waiting to take on his forces. Wayne now took charge of preparing his soldiers down to the last detail. He made sure their uniforms were clean and repaired if damaged. He ordered axes for the pioneers who would cut a swath through the forest as the Legion moved north. Tents were passed out, one for every eight men. More packhorses were purchased in Kentucky and brought north to haul the baggage. Wayne told his soldiers to take only their guns, bayonets, and swords, their blankets, and five days of rations. All personal items, which he had allowed his men to bring from Hobson's Choice, must be left at Fort Greeneville. Women would again be allowed to follow the Legion, but only if their children stayed behind.[21]

As the day of departure drew near, Wayne grew ever more anxious. His officers noticed he seemed lost in thought and preferred staying alone in his quarters. The pressure that both Knox and Washington had placed on him to defeat the Indians, and the British if he must engage them, was almost unbearable. He had placed even more pressure on himself to train his men perfectly so victory was assured. Yet he learned long ago in the darkest days of the Revolution that the "fortuitous events of War are very uncertain." Knowing that he might be writing to Knox for the last time, before Madame Fortune led him most probably to his own death, he was certain of only one thing. "I can promise that no conduct of mine will ever require the palliative of a friend," he vowed, "or cause that great & good man Our Virtuous President to regret the trust & confidence that he has pleased to repose in me."[22]

Wayne had faced death many times since first fighting Guy Carleton's redcoats at Three Rivers. He had been certain he would die on the cliffs below Stony Point and in the swamps outside Savannah. But the fear of those times paled in comparison to what he felt now. He was convinced beyond any doubt that he would die in the battle he must win. He wrote a last goodbye to Sharp Delany telling him that, somewhere in the dark woods north of Greeneville, thousands of "hostile savages of the West" and John Graves Simcoe himself, his old nemesis from the Virginia campaign, were waiting for him. He envisioned the battle, a "solemn and awful interview," unfolding before him. The "hour of action will be severe and bloody," he told his best friend. Certain he would fall in the battle, he wrote out his last will and testament, attaching it to his letter, and asking Delany to serve as the executor of his estate, along with his son, Isaac, and his lawyer William Lewis.[23]

To Isaac, he left Waynesborough, the great stone house and all its belongings, the tannery, the barns, the fenced-in fields and meadows, and all the horses and livestock. Margaretta would receive his house and adjoining lot in Philadelphia on Second Street between Market and Walnut. To his son-in-law William Atlee, and so to Margaretta and the children born to their union, he left a house in Harrisburg, Pennsylvania, the fifteen hundred acres in western Pennsylvania granted to him by the state's assembly, and fifteen hundred more acres given to him in Georgia, which he described one last time in his favorite imagery, "as some retribution for the loss of blood I have sustained in defense of the liberties of America on many a well-fought field from the frozen lakes of Canada to the burning sands of Florida."[24]

Wayne wrote an even more heartfelt letter to Isaac, much like the ones he had written to Polly before every battle. He described the modern-day Hydra, like the many-headed serpent of ancient lore, waiting to destroy his Legion. He could see the faces of the enemy even now: painted warriors more numerous than ever collected in America, British redcoats and Canadian militia, and in the middle of them, General Simcoe himself. If they did not attack him at the Grand Glaize or Roche de Boeuf, then they would at Fort Miamis. Repeating the words he had written to Knox, Wayne reminded Isaac that the "fortuitous events of War are very uncertain," and therefore he was "preparing for the worst." He asked his son to collect the letters that Polly had saved for him at Waynesborough, and to preserve them along with the many others he would leave behind in a leather trunk at Fort Greeneville. He also told him to destroy any letters he wrote when he was a boy. Wayne was reluctant to close this final letter to his son, whom he now addressed as his "dear friend." He wished he had more time to make this last "adieu," but his days were now filled with preparing for battle. Finally, telling Isaac to embrace his "amiable and lovely" sister one last time, he added a prayer for both of them. "Under those impressions, and with those sentiments," he wrote, "I am only left to implore the Omnipotent Governor of the Universe, to bestow his choicest blessings on, and to take into his protections, my only son & daughter."[25]

Leaving Fort Greeneville at dawn on July 28, Wayne knew that his Legion was not the only army on the move in the hot summer of 1794. One hundred and thirty-five miles to the north, upward of two thousand warriors from nine nations, along with their families, had camped between Fort Miamis and Swan Creek, a small stream to the north that emptied into the Maumee. Their chiefs were meeting even now with the British to decide the best place to defeat Wayne's Legion. Six hundred miles to the east, President Washington was determined to put down the Whiskey Rebellion in western Pennsylvania. Hundreds of angry farmers near Pittsburgh had just set fire to the home of the local tax collector. Their attack had come at the very moment Indian warriors laid siege to Fort Recovery. With no soldiers at his disposal, since the nation's only army was marching with General Wayne toward the Grand Glaize, Washington was ready to call out the state militias of Virginia, Maryland, and Pennsylvania.

By the time they were mustered out, there would be close to thirteen thousand of them, seven times more than Wayne's Legion. Washington, dressed again in his Continental Army uniform, would bid farewell to the troops at Carlisle, Pennsylvania, before handing them over to the man who had been so angry at Wayne's appointment as the Legion's commander, Governor Henry Lee of Virginia, with Alexander Hamilton, author of the whiskey tax, at his side. Terrified of the liberty poles with Jacobin caps on top of them going up on the frontier, Washington and his Federalists were determined to prevent the same upheaval spreading through America that had plunged France into chaos. Little did they know that on the day Wayne's Legion left Fort Greeneville, Robespierre, architect of the Reign of Terror, died at the hands of a guillotine in the heart of Paris.[26]

Cut off from communicating with Knox and Washington, Wayne knew he would be on his own as he marched his soldiers to victory or defeat. Following his scouts, who led the way, he rode out of Fort Greeneville with Lieutenant Harrison at his side, along with two other aides-de-camp, Captain Henry DeButts and Captain Thomas Lewis. General Wilkinson commanded the First and Third Sublegions marching in a long column on his right, while Lieutenant Colonel Hamtramck led the Second and Fourth Sublegions on his left. Light infantry and dragoons fanned out on all sides from the central columns. Around them, riflemen marched along the edges of the Legion. In the center column behind Wayne and his aides came packtrains loaded with rations and supplies, the artillery, herds of cattle, and women following their men into battle. General Scott's mounted volunteers arrived in time to join the march at the rear of the columns. Scott had listened well to Wayne's warning about the circumvallation of America's frontier. He brought nine hundred men from northern Kentucky, under the direct command of General Todd, to fight with the Legion. Another six hundred led by General Barbee would soon join them from southern Kentucky. Still worried that the militia might bolt and run, like they had while fighting with St. Clair, Wayne was greatly relieved that his army now outnumbered the warriors waiting to strike him.[27]

At the first sign of an Indian attack, Wayne's soldiers knew they must form their columns quickly in the direction of the gunfire. Listening to the signals pounded on the drums, they must maneuver into place just as they had practiced every Sunday. No matter how hot the temperature, they must never remove their coats or take off their hats. To act like soldiers, they must look like soldiers. They must keep up the pace of twelve to fifteen miles per day that Wayne set for them. Every

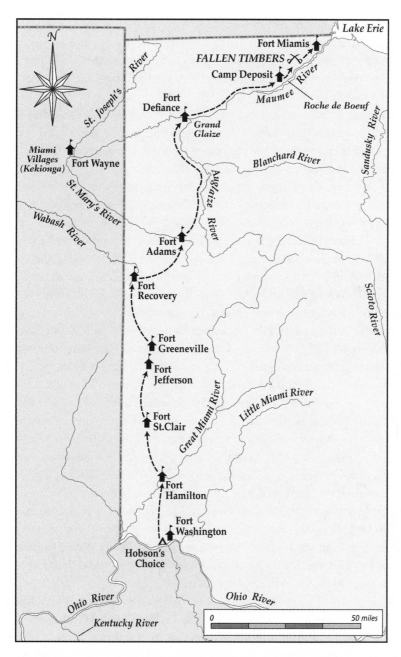

Wayne's Ohio campaign. Copyright © Roberta Stockwell, 2018.

afternoon, long before sunset, they must march onto the giant grid laid out by the quartermaster's staff, set up their tents, and then go off to build a breastwork around their camp. Once they cooked their evening meal, they could finally lay down on the ground and rest until the following morning when they must take up their march again.

At first, everything went according to Wayne's carefully laid plans. The Legion marched twelve miles on July 28, and by noon the next day, they passed Fort Recovery. But then the lay of the land changed and made marching difficult. The Legion had reached the edge of the Great Black Swamp, as settlers would later call the dark tangle of forests, grassy wetlands, and sandy soil that covered the Maumee watershed. Here the trees grew close together with weeds and nettles thick between them as high as a soldier's waist. Where the ground was wettest, the woods filled with maple, beech, and linden trees, interspersed with tulip poplars, all towering over the army. Marching on higher sandy ground, the Legion passed through stands of giant oak and hickory. Here the wide streams were deeper than Wayne's scouts had guessed. The mosquitoes and black flies seemed bigger, too, than anyone had ever seen. They bit right through a soldier's uniform and made life miserable for the horses and cattle. Wayne finally stopped early on the afternoon of July 29 at Beaver Creek to give the baggage train time to catch up. The army waited throughout the following two days as Major Burbeck's artillery corps built a bridge a hundred yards long and fourteen feet wide across the creek. At the same time, Wayne ordered the quartermaster's squad to head north and cut a path through the woods for the Legion to follow on the next morning.[28]

At dawn on August 1, the army was on the move again. After marching twelve miles, the soldiers came out from the tangled trees onto a wide prairie near the St. Mary's River. Here Wayne directed his men to build Fort Randolph, which he later renamed Fort Adams, high up on the south bank of the river. The small post, with its two opposing blockhouses shaped like diamonds, would serve as a way station for packtrains bringing supplies north. It would also house several dozen soldiers sick from swamp fever and heat exhaustion. While Wayne worried that it took two days to build the fort, his men were happy to spend their spare time swimming and fishing in the St. Mary's.[29]

While many of his soldiers were ill, no one was sicker than Wayne himself. From the moment he climbed onto his horse at Fort Greeneville, he suffered an acute attack of gout. The pain was so great that every morning his aides wrapped long flannel bandages tightly around his arms and legs. There was no medicine to ease his agony except for whiskey, which he drank long into the night. The pain in his body grew even worse after an accident befell him at the Legion's camp on the St. Mary's. On the afternoon of August 3, he retreated to his tent where, still wrapped in flannel bandages, he rested from the heat. Suddenly a large beech tree, just chopped down by his axmen, crashed onto his tent. Luckily for Wayne, the top of the huge trunk fell onto a stump rising a few feet from the ground. If not for the stump, the tree would have crushed Wayne into the ground. When his men finally pulled him out from under the heavy branches that had fallen on him, he was unconscious. A camp doctor put smelling salts under his nose and finally brought him around. His aides helped him up and, though limping and in greater pain than ever, he walked about the camp to let his men know he was all right. Soldiers who were glad he was still alive wondered if Wilkinson and his clique were behind the "accident."[30]

Setting out from the St. Mary's at dawn on August 4, the Legion followed a sharp diagonal to the northeast through the woods toward the Grand Glaize, some fifty miles away. Wayne, badly bruised and again wrapped in flannel, struggled to stay on his horse. He lost his appetite completely and could only keep down quinine and more whiskey. The heat and humidity were so oppressive that many packhorses collapsed and were left to die on the trail. Conditions were just as terrible the next day. When the Legion stopped for the night at Dog Creek, the water was too foul to drink. But after a two-day march in much cooler weather through a swamp near the Little Auglaize, Wayne's soldiers camped just six miles from the Auglaize River. Two hours after dawn, on August 8, they arrived at the Auglaize, a wide and shallow river that flowed north into the Maumee. Wayne ordered Wilkinson's column to cross over and head down the east bank, while he brought the bulk of the army along the west. General Todd's brigade of Kentucky volunteers also crossed the river to join Wilkinson's column. On the morning of August 9, Wayne's army, now camped on both sides of the Auglaize, awoke to a driving rainstorm. This was the first rain since the army left Fort Greeneville. Wayne's column to the west and Wilkinson's to the east pressed north through the downpour. They marched for six straight hours, until noon, when just as the sun broke through the clouds, they reached the Grand Glaize, which they found completely deserted.[31]

Wayne ordered Wilkinson's column to come back across the Auglaize. Together the two generals climbed the bluff that looked down over the valley where the river met the Maumee. Both men were overwhelmed at the beauty of the country. Corn grew everywhere along the bottomlands of the Auglaize. Apple trees lined the opposite bank of the Maumee. Row upon row of vegetable gardens extended back down the bluff behind them. Wayne had grown up in the rolling farm country of eastern Pennsylvania. He had also seen tobacco plantations along Virginia's James River. He had raised five hundred acres of rice on his Georgia plantation. But never had he seen so much land so perfectly cultivated.

His soldiers, who were equally amazed, guessed the cornfields along the Auglaize stretched five miles and covered at least a thousand acres.[32]

Overjoyed that his soldiers had taken the "Grand Imporium of the Hostile Indians of the West," Wayne ordered a gill of whiskey for every one of them. With whiskey the only ration in plentiful supply, Wayne encouraged his soldiers to gather as much corn, beans, squash, fruits, and vegetables, including potatoes, as they could find. There was so much corn that soldiers sold the surplus to the quartermaster for three dollars a bushel. The only thing that troubled Wayne was the fact that the village was deserted. The Indians seemed to have departed very quickly, with many families leaving food just prepared. Wayne assumed Indian scouts had been watching his army's every move and alerted the people gathered at the Grand Glaize to flee just in time. Knowing warriors might still be lurking nearby, probably with redcoats at their side, he ordered his soldiers to camp for the night as they always did, with a breastwork built around them. He also told General Scott to fortify the camp of his mounted volunteers.[33]

Still wrapping his arms and legs in flannel every morning and having difficulty walking, Wayne could not rest. He sent William Wells and a small party of scouts toward the council grounds at Roche de Boeuf. He directed five hundred mounted volunteers to reconnoiter the country on the western side of the Maumee where his Legion would soon march. But most important, he ordered his soldiers to construct a fort on the spot where he and Wilkinson had first looked out over the Auglaize and the Maumee River Valleys. He had only one requirement: the post must be strong. He made this request believing the fort might soon withstand an Indian attack like one against Fort Recovery, but this time with the blast of British artillery. In just ten days, its walls rose twelve feet high and extended sixty feet between each of the four blockhouses. Two of the blockhouses faced the Auglaize while the other two faced the Maumee. A covered walkway running from the juncture of the rivers back up to the fort would protect soldiers bringing supplies into the post. So would a deep trench dug around three sides of the fort and sharpened pickets pointing outward from the top of its walls. Wayne was so impressed with the post that he told his soldiers, "I defy the English, Indians, and all the devils of hell to take it." When General Scott heard the comment, he named the post Fort Defiance.[34]

As his men built the fort, Wayne spent much of his time resting in his tent. His gout had spread to his knee and made walking almost impossible. But when Wells returned with several captured Shawnee, he rose from his cot to interview them. He first asked them how the Grand Glaize came to be abandoned. They told him the Indians learned of Wayne's approach from a deserter from the Legion. He was Robert Newman, a civilian who worked for the quartermaster, who had run away when ordered to help open the road past Beaver Creek. He was not an Indian scout, they swore, but instead had come into the Grand Glaize of his own free will. Newman warned everyone that Wayne was on his way and gave specific instructions on how to defeat him. He said they should gun down the officers first, with Newman explaining how to identify them. They must never attack Wayne after he set up a fortified camp. Nor should they try to outflank him. Instead they must attack his soldiers as they marched, throwing their warriors in deep rows against his columns.

Certain Newman was a British spy, he asked the captured Shawnee about the Indians waiting to fight his army. They estimated there were seven hundred gathered at Fort Miamis along with the three hundred British soldiers stationed at the post. Another five hundred warriors were on their way from the northern lakes. But the Shawnee also told Wayne that the chiefs had not yet decided for war. Many wanted to step aside and let the Legion fight the redcoats at Fort Miamis or even Detroit. Some were ready to send out a white flag of truce and meet with Wayne. Finding the prisoners trustworthy, Wayne decided to try for peace one last time before pushing northward. He wrote out a speech that one of the Shawnee would carry down the Maumee to the chiefs gathered near Fort Miamis. Wells could not go along because he had injured his hand raiding an Indian camp on the way back from Roche de Boeuf. Instead another scout, Christopher Miller, who had been captured by the Shawnee and lived with them for a time, would take the message. The other captives would remain at Fort Defiance as hostages. Wilkinson hotly protested sending the speech, claiming a peaceful overture now would make the army appear weak and embolden the warriors. Wayne dismissed his concerns. Later he wagered his brigadier ten guineas and a quarter-cask of wine that he would get a treaty with the Indians before he had to fight them.[35]

"I, Anthony Wayne, Commander in chief of the Federal army at the Grand Glaize," the speech began, "extend the friendly hand of peace towards you." He urged the chiefs not to listen to the British who were lying about supporting them in the upcoming battle. He swore to the Indians that he had not come to take away their land in the Auglaize or Maumee River Valleys. He could make this promise because this country lay north of the Fort McIntosh treaty line. Instead he urged the warriors to think of how their women and children would suffer if they did not give up the fight against his soldiers. He summarized his plea in his simplest prose, saying the "army of the United States is strong and powerful but they love mercy and kindness more than war and desolation."[36]

The day after Miller and the Shawnee left for Fort Miamis, Wayne planned to lead his army out of Fort Defiance. A few soldiers would remain at the post, while hundreds of Kentuckians would head first down the Maumee's western bank, looking for any sign of Indians. The Legion's many columns would follow, with the rest of the Kentuckians right behind, just as they had marched from Fort Greeneville. Preparing to head north on the next day, Wayne committed himself and "his gallant" army to an "all-powerful and just God." But when he woke on the misty morning of August 14, he could not rise from his cot. He had suffered a painful attack of gout during the night and could not stand. So the army rested with him for one more day. But at dawn on August 15, Wayne struggled from his bed and ordered everyone across the Maumee, except a small brigade of Kentucky volunteers who would march on the opposite bank. Out of the view of his soldiers, Wayne's aides lifted him, again bound in flannel, onto his horse as tears rolled down his face. Seeing the state of Wayne's health, the Choctaw and Chickasaw warriors who had come from Fort Recovery to fight with the Legion refused to follow him any farther.

Riding away from them, Wayne was barely able to stay upright on his horse. As the day grew hotter, he became confused and almost delirious. His men were soon lost in a sea of huge white oak, maple, and walnut trees. Edward Butler, appointed as the Legion's surveyor, had marched the army due north instead of following the Maumee's flow toward the northeast. He finally led everyone back toward the river, but by mid-morning, after traveling for five hours, and with Wayne still incoherent, the army made camp. Wayne was carried to his tent where, with the help of whiskey, he slept through the night.[37]

August 16 proved just as trying as the previous day. Wayne was awake and coherent enough to launch the march at dawn. But by noon, with the sun beating down through the trees, the army stopped again so Wayne could rest in the shade. Fearing the worst for the Legion's commander, the brigade of Kentuckians crossed over the river to be with the rest of the army. At that very moment, Miller and the Shawnee returned with a letter responding to Wayne's speech. George White Eyes, who had come to Fort Greeneville the previous January, had signed the speech as its author. He thanked Wayne for his kind words and asked him to wait ten days at Fort Defiance for a formal response. Wayne became so angry at the Indian speech that he came out of his pain and delirium. He had not spent two years training the Legion to lead them into a massacre. But that is precisely what would happen if he gave the tribes ten days to recruit more warriors and find the perfect spot to attack his army. They would come at his soldiers with their painted faces and their screams like a thousand bells. They would surround and destroy his soldiers as they had done to St. Clair. He had vowed that his beloved America would "no longer be insulted with impunity." Instead blood would be "upon their own heads." After resting for only an hour, he ordered his aides to carry him from his cot, and now sitting astride his horse, he kept the army moving for another ten miles.[38]

On the much cooler morning of August 17, Wayne did not start the march until after seven o'clock. Paying careful attention to his surroundings, he was sure his men were drawing closer to the council grounds at Roche de Boeuf. There were signs of Indian life everywhere: abandoned cabins, patches of corn, and even flashes of warriors darting through the trees. The lay of the land also made marching difficult. Here the shallow river widened to three hundred yards from side to side. Thick woods covered the Maumee's left bank, which fell sharply from a high ridge to the bottomland below clogged with marsh grass. After marching for fourteen miles, Wayne ordered his men to camp for the night in dense woods overlooking the river. On the next day, after a nine-mile march, they came upon a huge limestone outcropping in the shallow waters. This was Roche de Boeuf, the giant rock so named by the French because it looked like a buffalo carved out of stone. The Indians had chosen this beautiful place, alongside the rapids and surrounded by apple, peach, and plum orchards, as their council grounds. Wayne's army, growing ever more anxious for "*Victory* or *Death*," would rest and make ready to march the last ten miles to Fort Miamis on the following morning.[39]

Wayne's spirits improved noticeably, especially now that he could walk on his own. He watched over the First Sublegion as they built a large stockade he named Camp Deposit. Here he would leave behind the sick, the heavy baggage, the cattle and packtrains, and the women when his army moved out the following morning. At dawn on August 19, when the soldiers of the First Sublegion appeared too exhausted to move, he delayed the march for twenty-four hours. He sent Major William Price and his company of Kentucky volunteers to reconnoiter the ground up ahead. He returned with descriptions of a broad plateau nearly a mile long about halfway between Roche de Boeuf and Fort Miamis. It sat on a ridge, marked by steep ravines on its right that tumbled more than a hundred feet down to a broad floodplain, maybe sixty to ninety yards wide, filled with grass that grew six feet high. Past the floodplain, silver rapids flowed down the center of the Maumee. The army could easily march through the giant oaks that were widely spaced on the plateau. But the dense woods to the left and a patch of fallen trees, probably leveled by a tornado, spread out over three hundred yards from the woods to the ridge on the right might slow the army's advance to Fort Miamis. While Price had seen a few Indians hiding there, he had no idea that the hostile tribes had chosen this spot as the place where they would fight Wayne's army.[40]

The tribes knew the place that Price had just reconnoitered as Presque Isle, so named by the French when they first explored the Maumee and more recently the site of Ottawa fishing villages. Wayne would have to pass this spot on his way to Fort Miamis. With his columns spread out across at least a half mile, he would face warriors waiting across an even wider front to attack him. Seventy Canadian militiamen, recruited in Detroit and dressed like Indians, hid in the thick woods to the left. More than a thousand warriors fanned out from the edge of the forest through the fallen trees and back toward the river. First came twenty-five Mingos and Mohawks, then Tarhe the Crane and his chiefs with two hundred and fifty Wyandot warriors, and next to them a hundred Miami under Little Turtle. Heading toward the river came Buckongehelas' two hundred Delaware and Bluejacket's two hundred Shawnee. The young warrior Tecumseh, who scouted the Legion's movements north from Fort Washington, stood ready to fight with his older brother Sauwauseekau. Toward the ridge on the far right, Le Petit Bled's twenty-five Pottawatomi waited along with Egushawa, Negig, and two hundred and twenty-five Ottawa. Down in the floodplain, twenty-five Chippewa from the northern lakes hid in the tall grass. The chiefs and warriors had waited for Wayne on the mornings of August 18 and 19, and after he failed to appear, they planned to wait for him again on the following day.[41]

Knowing none of this, Wayne met with his officers in the evening of August 19 to discuss the army's march at dawn. Everyone, including Wilkinson, was silent. Only Lieutenant Harrison spoke up, recommending that Captain Price's mounted volunteers march in front, followed by the Legion's advance guard, and then the Legion's multiple columns, all moving a hundred to a hundred and fifty yards apart. Wayne would lead the center column with the artillery and supply wagons behind him, while Wilkinson and Hamtramck's sublegions would march on the right and left. The dragoons and light infantry would march on both sides of the columns with the riflemen along the army's farthest edges. A rear guard and the rest of the Kentucky volunteers would follow behind them. Harrison found a large oak leaf and drew out the columns for Wayne. Approving the plan of his young lieutenant, who had learned so much from him, he ordered his men to sleep through the night with their arms ready. When they awoke before dawn to rain, Wayne delayed the march until a quarter past seven. Before wrapping his arms and legs in flannel, he called Harrison to his tent and tied a green satin sash around him. The rain had soaked through the drums and so they could not be used to signal the troops. Wayne told Harrison that he would have to carry his commands all day, sometimes going back and forth through the direct line of fire. His new adjutant Major John Mills would also carry his orders to the officers.[42]

Marching downriver from Roche de Boeuf for two hours, Wayne stopped several times to allow the columns to catch up with each other. He even ordered his

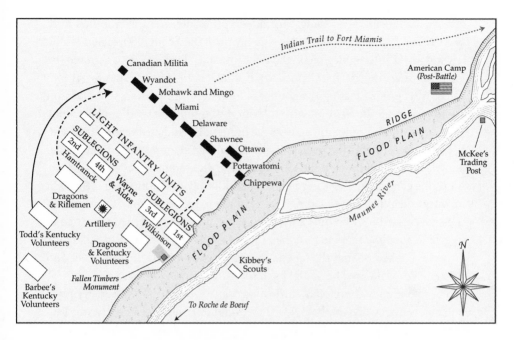

Battle of the Rapids (Fallen Timbers), August 20, 1794.
Copyright © Roberta Stockwell, 2018.

Legion to practice forming their battle lines. He also sent a company of scouts under Captain Ephraim Kibbey across the Maumee to protect the Legion's far right flank. Just as the leading edge of the army reached Presque Isle, a worried Lieutenant Harrison rode up to Wayne and said, "I am afraid you will go into the fight yourself and forget to give me the necessary field orders." "Perhaps I may," he answered back, "and if I do, recollect the standing order of the day is, 'Charge the damned rascals with the bayonet.'"[43] At that very moment, gunfire broke out from the direction of Price's mounted volunteers. Warriors, hiding behind the fallen trees, shot point-blank at them, killing two men instantly. Price ordered his men back toward Wayne's approaching army. For just a few moments, panic set in. The Legion's advance guard, seeing the Kentuckians hurrying their way, opened fire on them as Wayne had taught them to do if any soldier fled the battle-field. But most of the mounted volunteers rode straight through them into the front of Wilkinson's column. Soon the advance guard fled, too, racing to their respective sublegions as warriors chased them through the trees.[44]

At the first gunshots, Wayne ordered Wilkinson and Hamtramck to turn their columns toward the attack. Wilkinson lined up his two sublegions in a single row with the Third Sublegion next to Wayne and the First Sublegion trailing down into the floodplain. Hamtramck first lined up his sublegions in two rows front to back, but soon reformed them as one line with the Second Sublegion on the left and the Fourth Sublegion on the right. The line of soldiers now mirrored the long line of warriors facing them. They had taken only five minutes to get into place. Wayne, now tearing the bandages from around his arms, sent Harrison ahead to line up the light infantry in front of the sublegions. The soldiers took up their positions just in time to bear the brunt of the Indian attack on the right. In the floodplain near the river, Chippewa warriors, along with the Ottawa who joined them, raced through the tall grass waving their tomahawks and war clubs. Along the edge of the ridge, even more Ottawa and Pottawatomi fired at the light infantry and Wilkinson's men right behind them. Shawnee and Delaware warriors now closed in from only a hundred yards away. They hurried from tree to tree, hiding behind them to load their muskets and then stepping forward to fire. Others crouched behind the fallen logs, where they loaded their muskets, and then stood up and fired before falling back to the ground to reload.

The intention of the Indian warriors was clear to Wayne. They were trying to outflank his army first on the right. They would trap the light infantry and Wilkinson's sublegions in the steep ravines along the edge of the ridge and then push the whole line back toward the center. His men would die like Richard Butler with tomahawks buried in their skulls. But Wayne would not let this happen, for he had something the Indians did not have: artillery. As soon as the shooting started, he called up the guns from the rear. Sixteen howitzers were quickly pulled into place from the center of the American line all the way toward the floodplain. The guns first opened fire into the tall grass near the river, cutting down Chippewa and Ottawa warriors with every blast. They then pommeled the center of the enemy line with grapeshot and canister, which held back the onrushing Shawnee and Delaware.[45]

Even in the midst of the fight, Wayne was impressed that his soldiers never bolted, but instead stood their ground. They ran from tree to tree and over the fallen logs, quickly loading and reloading their muskets and firing at the warriors. But he knew this would not be enough to turn the battle in the Legion's favor. Even after the artillery blasts, Indian warriors still fought along the ridge to his right, while even more fought near the dense woods on his left. Wayne now called up his dragoons and riflemen, along with the Kentuckians waiting in the rear. He sent Captain Miscampbell and his dragoons forward along the ridge. He also ordered Price and the mounted volunteers who had not fled at the start of the battle to follow right behind them. Miscampbell was shot almost immediately, but the rest of the troops pressed on. Soldiers in the floodplain now raced up the ridge to join them.

Wayne ordered a similar press on his left, where the main bulk of the enemy was now fighting. Here the warriors were trying to turn the Legion back toward the ridge, down through the ravines and floodplain, and finally into the river. Hamtramck's sublegions pressed ahead first. To support them, Wayne sent the Sorrel Horse Dragoons under Solomon Van Rensselaer, riflemen led by Edward Butler and Fort Recovery's Captain Gibson, and finally General Todd's northern Kentuckians. For the first time in the battle, the Indians panicked, especially when they heard Wayne's trumpets blaring on the ridge to their left and in the woods to their right. With their leaders falling all around them, including every Wyandot chief but Tarhe shot dead, and Egushawa and Negig collapsing from head wounds, they fell back.[46]

Launching a final push up the middle, Wayne directed the seven hundred soldiers lined up on either side of him to move forward and "rouse the Indians from their coverts at the point of the bayonet." He became so excited that he reined in his horse, making ready to charge with his men. His aides DeButts and Lewis, who had stayed with him through the whole battle, grabbed hold of the bridle so he could not follow them. "Let me go. Damn them. Let me go. Give it to them, boys," he shouted at his soldiers as they raced ahead of him. At first, when moving over the first hundred yards, they took their time loading their muskets, aiming, and shooting. But then the whole line charged with their bayonets, running for nearly a mile, routing the last warriors from behind the fallen trees and striking them down without mercy. The dragoons rode ahead so quickly around the left and back toward the right that they cut off Ottawa warriors retreating along the river. General Barbee's men, who had been far in the rear, finally arrived, and also raced around Wayne's left, preparing to encircle the fleeing enemy completely.[47]

Realizing they would soon be surrounded, the last Indians and Canadian militia still on the battlefield finally took off down the trail toward Fort Miamis, abandoning their dead and wounded. One of the last men to depart was Tecumseh, who left his dead brother Sauwauseekau behind. They hurried past Colonel McKee, his assistant Matthew Elliot, and Simon Girty, who had watched the battle from a small hill at a distance. They ran four miles to Fort Miamis where they expected the British commander to welcome them. But after letting the Canadian militia into the fort, Major Campbell closed the gates in their faces. Having armed and encouraged them, the British told the Indians they did not know them. Some warriors fled downriver to protect their families along Swan Creek, but others headed deeper into the woods toward the northern lakes, escaping the general they now called the "Wind."[48]

Wayne did not pursue the Indians to Fort Miamis. Instead he collected a hundred wounded soldiers, sending them in wagons back to Camp Deposit, including the commanders of his dragoons, Robert Miscampbell, who died along the way, and Solomon Van Rensselaer, who survived. The dead, whom Wayne counted at thirty-three, were later buried in a common grave. Wayne could hardly believe that he had defeated the Hydra along the Maumee in a little over an hour. The Battle of the Rapids, as he named the fight, lasted longer than the final assault on Stony Point, but a little less than the last drive at Green Spring. He was immensely proud of his officers and soldiers, who except for the attack on Fort Recovery, had only fought imaginary Indians every Sunday. On this hot August morning near the rapids of the Maumee, they had done everything he had asked of them. Wayne camped his army a few miles north of the battlefield on the western bank of the river just across from McKee's trading post. Here his soldiers planted the flag of Wayne's beloved America: fifteen red and white stripes with fifteen stars on a field of blue. Here, too, they rested and talked long into the night about the glory of this day, no matter how fleeting.[49]

On the next day, August 21, 1794, a small party of redcoats from Fort Miamis bearing a white flag of truce came looking for Wayne. They handed him a note from their commander Major William Campbell, which calmly stated, "I know of no war existing between Great Britain and the United States." A drummer boy who had deserted from the fort told Wayne that the British had supplied guns, ammunition, and food to the Indians. Ignoring Campbell's note, Wayne rode with Lieutenant Harrison and a few soldiers toward Fort Miamis. He came so close to its walls that Harrison raced up to him and pointed at a gunner on the ramparts ready to fire directly at him. Major Campbell ordered his men to put down their weapons and then sent more notes denying any part in the battle. Wayne counted the guns of the fort, four facing the river and many more pointed at the woods to the rear, and surveying the moat that surrounded the walls, realized the illegal outpost built on American soil could only be taken with great loss of life. To show the British how little he feared them, he climbed down from his horse, walked over to the moat, and, scooping up a handful of water, drank it. He then ordered his men to destroy everything within sight of Fort Miamis right under the muzzle of the British guns. They spread south along both sides of the river, setting fire to Indian camps, the cornfields nearby, and finally all thirteen buildings of Colonel McKee's trading post. Major Campbell sent more notes, but gave no resistance.[50]

On the morning of August 23, the Legion played a solemn dirge alongside the Maumee Rapids and shot three rounds from howitzers into the dome of heaven to honor the dead. Then they headed back to Fort Defiance down the same path they had come. They took as much food as they could find before burning every Indian village, field, and orchard as they went. Wayne sent more detachments into the woods to set fire to even more towns. Eight days after the battle, with his army safely back at Fort Defiance, Wayne finally notified Secretary Knox, and through him President Washington, that the battle was won. "It is with infinite pleasure that I now announce to you the brilliant success of the Federal army under my command," he wrote, "in a general action with the combined force of the hostile Indians and a considerable number of the volunteers and militia of Detroit." Summarizing the fight in only three paragraphs, he spent most of his letter thanking his men. "The bravery and conduct of every officer belonging to the army, from the generals down to the ensigns, merit my approbation." He singled out many for their bravery, including Wilkinson, Hamtramck, and young Harrison and his friend Van Rensselaer. He praised the light infantry for bearing the brunt of the fighting early on, the fearless dragoons who turned the enemy's flanks, especially the "worthy and brave" Miscampbell, who fell in the first charge, and even the Kentucky volunteers who in the end showed a remarkable fighting spirit. For all his excitement, Wayne did not mention the one fact that amazed him most of all. He had not died in the last battle of his last campaign, as he had so feared, but had miraculously survived and remained very much alive.[51]

13

"LISTEN TO THE VOICE OF TRUTH AND PEACE"

In the winter of 1795, Anthony Wayne found himself wondering if he had actually won the battle along the Maumee Rapids. On that hot August day, when his men chased the Indians for a mile over fallen logs, he was sure his army had been victorious. But now as he wandered Fort Greeneville, he was not so certain. Even if he had won, his victory was not complete until the Indians signed a treaty allowing Americans to settle north of the Ohio River. Why had their chiefs not come to treat with him? He waited at the gates of his massive fort and scanned the snow-covered prairies that surrounded it for any sign of warriors bearing a flag of truce. But no matter how long he waited or how often he peered into the distance, no one ever came.

Perhaps the Indians did not come because he had made himself appear too powerful. He had transformed from the deadly Black Snake, who slithered in the grass from the Ohio to Greeneville, then to the Grand Glaize and Roche de Boeuf, and finally to the Maumee Rapids, into the Wind, who swept everything in front of him like the tornado that knocked down the trees on the battlefield where he fought the Indians. He was so frightening that even the British refused to send their soldiers against him. Instead, they hid behind the gates of Fort Miamis talking to him with bits of paper rather than meeting him face to face. But most terrifying of all, Wayne who battled the warriors like the wind also fought them with fire. Heading back down the Maumee, he torched every town, field, and orchard, setting them all ablaze like he once burned the rice fields and forage around Savannah.[1]

Wayne had done everything in his power to appear invincible when he led his men back from the Maumee Rapids to Fort Defiance the previous August. He marched them like they were still on their way to battle. They traveled in orderly columns as they had while heading north, and every evening they slept behind the same fortifications they had constructed just days before. Wayne hurried his men south for he still feared an attack, not just by the Indians but also the British, who would come from Fort Miamis with their artillery. A deserter who fled to his camp after the Battle of the Rapids told him that the chiefs were waiting along the Maumee for Governor Simcoe to arrive from Detroit. In council with him, they would decide for peace or war. Never doubting the deserter's report, Wayne pressed on toward the Auglaize. The weather had changed almost immediately after the battle, with the skies now a bright blue and the hint of fall already in the air, making marching easier than on the way north from Fort Greeneville. He hurried his men, too, because he did not want the Indians to realize the troubles that plagued his army. They might already know that his men were deserting, but he must not let them discover how many others were sick from fevers and how few rations he had left.[2]

When his army arrived back at Fort Defiance, Wayne still did not let his men rest. He ordered them to clean their guns and prepare to march on the parade ground on Sunday morning August 31, just as they had done at Legionville, Hobson's Choice, and Greeneville. Then he put them to work strengthening the post with a "good Parapet, sufficient to resist a twenty four pounder" around its top perimeter. With the parapet, along with abatis in the surrounding ditch, complete, Wayne was certain his men were protected from Indian and British attacks. But the defenses around his fort could not help him feed his troops. On the way to the Battle of the Rapids, he placed them on half rations and now he continued the practice at Fort Defiance. Every soldier and the women who followed them must survive on a half-pound of flour a day. The cattle were all gone. Even if more could be brought up quickly from the Ohio River, Wayne had no salt to preserve the meat. There was likewise not a drop of whiskey anywhere. Desperate to feed his men and knowing more angry letters to Elliott and Williams would do no good, he ordered the Kentucky volunteers to bring flour and cattle from Cincinnati. As humiliating as this task might be, they had to obey their commanding general, knowing if they refused, the army would starve.[3]

As weak as his army might be, Wayne knew there was still one more task that his soldiers must accomplish. They had to proceed to the Miami Villages and construct the fort at the headwaters of the Maumee that St. Clair had failed to build. Leaving Major John Hunt in charge of Fort Defiance, along with men too sick or hungry to march, Wayne departed for Kekionga with his Legion and the Kentucky mounted volunteers on September 14. As soon as they started on the fifty-mile trek to the river's headwaters, the weather changed dramatically. Now the skies opened and rain fell for a week just like during the Battle of the Clouds after Brandywine. When Wayne finally arrived at the Maumee's headwaters, he could not decide where a post should be built. He and Major Burbeck changed the location five times before finally placing the fort immediately west of the exact spot where the St. Mary's and St. Joseph's met. Each side measured two hundred and seventy-two feet long. Barracks were built adjacent to the interior walls, while earthen ramparts were pushed against the outer perimeter to make the fort invulnerable to cannon fire. Instead of blockhouses, Wayne ordered a guardhouse built directly over the main gate and four bastions at each of the corners. He also had a ditch sixteen feet wide around much of the post. He pressed every soldier into service, no matter how hungry or tired, chopping down trees and hauling the logs back to the building site.[4]

Wayne was disappointed when Todd and later Barbee arrived with little food. Barbee also brought news that Robert Elliott had been shot dead by warriors when leading a packtrain of four hundred horses north of Fort Hamilton. The Indians fired at Barbee's men when they tried to retrieve Elliott's body for burial. Later they came back and stole the body of Elliott's assistant, who had died with him, right out of his coffin. Having no rations to feed them, and knowing how desperately homesick they were, Wayne finally let the mounted volunteers, whom he now praised for behaving "better than any Militia I have heretofore seen in the field," go back to Kentucky on October 14. He tried to keep his hungry Legion occupied by taking some of them to search for ammunition that General Harmar left behind during his campaign against the Miami Villages. He also went looking for the quickest portage between the Maumee and Wabash. Finding the best spot, he climbed down from his horse and marked a tree where a fort should be built to protect the portage.

When he returned with news of his discovery, his exhausted men wondered how they could build another post when they were so hungry. With many convinced they would starve to death in this godforsaken wilderness, Wayne had Reverend Jones preach a sermon to them on the phrase, "If God is for us, who can be against us," from St. Paul's Epistle to the Romans. The silent prayers that went up for food were finally answered on October 16 when Captain Gibson arrived from Fort Recovery with 30,000 rations of flour, a hundred and fifty cows, and at least three hundred sheep. Ten days later, when the post at the Maumee's headwaters was finally finished, the soldiers of the Legion, now well fed if only for the moment, named the place Fort Wayne.[5]

After leaving his faithful officer Hamtramck in charge with a few soldiers, Wayne started the rest of his army down the seventy-mile trail to Fort Greeneville. The weather turned cold and rations again ran low. So many soldiers were sick that Wayne ran out of medical supplies. Hungry men who were desperate to go home deserted at an alarming rate. They were unaware of the fact that the British had offered a reward of £25 for each one of Wayne's soldiers brought into Fort Miamis. There a stark choice would be laid before them: either join His Majesty's army or work as a common laborer hauling wood and other supplies in a wheelbarrow. Both choices were preferable to what General Wayne would do if he caught them. They would be immediately court-martialed, sentenced to death with no mercy possible, and die by the hangman's noose. On the way back to Greeneville, the Legion stopped to witness a deserter meet his death on the gallows.[6]

Through it all, from Fort Defiance, to Fort Wayne, and back to Fort Greeneville, Wayne had seen no more than a handful of Indians. The few that did appear slipped away as quickly as they came. Now as he wandered Greeneville, as he once wandered Ticonderoga, he could not understand why the chiefs ignored his pleas to come into the fort and write a treaty. He had sent speeches to the Delaware, Shawnee, Wyandot, Miami, Ottawa, and the rest in the confederation, begging them to take the hand of friendship he offered them. His words were no longer full of the arrogance that marked his talks to the Creeks during the Georgia campaign. Now his tone was similar to the one he used to reach out to the Loyalists, redcoats, and Hessians in the swamps near Savannah. He opened a wide door to them to come to Greeneville and settle the trouble between their peoples.

"Listen to the voice of truth and peace," he wrote in speeches carried under white flags to the defeated chiefs. Surely it was clear to them by now that the British had lied to them. They encouraged the Indians to fight Wayne's army while they stayed safe in their forts. He had warned the warriors before the battle along the Maumee Rapids that the British could not be trusted, but they did not listen to him. Instead they hid themselves behind fallen logs and came after his soldiers in the tall grass. Wayne assured the chiefs that their warriors had only seen the "little finger" of the power of the United States. Come meet with me, he pleaded, and all would be forgiven. Together they would agree to honor the boundary set between their peoples at Fort Harmar, and before that at Fort Finney and Fort McIntosh. The Indians would live north of the line while Americans would finally cross the Ohio and settle south of it. He demanded only one condition for peace to reign. The Indians must return all the prisoners they had taken on the frontier. Wayne had collected the names of over fifty people taken since 1782 whose families demanded their return. If they brought these kidnapped Americans, mainly young men, women, and children, into Greeneville, the terrible events of the past, the murders on all sides, the battle high above the Maumee Rapids at Presque Isle and in the tall grass below, and all the towns set ablaze, would be forgotten, or as Wayne explained, "Permit me now to draw a veil over the late transaction and to bring in deep oblivion and to obliterate from the mind all remembrance of past injuries."[7]

Wayne did not tell the chiefs that they must come in and sign a treaty because he could not bear the thought of leading another campaign against them. Taking his Legion into the wilderness again was too horrific to imagine. But all he could do as he wandered Fort Greeneville was imagine. He could see the warriors even now gathering at Fort Miamis and Fort Detroit to plan their next move. This time they would have the full support of Carleton and Simcoe when they waited in some lonely place to strike his men. This time, too, they might defeat him, or another general chosen to lead the Legion. Once the army was lost, warriors would fall on unprotected settlements all along the Ohio frontier. The "fertile Country" that Wayne had "fought bled & conquered in vain" would be lost forever. As much as he loved his nation, he no longer wanted to be the general who must prevent this from happening. After trying for years to hide his many illnesses from Knox, and through him Washington, he now described his brokenness and how much he wished the Indians would simply disappear. "I sincerely wish that all the Indians would follow their brethren to the other side of the Mississippi," he confessed to Knox, "for it is a very unpleasant kind of warfare to contend with Savages, with famine & faction—and altho' I have hitherto sustained & baffled all the attacks of the Hydra, yet I feel both body & mind fatigued by the contest."[8]

In his growing despair, Wayne became convinced that the British and the Indians were working harder than ever to destroy America. They no longer wished merely to retain their hold on the Ohio Country, but to break off the frontier from Pittsburgh through Kentucky and down the Mississippi Valley. They had enlisted the help of the whiskey rebels in western Pennsylvania and lone wolves like George Rogers Clark, the Revolutionary War hero who offered his services to any foreign power west of the Appalachians. After Wayne had Robert Newman, the deserter who alerted the Indians of his approach, hunted down, arrested, and brought to him at Greeneville, he became convinced that Wilkinson was part of the grand scheme. According to Newman's confused testimony, Wilkinson was playing a key role in helping the British break off America's western territory. Newman mentioned that a mysterious man he met in the dark at Fort Greeneville had handed him instructions to give to the Indians at the Grand Glaize, including how to defeat Wayne. That man hidden in the shadows must have been James Wilkinson.[9]

Secretary Knox had not written to Wayne since the previous June. He had left Philadelphia two months later and traveled to Maine where he hoped to establish himself in business and raise his ever-growing family. Back in the nation's capital, i.e., by the late fall, after reading through Wayne's anxious letters, he decided to encourage him, and finally to reveal just how much Wilkinson despised him. In early December, he passed on Washington's congratulations for the victory along the Maumee Rapids four months previously. The president was most impressed with how carefully Wayne had prepared his men to fight Indian warriors. He also appreciated the fact that Wayne had been able to supply his men in the wilderness. Knox forwarded the congratulations just passed in Congress, too, for the victory at the Maumee Rapids. Knowing Wayne's depressed state of mind, he did not tell him that the House of Representatives passed resolutions thanking the officers and soldiers of the Legion as well as General Scott and his Kentucky volunteers, all who served "under the orders of Major General Wayne." However, after a lengthy debate, they refused to thank Wayne personally for the victory. Instead they defeated the proposal by arguing that congratulating a general for merely earning his pay would be a dangerous precedent for the young republic to set.[10]

But Knox believed he could no longer shield him from the fact that his second in command had been working against him. Along with his letter of congratulations, Knox sent another marked "private and confidential" with copies of Wilkinson's letters to the War Department dated June 30 and July 18, 1794. In these letters, Wilkinson asked Secretary Knox to bring formal charges against Wayne. Written in an outraged tone, they described Wayne's misconduct in vague terms. First, he was not a gentleman. He violated every principle of justice, law, and humanity. More specifically, as part of this bad behavior, he misappropriated government funds. Second, his strict discipline of the Legion's soldiers was brutal, but precisely in what way, the letters did not mention. Third, the summer campaign to the Maumee Rapids and back had been nothing short of a disaster. Rather than a careful plan, Wayne had led the army with "noise and gasconade." Even with all his bluster, he failed to send one command to Wilkinson throughout the entire fight. Finally, after the battle, Wayne had failed to attack the many Indian villages north of Fort Miamis. He might have captured upward of twenty-five hundred women and children if he had done so.[11]

Knox did not tell Wayne that these letters were only two of many that Wilkinson had sent since Wayne took command of the Legion. But he revealed enough to send Wayne into a fit of anguish and rage. All attempts to temper his language disappeared as he composed an eleven-page letter to defend himself. If he did not know these accusations were from Wilkinson, he would have thought they had come from a madman. He answered that the charges were as "unexpected as they were groundless," and they were as "false, as they were base & insidious." But most terrible to Wayne, Wilkinson's charges proved his brigadier was a traitor to his nation. Only a traitor would condemn Wayne for disciplining his soldiers so carefully. He noted that Wilkinson seemed to regret how deliberately the Legion had been trained to defeat the Indians. This was proof, Wayne now countercharged, that Wilkinson had joined, and perhaps was even leading, the grand conspiracy between the Indians, whiskey rebels, frontier malcontents, and the British to break off America's western frontier.[12]

For a few weeks, Wayne was inconsolable. The irony that he had spent his every waking moment since winning command of the Legion preparing his men for battle, while his brigadier general spent the same time weaving a fabric of lies about him, was almost too incredible to bear. Sharp Delany tried his best to keep his old friend on an even keel. Delany assured him that everyone in Philadelphia was overjoyed at his victory and gave him full credit for defeating the Indians. It was now obvious that the articles critical of Wayne in the Philadelphia newspapers were the handiwork of Wilkinson. Neither Wayne nor Delany knew that Wilkinson was writing far worse things to politicians across the nation than to Knox or the newspapers. As he explained to Harry Innes, a federal judge in Kentucky, General Wayne was a "liar, a drunkard, a Fool," a companion of the lowest order of society and their vices, "a coward, a Hypocrite," desperate to make a fortune for himself, and most truly "my Rancorous enemy."[13]

Knox made no suggestion to Wayne on how to handle his treacherous brigadier beyond hoping Wilkinson would take a leave of absence. For his part, Wilkinson promised to put down his pen only to take it up again. Just after the New Year in 1795, he wrote again to Secretary Knox that Wayne was a "worthless old scoundrel." His complaints, both to the War Department and to his many supporters, continued unabated. Wayne, still saddled with Wilkinson as his second in command, decided to ignore him. He sent him back to Fort Washington and turned his full attention to calling the chiefs into a council with him at Greeneville. This work, which he considered equal to the task of commanding the Legion, kept him so occupied from January 1795 onward that he soon set aside the outrage he felt for Wilkinson. His brigadier might still spew out his hatred for the "Old Man," but he was never again allowed into Wayne's confidence nor was he invited to attend the negotiations with the Indians. For all practical purposes, Wilkinson became an invisible man.[14]

Forgetting Wilkinson for the moment, Wayne learned that Tarhe the Crane might be willing to sue for peace. He sent another speech to the Wyandot on New Year's Day 1795, his fiftieth birthday, offering the same proposals he had made in the late summer. He added that he would build a fort on the Sandusky River to protect and supply the tribe if only Tarhe would come to Greeneville and sign a treaty. Something in this latest speech struck a chord in the chiefs who had opposed Wayne at the Maumee Rapids. Now Indians wrapped in threadbare blankets appeared before the walls of Greeneville. Their horses were so thin that the soldiers could see the ribs of the animals from high atop the walls of the fort. With their fields burned to the ground by Wayne, and with the British unwilling to support thousands of warriors with their wives and children, they had no choice but to come and beg for food. Wayne fed every Indian who came his way. Hamtramck sent a steady trickle of Indians, who came to his post also looking for the Wind, onto Greeneville. There were rumors that Little Turtle and other headmen also wanted peace. After the battle at the Maumee Rapids, the Delaware war chief Buckongehelas had met in Detroit with the British, who urged him to continue the war against the Americans in the spring when the enlistments of Wayne's soldiers were up. But remembering the gates of Fort Miamis shut in his face, Buckongehelas no longer trusted the British. He debated whether to take his people west to the White River or to meet first with General Wayne at Greeneville before leaving. He finally made up his mind to do whatever the Shawnee war chief Bluejacket did.[15]

On February 7, 1795, Bluejacket, at the head of a party of twenty people, rode through the gates of Fort Greeneville. Wayne was as impressed with the handsome chief as the officers who met him at Fort Defiance on his way south. Taller than Wayne, he was dressed in the coat of a British officer with golden epaulets, a woolen shirt and bright red pants, and moccasins. He wore a silver medal of George III at his throat. Wayne, who still believed Little Turtle was the sole leader of the Indian confederacy, shook Bluejacket's hand without knowing that this was the man who led the attacks at Fort Recovery and the Maumee Rapids. But Bluejacket well knew the speech that Wayne had just sent to Tarhe. One of his attendants pulled out a copy and asked Wayne if he truly meant these words. With no hesitation, Wayne answered yes. Bluejacket then said he had come to accept Wayne's terms. "Our hearts and minds are changed & we now consider ourselves your friends and brothers," he told Wayne. As a sign of good faith, he handed four people in his party, a woman and three men, over to him. He told Wayne they had been kidnapped by the Indians on the frontier during the last four years. On the next day, a Delaware chief, acting on behalf of Buckongehelas, arrived in Greeneville announcing his tribe's agreement with Bluejacket.

Three days later, on February 11, Bluejacket signed a preliminary peace treaty with Wayne agreeing to a cease-fire. He promised to return on June 15 with all the chiefs who had fought the Legion at the Maumee Rapids to sign a permanent treaty. Wayne again mentioned the conditions of peace. All prisoners, not just the four that Bluejacket had brought, must be returned. The boundary line agreed to most recently at Fort Harmar would serve as the starting point of discussions on the border between the Indians and the Americans. Wayne also promised that the Indians could return to their villages and plant their crops in the spring without interference from his soldiers or any settler. He then ordered his quartermaster to load the horses of Bluejacket's party with beef, flour, and salt. Before he left, Bluejacket wanted one more favor from Wayne. When the treaty was finally written, he asked if he could have a copy with seals on it, just like the one he had received from the British ten years before acknowledging him as a chief. Wayne, after dreading the possibility of fighting the Indians in the spring and trying always to speak respectfully to the chiefs, now found Bluejacket almost childlike in his concern for such trifles.[16]

Never doubting that the Indians would come to a council in June, as Bluejacket promised, Wayne came out of the dark mood that had haunted him since the fall. His health improved and he no longer walked with a limp. Even Wilkinson's treachery did not bother him. After doubting for so long that he had won the Battle of the Rapids, he now told Timothy Pickering, the new secretary of war, that the bayonets of his Legion had opened the eyes of the Indians. He threw himself into setting up the meeting with the tribes. He built a house at the center of Fort Greeneville where he would light the council fire. Working with his quartermaster James O'Hara, he carefully stored goods worth $25,000 that Pickering forwarded from Philadelphia for distribution to the Indians. He alerted his paymaster Caleb Swan to be ready to receive another $10,000, which would be distributed as the first annuity payment to the tribes.

Carefully studying the treaties of Fort McIntosh, Fort Finney, and Fort Harmar, along with a draft of the upcoming treaty sent from the War Department, Wayne noticed the southwestern boundary described in these agreements, which was to run along the Great Miami River, would place important posts and land already carved out for settlement in Indian country. He recommended that the line be adjusted to include Fort Recovery and then take a sharp diagonal to the southwest farther down the Ohio River. He also recommended that a buffer zone be set up along the treaty line to keep settlers and Indians apart. While Secretary Pickering accepted Wayne's changes to the boundary line, he could not agree to a buffer zone because it would be difficult to implement.[17]

Excited about the prospects of a treaty, Wayne found that his feelings toward his children suddenly became warmer. He wrote to Isaac with actual concern for his happiness, something he had never done in the young man's entire life. Instead of simply expecting Isaac to listen to his troubles, as he once did with Polly, he sympathized with Isaac's problems, especially his worry that his legal education was taking so long. Wayne encouraged him to continue his studies.

They might be difficult now, but as he assured him, they would guarantee him a high place in the government someday. He told Isaac to move back to Waynesborough, where Polly's mother and sister were currently living, and manage the estate if that would improve his worldly prospects.[18]

Wayne also answered letters that his son-in-law, William Atlee, had written to him in the fall. Atlee had told him that Margaretta was in a state of near despair. She never recovered from the death of her mother in April 1793 or from the death of her firstborn child who died when just five months old. Margaretta had recently written to her father describing the depression she felt. Her mother had suffered greatly in the final weeks of her life, and then her little son, "one of the finest boys perhaps in the world," had been taken from her within the same year. She could hardly eat and had lost a great deal of weight. Her husband sold the house in Harrisburg and bought a small farm, but she was too weak to move there. Compounding her sorrow was the fact that her father never wrote to her. While Wayne did not answer Margaretta, he now assured Atlee that he never stopped caring for his family, even though it might seem so. The terrible business of war and the equally difficult task of diplomacy had caused the silence, not a lack of concern for his family.[19]

After months of preparation, Wayne finally opened the council at Fort Greeneville on June 15, 1795. By then the Ottawa, led by their wounded chief Egushawa, along with their brother tribes the Pottawatomi and Chippewa, and many Delaware had arrived. Wayne thanked the Great Spirit for the glorious sun and the cloudless blue sky above them all. Surely the beauty of the day proved that God himself was smiling on them. He waited another week before officially starting the negotiations. Every day more chiefs and warriors, along with their families, came into the fort. He let them set up their camps in the redoubts around the post and kept them well fed. But recalling that Washington had warned him to remember Pontiac's treachery, Wayne kept the artillery trained on them.

However, it was clear to him that the chiefs arriving at Greeneville were determined to make peace, and not start up a war again. He also noticed that many of them, like New Corn of the Pottawatomi, who had come all the way from Lake Michigan, were tired old men. New Corn told Wayne how his young warriors tore the medals of George III from their throats after the British shut the gates of Fort Miamis. They threw them to the ground and would not rest until they wore those of the great chief Washington. Another old chief, Tetabockshe, the king of the Delaware, hoped the wampum he laid before Wayne would forever wipe the sorrow from his people's hearts. Asimethe, another Pottawatomi chief, apologized that he had so few warriors with him. Some had been lost along the Maumee Rapids, but many more had died in the starving time that followed.

They passed a peace pipe, a calumet three feet in length with eagle feathers tied about it, among themselves and Wayne in hopes of happier times to come.

Day after day Wayne waited in the council house for the rest of the chiefs to arrive. His officers sat at his side, perfectly dressed like himself with their hair powdered and their uniforms spotless. They included his three aides, Harrison, DeButts, and Lewis, who were to take down every word spoken at the council, his quartermaster O'Hara and paymaster Swan, his adjutant general John Mills, his artillery lieutenant George Demter, and the camp's minister Reverend Jones. General Wilkinson was nowhere in sight. Finally, after another month, the most important Indian leaders finally came into Fort Greeneville: Buckongehelas on June 21, Little Turtle two days later, Tarhe the Crane on July 13, and finally five days later Bluejacket, who was delayed, he explained, by the British at Detroit who begged him not to come.

Now the negotiations could begin in earnest. Wayne explained that the great chief Washington had appointed him to treat with the Indians. In this capacity, he was duty bound to tell them that the land they had fought for, meaning the country immediately north of the Ohio River, was no longer theirs. They had surrendered the territory in several treaties with the American government, including most recently the treaty signed at Fort Harmar on the Muskingum River in 1789. He reminded them that before this they had already given up their country to the French and later the British by allowing them to settle on their land. The British had in turn lost the country to the Americans in 1783 when they signed a treaty in Paris ending the war between them. He read portions of the treaty which stated that the land west of the Appalachians and south of the lakes now belonged to the United States. In this same treaty, the British promised to surrender their forts at Detroit, Niagara, Oswego, and Michillimackinac, but they had failed to do so. They stayed in these posts, urging the Indians to fight the Americans for the very country they had already ceded. They had even built another illegal fort below the Maumee Rapids.

To underscore their treachery, Wayne read aloud from Jay's Treaty just negotiated between Great Britain and the United States. In the document, which Secretary Hamilton had forwarded to him, the British finally surrendered all their forts on American soil. How could the Indians continue their war against the United States if soon there would be no British forts nearby where they could obtain guns and ammunition? Wayne offered his own character as proof he was telling the truth. "I have never yet, in a public capacity, told a lie. You will not be deceived, by placing the utmost confidence in what I shall tell you. I again repeat, that your own towns and villages could not afford you greater liberty, safety, and security, than you will enjoy, whilst you choose to remain with me."[20]

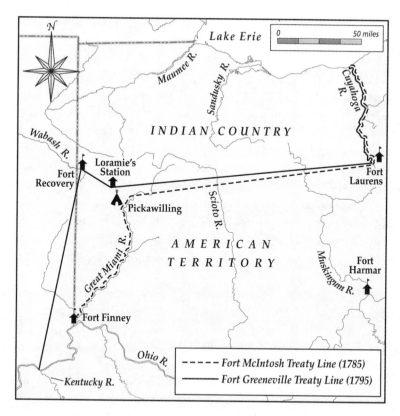

Greeneville Treaty Line. Copyright © Roberta Stockwell, 2018.

Much to Wayne's surprise, the Miami chief Little Turtle countered his argument point by point. A tall man, just about Wayne's age, with a high forehead and piercing eyes, he had not come dressed like a British soldier. He instead wore a breechcloth like most Miami men did; even in winter they threw only a blanket or buffalo robe around themselves. He wore a medal of George III around his throat along with a bear claw necklace. Little Turtle told a startled Wayne that he never heard of the treaty signed along the Muskingum. None of his chiefs had ever agreed to hand over their country to the Americans, or before that to the French or British. Day after day, with Little Turtle denying everything he said, Wayne patiently restated his same arguments. The Indians had surrendered much of the land across the Ohio River to the Americans at Fort McIntosh in 1785, at Fort Finney a year later, and finally at Fort Harmar in 1789, while the British had surrendered the entire western country to the Americans at the conclusion of the Revolution. There had been enough killing on both sides. Acknowledge your loss, accept the peace offered, Wayne pleaded, and take the money and gifts that the American government offered this summer and every year from now on.

As logical as Wayne's arguments might seem, Little Turtle continued to contradict him and swayed many chiefs to his side. He said again that he never heard of these treaties nor had any Miami chief ever signed them. Little Turtle was correct because the Miami had not attended the negotiations at Fort McIntosh, Fort Finney, or Fort Harmar. Nor had any Indian leader been present in Paris to witness the treaty between the British and the Americans. Agreeing with Little Turtle, chiefs among the Ottawa, Pottawatomi, and Chippewa now challenged Wayne. Maybe some of their warriors were at the forts where these treaties were signed, but these young men had no authority to negotiate for the tribes. They would only honor promises made by their headmen and greatest war chiefs. On the outside chance some of their leaders had actually signed the treaties, they added that the interpreters must have done a poor job of explaining what was in them.[21]

After the arguing went back and forth for a week, Tarhe the Crane finally rose to address the council. He was a tall and very thin man who had lost the use of his right arm when Wayne's soldiers shattered his elbow at the Battle of the Rapids. He had heard enough from Little Turtle and would now speak as the leader of the Wyandot, the grandfathers of the tribes, and the only chief among his people to come back from the bloody fight. His words were stark and poetic. The Indians must admit that they had murdered on behalf of the British. The redcoats might have placed the hatchet in their hands, but they buried it in the skulls of the Americans. He reminded everyone in the council house that many Wyandot chiefs, along with headmen of the Delaware, Ottawa, Pottawatomi, Chippewa, and Six Nations, had signed the treaty at Fort Harmar. He did not mention that he and Buckongehelas, along with many other leaders in this very room, had witnessed the treaty at Fort Finney three years previously. But he did tell his fellow chiefs to listen to Wayne. The Legion's commander was in a position to take away all their land. Instead he only asked for the land south of a line running from the Tuscarawas River to just below Loramie's Station. They must give Wayne, who had defeated them in battle, what he demanded. The killing, bloodshed, and war must end. They must turn their backs on the British and make friends with the Americans. An excited General Wayne agreed, urging the chiefs to throw the hatchet of war into the lake and bury it in the sand at the bottom. Better yet throw it into the center of the ocean where no man would ever find it again.[22]

A few chiefs still complained that if they had signed treaties, none of them had ever received the money and goods promised to them. But their arguments meant little now that Tarhe the Crane, the most respected chief of the most honored tribe, had spoken, and once Bluejacket rose to speak in support of him. When he arrived at the council house, Bluejacket had made a point of sitting between the Wyandot, the grandfathers of the tribes, and the Delaware, the uncles of the tribes. These three tribes, and not the Miami, had built the latest confederacy to stop the Americans from crossing the Ohio. As Bluejacket explained, Little Turtle may have led the warriors against St. Clair, but he himself, along with Tarhe and Buckongehelas, had organized the tribes against General Wayne. Defeated at both Fort Recovery and along the Maumee Rapids, and with the British locking them out of Fort Miamis, they must do what Wayne asked. They must bury their hatchets forever. Bluejacket, a war chief, said he would take his place behind the village chiefs who would lead his people from now on. All the Indians must follow his example and accept their place as "younger brothers" behind their "elder brothers," the Americans. "We must think of war no more," he told the chiefs. Then turning to Wayne, he said he had a deep desire to meet the "great man" Washington and asked if two chiefs from every tribe could go to Philadelphia and "take him by the hand."[23]

Once the Wyandot and Shawnee made peace with Wayne, the Delaware quickly agreed. Speaking for his tribe, Buckongehelas, a grave man with a downcast appearance, who like Tarhe had put his mark as a witness on the treaty at Fort Finney, promised he would be as good a friend to the Americans as he had once been their enemy. But he wryly added that he hoped the people of the United States would have "sense enough" to enjoy their "dawning happiness." Wayne, who had wondered if he won the Battle of the Rapids, now had no doubt that he secured a happy peace for his nation, mainly with the help of Tarhe and Bluejacket. In the treaty adopted on August 1, everyone present agreed to end hostilities and establish a "perpetual peace." Within ninety days, both sides would return all the prisoners taken on the frontier to the commanders at Fort Greeneville, Fort Wayne, or Fort Defiance. Ten chiefs would remain at Greeneville as hostages until all the captives were restored to their families. Most important in ending the war on the frontier, the Indians gave up all claims to the country lying south of a line running down the Cuyahoga to Fort Laurens, all the way west to Loramie's Station, then on a sharp diagonal toward the northwest to Fort Recovery, and finally along another sharp diagonal to the place where the Kentucky River met the Ohio.

By signing the treaty, the United States gave up its claims to the Indian country beyond the new boundary, which the British had granted to the Americans in 1783. But by signing the same treaty, the Indians effectively placed themselves under the protection of the United States. They promised to sell their land as tribes, not as individuals, and only to the American government. They were given full authority to drive squatters out of their country, but they must allow Americans to travel through their territory unmolested. Likewise, they could hunt on the land they had ceded without fear of harm. The government would send licensed traders into the Indian country to set up posts where the tribes could trade their furs and skins for manufactured goods. Violators of the treaty on either side were subject to punishment. Finally, the tribes would receive annual payments of $1,000 each for the Wyandot, Delaware, Shawnee, Miami, Ottawa, Pottawatomi, and Chippewa, and $500 each for smaller bands who had joined the negotiations, including the Wea, Eel River, and Piankeshaw, which were part of the Miami, along with the Kickapoo and Kaskaskia.[24]

Looking once again to the future of his nation, and with the full backing of Secretary Pickering, Wayne made sure an American footprint was laid down on the other side of the new Indian boundary. Six-mile-square plots of ground, belonging to the United States, would be drawn around Fort Defiance, Fort Wayne, Fort Detroit, Fort Michillimackinac, and old Fort Peoria on the Illinois River. They would also be located at the mouths of the Maumee and Sandusky Rivers on Lake Erie and at the Chicago River on Lake Michigan. A two-mile-by-two-mile square block would be carved out around the lower rapids of the Sandusky. Still more six-mile-by-six-mile square blocks would be designated at the head of the navigable waters of the St. Mary's and the Auglaize as well as the strait between Lake Huron and Lake Michigan. Finally, a twelve-mile-by-twelve-mile square block would be drawn around Fort Miamis on the Maumee as well as around the mouth of the Illinois where the river emptied into the Mississippi. The United States would retain Fort Vincennes on the Wabash and Fort Massac on the Ohio near the Mississippi. Finally, French settlers in the Indian country would keep their land, as would George Rogers Clark, who had been granted a 150,000-acre tract at the Falls of the Ohio.[25]

Before asking the chiefs to accept the treaty, Wayne had its ten articles read out in all the languages present. After making corrections based on the Indians' objections, he had the revised articles read aloud a second time. Wayne then asked, "You, Chippewas, do you approve of these articles of the treaty, and are you prepared to sign them? You, Ottawas, do you agree? You, Pattawatomies? You, Wyandots, do you agree? You, Delawares? You, Shawanese? You, Miamies, do you agree? You, Weas? And you, Kickapoos, do you agree?" One by one, each tribe answered yes.[26]

Two days later, on August 3, almost a year to the day since the men gathered in the council house fought him near the Maumee Rapids, Anthony Wayne signed his name to the Treaty of Greeneville. Below his large signature, the ninety chiefs present each made an "x" or a cross, with some also drawing their totems. The

Treaty of Greeneville. Chicago History Museum.

parchment soon filled up with tiny ink drawings of deer, snakes, wolves, turtles, fish, and eagles. Captain DeButts wrote the Indian names next to the marks and totems. After Wayne's aides and other officers, who had been present throughout the negotiations, added their signatures, so did the interpreters, with some writing their names and others drawing an "x." As the chiefs and their families departed from the fort, with their horses loaded down with the goods the government had provided them, Wayne promised each of them a new medal to replace the hated images of George III. They would show the symbol of his beloved America, the eagle clutching arrows and an olive branch in his talons. As the chiefs finally departed, Anthony Wayne, after accomplishing so much for his nation, suddenly realized that he, too, must go home.[27]

14

"I Will Write You More from Presque Isle"

Late in the afternoon of February 6, 1796, Anthony Wayne came to the crest of the hills outside of Philadelphia. He had asked for a furlough after the negotiations at Greeneville and finally received one. He was relieved that he arrived in the capital in time to make the case to Congress not to reduce the Legion. He even hoped that President Washington would appoint him the next secretary of war now that Timothy Pickering had resigned. But what he could not understand was why all the bells in every steeple in the city were ringing. There must be a celebration of some kind, but for what he did not know. He was more surprised when, looking down the road toward the capital, he saw three companies of soldiers heading his way. When Captain John MacPherson rode up to his side, he finally knew the bells were ringing for him. He had met MacPherson during the Revolution when the captain left the British army to fight with him. MacPherson had come with the Philadelphia Light Horse Brigade to escort his former commander into the city. When they crossed the Schuylkill, fifteen cannon boomed out a welcome from Centre Square. As Wayne made his way into the city, thousands lined the streets cheering his victory at Fallen Timbers.

In the letter he wrote to Henry Knox after the battle, Wayne described how the Legion had fought the Indians in "old fallen timber." When this letter was published in the Philadelphia newspapers, these words took hold of the public's imagination. The Battle of the Rapids, as Wayne called the fight, now became the Battle of Fallen Timbers. MacPherson's light horse brigade led him to the City Tavern where his oldest friends, including Sharp Delany, Richard Peters, and Benjamin Rush, were waiting, along with leading politicians, to toast his success. He was so popular that six days later, Vice President John Adams hosted a dinner in his honor. Adams was surprised at the outpouring of emotion for

Wayne from the sedate Pennsylvanians. "The man[']s feelings must be worth a guinea a minute," he wrote to his wife, Abigail. For Adams, who never received the praise he deserved, watching Wayne wrapped in glory was somewhat disconcerting.[1]

An even greater celebration in Wayne's honor came on February 18 at Richardet's Tavern. A Temple of Peace had been constructed near the tavern. Its columns rose twenty-six feet high. On its cornice, a dove sat on top of a globe with a banner marked "Peace" in its beak. A statue of a beautiful woman, representing America, stood at the pavilion's center. Ambroise and Company, the makers of the pavilion, could never have guessed that this was precisely how Wayne imagined his beloved country. Statues of five more women, wrapped in vines and holding baskets filled with flowers, stood near America. They represented Peace, Plenty, Liberty, Justice, and Reason. Later that night, as Wayne celebrated with many of his former officers, fireworks lit up the night sky over the tavern.[2]

The temple seemed a fitting symbol for the peace that reigned in America and the world. The tribes across the Ohio had signed the Treaty of Greeneville, while the British, who had agreed to Jay's Treaty, would soon abandon their illegal posts on American soil. Charles Coatesworth Pinckney, Washington's second choice to lead the Legion, had won a treaty with Spain opening New Orleans and the Mississippi River to American shipping. All along the frontier, the whiskey rebels were quiet, having fled at the sight of the huge army sent against them. The president had also opened negotiations with the Barbary States to win a comprehensive treaty ending attacks on American vessels in the Mediterranean. Peace had even come to France once Robespierre was toppled from power and a new constitution was adopted. Lafayette remained a prisoner of the Austrians at Olmütz, but Rochambeau had been saved at the last minute on his way to the guillotine. French armies now occupied the Netherlands and much of the Rhine Valley. Their victories had forced Spain, Austria, and the German states to sue for peace. Great Britain, Prussia, the Italian states, and Russia still opposed France, though perhaps not for long.[3]

But Wayne quickly realized there was little peace in the nation's capital. The city was deeply divided between Washington's supporters, now officially labeled the Federalists, and the president's many critics. Wayne finally understood that politicians who opposed the administration were not a faction to be mocked as "Demoncrats." Instead they were a full-fledged political party, the Democratic-Republicans. They were powerful enough to block Congress from thanking Wayne personally for the victory at Fallen Timbers. Later, seeing his great popularity among the people, they were wise enough to organize the elaborate celebration at Richardet's Tavern on his behalf. Their main goal was to elect

Thomas Jefferson, who had resigned from Washington's cabinet, as the next president. They drew much of their support from their continuing opposition to Jay's Treaty, an agreement they believed favored Great Britain and the old elitist order at the expense of France and the new democratic era dawning upon the world. Once the celebrations were over, Wayne found himself the target of the Democratic-Republicans. As Washington's appointee, who read aloud from Jay's Treaty during the negotiations at Greeneville, he was labeled a tool of bankers, monarchists, and Great Britain. Though he had spent his life fighting the British, and sympathized with the French in their attempt to establish a republic, this mattered not at all. Instead partisan newspapers mocked Wayne as a "pirate, a murderer, and a devil incarnate."[4]

What made the hatred of the Democratic-Republicans amazing to Wayne was the fact that they embraced General James Wilkinson as their sterling hero. He learned this when he appeared before the House's Committee of Military Establishment to defend maintaining the army at its current strength. Ignoring his arguments that Great Britain was still a danger to the United States, and that only trained soldiers, not militias, could protect the country, the committee recommended reducing its numbers to two thousand, a 60 percent reduction, and handing its command over to a brigadier general. Wayne's friend Thomas Hartley, now a representative in Congress, argued against the recommendations, but the measure passed the full House by a wide margin. If the bill passed the Senate, the Democratic-Republicans were certain Wayne would resign his post rather than submit to the disgrace of a lower rank. Wilkinson, who cultivated friendships among the Democratic-Republicans in Congress, would assume control of the smaller army. Wayne hoped that the Senate, where the president had greater support, would never accept these changes.[5]

Fleeing for a time from the troubled politics in Philadelphia, Wayne rode to Waynesborough. He was happy to see Isaac was now managing the estate. He was also working with William Henry Harrison back in Ohio to secure land for his son in the Symmes Purchase west of Cincinnati at thirty-three cents an acre. Margaretta paid a visit, but she could not restore her relationship with her father. Nothing she did pleased him and he was soon off to Philadelphia. Her distress deepened when she learned he had taken up again with Mary Vining, who lived in the city with her brother John, a Federalist Congressman from Delaware. Now thirty-six years old, Mary had turned down many suitors, always hoping that someday General Wayne would return to her.

Just like fifteen years earlier, she and Wayne were inseparable. They attended plays, ballets, and musicals staged in Wayne's honor throughout the capital. They visited Mary's family and friends, took sleigh rides through the countryside, and

Portrait of Wayne in 1796.
Courtesy of Independence National Historic Park.

left many in the highest ranks of society whispering that the couple was engaged. Women who chased after Wayne during the Revolution now wondered how a re-fined woman like Miss Vining could think of marrying a "weather-beaten, vulgar, affected old soldier." But while Wayne bought Mary an expensive set of china, he never announced his engagement nor did he set a wedding date.[6]

Even as he squired Mary Vining about town, he was invited to more celebra-tions for his victory at Fallen Timbers. One of the largest, organized by the Fed-eralists, came on February 25 at Weed's Tavern, a popular inn at Gray's Ferry on the Schuylkill River. Wayne dined with General Daniel Morgan and officers of Philadelphia's Light Horse Brigades. But in all the adulation, Wayne never crossed paths with Catharine Greene. She was still grateful to him for the part he played during his few months in Congress in winning money from the government to pay off her husband's debts. But after he headed to Pittsburgh in May 1792, their relationship was never the same. Wayne did his best to stay in touch with her during the Ohio campaign. He often teased her about failing to write to him, just as she had complained about his silence when he sank into despair on his plantation.

But as troubles came into Catharine's life, her letters to Wayne were fewer and farther between. In the spring of 1793, her oldest son George Washington Greene, just fifteen years old, died when his canoe overturned in the Savannah River. Struggling with the loss of her favorite child, Catharine threw herself into the business partnership she had formed with Phineas Miller, the tutor of her children, and his friend Eli Whitney, a young inventor from New England. Their goal was to manufacture cotton gins, the same kind of device that Wayne had seen on Mrs. Bolling's plantation when he traveled south to join Nathanael Greene twelve years before. Tensions soon arose among the partners, as Miller and Whitney were both in love with Catharine. On June 13, 1796, while visiting George and Martha Washington in Philadelphia, Catharine would marry Phineas Miller in a private ceremony in the president's house. Within the year, her company to manufacture cotton gins would go bankrupt.[7]

If Wayne felt any remorse that the beautiful Caty was bound to marry someone else, he never said so in letters to his friends. By the spring of 1796, he was more concerned about taking up command of the Legion again. He had hoped to become the new secretary of war, but after Dr. James McHenry, a Continental Army surgeon and Washington's former secretary, assumed the post, Wayne held out little hope of winning a position in the government. By May, he was ready to return to Fort Greeneville when, at Washington's request, he was invited to a private meeting with the new secretary of war. McHenry explained that the president had an important public service for Wayne to perform. He wanted him to oversee the transfer of the western forts from Great Britain to the United States. Wayne accepted the task gladly. But then McHenry added that the president also wished him to perform a "secret service." Not understanding what McHenry meant, Wayne was stunned when he laid documents before him revealing that General Wilkinson was most probably a paid agent of the Spanish government.

Wayne had rightly guessed that there was a conspiracy at work on the frontier, but Spain, not Great Britain, was behind it. That the Spanish were causing trouble out west, even after signing Pinckney's treaty, did not surprise him. He received several reports that their colonial governor at New Orleans was building a new fort on the Mississippi at Chickasaw Bluffs in Tennessee. He ordered Captain Zebulon Pike, the commander of Fort Massac, thirty-eight miles from the mouth of the Ohio River, to inspect every boat that passed by and keep an eye out for Spanish agents. He just sent William Clark, a promising officer who had been misled by the Wilkinson clique, west to check if the Spanish were building forts nearby. He now regretted that he released the mysterious Robert Newman, who had probably taken valuable information on Wayne's corrupt brigadier with him.[8]

But he never suspected that Wilkinson was working with the Spanish to wrest control of the American Southwest from the United States. He was now determined to ferret out Wilkinson's contacts and intercept any documents proving him a traitor beyond a shadow of a doubt. McHenry told Wayne to be on the lookout for Dr. Thomas Power, an Irishman born in the Canary Islands who was a well-known agent of Spain. He was probably Wilkinson's main contact with the Spanish government. McHenry added that Wayne must perform one more task in the president's "secret service." Washington had learned that France, now at peace with most of Europe, was determined to retake its empire in the Mississippi Valley lost to the British in 1763. Wayne had heard rumors of this, but never investigated them after Kentucky's Governor Shelby assured him they were untrue. McHenry now told Wayne to watch for two French agents, Victor Collot, an army officer, and Joseph Warin, an engineer who once worked for the American army. Both men were inspecting forts throughout the West as the advance guard of a French takeover.[9]

There were many times before when Washington had found himself in a difficult position where no one could help him. In those moments, he had always sent for Anthony Wayne. One of the worst came when Benedict Arnold, after failing to turn West Point over to the British, fled to Clinton's army in New York City. Then Washington had called Wayne to his side when he feared thousands of redcoats were heading up the Hudson to attack the Continental Army. This was a similar but far more dangerous situation. Wayne must outwardly play the part of the conquering hero as he passed from fort to fort, but behind the scenes he must act as a secret agent, tracking Wilkinson's every move, but never letting him know that Washington suspected him of treason. Taking command of the western posts from the British would be a mere formality compared to finding proof of Wilkinson's sedition.

Even though he no longer felt as well as he did during the treaty negotiations the previous summer, with gout and the old wound in his left leg bothering him again, he had never turned down a request for help from his commander in chief. He would not do so now, especially since Washington appeared older and more tired than Wayne himself. No matter how much he was suffering, he would move like the Wind, as the Indians called him, and get back to Fort Greeneville as quickly as possible. Six months earlier, before he left for Philadelphia, he had called Wilkinson, whom he now described as the "worst of all bad men," back from Cincinnati to Greeneville to assume command of the army in his absence. Before bidding a "Temporary Adieu" to his Legion, he had handed his untrustworthy brigadier a long list of instructions. He wondered at the time why Secretary McHenry had ordered him to tell Wilkinson not to waver from this list. He now understood why. He must hurry back to Greeneville and make certain that Wilkinson had done no further damage to his beloved America.[10]

By early June, Wayne was ready to leave Philadelphia. He rode out of the city just as he had entered it. He was still a major general in command of the American army. As he had hoped, the Senate did not accept the changes proposed by the House of Representatives. On May 30, 1796, Congress enacted a law supporting the army at slightly less than its present strength, but retaining a major general as its commander in chief, at least through February 1797. The act also kept the current level of daily rations for soldiers at a pound of beef or three-quarters of a pound of pork, a pound of bread or flour, and a half-gill of rum, brandy, or whiskey, plus two more ounces of beef or pork and two more ounces of bread or flour for men serving on the frontier. Troops out west would continue receiving an extra half-pint of salt for every hundred men beyond the standard ration of a quart of salt, two quarts of vinegar, two pounds of soap, and a pound of candles. Soldiers everywhere were still entitled to a new hat, coat, and vest, two pairs each of woolen and linen overalls, four pairs of shoes and socks, a blanket, one stock and clasp, and a pair of buckles each year.[11]

Wayne arrived in Pittsburgh on June 23 where he learned from his friend Judge Brackenridge that Thomas Power had just visited the town. The mysterious doctor happily proclaimed to everyone he met that Wilkinson would soon take command of the Legion. He then proceeded downriver to meet with the brigadier in person. On July 5, Wayne arrived at Fort Washington where he learned that Dr. Power had already paid a visit to Wilkinson at Fort Greeneville and was now on his way down the Ohio. Collot and Warin had also just passed through Cincinnati. They came looking for Wilkinson with a large packet of documents. They, too, were now traveling down the Ohio toward the Mississippi. Hurrying north to Fort Greeneville, Wayne rode through the gates on July 16. He immediately sent for Wilkinson and relieved him. Seething with hatred for the "old Man," whom he had mockingly referred to as "his Excellency" during his absence, Wilkinson quipped to his followers that Wayne was a laughable fool who would seduce, rather than reduce, the British from their posts with the honey of his lies. As soon as Wayne set out for Fort Recovery, Wilkinson left for Philadelphia. Once he arrived there, he would demand that the president court-martial Anthony Wayne.[12]

As Wayne headed past Fort Defiance toward Fort Miamis, Indians greeted him all along the way. The chiefs who signed the Treaty of Greeneville, as well as many of the warriors who fought him at the Maumee Rapids, now admired him. They no longer called him the Wind, nor the Black Snake, but instead greeted him as "Father." Some even named their children after him. They hurried to General Wayne's side knowing he brought gifts from the great chief Washington, including hundreds of pounds of beef, veal, suet, mutton, pork, and fish, which he gave freely to all who asked. Everywhere he traveled, from the prairies just north of Fort Recovery, through the tangled forests of the Black Swamp, and down the Auglaize and Maumee River Valleys, Wayne noticed that the tribes had returned to their villages. Corn was again planted in patches of sunlight in the forest and along the bottomlands. Traders, licensed by the American government, would soon set up stores along the trail, including on the former site of McKee's trading post at the Foot of the Rapids.[13]

Making his way north, as a hero among the Indians just as he had been among the crowds in Philadelphia, he finalized the transfer of Fort Miamis on August 7 in a simple ceremony. He then boarded the *Adventure* for the trip to Detroit. He sent several officers ahead of him, including Captain DeButts and Lieutenant Colonel Hamtramck, who had overseen the surrender of Fort Miamis. Wayne also ordered Henry Burbeck, his artillery chief, to take a small party to Michillimackinac and handle the transfer. He did not worry for the moment that Burbeck was part of the Wilkinson clique. He needed someone of Burbeck's caliber to evaluate the all-important fort at the Straits of Mackinac and rebuild it if necessary.[14]

When the *Adventure* landed at Springwells three miles south of Detroit, the largest crowd of Indians that Wayne had yet seen came out to meet him. He estimated at least twelve hundred people stood waiting for him. Dragoons rushed forward to protect him, but he waved them off. The Indians now surrounded him, hugging him and shaking his hand with all their might, while shouting, "Father." They let out loud "ear-piercing yells" and shot their rifles into the air. Wayne found Little Turtle and Bluejacket in the crowd and embraced them. He promised to send them to meet with Washington in the early fall. Later, in Detroit, Wayne was led from one celebration to another with soldiers, French settlers, American traders and politicians, more Indians, and even British officers who were about to depart for their new post across the Detroit River at Fort Malden in Amherstburg. He became so friendly with the British that he even asked them for a loan of fifty barrels of pork for Burbeck's expedition to Michillimackinac. Military bands, artillery salutes, toasts with fine wine, dinner and dancing long into the night, and all the food that Wayne brought with him kept the celebrations going for weeks on end.[15]

By the middle of August, Wayne reported to McHenry that the British had graciously surrendered every post to the United States without incident. Wayne, in turn, had wished them well and hoped that "happiness, life & laurels" would "attend them." But amidst all the celebrations, he was distressed at the state to which the Legion had fallen. Supplies were low, discipline had disappeared completely, and men were deserting in greater numbers than during the march to the Maumee Rapids. As he had done so many times before, he complained about the sorry state of the soldiers' uniforms. He was thinking seriously of having Indian blankets sewn into clothes to keep his army warm in the winter. Wayne vowed he would do everything in his power to get the army back into shape, especially now that many of his men would be heading south to defend the Tennessee border against the Spanish and their Indian allies. He was equally determined, as he had been during the Revolution's last days in Georgia, to establish the rule of law everywhere he went. He ordered Winthrop Sargent, the secretary of the Northwest Territory, to come up from Cincinnati to establish civil government first in Detroit and then in Michillimackinac.[16]

But Wayne was deeply disappointed that he failed to discover definitive proof of Wilkinson's intrigues with the Spanish. Dr. Power had traveled all the way down the Ohio, slipping past Fort Massac before Captain Zebulon Pike realized who he was. Later, he ascended the Ohio in a barge loaded with barrels of rice, sugar, and tobacco. Lieutenant John Steele stopped him between Fort Massac and the Falls of the Ohio. Although Steele thought the Irishman looked odd for a trader, he failed to inspect his cargo and let him go. Wayne was beside himself, knowing that he had probably lost the best chance to accuse Wilkinson of treason with Power's "royal Chest" of Spanish gold and incriminating documents. He felt just as terrible that Captain Pike had mistakenly let Collot and Warin go. What disappointed even more was the fact that he had failed to complete his secret service for Washington who, as he learned from McHenry, would soon retire from public life. He would never again have the chance to serve the best, most patriotic, and wisest commander ever to have lived, a far greater man than Julius Caesar.[17]

Wayne remained so focused on proving his brigadier's guilt that he barely reacted when McHenry told him Wilkinson had convinced Washington to court-martial him. At first, the president turned down the request, just as Knox, Pickering, and McHenry did before him, on the grounds that he had no authority to call one. But after Wilkinson threatened to go to Congress and lay his accusations in front of the House of Representatives, where he had many supporters, Washington relented, hoping that Wayne could defend himself against the charges. For his part, Wayne was certain Wilkinson's actions were part of his efforts to help Spain take control of the American Southwest. His success was more likely if he ousted Wayne from his post. "The fact is my presence with the army is very inconvenient," Wayne explained to McHenry, "to the nefarious machination of the Enemies of Government & may eventually prevent them from dissolving the Union."[18]

He had only one concern about what lay ahead of him and it was not a court-martial. He was sure he would be proved innocent of Wilkinson's charges, which he believed were the product of a twisted mind. The Democratic-Republicans might even end up commending him for training the army so diligently. Instead, he thought only of America's future. After worrying for years about the circumvallation of the Indians and British, he must now worry about threats from Spain and France. He must watch over the frontier even more diligently than when he was first appointed commander in chief of the Legion. He decided the best place to stand guard would be Pittsburgh.

After making sure every frontier post was well supplied, he planned to set up his headquarters there. He turned to the mathematics he loved since childhood to explain why he must proceed there with due haste. Pittsburgh sat at the corner of an equilateral triangle with Fort Washington and Fort Detroit on the other two corners. Each point was three hundred to three hundred and ten miles apart from the other locations. Orders could be sent from the War Department in Philadelphia to Wayne in Pittsburgh in only a week, and he could respond just as quickly. He in turn could send commands on to the other two forts in twelve to fifteen days. He did not have to tell McHenry that he could get to either post just as quickly if there was trouble anywhere on the frontier. He had already written to his friend from Georgia Joseph Habersham, now the nation's Postmaster General, about setting up post roads along the lines of the equilateral triangle. He also asked that another road be laid out from Pittsburgh to the mouth of the Sandusky and then on to Detroit. This new route would encourage trade between the United States and Canada, and rival the road from New York City up the Hudson to Albany, and then west along the Mohawk River Valley. He was already writing to Oliver Wolcott, Hamilton's successor as the secretary of the treasury, about the potential revenue that could be collected from trade on the new path.

In early November, Wayne was finally ready to leave Detroit for Pittsburgh. One of his last official acts was to hand three packets of documents to a promising young soldier he had just spotted. His name was Meriwether Lewis. Wayne told his ensign to deliver the packets to Major Isaac Craig, the deputy quartermaster general in Pittsburgh, who would mark them "Confidential" and then send them on to the War Department. On November 12, he wrote a last letter to McHenry, promising, "I will write you more from Presque Isle, which I mean to visit in the course of a few days." He signed the letter the same way he ended thousands of others written throughout his long military career, "Your Most Obedient and Humble Servant."[19]

The weather was warm and sunny with the sky a clear blue when Wayne boarded the *Detroit* on the morning of November 13. He and his aide Captain DeButts expected to arrive at the small fort on the eastern end of Lake Erie, also called Presque Isle like the place where he defeated the Indians along the Maumee Rapids, in just a few days. With the weather staying beautiful as he crossed the lake, Wayne, for the first time in a long while, looked forward to the future with no depression or fear. His only worry was a fever that lingered even after he took large quantities of quinine. A day out from Presque Isle, his left leg, with the musket ball lodged there since the night the French fleet sailed up the James River in 1781, became greatly swollen. By the time the *Detroit* docked, on November 18, he could not walk. Captain Russell Bissell, the commander of Fort Presque Isle and a veteran of Fallen Timbers, ordered Wayne carried up to the second floor of the blockhouse where he was put to bed. He also had the general's legs and arms wrapped in flannel.

Over the next two weeks, Wayne seemed to improve. He took an interest in the fort, originally constructed by the French at the start of the Seven Years' War, and the town of Erie growing up around the post. But on December 1, he complained of pains in his stomach and bowels. He was certain that the gout had settled there. He asked for brandy, but there was none at the fort. Soon his suffering was so intense that he begged Bissell to send for his friend Benjamin Rush in Philadelphia. Bissell wrote to Rush, but knowing he would not arrive for weeks, also sent for a doctor from Fort Fayette. Major Abraham Kirkpatrick, who had climbed up the cliffs of Stony Point with Wayne, raced from Pittsburgh to his side. So did an army surgeon, George Balfour, who upon arriving at the post bled Wayne. Weakened by the loss of blood, he finally slept, but upon waking, called again for brandy. Now in almost unbearable pain, he reached out for Captain Bissell, and grabbing hold of his hand, said, "I am dying. Bury me on the hill, at the foot of the flagpole." Finally, just after two o'clock in the morning on December 15, 1796, as Major Kirkpatrick held him in his arms, Anthony Wayne breathed his last.[20]

The following day, Captain Bissell did as Wayne had asked. He laid him to rest, dressed in his blue and white uniform, in an oak casket. He had golden nails pounded into the casket's lid marking the date of his death. He buried him facing

the flagpole on a windswept hill overlooking Lake Erie. He placed a simple head-
stone carved with the letters "A.W." over the grave, and, perhaps remembering
the fortifications Wayne had constructed around his men every night when the
Legion marched north through the wilderness, he built a small fence around the
grave. Two weeks later, when Isaac Wayne learned of his father's death, he could
hardly bear the thought of him buried on some lonely hillside. Remembering
the graves of other heroes, Achilles on the heights of Troy, General Montgomery
on the Plains of Abraham, and Richard Butler on a bluff near the Wabash, he
wrote a poem in his honor:

> Presque isle saw Wayne expire; & there
> The traveler shall see his monument
> At least his grave—To this coursing
> Jealousy will not detract
> But allow a mound—
> Some little swelling of the earth
> To mark the internment of his bones
> Brave honest soldier sleep
> And let the dews weep over thee
> And gales that swish across the lake
> 'Til men shall recognize thy worth
> And coming to the place will ask
> Is this where Wayne is buried—[21]

Epilogue: "A.W. 15 Dec. 1796"

The statue of Anthony Wayne that looks out over the Maumee Rapids where he won his battle for America on the morning of August 20, 1794, is a beautiful one. It is a far more fitting tribute to him than the simple phrase that Captain Bissell pounded into his coffin with golden nails: "A.W. 15 Dec. 1796." High on a pedestal, Wayne stands straight and tall, looking out past the floodplain toward the rising sun. On his right stands an Indian, probably representing one of his scouts, and to his left stands a frontiersman in buckskin, no doubt a Kentucky volunteer. But as beautiful as the statue might be, it bears little resemblance to the man sent west in 1792 to defeat the Shawnee, Delaware, Wyandot, Miami, and Ottawa and all the tribes who fought with them.

A more accurate portrait would show Wayne's legs and arms wrapped in flannel bandages so he could bear the pain of gout and the lead ball he still carried in his leg from the Yorktown campaign. No Indian would be standing with him, as his Choctaw and Chickasaw scouts, seeing how sick he was on the way north from Fort Defiance, abandoned him. Nor would a Kentucky volunteer, representing the militia that he so disliked for their bloodthirstiness and cowardice, stand at his side. Instead he would be with the soldiers of his Legion whom he carefully trained to march and maneuver, to load and shoot their muskets, and above all else, not to be afraid. Wayne would surely be far happier with a veteran officer on his right and a young recruit on his left.

But even the greatest artist could not portray the struggle that Wayne endured to bring his army to this place. Within himself, he stared down the demons of illness, despair, and an acute anxiety for America's future. Beyond himself, he faced a president and secretary of war who could not make up their minds for peace or war, a Congress that refused to feed and clothe the very army it had

Fallen Timbers. Photograph by the author.

raised, and turbulent politics at home and abroad that painted Wayne as a fiend bent on destroying the very republic he had helped to create. Given the task of leading a third American army into the Ohio Country, probably to its own destruction, he had few experienced officers, recruits who ran at the mere thought of Indians, and a second in command who not only despised him, but who was working against him as a foreign agent.

Despite these obstacles, Wayne trained his veterans and recruits alike to become not just soldiers but an army. He was ever determined to feed, clothe, and supply his men who, like himself, were forgotten and alone in the vast wilderness they had all come west to secure. When after training his Legion for two years, and finally leading them toward the Maumee Rapids, where warriors waited to attack them with the full support of the British at their illegal post of Fort Miamis, he still doubted if they could ever win the battle that lay ahead, even though he had prepared them for so long to fight it. A year later, he was only convinced he had actually won the battle when the chiefs he had defeated drew their marks and totems on the treaty at Greeneville.

The very real struggles that Anthony Wayne endured have been largely forgotten. If people still remember him, they think of him as the confident man portrayed in the statue at Fallen Timbers rather than the hard-pressed commander who took years to ready his soldiers for the battle near the Maumee Rapids. Fearless, daring, even reckless, never believing he might lose, and above all else, "mad," are words that come to mind when the name "Anthony Wayne" is mentioned. His trials during the Ohio campaign, and before that during the Revolution when he led a defeated army away from Three Rivers, played a pivotal role at Brandywine, Germantown, and Monmouth, foraged for the starving Continentals at Valley Forge and Bull's Ferry, supported Lafayette in Virginia before the Yorktown victory, and took on any challenge necessary to defend Washington and America, the commander and nation he so loved, are all forgotten in that one word: "mad."

Even if people recall the battles that he fought, few know that Wayne came to see war as a horrid trade of blood. From the moment his soldiers mutinied on New Year's Day 1781, then continuing on through the desperate fight to save his men at Green Spring, and most terrible of all, during his forgotten command in the burning swamps and rice fields of Georgia, he lost his fascination with war and its glory that he had known since childhood. In his long descent through brutality, sickness, and despair, the dashing Wayne, who rarely receives more than a mention in history books about the Revolution, disappeared. The man who emerged in his place was more often than not sick and depressed, haunted by loneliness and the wrong choices he had made, and prone more to failure than success. He remained determined to defend America, whom he still loved as a woman, but he was more somber, more careful, and more aware of the dark uncertainties of this world. This man was the unlikely general that President Washington grudgingly chose to lead the Legion in one great battle against the Indians who were blocking the advance of the United States across the Ohio River.

Wayne never lived to see how his victory at the Battle of the Rapids, his name for the contest at Fallen Timbers, helped his country move west. He also never knew that he had bought his nation time, ten years to be exact, before the next generation of warriors living from the Appalachians to the Mississippi rose up, again with the help of the British, to halt the advancing Americans. The last man to flee from the battlefield near the Maumee Rapids, and who later refused to attend the negotiations at Greeneville, would lead a larger confederation against the United States than Bluejacket, Tarhe, and Buckongehelas had ever imagined. That man was the Shawnee warrior Tecumseh. In the War of 1812, he would fight to the finish against the young man with the green sash tied about him who rode with Wayne's orders on that fateful day in August 1794: William Henry Harrison.

In the river valley where Wayne won his great battle for America, "mad" Anthony stands forever frozen in time. Perhaps only a madman would have come out into the wilderness to take on warriors who had already destroyed two armies, with frightened soldiers who were barely clothed and badly fed. Perhaps it was also madness for a man to give up wealth and security, health and comfort, and home and family, all to win the dream of a new nation founded on liberty. If it was, then madness did propel Anthony Wayne from Three Rivers to Ticonderoga, from Brandywine and Germantown to Monmouth and Yorktown, and finally from the horrors of Georgia to the impossible fight at Fallen Timbers. It led him to fill his letters, that to this day lay forgotten in libraries throughout the country he fought so hard to create, with pleas, more passionate than the rational arguments of his peers, for America to endure no matter what the cost. As he explained to the wife he lost in the fight:

> You must endeavor to keep up your spirits as well as possible—The times require great sacrifices to be made—the blessings of liberty cannot be purchased at too high a price—the blood & treasure of the choicest & best spirits of the land is but a trifling consideration for such a rich inheritance—Whether any of the present leaders will live to see it established in this once happy soil depends on Heaven;—but it must—it will at one day rise in America, & shine forth in its pristine luster.[1]

NOTES

CHAPTER ONE. "I HAVE FOUGHT AND BLED FOR THE LIBERTIES OF AMERICA"

1. Richard Rush, *Washington in Domestic Life: From Original Letters and Manuscripts* (Philadelphia: J. B. Lippincott, 1857), 65–68; George Washington Parke Custis, *Recollections and Private Memoirs of Washington, By His Adopted Son George Washington Parke Custis, With a Memoir of the Author, By His Daughter; and Illustrative and Explanatory Notes by Benson J. Lossing with Illustrations* (Philadelphia: J. W. Bradley, 1861), 214; Thomas Boyd, *Mad Anthony Wayne* (New York: Charles Scribner's Sons, 1929), 242.

2. Arthur St. Clair to Henry Knox, November 9, 1791, *The Life and Public Career of Arthur St. Clair*, volume 2 (hereafter *St. Clair Papers*), edited by William Henry Smith (Cincinnati: Robert Clarke & Co., 1882), 262–267; "The following circumstantial account of the last Illness and death of General Washington was noted by T. Lear, which happened on Saturday evening, Dec. 14, 177[9]9, between the hours of ten and eleven," *Tobias Lear Papers*, William L. Clements Library (WLCL).

3. Custis, *Recollections and Private Memoirs of Washington*, 417–418.

4. St. Clair to Knox, November 9, 1791, *St. Clair Papers*, volume 2, 262–263.

5. Ibid., 263–265.

6. Ibid., 265–267.

7. General Washington to the Senate and House of Representatives, December 12, 1791, *The Writings of George Washington from the Original Manuscript Sources, 1745–1799*, edited by Thomas Fitzpatrick (Washington, D.C.: Government Printing Office, 1931–1944), volume 31, 442.

8. *Dunlap's American Daily Advertiser*, December 9, 1791, page 2; Richard M. Lytle, *The Soldiers of America's First Army, 1791* (Lanham, Md.: Scarecrow Press, 2004), 120–125.

9. Martin West, director, Fort Ligonier, editor, "George Washington's 'Remarks': Tran-

scription and Annotation," *George Washington Remembers: Reflections on the French and Indian War,* edited by Fred Anderson (Lanham, Md.: Rowman & Littlefield, 2004), 31–32.

10. Ebenezer Denny, "Memoir," *Military Journal of Major Ebenezer Denny, with an Introductory Memoir* (Philadelphia: J. B. Lippincott for the Historical Society of Pennsylvania, 1859), 3, 5–18, 38.

11. Harrison Clark, *All Cloudless Glory: The Life of George Washington, Volume II, Making a Nation* (Washington, D.C.: Regnery, 1996), 218.

12. Washington's Administration Report of St. Clair's Defeat, *American State Papers, Indian Affairs,* volume I, 139–140.

13. Jefferson's account of the event can be found in the *Papers of George Washington (PGW): Presidential Series (Pres. Ser.),* edited by Ted Crackel et al., volume 10:169; James Flexner, *George Washington and the New Nation, 1783–1793* (Boston: Little, Brown, 1970), 301.

14. Denny, "Memoir," 3, 5–18, 38.

15. Ibid., 165.

16. Washington to Beverly Tucker, May 16, 1789, *St. Clair Papers,* volume 2, 114–115.

17. Denny, *Military Journal,* 167.

18. Denny, "Memoir," 18.

19. Benjamin Van Cleve, "Memoirs of Benjamin Van Cleve," edited by Beverly W. Bond, *Quarterly Publication of the Historical and Philosophical Society of Ohio,* 17, nos. 1 and 2 (January–June 1922), 7–29; Theodore Roosevelt, *The Winning of the West,* volume V (New York: Knickerbocker Press, 1907), 168; Fairfax Downey, *Indian Wars of the U.S. Army 1776–1865* (Garden City, N.Y.: Doubleday, 1963), 54–59; Fort Recovery State Museum (http://www.fortrecoverymuseum.com/); Denny, *Military Journal,* 178.

20. Denny, *Military Journal,* 152–177.

21. St. Clair to Washington, February 24, 1792, March 26, 1792, and April 7, 1792; Washington to St. Clair, March 28 and April 4, 1792; Tobias Lear to St. Clair, (without date) 1792; Report of a Special Committee of the House of Representatives on the Failure of the Expedition against the Indians, March 27, 1792, *St. Clair Papers,* volume 2, 279, 282–299.

22. John Armstrong to Washington, December 23, 1791, *St. Clair Papers,* volume 2, 276–277; "Extract of a Letter from Colonel ———, Commanding Officer of a Frontier County, to a Member of Congress—dated Lexington, January, 1792," *Dunlap's American Daily Advertiser,* February 10, 1792.

23. Washington, "Memorandum on General Officers, March 9, 1792," *PGW: Pres. Ser.,* 10: 74.

24. Lawrence Goldstone, *Dark Bargain: Slavery, Profits, and the Struggle for the Constitution* (New York: Walker, 2005), 1; Washington, "Memorandum on General Officers, March 9, 1792," *PGW: Pres. Ser.,* 10: 74.

25. Washington to Henry Lee, June 30, 1792, *PGW: Pres. Ser.,* 10: 506; Charles Royster, *Light-Horse Harry Lee and the Legacy of the American Revolution* (New York: Knopf, 1981).

26. For "Active," "brave," and "sober," see Memorandum on General Officers, March 9, 1792, *PGW: Pres. Ser.*, 10: 74.

27. Washington, Memorandum on General Officers, March 9, 1792, *PGW: Pres. Ser.*, 10: 74; David B. Mattern, *Benjamin Lincoln and the American Revolution* (Columbia: University of South Carolina Press, 1995), 76–109, 190–205; Paul Lockhart, *The Drillmaster of Valley Forge and the Making of the American Army* (New York: HarperCollins, 2008), 95–116; Don Higginbotham, *Daniel Morgan: Revolutionary Rifleman* (Chapel Hill: University of North Carolina Press, 1961).

28. Washington, Memorandum on General Officers, March 9, 1792, *PGW: Pres. Ser.*, 10: 74; C. L. Bragg, *Crescent Moon over Carolina: William Moultrie and American Liberty* (Columbia: University of South Carolina Press, 2013), 234–243; Washington to William Moultrie, March 14, 1792, *Writings of George Washington*, volume 39, 4–5; "Mordecai Gist," *American Generals of the Revolutionary War: A Biographical Dictionary*, edited by Robert P. Broadwater, reprint edition (Jefferson, N.C.: McFarland, 2007), 45–46; Harvey H. Jackson III, *Lachlan McIntosh and the Politics of Revolutionary Georgia* (Athens: University of Georgia Press, 2003).

29. Washington, Memorandum on General Officers, March 9, 1792, *PGW: Pres. Ser.*, 10: 74; Consul Willshire Butterfield, ed., *The Official Letters Which Passed Between George Washington and Brig.-Gen. William Irvine and Between Irvine and Others Concerning Military Affairs in the West from 1781 to 1783* (Madison, Wisc.: D. Atwood, 1882); Harry M. Ward, *Duty, Honor, or Country: General George Weedon and the American Revolution* (Philadelphia: American Philosophical Society, 1979); Harry M. Ward, *Charles Scott and the "Spirit of '76"* (Charlottesville: University Press of Virginia, 1988).

30. Washington, Memorandum on General Officers, March 9, 1792, *PGW: Pres. Ser.*, 10: 74; Rufus Putnam, *The Memoirs of Rufus Putnam and Certain Official Papers and Correspondence*, edited by Rowena Buell (Boston: Houghton Mifflin, 1903); "Jedidiah Huntington," *American Generals of the Revolutionary War*, 60–61; Higginbotham, *Daniel Morgan*, 180–181.

31. Isaac Wayne, "Biographical Memoir of Major General Anthony Wayne," *The Casket* (May 1829), 195; Horatio N. Moore, *Life and Services of Gen. Anthony Wayne: Founded On Documentary Evidence And Other Evidence Furnished By His Son, Col. Isaac Wayne* (Philadelphia: Leary, Getz & Co., 1845), 17.

32. I. Wayne, "Biographical Memoir," *The Casket* (May 1829), 197, 200–201; Moore, *Anthony Wayne*, 28–29, 40–46.

33. I. Wayne, "Biographical Memoir," *The Casket* (May 1829), 197–200; Moore, *Anthony Wayne*, 30–39.

34. Major John André, *Cow-chace in three cantos, published on occasion of the rebel general Wayne's attack of the refugees block-house on Hudson's river, on Friday the 21st of July, 1780* (New York: Printed by James Rivington, 1780); Boyd, *Mad Anthony Wayne*, 112; I. Wayne, "Biographical Memoir," *The Casket* (December 1829), 303–317; Moore, *Anthony Wayne*, 87–129.

35. I. Wayne, "Biographical Memoir," *The Casket* (December 1829), 493–505; Moore, *Anthony Wayne*, 130–151.

36. Donald Jackson and Dorothy Twohig, eds., *The Diaries of George Washington*, volume 6 (Charlottesville: University of Virginia Press, 1979), 135–145.

37. Archibald Henderson, *Washington's Southern Tour, 1791* (Boston: Houghton Mifflin, 1923), 208.

38. Washington, Memorandum on General Officers, March 9, 1792, *PGW: Pres. Ser.*, 10: 74.

39. Thomas Jefferson, "Memorandum of a Meeting of the Heads of the Executive Departments, March 9, 1792," *The Complete Anas of Thomas Jefferson*, edited by Franklin V. Sawvel (New York: Round Table Press, 1903), 61–62.

40. Wayne to Washington, April 6, 1789, *PGW: Pres. Ser.*, 2:36; Wayne to James Madison, June 15, 1789, *General Anthony Wayne and the Ohio Indian Wars: A Collection of Unpublished Letters and Artifacts*, edited by Tony DeRegnancourt and Tom Parker (Arcanum, Ohio: Occasional Monographs of the Upper Miami Valley Archaeological Research Museum, No. 4, 1995), 6–10.

41. Wayne to Asa Emmanuel, December 15, 1788, *Wayne Papers*, Georgia Historical Society (GHS); Wayne to Benjamin Rush, November 24, 1776, *Wayne Papers*, Bancroft Collection, New York Public Library (NYPL); Charles Stillé, *Major-General Anthony Wayne and the Pennsylvania Line in the Continental Army* (Philadelphia: Historical Society of Pennsylvania, 1893), 112–128; Anthony Wayne to Polly Wayne, March 4, 1782, *Wayne Papers* (NYPL).

42. Wayne to Polly Wayne, March 4, 1782, *Wayne Papers* (NYPL).

43. Wayne to Polly Wayne, April 24, 1792, *Wayne Papers*, Historical Society of Pennsylvania (HSP), volume 20.

CHAPTER TWO. "MAY GOD SHUT THE DOOR OF MERCY ON US"

1. Solomon Marache to Wayne, May 30, 1792, *Anthony Wayne Family Papers* (hereafter *Wayne Papers*) (WLCL).

2. Mary Marache to Wayne, May 30, 1792, *Wayne Papers* (WLCL); Wayne to Polly Wayne, April 24, 1792, *Wayne Papers* (HSP), volume 20; Helen Cooper, "The Restoration of Waynesborough," *Tredyffrin Easttown Historical Society History Quarterly* 16, no. 4 (Winter 1978): 67–75.

3. Wayne to Madison, 15 July 1789, *General Anthony Wayne and the Ohio Indian Wars*, 10.

4. Paris Peace Treaty, September 30, 1783 (http://avalon.law.yale.edu/18th_century/paris .asp).

5. Henry Knox to George Washington, June 15, 1789, *American State Papers, Indian Affairs*, I, 12–14.

6. Treaty with the Six Nations, October 22, 1784; Treaty with the Wyandot, Etc., January 21, 1785; Treaty with the Shawnee, January 31, 1786; Treaty with the Wyandot, Etc., January 9, 1789; Treaty with the Six Nations, January 9, 1789, *Indian Affairs: Laws and Treaties*, II, compiled and edited by Charles J. Kappler (Washington, D.C.: Government Printing Office, 1904), 5–8, 16–25.

7. Copies of the treaties can be found in the *Wayne Papers* (HSP), volume 15; Washington to Beverly Tucker, May 16, 1789, *St. Clair Papers*, volume 2, 114–115.

8. Wayne to George Handley, May 28, 1787, *Wayne Papers* (WLCL); Wayne to Nathanael Greene, June 24, 1789, *Wayne Papers* (HSP), volume 17.

9. Harry Emerson Wildes, *Anthony Wayne: Troubleshooter of the American Revolution* (New York: Harcourt, Brace, 1941), 350; William E. Peters, *Ohio Lands and Their Subdivisions* (Athens, Ohio: W. E. Peters, 1918), 237–258; George Knepper, *The Official Ohio Lands Book* (Columbus: Auditor of the State, 2002), 26–38; Patrick Griffin, "Reconsidering the Ideological Origins of Indian Removal: The Case of the Big Bottom Massacre," *The Center of a Great Empire: The Ohio Country in the Early American Empire*, edited by Andrew R. L. Cayton and Stuart D. Hobbs (Athens: Ohio University Press, 2005), 23–29; Knox to Josiah Harmar, January 31, 1791, *Josiah Harmar Papers* (WLCL).

10. William C. Reichel, "Introduction and Notes," in John Gottlieb Ernestus Heckewelder, *History, Manners, and Customs of the Indian Nations: Who Once Inhabited Pennsylvania and the Neighboring States*, volume 12 (Philadelphia: Publication Fund of the Historical Society of Pennsylvania, 1881), vii–xi.

11. Rob Harper, "Looking the Other Way: The Gnadenhutten Massacre and the Contextual Interpretation of Violence," *William and Mary Quarterly*, 3rd series, 64, no. 3 (July 2007), 621–644; Reichel, "Introduction and Notes," xii.

12. Heckewelder, *History, Manners, and Customs of the Indian Nations*, 187–192.

13. Ibid., 100–106, 163–180, 215–219, 277–289.

14. Consul Willshire Butterfield, *An Historical Account of the Expedition against Sandusky under Col. William Crawford in 1782* (Cincinnati: Robert Clarke & Co., 1873), 379–392.

15. Heckewelder, *History, Manners, and Customs of the Indian Nations*, 132–136, 150–153, 185–186.

16. Wayne to Knox, April 13, 1792, *Wayne Papers* (HSP), volume 20; Baron de Steuben, *Regulations for the Order and Discipline of the Troops of the United States* (Exeter, N.H.: Printed by Henry Ranlet for Thomas & Andrews, 1794).

17. Wayne to Bab McLaine, June 29, 1792, *Wayne Papers* (HSP), volume 20; Petition of James Jackson to the Speakers and Members of the House of Representatives, 1791, *Wayne Papers* (WLCL); Mathew McAlister to Anthony Wayne, January 15, 1792, ibid.; Anthony Wayne to William Lewis, February 29, 1792, ibid.

18. Frazer Ellis Wilson, *Arthur St. Clair: Rugged Ruler of the Old Northwest; An Epic of the American Frontier* (Richmond: Garrett and Massie, 1944), 97–99.

19. James Monroe to Thomas Jefferson, June 17, 1792, *The Writings of James Monroe*, volume 1, edited by Stanislaus Murray Hamilton (New York: G. P. Putnam's Sons, 1903), 232; James Madison to Henry Lee, April 15, 1792, *James Madison Papers*, Library of Congress (LOC).

20. Lee to Washington, 15 June 1792, *PGW: Pres. Ser.*, 10: 455; Washington to Lee, 30 June 1792, ibid., 506.

21. Wayne to Knox, June 4, 1792, *Wayne Papers* (WLCL).

22. Judith Ridner, *A Town In-Between: Carlisle, Pennsylvania, and the Early Mid-Atlantic Interior* (Philadelphia: University of Pennsylvania Press, 2010), 3; Wayne to Knox, June 4, 1792, *Wayne Papers* (WLCL).

23. Simon Gratz, "A Biography of Richard Butler," *Pennsylvania Magazine of History and Biography*, 7, no. 1 (1883): 7–10; Butler to Wayne, April 28, 1781, *Wayne Papers* (HSP), volume 12.

24. Richard Butler, "Colonel Butler's Journal," *An Authentic and Comprehensive History of Buffalo*, volume 1, edited by William Ketchum (Buffalo: Rockwell, Baker, & Hill, 1864), 25–26.

25. Harvey Lewis Carter, *The Life and Times of Little Turtle: First Sagamore of the Wabash* (Urbana: University of Illinois Press, 1987), 106–107, 110.

26. Wayne to Delany, June 8, 1792, *Wayne Papers* (WLCL).

27. Moore, *Anthony Wayne*, 5–8.

28. Douglas Southall Freeman, *George Washington: A Biography, Volume 1, Young Washington* (New York: Charles Scribner's Sons, 1948), 351–412; Second Virginia Charter, May 23, 1609 (http://avalon.law.yale.edu/17th_century/va02.asp).

29. I. Wayne, "Biographical Memoir," *The Casket* (May 1829), 193.

30. Ibid., 193–194.

31. Ibid., 194; for an example of his love of literature, see Wayne's handwritten copies of "1776 Verses on a Particular Occasion" (Sheridan's lyrics to "Had I a Heart to False-hood Fram'd" and "Friendship is the Bond of Reason"), *Wayne Papers* (HSP), volume 2.

32. Wayne to Sally Robinson, August 10, 1776, *Wayne Papers* (HSP), volume 2.

33. Wildes, *Anthony Wayne*, 13; Wayne's Surveys of Thomas Jones' Land (December 15, 1764), Isaac Wayne's Land (January 12, 1767), and Samuel Kennedy's Lands (January 9, 1768), *Wayne Papers* (WLCL).

34. Moore, *Wayne*, 12–13.

35. Wildes, *Anthony Wayne*, 20.

36. Wayne to Amesbury & Bard, December 19, 1766, *Wayne Papers* (WLCL); Crown Land Office Patents on the St. John's and Petitcodiac Rivers, *Wayne Papers* (HSP), volume 1; Les Bowser, "Anthony Wayne's Petitcodiac Adventure," *Generations: The Journal of the New Brunswick Genealogical Society* (Winter 2006): 51–55.

37. Gregory Evans Dowd, *The War Under Heaven: Pontiac, the Indian Nations, and the British Empire* (Baltimore: Johns Hopkins University Press, 2004), 1–21; Royal Proclamation, October 7, 1763 (http://avalon.law.yale.edu/18th_century/proc1763.asp).

38. Wayne to John Hunt, September 7, 1778, *Wayne Papers* (WLCL); Wayne to Washington, December 14, 1783, *Washington Papers* (LOC).

39. Wayne to Sharp Delany, June 22, 1792, *Wayne Papers* (WLCL).

40. George Hammond to John Graves Simcoe, April 21, 1792, *George Hammond Papers* (WLCL); Wayne to Thomas Robinson, April 11, 1776, *Wayne Papers* (NYPL).

CHAPTER THREE. "DESTINED TO EXIST . . . IN
A HOWLING WILDERNESS"

1. Wayne to Knox, June 15, 1792, *Wayne Papers* (WLCL); Wayne to Delany, June 22, 1792, ibid.
2. Wildes, *Anthony Wayne*, 366–369.
3. Francis Roy Harbison, *Flood Tides along the Allegheny* (Pittsburgh: Francis R. Harbison, 1941), 31–45.
4. Leland D. Baldwin, *Whiskey Rebels: The Story of a Frontier Uprising* (Pittsburgh: University of Pittsburgh Press, 1939), 56–75; Mary Stockwell, "First Report on Public Credit," "Second Report on Public Credit," "Tariff of 1790," and "Tariff of 1792," *Encyclopedia of Tariffs and Trade in U.S. History,* volume I, edited by Cynthia Clark Northrup and Elaine C. Prange Turney (Westport: Greenwood Press, 2003), 141–142, 334–335, 357–358.
5. Wayne to Knox, July 6, 1792, *Wayne Papers* (WLCL); Knox to Wayne with Instructions from the Treasury Department's Comptroller, August 3, 1792, ibid.
6. Wayne to Knox, June 15, 1792, ibid.
7. Wildes, *Anthony Wayne*, 40–42; Anthony Wayne, Speech, August 13, 1774, Draft of a Proclamation (1774), and Draft of a Speech (1774), *Wayne Papers* (HSP), volume 1.
8. Polly Wayne to Wayne, January 29, 1776, *Wayne Papers* (WLCL); Wayne, Speech, August 13, 1774, Draft of a Proclamation (1774), and Draft of a Speech (1774), *Wayne Papers* (HSP), volume 1.
9. Wayne, Draft of a Proclamation (1774), *Wayne Papers* (HSP), volume 1.
10. Wayne, Speech, August 13, 1774, and Draft of a Speech (1774), ibid.
11. I. Wayne, "Biographical Memoir," *The Casket* (May 1829), 195; Moore, *Anthony Wayne*, 15–17.
12. Delany to Wayne, September 5, 1776, *Wayne Papers* (NYPL); Wayne to Thomas Hartley, January 1, 1793, *Wayne Papers* (HSP), volume 24.
13. I. Wayne, "Biographical Memoir," *The Casket* (December 1829), 498; Moore, *Anthony Wayne*, 132–133.
14. Delany to Wayne, September 21, 1792, *Wayne Papers* (WLCL); Wayne to Delany, October 26, 1792, ibid.
15. J. A. Murray, "The Butlers of Cumberland Valley," *Historical Register: Notes and Queries, Biographical and Genealogical* I (January 1883): 9–13.
16. Harrison to James Brooks, July 30, 1839, *Harrison Papers* (New-York Historical Society); Freeman Cleaves, *Old Tippecanoe: William Henry Harrison and His Time* (New York: Charles Scribner's Sons, 1939), 3–9.
17. Cleaves, *Old Tippecanoe*, 10–14; Wayne to Knox, June 29, 1792, *Wayne Papers* (WLCL); Wayne to Wilkinson, July 7, 1789, ibid.
18. Marshal Herman Maurice de Saxe, *Reveries, or, Memoirs Concerning the Art of War* (Edinburgh: Printed by Sands, Donaldson, Murray, and Cochran for Alexander Donaldson at Pope's Head, 1759).
19. Wayne to Knox, July 6, 1792, *Wayne Papers* (WLCL); Wayne to Knox, September

13, 1792, *Anthony Wayne: A Name in Arms; Soldier, Diplomat, Defender of Expansion Westward of a Nation; The Wayne–Knox–Pickering–McHenry Correspondence*, edited by Richard C. Knopf (Pittsburgh: University of Pittsburgh Press, 1960), 92–94.

20. Wayne to Knox, July 20, 27, August 3, 10, 17, 24, September 7, 13, and 14, 1792, *Anthony Wayne: A Name in Arms*, 47–50, 55–59, 63–69, 71–81, 87–89, 91–94, 97–99.

21. Wayne, General Orders, August 8, 1792, *General Wayne's Orderly Book, 1792–1797*, edited by C. M. Burton, Historical Collections, *Michigan Pioneer and Historical Society* 24 (1905), 357.

22. Wayne to Wilkinson, July 7, 1792, *Wayne Papers* (WLCL); Wayne to Henry Knox, July 13, 1792, ibid.

23. Wayne to Knox, July 27, 1792, *Wayne Papers* (WLCL).

24. Wayne to Knox, August 10, 1792, ibid.

25. I. Wayne, "Biographical Memoir," *The Casket* (May 1829), 195; Moore, *Anthony Wayne*, 18.

26. Stillé, *Anthony Wayne*, 25–28.

27. Hal Shelton, *General Richard Montgomery and the American Revolution* (New York: New York University Press, 1994), 141–148, 164.

28. Wayne to Francis Johnston, May 14, 1776, *Wayne Papers* (HSP), volume 1; Wayne to Thomas Robinson, May 26, 1776, ibid.

29. Wayne to Polly Wayne, April 28, 1996, *Wayne Papers*, Detroit Public Library (DPL); Wayne to Knox, August 10, 1792, *Wayne Papers* (WLCL).

30. Wayne to Franklin, June 13, 1776, *Wayne Papers* (HSP), volume 1.

31. Ibid.

32. I. Wayne, "Biographical Memoir," *The Casket* (May 1829), 195; Moore, *Anthony Wayne*, 20; Paul David Nelson, *General Horatio Gates: A Biography* (Baton Rouge: Louisiana State University, 1976), 56–61.

33. Wayne to Knox, July 20, 1792, *Wayne Papers* (HSP), volume 20.

34. Knox to Wayne, July 27, 1792, ibid.; Wayne to Knox, August 10, 1792, *Wayne Papers* (WLCL).

35. Wayne, General Orders, August 4 and 12, and September 1, 1792, *General Wayne's Orderly Book*, 356, 360, 370–371.

36. Wayne to Polly Wayne, August 12, 1776, *Wayne Papers* (HSP), volume 1; Wayne to Abraham Robinson, December 15, 1776, ibid.; Polly Wayne to Wayne, April 29, 1776, *Wayne Papers* (WLCL).

37. Wayne to Franklin, July 29, 1776, *Wayne Papers* (HSP), volume 1.

38. Wayne to Franklin and Mr. Morton, October 2, 1776, ibid.; Wayne to Sharp, December 15, 1776, ibid., volume 2.

39. Wayne to Joseph Penrose, August 23, 1776, ibid.; Wayne to Delany, December 15, 1776, ibid., volume 2.

40. Wayne to George Clymer, December 15, 1776, *Wayne Papers* (NYPL).

41. Wayne to Rush, November 11, 1776, ibid.; Wayne to Peters, December 1, 1776, ibid.; Moore to Wayne, December 21, 1776, ibid.; Wayne to George Measom, January 1, 1777, ibid.; Wayne to Philip Schuyler, January 2, 1777, ibid.

42. Washington to Wayne, April 12, 1777, *Wayne Papers* (HSP), volume 3.
43. Wayne to Schuyler, January 22 and February 12, 1777, ibid., volume 2.
44. Wayne to Knox, August 17, 1792, *Wayne Papers* (WLCL).
45. Wayne to Knox, September 7, 1792, ibid.
46. Wayne to Knox, October 26, 1792, *Anthony Wayne: A Name in Arms*, 121–122.

CHAPTER FOUR. "I HAVE THE CONFIDENCE OF THE GENERAL"

1. "Journal of the Virginia Commissioners," *Virginia Magazine of History and Biography* 13 (1906): 154–173; "Treaty of Logg's Town, 1752," ibid., 173–174; "A Treaty Held at the Town of Lancaster, in Pennsylvania, etc.," *Indian Treaties Printed by Benjamin Franklin, 1736–1762*, edited by C. Van Doren and J. P. Boyd (Philadelphia: Historical Society of Pennsylvania, 1938), 41–79.
2. Nicholas Wainwright, *George Croghan: Wilderness Diplomat* (Chapel Hill: Published for the Institute of Early American History and Culture at Williamsburg by the University of North Carolina Press, 1959), 75; Wayne to Knox, November 2, 1792, *Wayne Papers* (WLCL).
3. Wayne to Knox, November 14, 1792; Wayne to Elliott and Williams, October 8, 1792, ibid.
4. Knox to Wayne, September 4, 1792, ibid.; Wayne, General Orders, September 11 and 28, 1792, *General Wayne's Orderly Book*, 382, 387–388.
5. Knox to Wayne, September 21, 1792, *Wayne Papers* (WLCL).
6. Wayne to Washington, September 2, 1777, *Wayne Papers* (HSP), volume 4, as an example.
7. Knox to Wayne, September 7, 1792, *Anthony Wayne: A Name in Arms*, 83.
8. Simcoe to Alured Clarke, July 3, 1792, including Henry Knox to Joseph Brant, July 27, 1792, *George Hammond Papers* (WLCL); Simcoe to Hammond, September 8, 1793, ibid.; Wayne to Knox, October 3, 1792, *Wayne Papers* (WLCL).
9. Knox to Alexander Trueman, April 3, 1792 and Speech of Henry Knox, Secretary of War, April 4, 1792, Colonial Office Records, *Michigan Pioneer and Historical Collections*, volume 24, 390–391.
10. Circular to the Lieutenants of the County Militias, June 23, 1792, *Wayne Papers* (HSP), volume 20.
11. Wayne to Knox, November 14, 1792, *Wayne Papers* (WLCL); Observations of President Washington on General Wayne's Letter of the 14th Instant, November 23, 1792, *Writings of Washington*, volume 32, 234–235.
12. Wayne to Knox, November 16, 1792, *Wayne Papers* (WLCL); Observations of President Washington on General Wayne's Letter of the 14th Instant, and On Wayne's of the 16th of November, November 23, 1792, *Writings of Washington*, volume 32, 235.
13. Alexander Graydon, *Memoirs of a Life, Chiefly Passed in Pennsylvania, etc.* (Harrisburg: John Wyeth, 1811), 277; Wayne to Colonel Varrick, April 22, 1777, *Wayne Papers* (NYPL).
14. Wayne to Polly Wayne, June 7, 1777, *Wayne Papers* (NYPL).

15. I. Wayne, "Biographical Memoir," *The Casket* (May 1829), 196; Moore, *Anthony Wayne*, 26–29; Stillé, *Anthony Wayne*, 62–64.

16. Wayne to Delany, June 7, 1777, *Wayne Papers* (HSP), volume 3.

17. Julius Caesar, *Caesar's Gallic War*, translated by W. A. McDevitte and W. S. Bohn, 1st edition (New York: Harper & Brothers, 1869), book 5, chapters 45 and 46; Wayne to the Board of War, June 3, 1777, *Wayne Papers* (HSP), volume 3; Wayne to Delany, June 7, 1777, ibid.

18. Plutarch, "Fabius," *Lives of Noble Grecians and Romans*, volume 1 (New York: Modern Library, 1992), 235–255.

19. St. Clair, *St. Clair Papers*, volume 1, 44, 61–65, 447–457n.

20. Council of War, August 24, 1777, *Writings of Washington*, volume 9, 109–110.

21. Wildes, *Anthony Wayne*, 115–116; Graydon, *Memoirs*, 291; Washington to Wayne, August 19, 1777, *Washington Papers* (LOC).

22. Wayne to Washington, October 4, 1777, *PGW: Rev. Ser.*, 11:389.

23. Washington to Continental Congress, September 11, 1777, *Washington Papers* (LOC).

24. Stillé, *Anthony Wayne*, 78–79; Anthony Wayne to Thomas Mifflin, September 15, 1777, *Wayne Papers* (HSP), volume 4.

25. Wayne to Thomas Mifflin, September 15, 1777, *Wayne Papers* (HSP), volume 4; George Washington to John Sullivan, October 24, 1777, *Writings of Washington*, volume 9, 425–426.

26. Sullivan to the Continental Congress, October 6, 1777, *Letters and Papers of Major General John Sullivan, Continental Army*, volume 1, edited by Otis G. Hammond (Concord: New Hampshire Historical Society, 1930), 475–476; Major John André, *André's Journal: An Authentic Record of the Movements and Engagements of the British Army in America from June 1777 to November 1778 as Recorded from Day to Day by Major John André*, edited by Henry Cabot Lodge (Boston: Issued by the Bibliophile Society for Members Only, 1903), 84–88.

27. I. Wayne, "Biographical Memoir," *The Casket* (May 1829), 197; Moore, *Anthony Wayne*, 28–29; Stillé, *Anthony Wayne*, 77–80.

28. Thomas J. McGuire, *The Battle of Paoli* (Mechanicsburg, Pa.: Stackpole Books, 2000), 28–37.

29. Wayne to Washington, September 19, 1777, *Washington Papers* (LOC).

30. Washington to Wayne, September 19, 1777, quoted in I. Wayne, "Biographical Memoir," *The Casket* (May 1829), 197.

31. I. Wayne, "Biographical Memoir," *The Casket* (May 1829), 197–198; Moore, *Anthony Wayne*, 31–34; Stillé, *Anthony Wayne*, 81–83.

32. Wayne to Washington, September 21, 1777, *Wayne Papers* (HSP), volume 4.

33. Wayne's Court-Martial Defense, October 25, 1777, ibid.

34. Wayne to Washington, September 27, 1777, ibid.

35. Tench Tilghman (on behalf of George Washington) to Wayne, September 27, 1777, ibid.; Wayne to Washington, October 22, 1777, ibid.; I. Wayne, "Biographical Memoir," *The Casket* (May 1829), 198–200; Moore, *Anthony Wayne*, 34–39; Stillé, *Anthony Wayne*, 84–92.

36. Wayne to Polly Wayne, October 6, 1777, *Wayne Papers* (NYPL); General Hunter, *History of the Fifty-Second British Regiment*, quoted in Stillé, *Anthony Wayne*, 97–98.

37. Wayne to Peters, November 30, 1777, *Wayne Papers* (HSP), volume 4.

38. Ibid.

39. Wayne to Polly Wayne, October 6, 1777, *Wayne Papers* (HSP), volume 4; Wayne to Washington, October 4, 1777, *Wayne Papers* (NYPL).

40. Wayne to Peters, November 18 and December 30, 1777, *Wayne Papers* (HSP), volume 4.

41. Ibid.

42. Ibid.

43. Wayne to Washington, October 27 and November 25, 1777, *Wayne Papers* (HSP), volume 4.

44. Wayne to Washington, December 4, 1777, ibid.

45. At a Court of Inquiry, October 13, 1777, ibid.; Wayne's Court-Martial Defense, October 25, 26, 27, and 30, 1777, ibid.

46. Wayne to Thomas Wharton, February 10, 1778, ibid.; Wayne to Casimir Pulaski, February 21, 1778, ibid.; Wayne to Washington, February 25 and March 14, 1778, ibid; Moore, *Anthony Wayne*, 115–116.

47. Wayne to Knox, December 12, 1792, *Wayne Papers* (HSP), volume 23.

48. Knox to Wayne (Private), December 22, 1792, ibid.

49. Knox to Wayne, December 22, 1792, ibid.; Wayne to Knox, January 15, 1793, ibid., volume 24; Wayne to Elliott and Williams, December 28, 1792, *Wayne Papers* (WLCL).

50. Wayne to Delany, December 25, 1792, *Wayne Papers* (WLCL).

CHAPTER FIVE. "I HAVE NOT BEEN PLEASED WITH MADAME FORTUNE"

1. Wayne to William Hazard, January 29, 1790, *Wayne Papers* (WLCL); Wayne to Delany, April 12, 1793, ibid.; Wayne to Bab McClaine, June 29, 1792, *Wayne Papers* (HSP), volume 20.

2. Joseph Strong's Sketch of Legionville (Beinecke Rare Book and Manuscript Library, Yale University), as cited in Alan Gaff, *Bayonets in the Wilderness: Anthony Wayne's Legion in the Old Northwest* (Norman: University of Oklahoma Press, 2008), 77.

3. Wayne to Elliott and Williams, October 8, 1792, *Wayne Papers* (WLCL).

4. Wayne, General Orders, September 11, 1792, *General Wayne's Orderly Book*, 382; *Pittsburgh Gazette*, March 9, 1793.

5. Wayne to Knox, February 8, 1793, *Wayne Papers* (WLCL); *Pittsburgh Gazette*, March 9, 1793.

6. Charles Prentiss, *The Life of the Late Gen. William Eaton; . . . Principally Collected from His Correspondence and Other Manuscripts* (Brookfield, Mass.: E. Merriam & Co., 1813), 15–17.

7. Cleaves, *Old Tippecanoe*, 10; Harrison to A. B. Howell, April 7, 1838, *Cincinnati Daily Gazette*, May 19, 1838; *Maryland Journal and Baltimore Advertiser*, April 18, 1793; Piercy Pope and Henry Towles to Wayne, March 29, 1793, *Wayne Papers* (HSP),

volume 26; Wayne to Piercy Pope and Henry Towles, March 30, 1793, ibid.; John Gassaway to Wayne, April 12, 1793, ibid.; Wayne to Gassaway, April 19, 1793, ibid.; Knox to Wayne, April 20, 1793, ibid.; Wayne to Knox, April 29, 1793, ibid.

8. Delany to Wayne, November 2, 1792, *Wayne Papers* (WLCL); Henry M. Brackenridge, "Biographical Notice of H. H. Brackenridge," *Southern Literary Messenger* 8 (January 1842): 1–19; Hugh Henry Brackenridge, *Modern Chivalry: Containing the Adventures of a Captain and Teague O'Regan, His Servant*, 2 volumes (Pittsburgh: R. Patterson & Lambdin, 1819), book I, chapter 5.

9. Delany to Wayne, January 4, 1793, *Wayne Papers* (WLCL); Wayne to Delany, March 30, 1793, ibid.

10. Wayne to Washington, September 2, 1777, *Wayne Papers* (HSP), volume 4.

11. Mike Dixon-Kennedy, *Encyclopedia of Greco-Roman Mythology* (Santa Barbara: ABC Clio, 1998), 133–134, 312; Wayne to William Thompson, September 1, 1776, *Wayne Papers* (NYPL).

12. Washington, Council of War, June 17, 1778, *Writings of Washington*, volume 12: 75–78; Wayne to Washington, June 18, 1778, *Wayne Papers* (HSP), volume 5.

13. Wildes, *Anthony Wayne*, 160–162.

14. Washington, Council of War, June 24, 1778, *Writings of Washington*, volume 12: 115–117; Wayne to Wayne, June 24, 1778, *Wayne Papers* (HSP), volume 5.

15. Alexander Hamilton to Washington, June 26, 1778, *Writings of Washington*, volume 12: 120n; Washington to Charles Lee, June 26, 1778, ibid., 120; Washington to Lee, June 27, 1778 (two letters written at 9 A.M. and 8:30 P.M.), ibid., 121–123.

16. Stillé, *Anthony Wayne*, 140–143.

17. Wayne to Polly Wayne, July 1, 1778, *Wayne Papers* (HSP), volume 5; Wayne to Richard Peters, July 12, 1778, ibid.; Wayne and Charles Scott to Washington, June 30, 1778, Jared Sparks, ed., *Correspondence of the American Revolution being letters of eminent men to George Washington from the time of his taking command of the army to the end of his presidency*, volume 2 (Boston: Little, Brown & Company, 1853), 150–152.

18. Mark Edward Lender and Garry Wheeler Stone, *Fatal Sunday: George Washington, the Monmouth Campaign, and the Politics of Battle* (Norman: University of Oklahoma, 2016), 184–189; Wayne to Polly Wayne, July 1, 1778, *Wayne Papers* (HSP), volume 5; Wayne to Richard Peters, July 12, 1778, ibid.; Wayne and Charles Scott to Washington, June 30, 1778, *Correspondence of the American Revolution*, 150–152.

19. George Washington Parke Custis, *Memoirs and Recollections of Washington* (New York: Derby & Jackson, 1860), 218; Ward, *Charles Scott and the Spirit of '76*, 50–51.

20. Lender and Stone, *Fatal Sunday*, 298–330; G. F. Scheer, ed., *Private Yankee Doodle Being a Narrative of the Adventures, Dangers, and Sufferings of a Revolutionary Soldier by Joseph Plumb Martin* (Boston: Eastern Acorn Press, 1962), 132–133.

21. Lender and Stone, *Fatal Sunday*, 331–352; Wayne to Polly Wayne, July 1, 1778, *Wayne Papers* (HSP), volume 5; Wayne to Richard Peters, July 12, 1778, ibid.; Wayne and Charles Scott to Washington, June 30, 1778, *Correspondence of the American Revolution*, 150–152.

22. Washington to President of Congress, July 1, 1778, *Writings of Washington*, volume 12, 139–145; Wayne to Polly Wayne, July 1, 1778, *Wayne Papers* (HSP), volume 5; Wayne to Richard Peters, July 12, 1778, ibid.

23. Wayne to William Irvine, July 14, 1778, ibid.; Wayne to Charles Lee, January 7, 1779, *Wayne Papers* (HSP), volume 6; Charles Lee to Wayne, January 9, 1779, ibid.

24. Washington to President of Congress, July 1, 1778, *Writings of Washington*, volume 12: 145.

25. Wildes, *Anthony Wayne*, 175; Wayne to Morris, January 24, 1779, *Wayne Papers* (HSP), volume 6.

26. Wayne to Irvine, November 12 and December 28, 1778, *Wayne Papers* (HSP), volume 6; Wayne to Pennsylvania Assembly, March 13, 1779, ibid.; Wayne to Committee of Field Officers, March 14, 1779, ibid.; "Brigadier Anthony Wayne," RG-17, *Records of the Land Office: Donation Claimant Papers and Miscellaneous Patents* (ca. 1785–1810) (series #17.168), Pennsylvania State Archives.

27. Henry P. John, "Christian Febiger: Colonel of the Virginia Line of the Continental Line," *Magazine of American History* 6 (1881): 188–203; Stillé, *Anthony Wayne*, 164–165.

28. John Archer (Signing by Order for General Wayne) to Butler, July 5, 1779, *Wayne Papers* (HSP), volume 7; Stillé, *Anthony Wayne*, 182–185.

29. Wayne to Washington, July 3, 1779, *Wayne Papers* (HSP), volume 7.

30. Washington to Wayne, July 9 and 10, 1779, *Writings of Washington*, volume 15, 386, 396–399; Washington to Wayne, July 15, 1779, *Wayne Papers* (HSP), volume 7.

31. Wayne to Washington, July 15, 1779, ibid.

32. Wayne, Order of Battle, July 15, 1779, ibid.

33. Wayne to Delany, July 15, 1779, ibid.

34. Ibid.

35. Moore, *Anthony Wayne*, 96–101.

36. Stillé, *Anthony Wayne*, 195; Wayne to Washington, July 16, 1779, *Wayne Papers* (HSP), volume 7.

37. Hamilton to Wayne, July 26, 1789, *Wayne Papers* (HSP), volume 7; James Mease, "Description of Some Medals, Etc.," *Collections of the Massachusetts Historical Society*, 3rd series, volume 4 (1834): 301–303; for the letters from Lafayette, Lee, St. Clair, and Rush, see Moore, *Anthony Wayne*, 102–105; Delany to Wayne, July 27, 1779, *Wayne Papers* (HSP), volume 7; Reed to Wayne, July 20, 1779, ibid.; *Pennsylvania Packet*, January 27, 1780.

38. Wayne to Return Jonathan Meigs, August 23, 1779, *Wayne Papers* (HSP), volume 7; Wayne to Thomas Posey, August 28, 1779, ibid.

39. Officers of the Light Infantry Corps to General Wayne, January 1, 1780, ibid., volume 11; Wayne to Officers of the Light Infantry Corps, January 2, 1780, ibid.

40. Wayne to Reed, July 26, 1780, ibid., volume 10; Stillé, *Anthony Wayne*, 241.

41. Wayne to Washington, July 19, 1780, *Wayne Papers* (HSP), volume 10; Wayne to Washington, July 22, 1780, *Washington Papers* (LOC).

42. André, *Cow-chace*, cantos I, II, and III.

43. Washington to President of Congress, September 26, 1780, *Writings of Washington*, volume 20, 91–93; George Washington to George Clinton, September 26, 1780, ibid., 93–94; Washington, General Orders, September 26, 1780, ibid., 94–96.

44. Wayne to Washington, September 27, 1780, *Wayne Papers* (HSP), volume 10; Wayne to Hugh Sheel, October 2, 1780, ibid.
45. "Diary of the Revolt," *Pennsylvania Archives*, 2nd series, volume 11, 631–674.
46. Moore, *Anthony Wayne*, 127n.
47. Wayne to Washington, January 2, 1781, *Wayne Papers* (HSP), volume 11.
48. Agreement, January 8, 1781, *Wayne Papers* (HSP), volume 11; Wayne to Washington, January 12, 1781, ibid., volume 12; Washington to Wayne, February 26, 1781, ibid.
49. *Journals of the Continental Congress*, 1774–1789, volume 19 (Washington, D.C.: Government Printing Office, 1912), 79; Wayne to Reed, May 16, *Wayne Papers* (HSP), volume 12; Wayne to Board of War, May 20, 1781, ibid.
50. Wildes, *Anthony Wayne*, 242–243; Moore, *Anthony Wayne*, 130–132; Wayne to Polly Wayne, May 25, 1781, *Wayne Papers* (HSP), volume 12.
51. Wayne to Benjamin Fishbourne, May 25, 1781, ibid.; Wayne to Lafayette, September 11, 1781, ibid., volume 14.

CHAPTER SIX. "AN EVENT OF THE UTMOST CONSEQUENCE"

1. Wayne to Delany, April 27, 1793, *Wayne Papers* (WLCL); Wayne to Knox, April 27, 1793, ibid.
2. "William Henry Harrison to Thomas Chilton, February 1834," John Stevens Cabot Abbott, *The History of the State of Ohio: From the Discovery of the Great Valley, to the Present Time* (Detroit: Northwestern Publishing Co., 1875), 371–373; Simcoe, "To the Americans of Massachusetts Bay, 1775," *Simcoe Papers* (WLCL).
3. Wayne to Knox, April 27, 1793, *Wayne Papers* (WLCL).
4. Ibid.
5. Ibid.
6. Washington to Gouverneur Morris, October 13, 1789, *Writings of Washington*, volume 30, 443.
7. Gen. H. L. V. Ducoudray, *Memoirs of Gilbert M. Lafayette* (Geneva, N.Y.: John Greves, 1839), 100–106.
8. "Declaration of the Rights of Man, 1789" (http://avalon.law.yale.edu/18th_century/rightsof.asp); Ducoudray, *Memoirs of Lafayette*, 107–109.
9. Ducoudray, *Memoirs of Lafayette*, 109–180.
10. Washington to Lafayette, June 10, 1792, *Writings of Washington*, volume 32, 53–55; Washington to Marquis de Lafayette, January 31, 1783, ibid., 322; Treaty of Alliance, February 6, 1778, *United States Statutes at Large*, 6–11.
11. Treaty of Amity and Commerce, February 6, 1778, *United States Statutes at Large*, 12–31.
12. "Alexander Hamilton on the French Revolution, 1794," *Liberty, Equality, Fraternity: Exploring the French Revolution*, edited by Lynn Hunt and Jack Censer (https://chnm.gmu.edu/revolution/d/593/); Alexander Hamilton (Titus Manlius), "The Stand, No. III, April 7, 1778," *The Papers of Alexander Hamilton*, edited by Harold C. Syrett, volume 21 (New York: Columbia University Press, 1974), 402–408; Jefferson to William Short, January 3, 1793, *Thomas Jefferson Papers* (LOC).

13. Wayne to Delany, June 2, 1791, *Wayne Papers* (WLCL); Wayne to Matthew Mc-Allister, August 29, 1791, ibid.; Delany to Wayne, June 22, July 24, October (no date), November 2, 1792, and April 6, 1793, ibid.; William Atlee to Wayne, March 19, 1793, ibid.; Richard Wayne to Wayne, April 10, 1793, ibid.; David Jones to Wayne, September 17, 1793, ibid.; Wilkinson to Wayne, December 11, 1793, ibid.

14. Delany to Wayne, November 2, 1792, ibid.; Mary Stockwell, "Washington at Valley Forge," *Companion to George Washington*, edited by Edward G. Lengel (Chichester, UK: Wiley-Blackwell, 2012), 209–225.

15. Lafayette to Wayne, March 7 and 13, April 7 and 26, May 5 and 31, 1781, *Wayne Papers* (NYPL).

16. Lafayette to Wayne, May 15 and 26, 1781, ibid.

17. Wayne to Washington, March 19, 1781, ibid.

18. Washington to Wayne, February 26, 1781, *Wayne Papers* (HSP), volume 12; Wayne to Washington, February 27, ibid., volume 12; Wayne to Washington, May 26, 1781, ibid., volume 13; Wayne to Polly Wayne, May 25, 1781, ibid., volume 12; Wayne to John Dickson, May 25, 1781, ibid., volume 12.

19. Excerpted letter in Wildes, *Anthony Wayne*, 260 (Fishbourne paraphrases a famous quote from Sheridan's *Cato*, act I, scene I).

20. Wayne to Lafayette, May 31 (two letters), June 1, 4, 6, and 7, 1781, *Wayne Papers* (HSP), volume 13.

21. Marie E. Morrison, *A History of the Old Brick Church, Blandford Cemetery, Petersburg, Va.* (Petersburg, 1901), 5–7.

22. Wildes, *Anthony Wayne*, 251–253.

23. Lafayette to Wayne, June 21, 22, 25, 26, 30, *Wayne Papers* (HSP), volume 13; Wayne to Lafayette, June 22, 25, 30, and July 2, 1781, ibid.

24. Wayne to William Irvine, July 8, 1781, *Magazine of American History with Notes and Queries*, 15 (January–June 1886): 201–202; Wayne to Washington, July 8, 1781, *Wayne Papers* (HSP), volume 13; Wayne to Peters, July 8, 1781, ibid.; William Galvan to Richard Peters, July 8, 1781, ibid.; Lafayette to the President of Congress, July 8, 1781, ibid.; Lafayette's General Orders, July 8, 1781, *Pennsylvania Gazette*, August 1, 1781; Wayne to Polly Wayne, July 11, 1781, *Wayne Papers* (HSP), volume 13.

25. Washington to Wayne, July 30, 1781, *Wayne Papers* (HSP), volume 13; Robert Morris' letter quoted in Stillé, *Anthony Wayne*, 272; Nathanael Greene to Wayne, July 24, 1781, *Wayne Papers* (HSP), volume 13.

26. Dr. Robert Wharry to Dr. Reading Beatty, July 27, 1781, "Letters from Continental Officers to Doctor Reading Beatty, 1781–1789," *Pennsylvania Magazine of History and Biography* 54 (1930), 159–162.

27. Henry Lee, *Memoirs of the War in the Southern Department of the United States* (New York: University Publishing Co., 1870), 420.

28. Wayne to His Officers, July 10, 1781, *Wayne Papers* (HSP), volume 13; Wounded Officers to Wayne, ca. July 1781, ibid.

29. Greene to Wayne, July 24, 1781, ibid.; Lafayette to Knox, August 18, 1781, *Lafayette in the Age of the American Revolution: Selected Letters and Papers, 1776–1790*, edited by Stanley J. Idzerda (Ithaca: Cornell University Press, 1980), volume 3, 332–333.

30. Wayne to Polly Wayne, July 11, 1781, *Wayne Papers* (HSP), volume 13; Wayne to Reed, July 16, 1781, ibid.; Lafayette to Wayne, July 13, 15, 21, 23, 24, 27, and 31, ibid.; Lafayette to Wayne, August 3, 4, and 6, 1781, *Wayne Papers* (HSP), volume 14; Wayne to Lafayette, July 22, 1781, ibid., volume 13.

31. Wayne to Morris, October 26, 1781, *Wayne Papers* (HSP), volume 14: Thomas Nelson to Lafayette, August 9, 1781; Wayne to Lafayette, August 9, 1781; Lafayette to Wayne, August 25, 1781, *Lafayette in the Age of the American Revolution*, volume 4, 307–309, 359–361.

32. Wayne to Polly Wayne, September 12, 1781, *Wayne Papers* (HSP), volume 14.

33. Lafayette to Wayne, August 25, 1781, ibid.

34. Wayne to Lafayette, September 2, 1781, ibid.

35. Wayne to Polly Wayne, September 12, 1781, ibid.

36. Wayne to Morris, September 14, 1781, ibid.

37. Wayne to Polly Wayne, September 12, 1781, ibid.

38. Hamilton to Lafayette, October 15, 1781, *Washington Papers* (LOC); Wayne, Diary, September 6 to October 17, 1777, *Wayne Papers* (HSP), volume 14; Wayne to ———, October 1781, *Wayne Papers* (NYPL).

39. Wildes, *Anthony Wayne*, 267; "The World Turned Upside Down, or the Old Woman Taught Wisdom," *Poems of American History*, edited by Burton Egbert Stevenson (Boston: Houghton Mifflin, 1908), 130.

40. Wildes, *Anthony Wayne*, 264–265; Arnold Whitridge, *Rochambeau* (New York: Macmillan, 1965), 299–303.

41. Proclamation of Neutrality 1793 (http://avalon.law.yale.edu/18th_century/neutra93.asp); Knox, "Instructions to Benjamin Lincoln, etc.," *American State Papers, Indian Affairs*, I, 341–342.

42. Knox to Anthony, April 13, 1793, *Wayne Papers* (HSP), volume 26.

CHAPTER SEVEN. "I HAVE NO ANXIETY
BUT FOR YOU AND OUR CHILDREN"

1. Knox to Wayne, April 20, 1793, *Wayne Papers* (WLCL).

2. Knox to Wayne, March 5, 1793, *Wayne Papers* (HSP), volume 25; Knox to Wayne, April 20, 1793, ibid., volume 26.

3. Wayne to Knox, January 24, 1793, ibid., volume 24; Wayne to Knox, April 5, 1793, ibid., volume 25; Wayne to Knox, April 20, 1793, ibid., volume 26.

4. Wayne to Knox, August 24, 1792, ibid., volume 21.

5. Lord Grenville to Hammond, March 1792, *Simcoe Papers* (WLCL).

6. Hammond, "Answer to Major General Knox on the Causes of the Present Indian War," 1792, *George Hammond Papers* (WLCL); Hammond to Simcoe, March 3 and April 21, 1792, ibid.; Grenville to Hammond, April 25, 1792, ibid.

7. Gaff, *Bayonets in the Wilderness*, 110; Wayne, General Orders, April 28, 1792, *General Wayne's Orderly Book*, 411–412.

8. Delany to Wayne, April 19, 1793, *Wayne Papers* (HSP), volume 34.

9. William Atlee to Wayne, April 19, 1793, ibid.; William Hayman to Wayne, April 20, 1793, *Wayne Papers* (WLCL).

10. William Atlee to Wayne, November 6, 1793, ibid.; Margaretta Atlee to Wayne, January 16, 1793, *Wayne Papers* (DPL); I. Wayne, "Biographical Memoir," *The Casket* (May 1829), 119.

11. Wayne to Knox, April 29, 1793, *Wayne Papers* (HSP), volume 34.

12. I. Wayne, "Biographical Memoir," *The Casket* (May 1829), 194–195; Stillé, *Anthony Wayne*, 10; Josiah Granville Leach, *The Penrose Family of Philadelphia* (Philadelphia: D. Biddle, 1903), 19–21.

13. Wildes, *Anthony Wayne*, 25–29; Accounts and Receipts, 1760–1780 and Account Book of Wayne Family Tannery Business, *Wayne Papers* (WLCL).

14. Sue Andrews, "Howellville," Easttown Historical Society, *History Quarterly* Digital Archives 39, no. 3 (July 2002): 75–103.

15. William Moore, "Chester County Docket, 1719–1722" (HSP).

16. Boston Port Act, March 31, 1774 (http://avalon.law.yale.edu/18th_century/boston _port_act.asp); Massachusetts Government Act, May 20, 1774 (http://avalon.law.yale .edu/18th_century/mass_gov_act.asp); Administration of Justice Act, May 20, 1774 (http://avalon.law.yale.edu/18th_century/admin_of_justice_act.asp); Quartering Act, June 2, 1774 (http://avalon.law.yale.edu/18th_century/quartering_act_1774.asp); Quebec Act, October 7, 1774 (http://avalon.law.yale.edu/18th_century/quebec_act_1774 .asp); Polly Wayne to Wayne, January 29, 1776, *Wayne Papers* (WLCL).

17. Wildes, *Anthony Wayne*, 42–43.

18. Mary Keating to Wayne, March 8, 1795 and April 24, 1796, *Wayne Papers* (WLCL); Wayne to Sally Robinson, August 10, 1776, *Wayne Papers* (HSP), volume 1.

19. John Randolph Spears, *Anthony Wayne: Sometimes Called "Mad Anthony"* (New York: D. Appleton and Co., 1903), 24; Wayne to Delany, April 22, 1776, *Wayne Papers* (HSP), volume 1; Wayne to Thomas Robinson, April 11, 1776, *Wayne Papers* (NYPL).

20. Wayne to Morgan Lems, March 3, 1777, *Wayne Papers* (NYPL); Wayne to Colonel Lewis, March 3, 1777, *Wayne Papers* (HSP), volume 2; Colonel Jeduthun Baldwin, *The Revolutionary Diary of Col. Jeduthun Baldwin, 1775–1778, Edited with a Memoir and Notes by Thomas William Baldwin* (Bangor: De Burians, 1906), 97–98.

21. Wayne to Sally Robinson, August 10, 1776, *Wayne Papers* (HSP), volume 1.

22. Sally Peters to Wayne, September 20, 1776, ibid.; Wayne to Joseph Wood, March 3, 1777, *Wayne Papers* (NYPL).

23. Wayne to Sally Peters and Hetty Griffits, February 16, 1777, quoted in Wildes, *Anthony Wayne*, 91–92.

24. Griffits to Wayne, October 30, 1776, *Wayne Papers* (HSP), volume 1; Griffits to Wayne, July 18, 1777, ibid., volume 3; "To a young Lady on her expressing some doubts of the Sincerity of a lasting Fidelity in Her Admirer," *Wayne Papers* (HSP), volume 1; *London Magazine or Gentlemen's Monthly Intelligencer*, 44, 1775; Richard Sheridan, *La Duenna, or the Elopement: A Comic Opera: As it is Acted at the Theatre, at Smoke-Alley, Dublin* (Dublin: Printed for the Booksellers, 1786); "To a Friend when accused of Endeavouring to Supplant Him in the Affections of a Lady—and deemed by him a breach of Faith and Friendship," Wayne Papers (HSP), volume 1.

25. Wayne to Polly Wayne, May 30, 1789, *Wayne Papers* (NYPL).

26. Wayne to Polly Wayne, October 3, 1777, ibid.

27. Ibid.

28. Wayne to Polly Wayne, October 6, 1777, ibid.

29. Polly Wayne to Wayne, October 6, 1776, *Wayne Papers* (WLCL); Wayne to Polly Wayne, October 6, 1777, *Wayne Papers* (NYPL).

30. Polly Wayne to Wayne, April 26 and May 6, 1776, *Wayne Papers* (WLCL).

31. Elizabeth Ferguson to Wayne, August 25, 1777, *Wayne Papers* (HSP), volume 3; Ruth Hoover Seitz, *Pennsylvania's Historic Places* (Intercourse, Pa.: Good Books, 1989), 22–25; William Draper Brinkloe, "The House in the Farm Journal Heading," *Farm Journal* (October 1917), *Wayne Papers* (WLCL).

32. Wayne to Polly Wayne, September 30, 1777, *Wayne Papers* (HSP), volume 4.

33. Polly Wayne to Wayne, September 7, 1778, *Wayne Papers* (WLCL).

34. Wayne to Polly Wayne, August 26, 1777, *Wayne Papers* (HSP), volume 3; Wayne to Polly Wayne, February 7, 1778, ibid., volume 4.

35. John F. Stegeman and Janet A. Stegeman, *Caty: A Biography of Catharine Littlefield Greene* (Athens: University of Georgia Press, 1977), 1–59.

36. Wayne to Catharine Greene, March 10, 1789, and February 17, 1793, in *Letters by and to Nathanael Greene with Some to His Wife* (New York: George H. Richmond, 1906).

37. Stegeman and Stegeman, *Caty*, 55–56, 99–101, 106–107.

38. Mabel Lloyd Ridgely, *What Them Befell: The Ridgelys of Delaware and Their Circle in Colonial and Federal Times: Letters 1751–1890* (Portland, Me.: Anthoensen Press, 1949), 159–164; To Anthony Wayne, May 20, 1778, *Wayne Papers* (HSP), volume 5.

39. Stewart to Wayne, November 29, 1778, *Wayne Papers* (NYPL); Wayne to Stewart, February 28, 1779, *Wayne Papers* (HSP), volume 6.

40. Wayne to Stewart, June 7, 1779, *Wayne Papers* (HSP), volume 6.

41. Wayne to Richard Butler, June 7, 1779, ibid.; Wayne to Polly Wayne, June 24, 1779, ibid.

42. Wayne to Colonel Robert Magaw, March 12, 1780, *Wayne Papers* (HSP), volume 9; Elizabeth Johnson Wright, "Mary Vining: An Account of Her Life," *Society Miscellaneous Collection* (Georgia Historical Society).

43. Wayne to Francis Johnston, March 25, 1780, *Wayne Papers* (HSP), volume 10.

44. Wayne to Polly Wayne, June 9, 1780, ibid.

45. André, *Cow-chace*, 25; Wildes, *Anthony Wayne*, 206; Delany to Wayne, October 29, 1780, *Wayne Papers* (WLCL).

46. Wayne to Robert Magaw, March 12, 1780, *Wayne Papers* (HSP), volume 9; Wayne to Fishburne, May 25, 1781, ibid., volume 12; Wayne to Bab McClaine, June 29, 1792, ibid., volume 20; Mary Byrd to Wayne, August 28, 1781, ibid., volume 14.

47. Hartley to Wayne, December 21, 1792, *Wayne Papers* (HSP), volume 23; Wayne, General Orders, September 17, 1792 (Countersign: Vining), *General Wayne's Orderly Book*, 383, and General Orders, September 28, 1792 (Parole: Alexander), ibid., 387.

48. Wayne to Delany, May 21, 1778, *Wayne Papers* (HSP), volume 5.

49. Wayne quotes "The Old Soldier" in Wayne to Polly Wayne, July 5, 1790, *Wayne Papers* (NYPL).

50. Wildes, *Anthony Wayne*, 382–384.

51. Wayne to Knox, April 27, 1793, *Wayne Papers* (HSP), volume 26; Wayne, General Orders, May 6, 1793, ibid.; Delany to Wayne, May 11, 1793, *Wayne Papers* (WLCL); William Hayman to Wayne, May 31, 1793, ibid.; Margaretta Atlee to Wayne, January 16, 1793, *Wayne Papers* (DPL); I. Wayne, "Biographical Memoir," *The Casket* (May 1829), 119.

CHAPTER EIGHT. "THEY OUGHT TO UNITE AS A BAND OF BROTHERS"

1. Wayne to Knox, May 9, 1793, *Wayne Papers* (HSP), volume 26.

2. Knox to Wayne, June 28, 1793, ibid., volume 27.

3. Wayne to Knox, November 9, 1792, ibid., volume 22.

4. George Knepper, *Ohio and Its People* (Kent, Ohio: Kent State University Press, 2003), 17–19.

5. John Vogel, *The Indians of Ohio and Wyandot County* (New York: Vantage Press, 1975), 1–4; Carter, *Little Turtle*, 11–27; Anthony F. C. Wallace, *The Death and Rebirth of the Seneca* (New York: Alfred A. Knopf, 1970), 149–179.

6. Robert F. Bauman, *The Ottawas of Ohio: 1704–1840*, volume 6 (Toledo: University of Toledo, 1984); Henry Harvey, *History of the Shawnee Indians: from the year 1681 to 1854, Inclusive* (Cincinnati: E. Morgan & Co., 1855), 81–85; C. A. Weslager, *The Delaware Indian Westward Migration* (Wallingford, Pa.: Middle Atlantic Press, 1978), 1–25.

7. Wayne to Knox, July 2, 1793, *Wayne Papers* (HSP), volume 27; Carter, *Little Turtle*, 82–103.

8. Carter, *Little Turtle*, 72–74.

9. Ibid., 101–110; Benjamin Drake, *Life of Tecumseh, and His Brother the Prophet* (Cincinnati: E. Morgan & Co., 1841), 71; David Stothers and Patrick Tucker, *The Fry Site: Archaeological and Ethnohistorical Perspectives on the Maumee River Ottawa of Northwest Ohio* (Morrisville, N.C.: LuLu Press, 2006), 31–32; Robert F. Bauman, "Pontiac's Successor: Au-goosh-away," *Northwest Ohio Quarterly*, 26 (1954): 8–38.

10. Carter, *Little Turtle*, 112; Wayne to Knox, September 17, 1793, *Wayne Papers* (HSP), volume 29.

11. Wayne to Knox, August 7, 1792, *Wayne Papers* (HSP), volume 20 (first mention of Girtys); Consul Willshire Butterfield, *History of the Girtys* (Cincinnati: Clarke, 1890), 8–53, 60, 64, 91–92, 105–107, 117, 177–182.

12. Wayne to Knox, July 2, 1793, *Wayne Papers* (HSP), volume 27 (first mention of McKee); Wayne to Knox, September 17, 1793, ibid., volume 29 (first mention of Matthew Elliott).

13. Wayne to Knox, July 2, 1793, ibid., volume 27.

14. Wayne to Knox, June 20, 1793, ibid.; Wayne to Henry Knox, July 2, 1793, ibid.

15. Wayne to Elliott and Williams, October 8, 1792, *Wayne Papers* (WLCL); Anthony Wayne Accounts with Elliott and Williams 1792–1796, ibid.

16. Knox to Wayne, August 16, 1793, *Wayne Papers* (HSP), volume 28.

17. Indian Commissioners to Knox, July 10, 1793, *Wayne Papers* (WLCL); Knox to Wayne, June 7, 1793, *Wayne Papers* (HSP), volume 28.
18. Knox to Wayne, July 20, 1793, *Wayne Papers* (HSP), volume 28.
19. Wayne wrote two versions: August 7, 1793 and August 8, 1793 (the latter was sent to Knox). See Wayne to Knox, August 7, 1793, *Wayne Papers* (HSP), volume 28, and Wayne to Knox, August 8, 1793, *Wayne Papers* (WLCL); for a combined letter, see *Anthony Wayne: A Name in Arms*, 260–265.
20. Wayne to Knox, August 8, 1793, *Wayne Papers* (WLCL).
21. Ibid.
22. Knox to Wayne, August 16, 1793, *Wayne Papers* (HSP), volume 28; Knox to Wayne, May 17, 1793, ibid., volume 26.
23. Knox, "Instructions to Benjamin Lincoln, etc.," *American State Papers: Indian Affairs*, I, 340–342.
24. Knox to Wayne, May 17, 1793, *Wayne Papers* (HSP), volume 26.
25. John Armstrong to Wayne, March 28, 1793, *Wayne Papers* (WLCL).
26. Ibid.
27. James Wilkinson, *Memoirs of My Own Times*, volume I (Philadelphia: Abraham Small, 1816), 49–53.
28. Ibid., 53–54.
29. Wayne to Wilkinson, June 16, 1792, *Wayne Papers* (WLCL).
30. Wilkinson to Wayne, August 24, September 12, October 9, and 23, 1792, ibid.
31. Wayne, General Orders, October 14, 1793, *General Wayne's Orderly Book*, 492; Richard Knopf, *Anthony Wayne and the Founding of the United States Army* (Columbus: Anthony Wayne Parkway Board, 1961), 53–55.
32. Gaff, *Bayonets in the Wilderness*, 117–118, 175–176, 208–209.
33. Wildes, *Anthony Wayne*, 401–407.
34. Wayne to Wilkinson, July 31, 1792, *Wayne Papers* (WLCL).
35. Wayne to Knox, January 24, 1793, ibid.; Wayne to Delany, March 30, 1793, ibid.; Wayne to Isaac Wayne, September 10, 1794, *Wayne Papers* (HSP), volume 37.
36. In Council at Captain Elliot[t]'s, etc., July 31, 1793, *American State Papers, Indian Affairs*, I, 352; Speech of the Commissioners of the United States, Etc., August 1, 1793, ibid., 352–354; To the Commissioners of the United States, August 16, 1793, ibid., 356–357.
37. Knox to Wayne, September 3, 1793, *Wayne Papers* (HSP), volume 28.

CHAPTER NINE: "THEY SHALL NOT BE LOST"

1. Julius Caesar, *First Eight Books of Caesar's Commentaries on the Gallic War*; literally translated with an introduction by Edward Brooks, Jr., volume VII (Philadelphia: David McKay, 1896), 285–305.
2. Wayne to Charles Scott, September 26, 1793, *Wayne Papers* (HSP), volume 28.
3. Wayne to Knox, August 24, 1792, *Wayne Papers* (HSP), volume 30; Merrill Gilfillan, *Moods of the Ohio Moons* (Kent, Ohio: Kent State University Press, 1991), 16–23.
4. Wayne, General Orders, August 29, 1793, *Wayne Papers* (HSP), volume 28.

5. Wayne to Knox, May 9, 1793, ibid., volume 26.

6. Wayne, General Orders, August 25, 1793, ibid., volume 28.

7. Wayne to Knox, October 5, 1793, ibid.

8. Wayne, General Orders, August 25, ibid.; John Scott to Josiah Harmar, October 6, 1793, *Josiah Harmar Papers* (WLCL).

9. Wayne to Knox, October 5, 1793, *Wayne Papers* (HSP), volume 29.

10. St. Clair to Edmund Randolph (no date), *St. Clair Papers*, I, 327.

11. Wayne, General Orders, August 22 and 25 and September 13 and 16, 1793, *General Wayne's Orderly Book*, 465–470, 477–484.

12. Wayne, General Orders, August 25, 1793, ibid., 467–470.

13. Wayne, General Orders, October 9, 1793, ibid., 491–492; "General Wayne's Daily Encampment," *American Pioneer*, 2 (July 1843): 290; Gaff, *Bayonets in the Wilderness*, 159.

14. Richard C. Knopf, ed., "Two Journals of the Kentucky Volunteers, 1793–1794," *Filson Club History Quarterly*, 27 (July 1953): 247–281; Douglas Frazier Wilson, ed., *The Journal of Daniel Bradley: An Epic of the Ohio Frontier* (Greenville, Ohio: F. H. Jobes, 1935), (not paginated).

15. Wayne, General Orders, October 9, 1793, *General Wayne's Orderly Book*, 491–492.

16. John Hutchinson Buell, "A Fragment from the Diary of John Hutchinson Buell, U.S.A., who Joined the American Army at the Start of the Revolutionary War and Remained in Service until 1803," *Journal of the Military Service Institution of the United States*, 40 (1907): 104.

17. Wayne to Knox, November 15, 1793, *Wayne Papers* (HSP), volume 31.

18. Wayne to Elliott and Williams, October 14, 16, and 23, 1793, *Wayne Papers* (HSP), volume 30; Elliott and Williams to Wayne, October 15, 1793, ibid.; James O'Hara to Wayne, October 17, 1793, ibid.

19. Report of a Staff Council, October 31, 1793, *Wayne Papers* (HSP), volume 30; Scott to Wayne, November 1, 1793, ibid.; Thomas Barbee to Wayne, November 1, 1793, ibid.; Robert Todd to Wayne, November 2, 1793, ibid.; Knopf, ed., "Two Journals," 253; John McDonald, *Biographical Sketches of General Nathaniel Massie, Captain William Wells, and General Simon Kenton* (Dayton: D. Osborn & Son, 1852), 261–263.

20. Wayne to Charles Scott, November 2, 1793, *Wayne Papers* (HSP), volume 30; Wayne to St. Clair, November 7, 1793, ibid.

21. Charles Theodore Greve, *Centennial History of Cincinnati and Representative Citizens*, volume I (Chicago: Biographical Publishing Co., 1904), 290–291.

22. James McMahon to Wayne, October 9, 1793, *Wayne Papers* (HSP), volume 30; Jacob Melcher to Wilkinson, October 9 and 10, 1793, ibid.; Melcher to Wayne, December 11, 1793, ibid.; Wayne, General Orders, December 13, 1793, ibid.

23. Scott, "Unaddressed Letter, October 22, 1793," *Cincinnati Miscellany, or Antiquities of the West*, volume II, edited by Charles Cist (Cincinnati: Robinson & Jones, 1846), 55–56.

24. Buell, *Diary*, 104–105.

25. Hamtramck to Wayne, November 22, 1793, *Wayne Papers* (HSP), volume 31; Wayne to Hamtramck, November 23, 1793, ibid.; Wildes, *Anthony Wayne*, 404.

CHAPTER TEN: "THIS HORRID TRADE OF BLOOD"

1. John Armstrong to Wayne, November 1, 1792, *Wayne Papers* (WLCL); Erkurius Beatty to Wilkinson, November 22, 1792, ibid.; Beatty to Wayne, January 7, 1793, ibid.; John Hunt to Wayne, December 5, 1793, ibid.

2. Wayne to Polly Wayne, November 12, 1778, Wayne Papers (HSP), volume 6; Wayne to Greene, November 4, 1781, ibid., volume 14.

3. Wayne to Washington, November 4, 1781 (first note), *Wayne Papers* (HSP), volume 14.

4. Washington to Wayne, November 4, 1781 (first note), *Washington Papers* (LOC).

5. Wayne to Washington, November 4, 1781 (second note), *Wayne Papers* (HSP), volume 14.

6. Douglas Southall Freeman, *George Washington: A Biography, Volume 5, Victory with the Help of France* (New York: Charles Scribner's Sons, 1948), 401–412.

7. Washington to Wayne, November 4, 1781 (second note), *Washington Papers* (LOC).

8. Wayne to Greene, November 30, 1781, *Greene Papers* (WLCL); Wayne to Henry Archer, December 14, 1781, *Wayne Papers* (HSP), volume 14; Wayne to Margaretta Wayne, November 18, 1781, ibid.

9. Wildes, *Anthony Wayne*, 268–272; Wayne to St. Clair, December 20, 1781, *Wayne Papers* (HSP), volume 14; Rush to Wayne, October 30, 1781, ibid.

10. Theodore Thayer, *Nathanael Greene: Strategist of the American Revolution* (New York: Twayne, 1960), 24–27.

11. Greene to Wayne, January 9, 1782, *Wayne Papers* (HSP), volume 14.

12. Greene to John Martin, January 9, 1782, *Greene Papers* (WLCL).

13. Kenneth Coleman, *A History of Georgia* (Athens: University of Georgia Press, 1977), 71–88; Thomas Hobbes, *Elementa philosophica de cive* (Paris, 1642); John Locke, *Two Treatises of Government* (London, 1690).

14. Greene to Wayne, January 9, 1782, *Wayne Papers* (NYPL).

15. Stillé, *Anthony Wayne*, 287.

16. Wayne to Martin, January 14, 1782, *Wayne Papers* (HSP), volume 14.

17. Wayne to John Twiggs, January 14, 1782, ibid.; Wayne to Jackson, January 14 and 17, 1782, ibid., volume 15.

18. Wayne to Martin, January 14, 1782, *Wayne Papers* (HSP), volume 14; Suetonius, *The Lives of the Twelve Caesars*, edited by Joseph Cavorse (New York: Modern Library, 1951), 20–21.

19. Wayne to Lee, January 17, 1782, *Wayne Papers* (HSP), volume 15.

20. Reverend P. A. Strobel, *The Salzburgers and Their Descendants* (Baltimore: T. Newton Kurtz, 1855), 125–147, 201–217; Orders of Alured Clarke, January 13, 1782 (GHS); James Wright to George Germain, January 25, March 5 and 9, April 24, May 1, 21, 25, and 30, 1782, *Letters of James Wright* (GHS).

21. Wayne to Greene, January 17, 1781, *Wayne Papers* (HSP), volume 15.

22. Edward J. Cashin, *The King's Ranger: Thomas Brown and the American Revolution on the Southern Frontier* (New York: Fordham University Press, 1999), 145–161.

23. Anthony Wayne, "Proclamation," attached to the letter of Wayne to Greene, March 11,

1782, *Nathanael Greene Papers* (WLCL). Wayne wrote proclamations which Martin endorsed and distributed; see John Martin, "A Proclamation to Loyalists, February 1782," and "A Proclamation to Hessians, February 1782," in Daniel T. Elliot, "Ebenezer Revolutionary War Headquarters: A Quest to Locate and Preserve," *LAMAR Institute Publication Series*, report 73, 2003, 103.

24. Allen Daniel Candler and Clement Anselm Evans, *Georgia: Comprising Sketches of Counties, Towns, Events, Institutions, and Persons, Arranged in Cyclopedic Form*, volume II (Atlanta: State Historical Association, 1906), 310–311.

25. Martin to Wayne, January 29, 1782, *John Martin Papers* (GHS).

26. Wayne to Greene, January 22, 23, 24, and 26, 1782, *Wayne Papers* (HSP), volume 15; Wayne to Greene, February 11, 22, 28, and March 4, 1782, *Greene Papers* (WLCL).

27. Wayne to Stewart, February 25, 1782, *Wayne Papers* (NYPL).

28. Ibid.

29. Wildes, *Anthony Wayne*, 276; Wayne to Greene, February 11, 1782, *Greene Papers* (WLCL).

30. Kathryn E. Holland Braund, *Deerskins and Duffels: The Creek Indian Trade with Anglo-America, 1685–1815*, 2nd edition (Indians of the Southeast) (Lincoln: University of Nebraska Press, 2008); Coleman, *History of Georgia*, 268–289.

31. Wayne's Speech to Creeks and Choctaws, February 19, 1782, *Emmett Collection* (NYPL); Wayne to Irvine, February 24, 1782, *Wayne Papers* (NYPL); Wayne to Greene, February 22 and 28, ibid.

32. Wayne to Polly Wayne, March 2, 1782, *Wayne Papers* (HSP), volume 15; Laurence Sterne, *A Sentimental Journey through France and Italy, Volume I* (London: Printed for T. Becket and P. A. De Hondt in the Strand, 1768).

33. Wayne to Greene, February 28, 1782, *Greene Papers* (WLCL); Wayne to Greene, March 4, 1782, *Wayne Papers* (WLCL); Greene to Wayne, March 6, 1782, *The Papers of General Nathanael Greene, volume 10*, edited by Dennis M. Coward (Chapel Hill: University of North Carolina Press, 1998), 456–457.

34. Francis Moore to Wayne, March 11, 1782, *Wayne Papers* (NYPL).

35. Wayne to Sir (no name), April 1782 (no date), *Wayne Papers* (HSP), volume 16; Greene to Wayne, May 21, 1782, *Greene Papers* (WLCL).

36. Wayne to Greene, March 25, 1782, *Greene Papers* (WLCL).

37. Wayne to Greene, May 24, 1782, ibid.

38. Wildes, *Anthony Wayne*, 282; Wayne to Rush, April 10, 1782, *Wayne Papers* (HSP), volume 16; Wayne to Greene, April 28, 1792, Greene Papers (WLCL).

39. Extract of a Letter from the Right Honorable Wilbore Ellis, One of His Majesty's Principal Secretaries of State to Sir Henry Clinton K.B. Dated White Hall 6th March 1782, *Wayne Papers* (HSP), volume 15; "Two Resolutions of the House of Commons, 27th February and 4th March, 1782," ibid.; Wayne to Greene, May 27, 1782, *The First Overtures of the Cessation of Hostilities in the American War of Independence*, No. 9, Greene Papers (WLCL).

40. Alured Clarke to Wayne, May 29, 1782, *First Overtures*, No. 10, Greene Papers (WLCL); Wright to Wayne, ibid., No. 11; Wayne to Greene, May 30, 1782, ibid., No. 14; Greene to Wayne, ibid., No. 15.

41. Wayne to Greene, June 24, 1782, in Moore, *Anthony Wayne*, 155–156.
42. Lee, *Memoirs of the War in the Southern Department*, 557–561.
43. Wayne to Greene, March 11, 1782, *Greene Papers* (WLCL).
44. Wayne to the Merchants of Savannah and Orders for Occupying Savannah, June 17, 1782, *Wayne Papers* (WLCL).
45. Wayne to Mary Maxwell, April 25, 1782, *Wayne Papers* (HSP), volume 16; William Eustace to Wayne, May 29, 1782, ibid., volume 17; Wayne to Mary Maxwell, May 29, 1782, ibid.; Mary Maxwell to Wayne, May 29, 1782, ibid.; Wayne to Mary Maxwell, July 13, 1782, ibid., volume 18; Martin to Wayne, October 1782 (no date), ibid.
46. Wayne to Greene, June 18, 1782, *Greene Papers* (WLCL).
47. Ibid.; Martha Barnwell to Anthony Wayne, July 23, 1782, *Wayne Papers* (HSP), volume 18; Sarah Harden to Wayne, October 28, 1782, ibid.; Greene to Wayne, November 30, December 6 and 14, 1782, ibid.; Wayne to Sharp Delany, December 17, 1782, ibid.; Stegeman and Stegeman, *Caty*, 99–103.
48. Wayne to Greene, May 23, 1783, *Wayne Papers* (HSP), volume 15.
49. Wayne to John Dickinson, April 20, 1783, *Wayne Papers* (HSP), volume 19; Dickinson to Wayne, May 17, 1782, ibid.; Morris to Wayne, February 4, 1783, ibid.; Delany to Wayne, April 23, 1787, *Wayne Papers* (WLCL).
50. "Sale of Confiscated Estates, 1782," *Revolutionary Records of the State of Georgia*, volume I, edited by Alan D. Candler (Atlanta: Franklin Turner Co., 1908), 418–419.
51. Wayne to Unknown Recipient (Date Unknown), *Wayne Papers* (WLCL); "Recollections of General Wayne's Campaign against the Northwestern Indians in the years 1793 & 1794," *Native American Collection* (WLCL); Wayne to Knox, November 15, 1793, *Wayne Papers* (HSP), volume 30.

CHAPTER ELEVEN. "PERSECUTION HAS ALMOST DROVE ME MAD"

1. Simmons, *Forts of Anthony Wayne*, 12.
2. Wayne to Scott, September 26, 1793," *Wayne Papers* (HSP), volume 28.
3. Simmons, *Forts of Anthony Wayne*, 12–13; Wayne, General Orders, November 2, 3, 4, 6 (two orders), 8, 9, 10, 11, 12, 13, 18, and 26, *General Wayne's Orderly Book*, 496–501.
4. Wayne to Henry Burbeck, December 11, 1793, *Wayne Papers* (HSP), volume 31; Map of Fort Recovery, *Small Maps Collection* (WLCL).
5. Thomas Taylor Underwood, *Journal, Thomas Taylor Underwood, March 26, 1792 to March 18, 1800: An Old Soldier in Wayne's Army* (Cincinnati: Society of Colonial Wars in the State of Ohio, 1945), 9–10.
6. Ibid.
7. "George Will, Jr. to John Williams, May 25, 1842," *American Pioneer*, 1, no. 8 (August 1842): 293–294.
8. Wayne to Wilkinson, December 22, 1793, *Wayne Papers* (HSP), volume 31; Moore, *Anthony Wayne*, 284; Wayne to Knox, January 8, 1794, *Wayne Papers* (HSP), volume 32; Buell, *Journal*, 14.
9. Wayne to Alexander Gibson, January 17 and 29, 1795, *Wayne Papers* (HSP), volume 39.

10. St. Clair to Wayne, December 9, 1793, *Wayne Papers* (WLCL); Isaac Shelby to Wayne, February 10, 1794, ibid.

11. John Smith to Wilkinson, July 8, 1792, *Wayne Papers* (WLCL); Daniel Bradley to Wilkinson, October 23, 1792, ibid.; Wilkinson to Bradley, October 25, 1792, ibid.; Armstrong to Wayne, November 14, 1792; John Adair's report to Wilkinson, October 29 and November 7, 1792, ibid.

12. Knox to Wayne, March 31, 1794, *Wayne Papers* (WLCL); Knox to Wayne, March 20 and April 3, 1794, *Wayne Papers* (HSP), volume 33.

13. Wayne to Polly Wayne, July 5, 1790, *Wayne Papers* (HSP), volume 30.

14. Wayne to James Jackson, October 1, 1783, ibid., volume 19; Wayne to Joseph Habersham, October 1, 1783, ibid.

15. Wayne to Francis Johnston, September 17, 1783, *Wayne Papers* (HSP), volume 15; Wayne to Habersham, October 1, 1783, ibid.; Wayne to Jackson, December 9, 1783, ibid.; Wayne to Irvine, December 9, 1783, ibid.; Wayne to Washington, November 1 and December 14, 1783, ibid.

16. Wildes, *Anthony Wayne*, 305.

17. Constitution of the Commonwealth of Pennsylvania, 1776, *Pennsylvania State Archives*, volume 10 (1896), 767–784; Robert Lever Brunhouse, *The Counter-Revolution in Pennsylvania, 1776–1790* (Harrisburg: Pennsylvania Historical Commission, 1942), 15.

18. Brunhouse, *Counter-Revolution in Pennsylvania*, 143–145.

19. Wayne to James Jackson, October 1, 1783, *Wayne Papers* (HSP), volume 19.

20. Sharp Delany to Wayne, September 5, 1776, *Wayne Papers* (NYPL); Rush to Wayne, September 24, 1776, ibid.; Richard Peters to Anthony Wayne, October 16, 1776, ibid.

21. Constitution of the Commonwealth of Pennsylvania, 1776, 771–784.

22. Minutes, Council of Censors, November 10, 1783 to September 1, 1784, *Wayne Papers*, Burton Historical Collection (DPL); *Pennsylvania Packet; or the General Advertiser* (Philadelphia), January to March 1784.

23. RG-17, *Records of the Land Office: Donation Claimant Papers and Miscellaneous Patents* (ca. 1785–1810) (series #17.168), Pennsylvania State Archives.

24. *Minutes of the First Session of the Ninth General Assembly of the Commonwealth of Pennsylvania, etc.*, April 8, 1785, 302–305; *Minutes of the First Session of the Eleventh General Assembly of the Commonwealth of Pennsylvania, etc.*, November 11, 23, and 25, December 13, 1786, 38–40, 54–56, 66–70, 92–93; *Pennsylvania Packet, and Daily Advertiser* (Philadelphia), October 16, November 15, December 6, 9, and 30, 1784, January 19, 1785; *New York Packet* (New York City), December 5, 1785, February 6 and 9, April 6 and 10, 1786.

25. Savannah Unit, Georgia Writers' Project, Work Projects Administration of Georgia, "Richmond Oakgrove Plantation, Part 1," *Georgia Historical Quarterly*, 24, no. 1 (March 1940): 22–42, and "Richmond Oakgrove Plantation Part II," *Georgia Historical Quarterly*, 24, no. 2 (June 1940): 124–144; Stephanie Joyner, "Slave Housing Patterns within the Plantation Landscape of Coastal Georgia" (master's thesis: University of Florida, 2003), 25–38; "Early Georgia Plantations and the Township of

Savannah, 1752–1871," Chatham County Map Portfolio, Georgia Archives, University System of Georgia, 8.

26. Wilhelm and Jan Willink to Morris, March 26, 1784, *Wayne Papers* (WLCL).

27. Wilhelm and Jan Willink to Wayne, March 26, 1785, July 29, 1795, and May 14, 1790, ibid.; Anthony Wayne's Memorandum Book (1786–1790), ibid.

28. Wayne to Polly Wayne, June 18, 1786, *Wayne Papers* (DPL); Wayne to Delany, June 18, 1786, *Wayne Papers* (WLCL).

29. Wayne to Delany, June 7, 1785, *Wayne Papers* (WLCL); Delany to Wayne, August 12, 1785, ibid.

30. *Georgia Gazette* (Savannah), July 7, 1785.

31. Stegeman and Stegeman, *Caty*, 123.

32. Catharine Greene to Wayne, December 30, 1789, *Wayne Papers* (HSP), volume 19, and Wayne to Catharine Greene, February 4, 1790, ibid.; Wayne to Margaretta Wayne, June 28, 1786, ibid.

33. Wayne to Catharine Greene, August 1, 1786, *Greene Papers* (WLCL).

34. Edward Penman to Wayne, August 30, 1787, *Wayne Papers* (WLCL).

35. Wayne to Delany, May 24, 1787, ibid.

36. Wayne to Polly Wayne, May 26, 1787, ibid.

37. Aedanus Burke to Wayne, September 3, 1787, ibid.; Wayne to Burke, October 2, 1787, ibid.; Wayne to Delany, October 23, 1787, ibid.

38. Constitution of the Commonwealth of Pennsylvania, 1790, *Pennsylvania State Archives*, volume 10 (1896), 737–749; William A. Benton, "Pennsylvania Revolutionary Officers and the Federal Constitution," *Pennsylvania History: A Journal of Mid-Atlantic Studies*, 31, no. 4 (October, 1964), 419–435; Wayne's Notes at the Pennsylvania Ratifying Convention, November 27 to 30, 1787, *Wayne Papers* (WLCL); Wayne to George Handley, May 28, 1788, ibid.; William Littlefield to Wayne, Newport, September 22, 1788, ibid.; Catherine McLean to Wayne, April 7, 1786, *Greene Papers* (WLCL).

39. Wayne to Delany, February 20, 1788, *Wayne Papers* (WLCL); For sale, Etc., Charleston (January 21, 1788), ibid.; Wayne to William Lewis, February 20, 1788, ibid.; Delany to Wayne, April 7, 1788, ibid.; Wayne to Delany, May 14, 1788, ibid.

40. Wayne to Delany, July 16, 1788, *Wayne Papers* (WLCL).

41. Delany to Wayne, October 7, 1788, July 13 and November (no date), 1789 and May 14 and August 11, 1790, *Wayne Papers* (WLCL); Wayne to Elizabeth Wayne, June 28, 1790, ibid.; Wayne to Delany, April 13, 1791 (two letters), ibid.; Edward Penman Memo, April 16, 1791, ibid.; Notarial Copy of Edward Penman's Bond to Wayne, April 16, 1791, ibid.

42. Delany to Wayne, March 21, 1789, August 11 and 30, and November 6, 1790, *Wayne Papers* (WLCL); Catharine Greene to Wayne, February 21, 1790, *Greene Papers* (WLCL).

43. Wayne to Madison, July 15, 1789, in DeRegnancourt and Parker, eds., *General Anthony Wayne and the Ohio Indian Wars*, 10.

44. Georgia Superior Court Commission, Relinquishment of Right of Dower by Mary

Penrose Wayne, April 7, 1791, *Wayne Papers* (WLCL); Mary Penrose Wayne to Penman, May 7, 1781, ibid.

45. Wayne to Richard Wayne, August 18, 1791, *Wayne Papers* (WLCL); Wayne to Matthew McAllister, November 18, 1791, ibid.; Wayne, "Notes on Testimony re election irregularities in Georgia," ibid.; Wayne, "The Old Georgians Analyzed, 1791," ibid.

46. "Wayne to the Western Indians, January 14, 1794," *The Correspondence of Lieut. Governor John Graves Simcoe*, edited by E. Cruickshank, volume 2 (Toronto: The Society, 1923), 131–132.

47. Wildes, *Anthony Wayne*, 408–410.

48. Carter, *Little Turtle*, 134.

CHAPTER TWELVE. "A SAVAGE ENEMY IN FRONT, FAMINE IN THE REAR"

1. Wayne to Catharine Greene, December 17, 1793, *Greene Papers* (WLCL).

2. Wayne to Delany, January 1, 1794, *Wayne Papers* (HSP), volume 31.

3. Wildes, *Anthony Wayne*, 406–407.

4. Wayne to Knox, July 27, 1794, *Wayne Papers* (HSP), volume 36; United States Army Incomplete Copy of a Court Martial, June 17 and 18, 1793, *Wayne Papers* (WLCL); William McMahon to Wayne, January 16, 1794; Cornet Blue to Wayne, January 11, 1794; Thomas Posey to Wayne, January 11, 1794, *Wayne Papers* (HSP), volume 32.

5. Andro Linklater, *An Artist in Treason: The Extraordinary Double Life of General James Wilkinson* (New York: Walker, 2009), 134–135; Wilkinson to John Brown, August 28, 1794, *Innes Papers* (LOC); *Centinel of the Northwestern Territory*, April 12, May 17, June 6 and 14, 1794.

6. Stubborn Facts, "A gentleman in General Wayne's camp, who may be depended upon," quoted in Wildes, *Anthony Wayne*, 405–406; Gaff, *Bayonets in the Wilderness*, 203–204.

7. Wayne to Knox (Private), November 15, 1793, quoted in Gaff, *Bayonets in the Wilderness*, 181; Wildes, *Anthony Wayne*, 399–406; Wilkinson to Robin (Robert Williams), April 15, 1794, *Wayne Papers* (HSP), volume 34; Wildes, *Anthony Wayne*, 402.

8. Scott to Knox, April 30, 1794, *Scott Papers*, King Library (University of Kentucky); Knox to Wayne, April 3, 1794, *Wayne Papers* (HSP), volume 33; "A Friend to Truth," *Gazette of the United States*, July 19, 1794.

9. Wayne to Delany, July 10, 1794, *Wayne Papers* (WLCL).

10. Delany to Wayne, September 21, 1792; January 4, 1792; May 11 and June 14, 1789, ibid.

11. Polly Wayne to Wayne, January 28, 1776, ibid.; Wayne to Polly Wayne, October 21 and November 12, 1778, *Wayne Papers* (HSP), volumes 5–6; Polly Wayne to Wayne, April 29, July 6, October 6, 1776, and September 7, 1778, *Wayne Papers* (WLCL); Polly Wayne to Isaac Wayne, 1792 (no date), ibid.

12. Wayne to Isaac Wayne, May 9, 1794, *Wayne Papers* (WLCL); Shakespeare, *Hamlet*, I.iii.55–81.

13. Jonathan Alder, *A History of Jonathan Alder: His Captivity and Life with the Indians*, edited by Larry Nelson (Akron: University of Akron Press, 2002), 13, 109; Carter, *Little Turtle*, 120; Stothers and Tucker, *The Fry Site*, 31–32; Basil Meek, "Tarhe the Crane," *Ohio Archaeological and Historical Society Quarterly*, 20 (1911): 64–73.

14. Lord Dorchester to the Seven Nations, February 10, 1794, *Correspondence of Simcoe*, volume 2, 149–150; Wayne to Knox, March 3, 1793, *Wayne Papers* (HSP), volume 33.

15. F. Clever Bald, "Fort Miamis, Outpost of Empire," *Northwest Ohio Quarterly*, 16, no. 2 (1944): 73–116.

16. Wayne to Knox (Private and Confidential), May 30, 1794, and June 10, 1794, *Wayne Papers* (HSP), volume 35; George Washington, Seventh Annual Message to Congress, December 8, 1795 (http://avalon.law.yale.edu/18th_century/washs07.asp) and Eighth Annual Message to Congress, December 7, 1796 (http://avalon.law.yale.edu/18th_century/washs08.asp); John Adams, First Annual Message to Congress, November 22, 1797 (http://avalon.law.yale.edu/18th_century/adamsme1.asp).

17. Knox to Wayne, June 7, 1794, *Wayne Papers* (HSP), volume 35.

18. Wayne to Knox, July 16, 1794, *Wayne Papers* (WLCL).

19. Alexander Gibson to Wayne, June 30, July 1, 2, 5, 10, and 18, 1794, *Wayne Papers* (HSP), volume 36; Wayne to Gibson, June 27 and July 2, 1794, ibid.

20. Wayne to Knox, July 7, 1794, ibid.

21. Wayne, General Orders, July 20, 21, 26, and 27, 1794, ibid.

22. Wayne to Knox, July 27, 1794, ibid.

23. Wayne to Delany, July 10, 1794, *Wayne Papers* (WLCL).

24. Wayne, Draft of the Last Will & Testament of Major General Anthony Wayne, Etc., July 14, 1794, ibid.

25. Wayne to Isaac Wayne, July 14, 1794, ibid.

26. Thomas P. Slaughter, *The Whiskey Rebellion: Frontier Epilogue to the American Revolution* (New York: Oxford University Press, 1986), 205–214; David Jones to Wayne, August 11, 1794, *Wayne Papers* (WLCL); Peter McPhee, *Robespierre: A Revolutionary Life* (New Haven: Yale University Press, 2012), 201–221.

27. Wayne, General Orders, July 20, 21, 26, and 27, 1794, *Wayne Papers* (HSP), volume 36.

28. Kaycee Hallett, "History of the Black Swamp," *Black Swamp Journal* (April 14, 2011); July 27 and July 28, 1794 entries in the anonymous *Recollections of General Wayne's Campaign against the Northwest Indians in the years 1793 & 1794*; Randolph, *Journal*; and Edward Miller, *Journal, Wayne Family Papers* (WLCL); Lieutenant (John) Boyer, "Daily Journal of Wayne's Campaign," *Michigan Pioneer and Historical Collections*, 34 (1965): 539–540.

29. Simmons, *Forts of Anthony Wayne*, 14–15; August 3 and 4, 1794, entries in Boyer, "Daily Journal," 540–542.

30. J. Porter to Thomas R. Peters, November 6, 1817, *Wayne Papers* (HSP), volume 48; Wayne to Isaac Wayne, September 10, 1794, ibid., volume 36.

31. August 4–9, 1794 entries in *Recollections*, Randolph and Miller Journals; Boyer, "Daily Journal," 542–543.

32. Wayne to Knox, August 14, 1794, *American State Papers, Indian Affairs*, I, 490.

33. Wayne, General Orders, August 8, 1794, *Wayne Papers* (HSP), volume 36.

34. Simmons, *Forts of Anthony Wayne*, 45–46; August 9 and 10, 1794 entries in Boyer, "Daily Journal," 543–544; Paul David Nelson, "General Charles Scott, the Kentucky Mounted Volunteers, and the Northwest Indian Wars, 1784–1794," *Journal of the Early Republic*, 6, no. 3 (Autumn 1986), 246.

35. Report on Wells' Scouting Mission, *Correspondence of Simcoe*, II, 372–373; Examination of the Shawnee Prisoner, *Wayne Papers* (HSP), volume 37; Wildes, *Anthony Wayne*, 421.

36. Wayne, To the Delawares, Shawanese, Miamies, and Wyandots, Etc., August 13, 1794, *American State Papers, Indian Affairs*, I, 490.

37. Moore, *Anthony Wayne*, 189; August 14 and 15, 1794 entries in *Recollections*, Randolph and Miller Journals.

38. August 16, 1794 entries in *Recollections* and Randolph Journal; Moore, *Life and Services of Gen. Anthony Wayne*, 189; George White Eyes to Anthony Wayne (document 7), *Wayne Papers* (HSP), volume 36.

39. August 17 and 18, 1784 entries in *Recollections* and Randolph Journal. The direct quote is from the August 17, 1794, entry in Randolph's journal.

40. Benson J. Lossing, *Pictorial Fieldbook of the War of 1812* (New York: Harper & Brothers, 1868), 55; Simmons, *Forts of Anthony Wayne*, 18–19; General Wayne's Encampment & Establishment at Roche de Bout, *Small Maps Collection* (WLCL); Gaff, *Bayonets in the Wilderness*, 296–297.

41. Fallen Timbers and Fort Miamis National Historic Park (http://www.nps.gov/fati/in dex.htm); John F. Winkler, *Fallen Timbers 1794: The U.S. Army's First Victory* (Oxford: Osprey, 2013), 62.

42. Lossing, *Pictorial Fieldbook of the War of 1812*, 53–54n; Anthony Wayne, General Orders, August 19, 1794, *General Wayne's Orderly Book*, 535; William Henry Harrison to John Tipton, December 6, 1833, *Governors Messages and Letters: Messages and Letters of William Henry Harrison*, volume II, edited by Logan Esary (Indianapolis: Indiana Historical Commission, 1922), 746.

43. Cleaves, *Old Tippecanoe*, 18.

44. Nevin O. Winter, *History of Northwest Ohio*, volume I (Chicago: Lewis, 1917), 85.

45. Wayne to Knox, August 28, 1794, *Wayne Papers* (HSP), volume 36; James Wilkinson, "Journal," in *From Greene Ville to Fallen Timbers: A Journal of the Wayne Campaign, July 28–September 14, 1794*, edited by Dwight L. Smith (Indianapolis: Indiana Historical Society, 1962), 289, 291–292, 294, and 297; August 20 entry in *Recollections*, Randolph and Miller Journals. Other eyewitness journals include: Joseph G. Andrews, "Journal," *Manuscript Division* (LOC); John Boyer, *A Journal of Wayne's Campaign* (Cincinnati: Printed for William Dodge, 1866); Wilson, ed., *The Journal of Daniel Bradley*; William Clark, "A Journal of Major-General Anthony Wayne's Campaign against the Shawnee Indians in 1794–1795," *Mississippi Valley Historical Review*, 1 (1914): 419–444; John Cooke, "General Wayne's Campaign in 1794 & 1795: Captain John Cooke's Journal," *American Historical Record*, 2 (1873): 311–316, 339–

345; James Elliot, "Diary of James Elliot," *Works of James Elliot* (Greenfield, Mass., 1798); Nathaniel Hart Journal, *Draper Manuscript Collection;* James Wilkinson, "General James Wilkinson's Narrative of the Fallen Timbers Campaign," *Mississippi Valley Historical Review,* 16 (1929): 81–90; Dresden W. H. Howard, ed., "The Battle of Fallen Timbers, as Told by Chief Kin-Jo-I-No," *Northwest Ohio Quarterly,* 20 (1948): 37–40.

46. August 20, 1794 entries in *Recollections,* Randolph and Miller Journals; Wayne to Knox, August 28, 1794, *Wayne Papers* (HSP), volume 36; *American State Papers, Indian Affairs,* II, 491.

47. Anthony Wayne to Knox, August 28, 1794, Wayne Papers (HSP), volume 36; Gaff, *Bayonets in the Wilderness,* 309–310.

48. John Sugden, *Tecumseh: A Life* (New York: Henry Holt, 1997), 90; Hamtramck to Wayne, March 5, 1795, *Wayne Papers* (WLCL).

49. Wayne to Knox, August 28, 1794, *Wayne Papers* (HSP), volume 36; "Return of Killed, Wounded, and Missing," *American State Papers, Indian Affairs,* II, 492; "An Act Making an Alteration in the Flag of the United States," January 13, 1794, 3rd Congress, 1st session.

50. William Campbell to Wayne, August 21 and 22, 1794, *Correspondence of Simcoe,* volume II, 406–407; Wayne to Campbell, August 21 and 22, 1794, *Wayne Papers* (HSP), volume 36; August 21 and 22, 1794 entries in *Recollections* and Randolph and Miller Journals.

51. August 23 entries in *Recollections* and Randolph and Miller Journals; Wayne to Knox, August 28, 1794, *Wayne Papers* (HSP), volume 36.

CHAPTER THIRTEEN. "LISTEN TO THE VOICE OF TRUTH AND PEACE"

1. Hamtramck to Wayne, March 5, 1795, *Wayne Papers* (WLCL).

2. August 24 through 31, 1794 entries in Miller Journal; Wayne to Knox, September 20, 1794, *Wayne Papers* (HSP), volume 37.

3. Wayne to Knox, September 20, 1794, *Wayne Papers* (HSP), volume 37; September 19, 1794 entry in Miller Journal.

4. Simmons, *Forts of Anthony Wayne,* 19–22; October 12 through 17, 1794 entries in Miller Journal; Wayne to Knox, September 20, October 12, 15, 16, and 19, 1794, *Wayne Papers* (HSP), volume 37; Richard Battin, "Drawing of Original Fort Wayne Found," *Fort Wayne News-Sentinel,* March 1, 1993 (describes donation of Burbeck's map to U.S. Military Academy).

5. September 21 and October 16, 1794 entries in Miller Journal.

6. October 27, 1794 entry in Miller Journal.

7. Wayne to the Sachems & Warriors, Etc., September 12, 1794, *Wayne Papers* (WLCL); Wayne to Tarhe, Etc., November 14, 1794, ibid.; Wayne to Sachems, Chiefs & Warriors Etc., January 19, 1795, ibid.

8. Wayne to Knox, December 23, 1794, *Wayne Papers* (HSP), volume 38.

9. Wayne to Knox, October 17, 1794, ibid.; John Stagg to Wayne, October 4, 1781, ibid.; Newman's Deposition, December 1, 1794, ibid.

10. Knox to Wayne, December 5, 1792, ibid.; Debate over Thanks to General Wayne, *Annals of Congress*, House of Representatives, 3rd Congress, 2nd session December 1794, 957–966.

11. Knox to Wayne, December 5, 1794, *Wayne Papers* (HSP), volume 38; Knox attached Wilkinson's June 30 and July 18, 1795 letters to his December 5, 1794 letter to Wayne. James Ripley Jacobs is correct in his work *Tarnished Warrior: Major-General James Wilkinson* (New York: Macmillan, 1938), 144, that Wilkinson's charges in their final form have never been found; Wildes, *Anthony Wayne*, 427–428.

12. Wayne to Knox, January 25, 1794, *Wayne Papers* (WLCL).

13. Delany to Wayne, December 17, 1794 and April 13, 1795, *Wayne Papers* (WLCL); Wilkinson to Harry Innes, November 10, December (no date) 1794, *Innes Papers* (LOC).

14. Knox to Wilkinson, October 10, 1794, *James Wilkinson Papers* (Chicago Historical Society); Knox to Wilkinson, December 4 and 5, 1795, *Innes Papers* (LOC); Wilkinson to Innes, January 1, 1795, ibid.; Wilkinson to Knox, January 2, 1795 (Private), ibid.; Jacobs, *Tarnished Warrior*, 145.

15. Wayne to Tarhe and Sandusky Chiefs, January 1, 1795, *Wayne Papers* (HSP), volume 39; Wayne to Chippewa, Ottawa, Pottawatomi Chiefs, Etc., January 19, 1795, ibid.; Tarhe, Chief of the Hurons to Reverend Edmund Burke, February 6, 1795, *Wayne Papers* (WLCL); Hamtramck to Wayne, March 5, 1795, ibid.; Carter, *Little Turtle*, 145; John Sugden, *Blue Jacket: Warriors of the Shawnees* (Lincoln: University of Nebraska Press, 2000), 190.

16. Bluejacket's Speech, February 18, 1795, *Wayne Papers* (WLCL); A Proclamation (Cessation of Hostilities), February 22, 1795, ibid.

17. Pickering to Wayne, April 8, May 15, and June 29, 1795, *Wayne Papers* (HSP), volumes 40 and 41; Wayne to Pickering, May 15, ibid., volume 40; Pickering, "Draft of a Treaty," *Northwest Territory Collection* (Indiana Historical Society).

18. Wayne to Isaac Wayne, November 10 and December 23, 1794, *Wayne Papers* (HSP), volume 38.

19. Margaretta Atlee to Wayne, February 29, 1795, *Wayne Papers* (WLCL); William Atlee to Wayne, September 27, 1794, *Wayne Papers* (DPL); Wayne to William Atlee, February 22, 1795, *Gunther Collection* (Chicago Historical Society).

20. Minutes of a Treaty with the Tribes of Indians, Etc., August 10, 1795, *American State Papers, Indian Affairs*, I, 564–567.

21. Ibid., 567–571.

22. Ibid., 571–572.

23. Ibid., 572–578.

24. Articles I through VIII, Treaty with the Wyandot, Etc. (Treaty of Greeneville), *Indian Affairs: Laws and Treaties*, II, 39–45.

25. Articles III and IV, ibid., 39–42.

26. Minutes of a Treaty, ibid., 578.

27. Signatures, Treaty of Greeneville, ibid., 44–45; Francis Paul Prucha, *Indian Peace Medals in American History* (Norman: University of Oklahoma Press, 2000), 88, figure 36.

CHAPTER FOURTEEN. "I WILL WRITE YOU MORE FROM PRESQUE ISLE"

1. Wayne to Knox, August 28, 1794, *Wayne Papers* (HSP), volume 37; *Pennsylvania Gazette* (Philadelphia), February 10, 1796; *American Daily Advertiser* (Philadelphia), February 8 and 20, 1796; John Adams to Abigail Adams, February 13, 1796, *Adams Family Papers* (Massachusetts Historical Society).
2. J. Thomas Scharf and Thompson Westcott, *History of Philadelphia, Volume I, 1609 to 1884* (Philadelphia: J. B. Lippincott & Co., 1884), 486; *History of the First Troop Philadelphia City Cavalry: 1774, November 17, 1784* (Philadelphia: Printed for the Troop by Hallowell & Co., 1875), 36.
3. Jay Treaty, November 19, 1794 (http://avalon.law.yale.edu/18th_century/jay.asp); Treaty of Friendship, Limits, and Navigation Between Spain and the United States, October 27, 1795 (http://avalon.law.yale.edu/18th_century/sp1795.asp); David Jones to Wayne, August 11, 1794, *Wayne Papers* (WLCL); Barbary Treaties (http://avalon.law .yale.edu/subject menus/barmenu.asp); William Doyle, *Oxford History of the French Revolution* (Oxford: Clarendon Press, 1989), 272–296.
4. Knopf, "Preface to Correspondence of 1796," *Anthony Wayne: A Name in Arms*, 477.
5. Paul David Nelson, *Anthony Wayne: Soldier of the Early Republic* (Bloomington: Indiana University Press, 1989), 291; Organization of the Army (No. 27), 4th Congress, 1st Session, *American State Papers: Military Affairs*, I, 112–115.
6. Harrison to Wayne, November 1, 1794, *Wayne Papers* (WLCL); Margaretta Atlee to Wayne, June 2, 1796, ibid.; Wildes, *Anthony Wayne*, 449–452; Williamina Cadwalader to Ann Ridgely, February 20, 1796, *Cadwalader Collection* (HSP).
7. Stegeman and Stegeman, *Caty*, 146–156, 162–170; Wayne to Catharine Greene, February 21, 1790, *Greene Papers* (WLCL).
8. Wayne to Zebulon Pike, November 25, 1795 and May 25, 1796, *Northwest Territory Collection* (Indiana Historical Society); Wayne to William Clark, September 10, 1795, ibid.
9. McHenry to Wayne, May 25, 1796 (Private), *Wayne Papers* (HSP), volume 44.
10. Pickering to Wayne, October 24, 1795, *Wayne Papers* (HSP), volume 43; Wayne to Wilkinson, November 30 and December 14, 1795, ibid.; Anthony Wayne, General Orders, December 14, 1795, *General Wayne's Orderly Book*, 659.
11. Captain A. R. Hetzel, "An Act to Ascertain and Fix the Military Establishment of the United States," May 30, 1796, *Military Laws of the United States*, 3rd edition (Washington, D.C.: George Templeman, 1846), 62–66; Nelson, *Anthony Wayne*, 291.
12. Wayne to McHenry, July 8 (Private), 22 and 27, 1796, *Wayne Papers* (HSP), volumes 44 and 45; Wilkinson to Burbeck, July 12 and 20, 1796, *Wilkinson-Burbeck Letters* (WLCL); James Wilkinson, General Orders, December 15, 1796, *General Wayne's Orderly Book*, 660.

13. Accounts and Receipts for 1796, *Wayne Papers* (WLCL); Register Warrants Drawn by Major General Wayne on the Paymaster Commencing the 19th July (1796) at Greeneville, ibid.; James Ross to Isaac Wayne, December 29, 1810, ibid.

14. Burbeck to Wayne, September 1 and 6, October 25, 1796 (two letters), *Wayne Papers* (HSP), volume 47.

15. Wayne to Isaac Wayne, September 10, 1796, *Wayne Papers* (HSP), volume 46; Wayne to McHenry, September 29, October 3, and November 7, 1796, *Wayne Papers* (HSP), volumes 46–47; F. Clever Bald, *A Portrait of Anthony Wayne: Painted from Life by Jean Pierre Henri Elouis in 1796 and now reproduced from a unique print for the schoolchildren of Detroit: with a historical essay on General Wayne at Detroit* (Ann Arbor: Bulletin of the Clements Library, 1948), 7–14.

16. Wayne to Henry DeButts, July 10, 1796, *Wayne Papers* (WLCL); Wayne to McHenry, July 22, 1796, *Wayne Papers* (HSP), volume 45; Winthrop Sargent to Anthony Wayne, November 1, 1796, *Wayne Papers* (WLCL).

17. Zebulon Pike to Wayne, August 6 and 22, 1796, *Wayne Papers* (WLCL); John Steele to Wayne, August 28, 1794, *Wayne Papers* (HSP), volume 45; Wayne to McHenry, July 28, 1796 (Private), ibid.; Pickering to Wayne, September 10, 1796 (Private), *Wayne Papers* (WLCL); Wayne to McHenry, September 20, 1796, *Wayne Papers* (HSP), volume 46.

18. McHenry to Wayne, July 9, 1796 (Private Note), *Wayne Papers* (HSP), volume 44; Wayne to McHenry, July 28, 1796, ibid., volume 45.

19. Oliver Wolcott to Wayne, July 19, 1796, *Northwest Territory Collection* (WLCL); Wayne to McHenry, November 12, 1795, *Wayne Papers* (HSP), volume 47; DeButts to Isaac Craig, November 7, 1796, "Letters Relating to the Death of Major General Anthony Wayne," *Pennsylvania Magazine of History and Biography*, 19 (1895): 112.

20. Russell Bissell to Craig, November 29, 1796, "Letters Relating to the Death of Major General Anthony Wayne," 113; DeButts to Craig, December 14 and 15, 1796, ibid., 114–115; George Balfour to Craig, December 14, 1796, ibid., 114; *Major Abraham Kirkpatrick and His Descendants, Compiled by One of His Descendants* (Pittsburgh: J. P. Durbin, 1911), 9.

21. DeButts to Craig, December 15, 1796, "Letters Relating to the Death of Major General Anthony Wayne"; Delany to Isaac Wayne, December 30, 1796, *Wayne Papers* (HSP), volume 47; Laura Sanford, *The History of Erie County, Pennsylvania, from Its First Settlement* (Published by the Author, 1894), 89–90; *Claypoole's American Daily Advertiser* (Philadelphia), December 31, 1796; Isaac Wayne, "Died on Wednesday the 14th instant at Presque Isle His excellency Anthony Wayne Commander in Chief of the Army" (no date), *Wayne Papers* (WLCL).

EPILOGUE. A. W. 15 DEC. 1796

1. Anthony Wayne to Polly Wayne, June 7, 1777, *Wayne Papers* (NYPL).

BIBLIOGRAPHY

PRIMARY SOURCES

ARCHIVES

Adams Family Papers, Massachusetts Historical Society.
Andrews, Joseph G. "Journal." *Manuscript Division*, Library of Congress.
Henry Burbeck Papers, William L. Clements Library.
Cadwalader Papers, Historical Society of Pennsylvania.
Lewis Cass Papers, William L. Clements Library.
"Early Georgia Plantations and the Township of Savannah, 1752–1871." Chatham County
    Map Portfolio, Georgia Archives, University System of Georgia.
Emmett Collection, New York Public Library.
Great Britain Indian Department Collection, William L. Clements Library.
Nathanael Greene Papers, William L. Clements Library.
Gunther Collection, Chicago Historical Society.
George Hammond Papers, William L. Clements Library.
Josiah Harmar Papers, William L. Clements Library.
William Henry Harrison Papers, New-York Historical Society.
Nathaniel Hart Journal, *Draper Manuscript Collection*.
John Hughes Papers, Historical Society of Pennsylvania.
Innes Papers, Library of Congress.
Thomas Jefferson Papers, Library of Congress.
Henry and Lucy Knox Papers, William L. Clements Library.
Tobias Lear Papers, William L. Clements Library.
James Madison Papers, Library of Congress.
John Martin Papers, Georgia Historical Society.
James McHenry Papers, William L. Clements Library.
Miller, Edward. *Journal, Anthony Wayne Family Papers*, William L. Clements Library.
Native American History Collection, William L. Clements Library.

Northwest Historical Collection, William L. Clements Library.

Northwest Territory Collection, Indiana Historical Society.

"Orders of Alured Clarke, January 13, 1782," Georgia Historical Society.

Rufus Putnam Papers, William L. Clements Library.

Randolph, *Journal, Anthony Wayne Family Papers*, William L. Clements Library.

Recollections of General Wayne's Campaign against the Northwestern Indians in the years 1793 & 1794, Native American Collection, William L. Clements Library.

Records of the Land Office: Donation Claimant Papers and Miscellaneous Patents (ca. 1785–1810) (series #17.168), Pennsylvania State Archives.

Schoff Revolutionary War Collection, William L. Clements Library.

Scott Papers, King Library, University of Kentucky.

John Graves Simcoe Papers, William L. Clements Library.

Small Maps Collection, William L. Clements Library.

George Washington Collection, William L. Clements Library.

George Washington Papers, Library of Congress.

Anthony Wayne Family Papers, William L. Clements Library.

Wayne Papers, Bancroft Collection, New York Public Library.

Wayne Papers, Burton Historical Collection, Detroit Public Library.

Wayne Papers, Historical Society of Pennsylvania.

James Wilkinson Papers, Chicago Historical Society.

Wilkinson-Burbeck Letters, William L. Clements Library.

Wright, Elizabeth Johnson. "Mary Vining: An Account of Her Life." *Society Miscellaneous Collection*, Georgia Historical Society.

Letters of James Wright, Georgia Historical Society.

PRINTED WORKS

Adams, John. "First Annual Message to Congress, November 22, 1797 (http://avalon.law .yale.edu/18th_century/adamsme1.asp).

Alder, Jonathan. *A History of Jonathan Alder: His Captivity and Life with the Indians*, edited by Larry Nelson. Akron: University of Akron Press, 2002.

American State Papers, Indian Affairs, I.

American State Papers, Military Affairs, I.

André, Major John. *André's Journal: An Authentic Record of the Movements and Engagements of the British Army in America from June 1777 to November 1778 as recorded from day to day by Major John André*, edited by Henry Cabot Lodge. Boston: Issued by the Bibliophile Society for Members Only, 1903.

———. *Cow-chace in Three Cantos, published on occasion of the rebel general Wayne's attack of the refugees block-house on Hudson's river, on Friday the 21st of July, 1780*. New York: James Rivington, 1780.

Annals of Congress, House of Representatives, 3rd Congress, 2nd Session.

Baldwin, Colonel Jeduthun. *The Revolutionary Diary of Col. Jeduthun Baldwin, 1775–1778*. Bangor: Printed for the De Burians, 1906.

Boyer, Lieutenant [John]. "Daily Journal of Wayne's Campaign." *Michigan Pioneer and Historical Collections*, 34 (1965): 539–659.

———. *A Journal of Wayne's Campaign*. Cincinnati: Printed for William Dodge, 1866.

Brackenridge, Henry M., "Biographical Notice of H. H. Brackenridge." *Southern Literary Messenger* 8 (January 1842): 1–19.

Brackenridge, Hugh Henry. *Incidents of the Insurrection in the Western Parts of Pennsylvania, in the Year 1794, Vol. 1.* Philadelphia: John McCulloch, 1795.

———. *Modern Chivalry: Containing the Adventures of a Captain and Teague O'Regan, His Servant,* 2 vols. Pittsburgh: R. Patterson & Lambdin, 1819.

Buell, John Hutchinson, "A Fragment from the Diary of John Hutchinson Buell, U.S.A., who Joined the American Army at the Start of the Revolutionary War and Remained in Service until 1803." *Journal of the Military Service Institution of the United States*, 40 (1907): 102–113.

Burnett, Jacob. *Notes on the Early Settlement of the North-West Territory.* Cincinnati: Derby, Bradley, & Co., 1940.

Butterfield, Consul Willshire, ed. *The Official Letters Which Passed Between George Washington and Brig.-Gen. William Irvine and Between Irvine and Others Concerning Military Affairs in the West from 1781 to 1783.* Madison: D. Atwood, 1882.

Candler, Alan D., ed. *Revolutionary Records of the State of Georgia,* volume I. Atlanta: Franklin Turner Co., 1908.

Cist, Charles, ed. *Cincinnati Miscellany, or Antiquities of the West,* volume II. Cincinnati: Robinson & Jones, 1846.

Clark, William. "A Journal of Major-General Anthony Wayne's Campaign against the Shawnee Indians in 1794–1795." *Mississippi Valley Historical Review,* 1 (1914): 419–444.

Coward, Dennis M. *The Papers of General Nathanael Greene,* volume 10. Chapel Hill: University of North Carolina Press, 1998.

Cooke, John. "General Wayne's Campaign in 1794 & 1795: Captain John Cooke's Journal." *American Historical Record,* 2 (1873): 311–316, 339–345.

Custis, George Washington Parke. *Memoirs and Recollections of Washington.* New York: Derby & Jackson, 1860.

———. *Recollections and Private Memoirs of Washington, By His Adopted Son George Washington Parke Custis, With a Memoir of the Author, By His Daughter; and Illustrative and Explanatory Notes by Benson J. Lossing with Illustrations.* Philadelphia: J. W. Bradley, 1861.

Denny, Ebenezer. *Military Journal of Major Ebenezer Denny, with an Introductory Memoir.* Philadelphia: J. B. Lippincott & Co. for the Historical Society of Pennsylvania, 1859.

DeRegnancourt, Tony and Tom Parker, eds. *General Anthony Wayne and the Ohio Indian Wars: A Collection of Unpublished Letters and Artifacts.* Arcanum, Ohio: Occasional Monographs of the Upper Miami Valley Archaeological Research Museum, No. 4, 1995.

"Diary of the Revolt." *Pennsylvania Archives,* 2nd series, vol. 11, 631–674.

Drake, Benjamin. *Life of Tecumseh, and His Brother the Prophet.* Cincinnati: E. Morgan & Co., 1841.

Ducoudray, Gen. H. L. V. *Memoirs of Gilbert M. Lafayette.* 2nd edition. Geneva, N.Y.: John Greves, 1839.

Elliot, James. "Diary of James Elliot." *Works of James Elliot*. Greenfield, Mass., 1798.

Esary, Logan, ed. *Governors Messages and Letters: Messages and Letters of William Henry Harrison*, II. Indianapolis: Indiana Historical Commission, 1922.

Fitzpatrick, Thomas, ed. *The Writings of George Washington from the Original Manuscript Sources, 1745–1799*, 39 vols. Washington, D.C.: Government Printing Office, 1931–1944.

Foster, Emily, ed. *The Ohio Frontier: An Anthology of Early Writings*. Lexington: University Press of Kentucky, 1996.

"General Wayne's Daily Encampment," *American Pioneer*, 2 (July 1843): 290.

General Wayne's Orderly Book, 1792–1797. Edited by C. M. Burton, *Michigan Pioneer and Historical Collections*, 34 (1965): 341–501.

"George Will, Jr. to John Williams, May 25, 1842." *American Pioneer*, 1, no. 8 (August 1842): 293–294.

Graydon, Alexander. *Memoirs of a Life, Chiefly Passed in Pennsylvania, within the last sixty years, with occasional remarks upon the general occurrences, character and spirit of that eventful period*. Harrisburg: John Wyeth, 1811.

Harvey, Henry. *History of the Shawnee Indians from the Year 1681 to 1854*. Cincinnati: E. Morgan and Sons, 1855.

Heckewelder, John Gottlieb Ernestus. *History, Manners, and Customs of the Indian Nations: Who Once Inhabited Pennsylvania and the Neighboring States*, volume 12. Philadelphia: Publication Fund of the Historical Society of Pennsylvania, 1881.

Hobbes, Thomas. *Elementa philosophica de cive*. Paris, 1642.

Howard, Dresden W. H., ed. "The Battle of Fallen Timbers, as Told by Chief Kin-Jo-I-No." *Northwest Ohio Quarterly*, 20 (1948): 37–40.

Howe, Henry. *Historical Collections of Ohio*, 2 volumes. Cincinnati: C.H. Krehbiel, 1889.

Hunt, Lynn and Censer, Jack, eds. *Liberty, Equality, Fraternity: Exploring the French Revolution* (https://chnm.gmu.edu/revolution/d/593/).

Idzerda, Stanley J., ed. *Lafayette in the Age of the American Revolution: Selected Letters and Papers, 1776–1790*, volume III. Ithaca: Cornell University Press, 1980.

Jackson, Donald and Twohig, Dorothy, eds. *The Diaries of George Washington, 6 Volumes*. Charlottesville: University of Virginia Press, 1976–1980.

Jefferson, Thomas. *The Complete Anas of Thomas Jefferson*, edited by Franklin V. Sawvel. New York: Round Table Press, 1903.

"Journal of the Virginia Commissioners." *Virginia Magazine of History and Biography* 13 (1906): 154–173.

Journals of the Continental Congress, 1774–1789, volume 19. Washington, D.C.: Government Printing Office, 1912.

Julius Caesar. *Caesar's Gallic War*. 1st edition, Translated by W. A. McDevitte and W. S. Bohn. New York: Harper & Brothers, 1869.

———. *First Eight Books of Caesar's Commentaries on the Gallic War; literally translated with an introduction by Edward Brooks, Jr.*, Volume VII. Philadelphia: David McKay, 1896.

Kappler, Charles J., comp. and ed. *Indian Affairs: Laws and Treaties*, II. Washington, D.C.: Government Printing Office, 1904.

Ketchum, William, ed. "Colonel Butler's Journal." *An Authentic and Comprehensive History of Buffalo*, volume I. Buffalo: Rockwell, Baker, & Hill, 1864.

Knopf, Richard C., ed. *Anthony Wayne: A Name in Arms; Soldier, Diplomat, Defender of Expansion Westward of a Nation; The Wayne-Knox-Pickering-McHenry Correspondence.* Pittsburgh: University of Pittsburgh Press, 1960.

———. "Two Journals of the Kentucky Volunteers, 1793–1794." *Filson Club History Quarterly*, 27 (July 1953): 247–281.

Lee, Henry. *Memoirs of the War in the Southern Department of the United States.* New York: University Publishing Co., 1870.

Letters by and to Nathanael Greene with Some to His Wife. New York: George H. Richmond, 1906.

"Letters from Continental Officers to Doctor Reading Beatty, 1781–1789." *Pennsylvania Magazine of History and Biography* 54 (1930): 159–162.

"Letters Relating to the Death of Major General Anthony Wayne." *Pennsylvania Magazine of History and Biography*, 19 (1895): 112–115.

The Life of Major-Gen. Israel Putnam to which is added a Biographical Sketch of the Late Major General Anthony Wayne. Pittsburgh: Cramer, Spear & Richbaum, no date.

Locke, John. *Two Treatises of Government.* London, 1690.

Lossing, Benson J. *Pictorial Fieldbook of the War of 1812.* New York: Harper & Brothers, 1868.

Major Abraham Kirkpatrick and His Descendants, Compiled by One of His Descendants. Pittsburgh: J. P. Durbin, 1911.

Maurice de Saxe, Marshal Herman. *Reveries, or, Memoirs Concerning the Art of War.* Edinburgh: Printed by Sands, Donaldson, Murray, and Cochran for Alexander Donaldson at Pope's Head, 1759.

McDonald, John. *Biographical Sketches of General Nathaniel Massie, Captain William Wells, and General Simon Kenton.* Dayton: D. Osborn & Son, 1852.

Military Laws of the United States, Third Edition. Washington, D.C.: George Templeman, 1846.

Minutes of the First Session of the Ninth General Assembly of the Commonwealth of Pennsylvania.

Minutes of the First Session of the Eleventh General Assembly of the Commonwealth of Pennsylvania.

Monroe, James. *The Writings of James Monroe: Including a Collection of His Public And Private Papers And Correspondence Now for the First Time Printed.* New York: G. P. Putnam's Sons, 1898–1903.

Moore, Henry. *Life and Services of Gen. Anthony Wayne, Founded on Documentary and Other Evidence, Published by His Son, Col. Isaac Wayne.* Philadelphia: Leary, Getz, & Co., 1845.

Moore, William. "Chester County Docket, 1719–1722." Historical Society of Pennsylvania.

Plutarch. *Lives of Noble Grecians and Romans*, Volume 1. New York: Modern Library Series, 1992.

Putnam, Rufus. *The Memoirs of Rufus Putnam and Certain Official Papers and Correspondence*, Compiled and Annotated by Rowena Buell. New York: Houghton Mifflin, 1903.

Rush, Richard. *Washington in Domestic Life: From Original Letters and Manuscripts.* Philadelphia: J. B. Lippincott, 1857.

Scheer, G. F., ed. *Private Yankee Doodle Being a Narrative of the Adventures, Dangers and Sufferings of a Revolutionary Soldier by Joseph Plumb Martin.* Boston: Eastern Acorn Press, 1962.

Sheridan, Richard. *La Duenna, or the Elopement: A Comic Opera: As it is Acted at the Theatre, at Smoke-Alley, Dublin.* Dublin: Printed for the Booksellers, 1786.

Smith, Dwight L., ed. *From Greene Ville to Fallen Timbers: A Journal of the Wayne Campaign, July 28–September 14, 1794.* Indianapolis: Indiana Historical Society, 1962.

Smith, William Henry. *Life and Public Career of Arthur St. Clair,* Volumes 1 and 2. Cincinnati: Robert Clarke & Co., 1882.

Sparks, Jared, ed., *Correspondence of the American Revolution being letters of eminent men to George Washington from the time of his taking command of the army to the end of his presidency,* volume 2. Boston: Little, Brown & Company, 1853.

Steiner, Bernard C. *The Life and Correspondence of James McHenry: Secretary of War under Adams and Jefferson.* Cleveland: Burrows Brothers Co., 1907.

Sterne, Laurence. *A Sentimental Journey Through France and Italy, Volume I.* London: Printed for T. Becket and P. A. De Hondt in the Strand, 1768.

Steuben, Baron de. *Regulations for the Order and Discipline of the Troops of the United States.* Exeter, New Hampshire: Printed by Henry Ranlet for Thomas & Andrews, 1794.

Stevenson, Burton Egbert, ed. *Poems of American History.* Boston: Houghton Mifflin, 1908.

Suetonius. *The Lives of the Twelve Caesars,* edited by Joseph Cavorse. New York: Modern Library, 1951.

Sullivan, John. *Letters and Papers of Major General John Sullivan, Continental Army,* Volume 1, Edited by Otis G. Hammond. Concord: New Hampshire Historical Society, 1930.

Syrett, Harold C., ed. *The Papers of Alexander Hamilton,* Volume 21. New York: Columbia University Press, 1974.

Underwood, Thomas Taylor. *Journal, March 26, 1792 to March 18, 1800: An Old Soldier in Wayne's Army.* Cincinnati: Society of Colonial Wars in the State of Ohio, 1945.

Van Cleve, Benjamin. "Memoirs of Benjamin Van Cleve," edited by Beverly W. Bond. *Quarterly Publication of the Historical and Philosophical Society of Ohio,* 17, nos. 1–2 (January–June 1922), 7–29.

Washington, George. *The Diary of George Washington, 1789 to 1791.* New York: Charles B. Richardson, 1850.

———. "Eighth Annual Message to Congress," December 7, 1796 (http://avalon.law.yale.edu/18th_century/washs08.asp).

———. *Papers of George Washington,* Digital Edition, edited by Theodore J. Crackel, et al. Charlottesville: University of Virginia Press, Rotunda, 2007–.

———. "The Proclamation of Neutrality 1793" (http://avalon.law.yale.edu/18th_century/neutra93.asp).

———. "Seventh Annual Message to Congress, December 8, 1795" (http://avalon.law.yale.edu/18th_century/washs07.asp).

Wayne, Isaac. "Biographical Memoir of General Anthony Wayne." *The Casket: Flowers of Wisdom, Wit and Sentiment* 4 (1829): 193–203, 241–251, 297–397, 349–361, 389–411, 445–457, 493–505, and 5 (1830), 4–14, 61–72, 109–120.

West, Martin, director, Fort Ligonier, ed. "George Washington's 'Remarks': Transcription and Annotation." *George Washington Remembers: Reflections on the French and Indian War,* edited by Fred Anderson. Lanham: Rowman & Littlefield, 2004.

Wilkinson, James. "General James Wilkinson's Narrative of the Fallen Timbers Campaign." *Mississippi Valley Historical Review,* 16 (1929): 81–90.

———. *Memoirs of My Own Times.* 3 volumes. Philadelphia: Abraham Small, 1816.

Wilson, Douglas Frazier, ed., *The Journal of Daniel Bradley: An Epic of the Ohio Frontier.* Greenville: F. H. Jobes, 1935.

PERIODICALS

American Daily Advertiser (Philadelphia)

Centinel of the Northwestern Territory

Cincinnati Daily Gazette

Claypoole's American Daily Advertiser (Philadelphia)

Dunlap's American Daily Advertiser

Fort Wayne News-Sentinel

Gazette of the United States (Philadelphia)

Georgia Gazette (Savannah)

London Magazine or Gentlemen's Monthly Intelligencer

Magazine of American History with Notes and Queries

Maryland Journal and Baltimore Advertiser

New York Packet (New York City)

Pennsylvania Packet, and Daily Advertiser (Philadelphia)

Pittsburgh Gazette

ACTS, PROCLAMATIONS, AND TREATIES

"An Act Making an Alteration in the Flag of the United States," January 13, 1794; 3rd Congress, 1st Session.

Administration of Justice Act; May 20, 1774.

Barbary Treaties (http://avalon.law.yale.edu/subject_menus/barmenu.asp).

Boston Port Act: March 31, 1774 (http://avalon.law.yale.edu/18th_century/boston_port_act .asp).

Constitution of the Commonwealth of Pennsylvania, 1776, *Pennsylvania State Archives,* 10 (1896): 767–784.

Declaration of the Rights of Man, 1789 (http://avalon.law.yale.edu/18th_century/rightsof .asp)

Jay Treaty, November 19, 1794 (http://avalon.law.yale.edu/18th_century/jay.asp).

Massachusetts Government Act; May 20, 1774 (http://avalon.law.yale.edu/18th_century /mass_gov_act.asp).

Paris Peace Treaty of September 30, 1783 (http://avalon.law.yale.edu/18th_century/paris .asp).

Royal Proclamation, October 7, 1763 (http://avalon.law.yale.edu/18th_century/proc1763 .asp).

Quartering Act; June 2, 1774 (http://avalon.law.yale.edu/18th_century/quartering_act_17 74.asp).

Quebec Act: October 7, 1774 (http://avalon.law.yale.edu/18th_century/quebec_act_1774 .asp).

Second Virginia Charter, May 23, 1609 (http://avalon.law.yale.edu/17th_century/va02.asp).

"Treaty Held at the Town of Lancaster, in Pennsylvania, By the Honourable, the Lieutenant Governor of the Province, and the Honourable the Commissioners for the Provinces Virginia and Maryland, with the Indians of the Six Nations, in June 1744," in *Indian Treaties Printed by Benjamin Franklin, 1736–1762,* C. Van Doren and J. P. Boyd, Editors. Philadelphia: Historical Society of Pennsylvania, 1938, 41–79.

Treaty of Alliance between the United States and His Most Christian Majesty, February 6, 1778, *United States Statutes at Large.*

Treaty of Amity and Commerce between the United States and His Most Christian Majesty, February 6, 1778, *United States Statutes at Large.*

Treaty of Friendship, Limits, and Navigation Between Spain and The United States; October 27, 1795 (http://avalon.law.yale.edu/18th_century/sp1795.asp).

Treaty of Logg's Town, 1752, *Virginia Magazine of History and Biography,* 13 (1906): 173–174.

SECONDARY SOURCES

Abbott, John Stevens Cabot. *The History of the State of Ohio: From the Discovery of the Great Valley, to the Present Time.* Detroit: Northwestern, 1875.

Andrews, Sue. "Howellville." Easttown Historical Society, *History Quarterly* Digital Archives 39, no. 3 (July 2002): 75–103.

Bald, F. Clever. "Fort Miamis, Outpost of Empire." *Northwest Ohio Quarterly,* 16, no. 2 (1944): 73–116.

———. *A Portrait of Anthony Wayne: Painted from Life by Jean Pierre Henri Elouis in 1796 and now reproduced from a unique print for the schoolchildren of Detroit: with a historical essay on General Wayne at Detroit.* Ann Arbor: Bulletin of the Clements Library, 1948.

Baldwin, Leland D. *Whiskey Rebels: The Story of a Frontier Uprising.* Pittsburgh: University of Pittsburgh Press, 1939.

Bauman, Robert F. "Pontiac's Successor: Au-goosh-away." *Northwest Ohio Quarterly,* 26 (1954): 8–38.

———. *The Ottawas of Ohio: 1704–1840,* Volume 6. Toledo: University of Toledo, 1984.

Benton, William A. "Pennsylvania Revolutionary Officers and the Federal Constitution." *Pennsylvania History: A Journal of Mid-Atlantic Studies,* 31, no. 4 (October 1964): 419–435.

Bowser, Les. "Anthony Wayne's Petitcodiac Adventure." *Generations: The Journal of the New Brunswick Genealogical Society* (Winter 2006): 51–55.

Boyd, Thomas. *Mad Anthony Wayne*. New York: Charles Scribner's Sons, 1929.

Bragg, C. L. *Crescent Moon over Carolina: William Moultrie and American Liberty*. Columbia: University of South Carolina Press, 2013.

Braund, Kathryn E. Holland. *Deerskins and Duffels: The Creek Indian Trade with Anglo-America, 1685–1815*, 2nd edition (Indians of the Southeast). Lincoln: University of Nebraska Press, 2008.

Brinkloe, William Draper. "The House in the Farm Journal Heading." *Farm Journal* (October 1917).

Broadwater, Robert P. *American Generals of the Revolutionary War: A Biographical Dictionary*. Reprint edition. Jefferson, N.C.: McFarland, 2007.

Brunhouse, Robert Lever. *The Counter-Revolution in Pennsylvania, 1776–1790*. Harrisburg: Pennsylvania Historical Commission, 1942.

Butterfield, Consul Willshire. *An Historical Account of the Expedition Against Sandusky under Col. William Crawford in 1782*. Cincinnati: Robert Clarke & Co., 1873.

———. *History of the Girtys*. Cincinnati: Clarke, 1890.

Candler, Allen Daniel and Clement Anselm Evans. *Georgia: Comprising Sketches of Counties, Towns, Events, Institutions, and Persons, Arranged in Cyclopedic Form*, Volume II. Atlanta: State Historical Association, 1906.

Carter, Harvey Lewis. *The Life and Times of Little Turtle: First Sagamore of the Wabash*. Urbana: University of Illinois Press, 1987.

Cashin, Edward J. *The King's Ranger: Thomas Brown and the American Revolution on the Southern Frontier*. New York: Fordham University Press, 1999.

Cayton, Andrew R. L. and Stuart D. Hobbs, eds. *The Center of a Great Empire: The Ohio Country in the Early American Empire*. Athens: Ohio University Press, 2005.

Clark, Harrison. *All Cloudless Glory: The Life of George Washington, Volume II, Making a Nation*. Washington, D.C.: Regnery, 1996.

Cleaves, Freeman. *Old Tippecanoe: William Henry Harrison and His Time*. New York: Charles Scribner's Sons, 1939.

Coleman, Kenneth. *The American Revolution in Georgia*. Athens: University of Georgia Press, 1958.

———. *A History of Georgia*. Athens: University of Georgia Press, 1977.

Cooper, Helen. "The Restoration of Waynesborough." *Tredyffrin Easttown Historical Society History Quarterly* 16, no. 4 (Winter 1978): 67–75.

Dittmann, Stephen. "A Brief Look at the History of Waynesborough and the Recent Reconstruction of Its Barn Tredyffrin." Easttown Historical Society *Historical Quarterly* Digital Archives 39, no. 2 (April 2001):63–68.

Dixon-Kennedy, Mike. *Encyclopedia of Greco-Roman Mythology*. Santa Barbara, Calif.: ABC Clio, 1998.

Dowd, Gregory Evans. *The War Under Heaven: Pontiac, the Indian Nations, and the British Empire*. Baltimore: Johns Hopkins University Press, 2004.

Downey, Fairfax. *Indian Wars of the U.S. Army 1776–1865*. Garden City, N.Y.: Doubleday, 1963.

Doyle, William. *Oxford History of the French Revolution.* Oxford: Clarendon Press, 1989.

Elliot, Daniel T. "Ebenezer Revolutionary War Headquarters: A Quest to Locate and Preserve." *LAMAR Institute Publication Series,* Report 73, 2003: 1–255.

Fallen Timbers and Fort Miamis National Historic Park (http://www.nps.gov/fati/index.htm).

Faris, John T. *Old Trails and Roads in Penn's Land.* Philadelphia: J. P. Lippincott, 1927.

Flexner, James. *George Washington and the New Nation, 1783–1793.* Boston: Little, Brown, 1970.

Freeman, Douglas Southall. *George Washington: A Biography,* 7 volumes. New York: Charles Scribner's Sons, 1948–1953.

Gaff, Alan. *Bayonets in the Wilderness: Anthony Wayne's Legion in the Old Northwest.* Norman: University of Oklahoma Press, 2008.

Gilfillan, Merrill. *Moods of the Ohio Moons.* Kent, Ohio: Kent State University Press, 1991.

Goldstone, Lawrence. *Dark Bargain: Slavery, Profits, and the Struggle for the Constitution.* New York: Walker, 2005.

Gratz, Simon. "A Biography of Richard Butler." *Pennsylvania Magazine of History and Biography* 7, no. 1 (1883).

Greve, Charles Theodore. *Centennial History of Cincinnati and Representative Citizens,* volume I. Chicago: Biographical Publishing Co., 1904.

Hallett, Kaycee. "History of the Black Swamp." *Black Swamp Journal* (April 14, 2011).

Harbison, Francis Roy. *Flood Tides Along the Allegheny.* Pittsburgh: Francis R. Harbison, 1941.

Harper, Rob. "Looking the Other Way: The Gnadenhutten Massacre and the Contextual Interpretation of Violence." *William and Mary Quarterly* 3rd series, 64, no. 3 (July 2007): 621–644.

Hay, Thomas R. *The Admirable Trumpeter: A Biography of General James Wilkinson.* New York: Doubleday, 1941.

Henderson, Archibald. *Washington's Southern Tour, 1791.* Boston: Houghton Mifflin, 1923.

Higginbotham, Don. *Daniel Morgan: Revolutionary Rifleman.* Chapel Hill: University of North Carolina Press, 1961.

History of the First Troop Philadelphia City Cavalry: 1774, November 17, 1784. Philadelphia: Printed for the Troop by Hallowell & Co., 1875.

Hurt, R. Douglas. *The Ohio Frontier: The Crucible of the Old Northwest, 1720–1830.* Bloomington: Indiana University Press, 1996.

Jackson III, Harvey H. *Lachlan McIntosh and the Politics of Revolutionary Georgia.* Athens: University of Georgia Press, 2003.

Jacobs, James Ripley. *Tarnished Warrior: Major-General James Wilkinson.* New York: Macmillan, 1938.

John, Henry P. "Christian Febiger: Colonel of the Virginia Line of the Continental Line." *Magazine of American History* 6 (1881): 188–203.

Jones, Robert Ralston. *Fort Washington at Cincinnati, Ohio.* Cincinnati: Society of Colonial Wars in Ohio, 1902.

Jordan, J. W. *Colonial Families of Philadelphia.* New York: Lewis Publishing Co., 1911.

Joyner, Stephanie. "Slave Housing Patterns within the Plantation Landscape of Coastal Georgia." Master's thesis, University of Florida, 2003.

Knepper, George. *The Official Ohio Lands Book*. Columbus: Auditor of the State, 2002.

———. *Ohio and Its People*. Kent, Ohio: Kent State University Press, 2003.

Knopf, Richard. *Anthony Wayne and the Founding of the United States Army*. Columbus: Anthony Wayne Parkway Board, 1961.

Leach, Josiah Granville. *The Penrose Family of Philadelphia*. Philadelphia: D. Biddle, 1903.

Lender, Mark Edward and Garry Wheeler Stone. *Fatal Sunday: George Washington, the Monmouth Campaign, and the Politics of Battle*. Norman: University of Oklahoma Press, 2016.

Lengel, Edward G., ed. *Companion to George Washington*. Chichester: Wiley-Blackwell, 2012.

Linklater, Andro. *An Artist in Treason: The Extraordinary Double Life of General James Wilkinson*. New York: Walker, 2009.

Lockhart, Paul. *The Drillmaster of Valley Forge and the Making of the American Army*. New York: HarperCollins, 2008.

Lytle, Richard M. *The Soldiers of America's First Army, 1791*. Lanham, Md.: Scarecrow Press, 2004.

Mattern, David B. *Benjamin Lincoln and the American Revolution*. Columbia: University of South Carolina Press, 1995.

McDonald, Robert M. S., ed. *Sons of the Father: George Washington and His Protégés*. Charlottesville: University of Virginia Press, 2013.

McGuire, Thomas J. *The Battle of Paoli*. Mechanicsburg, Pa.: Stackpole Books, 2000.

McPhee, Peter. *Robespierre: A Revolutionary Life*. New Haven: Yale University Press, 2012.

Mease, James, "Description of Some Medals, Etc." *Collections of the Massachusetts Historical Society*, 3rd series, 4 (1834): 301–303.

Meek, Basil. "Tarhe the Crane." *Ohio Archaeological and Historical Society Quarterly*, 20 (1911): 64–73.

Montgomery, Elizabeth. *Reminiscences of Wilmington, in Familiar Village Tales, Ancient and New*. Wilmington, Del.: Johnson & Bogia, 1872.

Morrison, Marie E. *A History of the Old Brick Church, Blandford Cemetery, Petersburg, Va.* Petersburg, Va., 1901.

Murray, J. A. "The Butlers of Cumberland Valley." *Historical Register: Notes and Queries, Biographical and Genealogical* 1 (January 1883): 9–13.

Nelson, Paul David. *Anthony Wayne: Soldier of the Early Republic*. Bloomington: Indiana University Press, 1989.

———. "General Charles Scott, the Kentucky Mounted Volunteers, and the Northwest Indian Wars, 1784–1794." *Journal of the Early Republic*, 6, no. 3 (Autumn 1986): 219–251.

———. *General Horatio Gates: A Biography*. Baton Rouge: Louisiana State University, 1976.

Northrup, Cynthia Clark and Elaine C. Prange Turney, eds. *Encyclopedia of Tariffs and Trade in U.S. History*. Volume I. Westport: Greenwood Press, 2003.

Peters, William E. *Ohio Lands and Their Subdivisions*. Athens: W. E. Peters, 1918.

Peterson, Edwin. *Penn's Woods West*. Pittsburgh: University of Pittsburgh Press, 1958.

Posey, John T. *General Thomas Posey: Son of the Revolution*. East Lansing: Michigan State University Press, 1992.

Preston, John Hyde. *A Gentleman Rebel: The Exploits of Anthony Wayne*. New York: Farrar & Rinehart, 1930.

Prucha, Francis Paul. *Indian Peace Medals in American History*. Norman: University of Oklahoma Press, 2000.

Ridgely, Mabel Lloyd, ed. *The Ridgelys of Delaware and Their Circle; What Them Befell; In Colonial & Federal Times: Letters 1751–1890*. Portland, Me.: Atheneum Press, 1949.

Ridner, Judith. *A Town In-Between: Carlisle, Pennsylvania, and the Early Mid-Atlantic Interior*. Philadelphia: University of Pennsylvania Press, 2010.

Royster, Charles. *Light-Horse Harry Lee and the Legacy of the American Revolution*. New York: Knopf, 1981.

Sanford, Laura. *The History of Erie County, Pennsylvania, from Its First Settlement*. Author, 1894.

Scharf, J. Thomas, and Westcott Thompson. *History of Philadelphia*, Volume I, 1609 to 1884. Philadelphia: J. B. Lippincott, 1884.

Seitz, Ruth Hoover. *Pennsylvania's Historic Places*. Intercourse, Pa.: Good Books, 1989.

Shelton, Hal. *General Richard Montgomery and the American Revolution*. New York: New York University Press, 1994.

Simmons, David A. *The Forts of Anthony Wayne*. Fort Wayne: Historic Fort Wayne, 1977.

Slaughter, Thomas P. *The Whiskey Rebellion: Frontier Epilogue to the American Revolution*. New York: Oxford University Press, 1986.

Slocum, Charles E. *History of the Maumee River Basin from the Earliest Account to Its Organization into Counties*. Indianapolis: Bowen and Slocum, 1905.

Spears, John Randolph. *Anthony Wayne: Sometimes Called "Mad Anthony."* New York: D. Appleton and Co., 1903.

Stegeman, John F., and Janet A. Stegeman. *Caty: A Biography of Catharine Littlefield Greene*. Athens: University of Georgia Press, 1977.

Stillé, Charles. *Major-General Anthony Wayne and the Pennsylvania Line in the Continental Army*. Philadelphia: Historical Society of Pennsylvania, 1893.

Stothers, David, and Patrick Tucker. *The Fry Site: Archaeological and Ethnohistorical Perspectives on the Maumee River Ottawa of Northwest Ohio*. Morrisville, N.C.: LuLu Press, 2006.

Strobel, Reverend P. A. *The Salzburgers and Their Descendants*. Baltimore: T. Newton Kurtz, 1855.

Sugden, John. *Blue Jacket: Warriors of the Shawnees*. Lincoln: University of Nebraska Press, 2000.

———. *Tecumseh: A Life*. New York: Henry Holt, 1997.

Thayer, Theodore. *Nathanael Greene: Strategist of the American Revolution*. New York: Twayne, 1960.

Vogel, John. *The Indians of Ohio and Wyandot County*. New York: Vantage Press, 1975.

Wainwright, Nicholas. *George Croghan: Wilderness Diplomat*. Chapel Hill: Published for the Institute of Early American History and Culture at Williamsburg by the University of North Carolina Press, 1959.

Wallace, Anthony F. C. *The Death and Rebirth of the Seneca*. New York: Alfred A. Knopf, 1970.

Ward, Harry M. *Charles Scott and the "Spirit of '76."* Charlottesville: University Press of Virginia, 1988.

——. *Duty, Honor, or Country: General George Weedon and the American Revolution*. Philadelphia: American Philosophical Society, 1979.

Weslager, C. A. *The Delaware Indian Westward Migration*. Wallingford, Pa.: Middle Atlantic Press, 1978.

Whitridge, Arnold. *Rochambeau*. New York: Macmillan, 1965.

Wildes, Harry Emerson. *Anthony Wayne: Troubleshooter of the American Revolution*. New York: Harcourt, Brace, 1941.

Wilson, Frazer Ellis. *Arthur St. Clair: Rugged Ruler of the Old Northwest; An Epic of the American Frontier*. Richmond: Garrett and Massie, 1944.

Winkler, John F. *Fallen Timbers 1794: The U.S. Army's First Victory*. Oxford: Osprey, 2013.

Winter, Nevin O. *History of Northwest Ohio*, volume I. Chicago: Lewis, 1917.

INDEX